The Final Nephilim

Ryan Pitterson

The Final Nephilim

Published by Days of Noe Publishing
New York, NY, USA

Cover Illustration by: Teshingul - Pakistan
Edited by: Angie Peters
Formatting by: Polgarus Studio

DEDICATION

Once again, I give all thanks, praise and honor to my Lord and Savior Jesus Christ for being able to complete this book. I pray that my work is pleasing to Him. Thank you to my mother Olga Pitterson, my first Bible teacher, for your continued support and love through another project. I would also like to thank God for my own bloodline: starting with my grandfather, the late artist Lloyd Van Pitterson, my father Donovan Lloyd Pitterson and my brothers Sean and Adam. To my children Nya and Luke, the constant source of my inspiration – thank you. You have both gone from sitting next to me in your baby carriers in the middle of the night while I research, to amazing children who can now discuss the Nephilim in detail with your Dad. I am so incredibly proud of you and honored to have the blessing of raising you. And finally thank you to my best friend and the love of my life, my beautiful wife Erika. 2020 was an unforgettable year for so many reasons and I could have never made it, much less written an entire book in such a short time without your love, patience, wisdom and encouragement. Thank you for being a constant reminder of how good God is to me. I love you.

Contents

“It is the glory of God to conceal a thing: but the honour of kings is to search out a matter.” – Proverbs 25:2

“Religion and natural science are fighting a joint battle in an incessant, never relaxing crusade against skepticism and against dogmatism, against disbelief and against superstition, and the rallying cry in this crusade has always been, and always will be: “On to God!” – Max Planck, the father of Quantum Physics

INTRODUCTION

"And I will put enmity between thee and the woman, and between thy seed and her seed; it shall bruise thy head, and thou shalt bruise his heel." – Genesis 3:15

Throughout biblical history, two lineages—the line of the prophesied Messiah (the "Seed of the Woman") and the bloodline of Satan (the "serpent") waged battles all focused on one goal—the prophesied birth of the Messiah, who would one day defeat the Devil and redeem humanity. The Savior—Jesus Christ, in His First Advent, died on the cross to take the sins of humanity as predicted by the words of the ancient prophets. However, the battle is far from over.

Though the human race was redeemed at His First Advent, Satan and his fallen angelic army remain. They will be defeated at the Second Advent, when the Messiah returns to conquer His enemies and rightfully reclaim rulership over earth. All Bible prophecy points to this day when Jesus will execute judgment and punish the rebel angels who have led humanity into evil for millennia. End-times prophecy reveals that day is swiftly approaching.

During His First Advent, Jesus Christ forewarned His disciplesas to what will take place in the final years of history before His return:

"But as the days of Noah were, so shall also the coming of the Son of man be." – Matthew 24:37

What made the "days of Noah" so unique? It was an era in which fallen angels openly interacted with humanity—many of them taking wives and giving birth to the Nephilim. This corruption of human morality and genetics pushed humanity to the brink of destruction and almost thwarted God's plan of redemption. However, the Lord, in love, sent the Flood judgment to destroy the angelic invaders, their giant offspring, restarting the human population through faithful Noah.

Now, as the end times rapidly approach, the prophecies of the final confrontation are coming to life. In the mysterious prophecy of Genesis 3:15, there was a second "seed" predicted— Antichrist, the son of Satan. Thus, the prophesied Seed of the Woman will ultimately confront the seed of the Serpent. Thousands of years after the Flood, many questions remain about exactly how these prophecies will unfold in the end times:

- Will the fallen angels once again attempt to "mingle themselves with the seed of men"?
- Does the Bible prophesy that Satan himself will have a seed?
- Who or what is the Antichrist? Does he have a supernatural origin?
- What is the startling connection between Quantum Physics and the Biblical symbolism of the scroll in end times prophecy?
- Is the modern scientific movement of genetic research and life-extension technology a precursor for the Mark of the Beast?
- What role will the UFO and alien phenomena play in the end times?
- How are Jesus' warnings about the Days of Noah the key to deciphering the prophecies of Revelation?

The answers to all these questions are in **the Holy Bible**. Using **only Scripture**, we are able to uncover and unravel the many mysterious prophecies from the Book of Revelation that identify the Antichrist, the return of the fallen angels, and how all of the judgments and supernatural predictions of the Apocalypse will unfold before the final Battle of Armageddon.

This is the culmination of God's plan to redeem humanity from sin and judge the fallen angels. It is the fulfillment of Jesus' mission to restore righteousness, hope, and love in the Earth forever. This is THE FINAL NEPHILIM.

CHAPTER 1

THE BEGINNING IS THE END

"And I will put enmity between thee and the woman, and between thy seed and her seed." – Genesis 3:15

"In Gen 3:15 we find the Redeemer of mankind promised as the seed of the woman, and we also read of the seed of the serpent, and everlasting antagonism existing between them. Now the seed of the woman is confessedly one, our Lord Jesus Christ; and consequently the seed of the serpent must be also an individual, and as all the good are headed up in Christ, the representative Man, so all evil will be headed up, and will find its development, in the seed of the serpent, the Antichrist who shall come." – *Things That Must Be – 4 Advent Sermons,* Francis Tilney Bassett, 1873, p. 33

THE END FROM THE BEGINNING: BIBLE PROPHECY REPEATS EARLY EVENTS IN SCRIPTURE

In the book of Isaiah, chapter 46, God rebukes Israel for their worship of false gods and makes a fascinating proclamation. In order to demonstrate to the twelve tribes that He, Yahweh, is the True and Living God, the Lord used prophecy as evidence of His power and might:

"To whom will ye liken me, and make me equal, and compare me,

> that we may be like. **Remember the former things of old**: for I am God, and there is none else; I am God, and there is none like me, **Declaring the end from the beginning, and from ancient times the things that are not yet done**, saying, My counsel shall stand, and I will do all my pleasure:" – Isaiah 46:5, 9–10

What distinguishes God from every other false "god" (truly just created beings made by the Lord) is that Yahweh revealed the future through prophecy. The Lord declared "the end from the beginning, and from ancient times things that are not yet done." In fact, the supernatural predictions of Scripture are evidence that He alone is Creator:

> "I know no subject more sublime, more important, more glorious than this of the Revelation.... The peculiar glory of the true God in foretelling future events, is thus asserted by God himself: '*Let them bring them forth, and shew us what shall happen. Shew the things that are to come hereafter that we may know that ye are gods.*' (Isaiah 41:22). '*I am God, there is none like me, declaring the end from the beginning, and from ancient times the things that are not yet done, saying, My counsel shall stand and I will do all my pleasure.*' (Isaiah 46:9–10).
>
> Would anyone know what is the religion that comes from Jehovah, and what is not; Jehovah bids him make use of this test of prophecy. He only who is omnipotent and omniscient can at once predestinate, foretell, and execute in due season his own decrees. **This is the peculiar proof of the Divinity of the Scriptures.**" – *A Selection of Tracts and Essays, Theological and Historical, Volume 8*, Rev. Joseph Milner, 1810, p. 27

Thus, we can know the meaning of end-times Bible prophecy by going back to events and prophecies from the earliest times in Scripture.

A RIPPLE THROUGH TIME: TYPES AND SHADOWS FORESHADOW PROPHETIC EVENTS

> "I have also spoken by the prophets, and I have multiplied visions, and used similitudes, by the ministry of the prophets." – Hosea 12:10

Not only has God declared the final events in human history from the beginning, He also uses "similitudes"—a repetition of prophetic events through types and shadows—to demonstrate His sovereignty. When John the Baptist saw the Lord Jesus Christ at the beginning of His earthly ministry, he proclaimed:

> "Behold the Lamb of God, which taketh away the sin of the world." – John 1:29

This pronouncement stretched back through time almost two thousand years before the arrival of John the Baptist, when Abraham was hiking up Mount Moriah with his son Isaac (a son born under divine power in fulfillment of prophecy) to offer him as a sacrifice to God. When Isaac (not knowing he was being offered) asked his father where the required animal was, Abraham replied: "**My son, God will provide Himself a lamb for the burnt offering**." God did indeed provide an animal to die in the place of Isaac that day, in a prophetic foreshadow of the ultimate, true Lamb of God, Jesus Christ, who would give His own life, serving as a substitutionary atonement for the sins of all who believe upon Him.

John the Baptist's words also acknowledged that all the sacrificial lambs used in the first Passover, in the thousands of subsequent observations of Passover, and in all of the Temple atonement offerings **were a foreshadow of the Messiah**, the true Lamb of God who would be a sacrifice for the sins of the whole world. This is a *type* or *similitude*.

We see other examples of this throughout the Bible:

- **Joseph**, who was favored by his father and betrayed by his brothers (the patriarchs of the twelve tribes of Israel), was sold into slavery and punished for a crime he did not commit. However, he ultimately rose to such prominence that he sat at the right hand of Pharaoh as the second-most-powerful ruler in Egypt. He was also able to save Israel and many other nations of the world through his divinely endowed power of interpreting dreams. This was a foreshadow of Jesus Christ, who came to the twelve tribes who "received him not." Jesus was similarly punished unjustly, and in His death and resurrection, He won salvation for all who believe in Him.
- **Moses**, who led the Israelites out of bondage, was such a similitude of Christ that when he delivered a prophecy of the coming Messiah, the Holy Spirit inspired him to proclaim: "The LORD thy God will raise up unto thee a Prophet from the midst of thee, of thy brethren, **like unto me**; unto him ye shall hearken" – Deuteronomy 18:15.
- **Joshua,** the faithful servant of God, led the Israelites across the Jordan after the death of Moses. His Hebrew name, *Yeshua,* is the same name as the Messiah. Joshua was chosen by God to conquer the Nephilim—enemies of God—and lead the Israelites into the Promised Land. This all foreshadows and serves as a picture of Jesus, *Yeshua Ha Meshiach*, who leads all who trust and believe in Him into Heaven and the true Promised Land.

Thus, a prophecy can have more than one fulfillment throughout time. This should not be difficult to believe when one understands that **God exists outside of time**. Consider Genesis 1:1:

> "In the beginning God created the heaven and the earth."

God started "the clock" for human history in that verse, yet He existed before that "timer" was instituted. We know from Scripture that Jesus Christ created all things by His Word. In Revelation chapter 4, the twenty-four elders who sit before the throne of God worship by acknowledging both of these attributes of God:

> "The four and twenty elders fall down before him that sat on the throne, and worship him that liveth for ever and ever, and cast their crowns before the throne, saying, Thou art worthy, O Lord, to receive glory and honour and power: for thou hast created all things, and for thy pleasure they are and were created." – Revelation 4:10–11

Writing about the end of the Earth and Heaven that presently exist, the Apostle Peter provided a glimpse of Jesus existing outside of time:

> "But the heavens and the earth, which are now, by the same word are kept in store, reserved unto fire against the day of judgment and perdition of ungodly men. But, beloved, be not ignorant of this one thing, **that one day is with the Lord as a thousand years, and a thousand years as one day**." – 2 Peter 3:7–8

Also consider the language the Lord Jesus Christ used that demonstrates this divine bending of time and space. In Luke 11, He rebuked the Pharisees and laid the blame on them for the murder of the prophets of God who were sent to Israel in the Old Testament. Yet interestingly, the Lord declared that their deaths took place *at the beginning of time*:

> "That the blood of all the prophets, **which was shed from the foundation of the world,** may be required of this generation." –

> Luke 11:50

Also consider what was said about Jesus' death on the cross in a prophecy of the Antichrist:

> "And it was given unto him [the Antichrist] to make war with the saints, and to overcome them: and power was given him over all kindreds, and tongues, and nations. And all that dwell upon the earth shall worship him, whose names are not written in the book of life of the **Lamb slain from the foundation of the world**." – Revelation 13:7–8

In this verse, the death of the Lord Jesus Christ on the cross is described as having taken place "from the foundation of the world." Before the world was even created, Jesus was slain. How could this be? What is God revealing with these verses? Is it possible that He is expressing His existence in relation to time—that, as God exists outside of time, all events in human history are taking place at once for Him?

Rather than time being linear, as humans commonly perceive it, could time be more *circular* from the divine perspective? Is time, rather than a straight line, more like a rolled scroll that cycles through itself, where the beginning is the end and the end is the beginning? In fact, we see Jesus Christ give Himself this very title in Scripture:

> "I am Alpha and Omega, **the beginning and the ending**, saith the Lord, which is, and which was, and which is to come, the Almighty." – Revelation 1:8

Three times in the book of Revelation (which, of course, is mostly dedicated to prophesying the future of all existence and was written outside of time, as the Apostle John recorded it in Heaven), the Messiah uses this "beginning and ending" appellation. Notice that He not only expresses Himself as "the beginning and ending," but He also proclaims that He "is…was, and…is to come"—identifying Himself as **existing in the past, the present, and the future simultaneously**.

Similarly, the Trinity—God the Father, the Son, and the Holy Spirit—is comprised of separate beings who are "One" at the same time:

> "For there are three that bear record in heaven, the Father, the Word, and the Holy Ghost: **and these three are one**." – 1 John 5:7

When challenged by the Pharisees as to whether He truly was the prophesied Messiah, the Lord gave a response that made them want to try to assassinate Him:

> "My sheep hear my voice, and I know them, and they follow me: And I give unto them eternal life; and they shall never perish, neither shall any man pluck them out of my hand. My Father, which gave them me, is greater than all; and no man is able to pluck them out of my Father's hand. **I and my Father are one**. Then the Jews took up stones again to stone him." – John 10:27-31

Enraged at this statement, the Pharisees accused Jesus: "Because that thou, being a man, makest thyself God." In this statement, Jesus was indeed proclaiming Himself God, but He was also revealing that God can exist as Father and Son at the same time. Jesus would later declare: "Not that any man hath seen the Father, save he which is of God, he hath seen the Father" (John 6:46). This would make sense after all, since no human can claim to have gone to the throne of God in Heaven to behold Him. But in a later conversation with one of His disciples, the Lord made quite an interesting revelation:

> "Philip saith unto him, Lord, show us the Father, and it sufficeth us. Jesus saith unto him, Have I been so long time with you, and yet hast thou not known me, Philip? **he that hath seen me hath seen the Father**; and how sayest thou then, Show us the Father? Believest thou not that I am in the Father, and the Father in me? the words that I speak unto you I speak not of myself: but the Father that dwelleth in me, he doeth the works." – John 14:8–10

Even the description of a born-again Christian's salvation possesses time-bending properties:

> "Verily, verily, I say unto you, He that believeth on me **hath** everlasting life." – John 6:47

Notice that, in this verse, Jesus speaks in present tense: If you believe in Him, you have eternal life. It is not awaiting you at death; you have it already.

BIBLE PROPHECY AND QUANTUM PHYSICS: PROPHETIC EVENTS REPEAT THROUGH TIME AND GIVE EVIDENCE OF GOD AS CREATOR

> "Every particle, atom and molecule [photons, electrons, or whole atoms] behave in accordance with the laws of quantum mechanics—as does everything. However, this only becomes important when broken down to the atomic, sub-atomic and molecular scales. Quantum mechanics is trying to use the physics of things at the atomic level to create effects in the macroscopic world—which is our world.
>
> [Quantum] Superposition is a system that has two different states

> that can define it and it's possible for it to exist in both. For example, in physical terms, an electron has two possible quantum states: spin up and spin down. When an electron is in superposition, it is both up and down at once—it is a complex combination of both." – *Quantum for Dummies, the Basics Explained,* Alan Woodward, https://eandt.theiet.org/content/articles/2019/04/quantum-for-dummies-the-basics-explained/

> "**The thing that hath been, it is that which shall be**; and that which is done is that which shall be done: and there is no new thing under the sun. Is there any thing whereof it may be said, See, this is new? **it hath been already of old time, which was before us.**" – Ecclesiastes 1:9–10

"There is more of literal truth than is commonly supposed, in the remark of Israel's royal preacher that 'the thing that hath been, it is that which shall be; and that which is done, is that which shall be done; and there is no new thing under the sun.' There are great cycles in the moral world. As events roll on to the same point in the cycle, the same events rise to meet the eye; the careful student of the past, finds on almost every page of the records of other days, scenes which not inaptly lead him to feel that he is reading prophecy. The age in which he lives, and in whose scenes he participates, seems to him to have sat for the picture which was spread upon the canvas by the artists of centuries long gone by." – *The Biblical Repository and Classical Review, Third Series,* Reverend W. H. Bidwell, 1847, p. 728

Quantum physics, which observes the subatomic level of our world, is often used in an effort to explain the origin of time, space, and the universe itself. In fact, it is the one scientific discipline that has come closest to defining the spiritual realm, where the laws of physics no longer apply and subatomic particles behave differently once they are observed.

Meanwhile, the Bible contains all the answers to these questions and the many, many more mysteries that some of the most dedicated and learned minds have struggled with for centuries. Subatomic particles have been identified as the building blocks of the entire universe. All matter is explained through their interaction. In Romans 1:20, the Apostle Paul declares:

> "For the invisible things of him from the creation of the world are clearly seen, being understood by the things that are made, even his eternal power and Godhead; so that they are without excuse." – Romans 1:20

This passage illustrates that the visible, material world is made from invisible, immaterial elements. And Bible prophecy provides recorded evidence of God's power and sovereignty over the universe.

Quantum superposition, described above, is the principle that quantum particles (a beam of electrons, for example), can exist in two states at once. This is startlingly similar to how God reveals Himself in Scripture. Jesus proclaims that He is "Alpha and Omega, the beginning and the end"—all in one. In physics, there is even a much-debated theory called the Omega Point, which holds that all of the universe must "spiral toward a final point of unification." The Bible proclaims that Jesus Christ is the literal source of the entire creation, holding the universe together in His power:

> "For by him were all things created, that are in heaven, and that are in earth, visible and invisible, whether they be thrones, or dominions, or principalities, or powers: all things were created by him, and for him: **And he is before all things, and by him all things consist.**" – Colossians 1:16–17

Jesus proclaimed: "I am he that liveth, and was dead; and, behold, I am alive for evermore," (Revelation 1:18), again demonstrating His existing in seemingly opposite states. The world of physics teaches a famous thought experiment known as "Schrodinger's cat" that postulates a simulation in which a cat is both dead and alive at the same time.

We even find quantum superposition in the name of God. When Moses encountered God at the burning bush and was told to deliver a message to the Israelites, the man asked for God's name. The Lord provided a fascinating answer.

> "And Moses said unto God, Behold, when I come unto the children of Israel, and shall say unto them, The God of your fathers hath sent me unto you; and they shall say to me, What is his name? what shall I say unto them? And God said unto Moses, I AM THAT I AM: and he said, Thus shalt thou say unto the children of Israel, I AM hath sent me unto you." – Exodus 3:13–14

The name "I AM THAT I AM" again speaks to God existing outside of time. It is a declaration that He has always existed (even before what humans define as "existence"), and thus all creation flows from His power and will. This was an early affirmation of Jesus' declaration in the book of Revelation that He is "which is, which was and which is to come, the Almighty" (Revelation 1:8). A nineteenth-century sermon by the president of the College of New Jersey agrees with this very concept:

> "The name Jehovah is derived from the Hebrew verb, *to be;* and therefore the meaning of the word Jehovah is, *The existent the being or He that is.* Thus it seems explained in [Exodus 3:14]: I AM THAT I AM or 'I am because I am;' that is, I exist and have being in and of myself without dependence upon any cause; and my existence or being is always the same, unchangeable and eternal. St. John well explains this name by the *Who is, who was, and who is to come* or as the passage might be rendered, 'The present Being, the past Being, and the future Being,' or 'The Being that is, the Being that was, and

the Being that will be;' that is, the perpetual, the eternal, and unchangeable Being." "The Name of God," as printed in *Sermons, Vol. 1*, Reverend Samuel Davies, 1864, p. 455

A modern Jewish writer studying the name of God arrived at a similar conclusion:

"Another possible similarity between quantum physics and the Hebrew Bible relates to the four-letter name of God— יהוה (YHWH). People have wondered about and argued over this name for many centuries. A great number of different theories try to define its proper pronunciation and original meaning. **One of the most popular ideas is that the Hebrew Bible's name for God is a verb that expresses past, present, and future tenses all at once!** According to this interpretation, the name *YHWH* means something like 'the one who was-is-will be.' This is a very old idea that may go back as far as the Jewish-Greek Septuagint translation (ca. 200 BCE/BC) and the Book of Revelation (1st century AD/CE).

If we were to translate this understanding of God's name into the language of quantum physics, we might call it 'a superposition of all possible states.' Indeed, quantum mechanics posits that the particles or waves that apparently make up our universe (and us) can exist in all possible states at once—until someone carries out a 'measurement.' Once you measure the location of a particle, it 'collapses' to a single specific location. Perhaps the name of God, YHWH, is similar: it communicates Being in all states, dimensions, and times simultaneously—and if you try to define the meaning more specifically, you end up reducing it to just one aspect." – "God's Name and Quantum Physics?" https://weekly.israelbiblecenter.com/gods-name-quantum-physics/

So why does all this talk of physics and bending time matter for this study? In His mercy and wisdom, *Yeshua*, the Messiah, provided some important guidelines of where to look "in the beginning" in order to discern the times of His Second Coming:

> "For as the lightning, that lighteneth out of the one part under heaven, shineth unto the other part under heaven; **so shall also the Son of man be in his day**. But first must he suffer many things, and be rejected of this generation. **And as it was in the days of Noe, so shall it be also in the days of the Son of man**. They did eat, they drank, they married wives, they were given in marriage, until the day that Noah entered into the ark, and the flood came, and destroyed them all.
>
> **Likewise also as it was in the days of Lot**; they did eat, they drank, they bought, they sold, they planted, they builded; But the same day that Lot went out of Sodom it rained fire and brimstone from heaven, and destroyed them all. **Even thus shall it be in the day when the Son of man is revealed**." – Luke 17:24–30

Jesus pointed specifically to the days of Noah and Lot as an indication of what the world will be like in the final years before His Second Coming. What was so unique about these eras that, in more than one teaching, the Lord pointed directly to these two accounts from the book of Genesis as a guide to understanding the end times? This study will explore that and two other key events from "the beginning" that will help us understand the end of biblical history.

EVENTS FROM EARLY SCRIPTURE HELP EXPLAIN END-TIME PROPHECY

Like a wave of light, a prophecy can ripple through various points in history confirming God's Word. These are sometimes called "double fulfillments," but in reality, a single prophecy can have several fulfillments throughout Scripture. With this understanding, we can now turn to the events of Revelation that will deal with the final confrontation between Jesus Christ and the Final Nephilim.

Scripture clearly tells us that God has declared the end of all things "from the beginning." By going back to Genesis and Exodus and examining four key events, we are able to discern and understand the final events of human history as detailed in the book of Revelation and the major role the Nephilim have played and will play as we race towards the end times:

- Genesis 3:15: The judgment of Satan and prophecy of Messiah
- Genesis 6: The days of Noah, the birth of the Nephilim, and the Flood
- The judgment of Sodom and Gomorrah
- The Exodus

Viewing the book of Revelation through the lens of these events from the earliest parts of scriptural history, while understanding that God has rippled types and shadows of prophecy throughout the pages of the Old Testament, will provide us with an entirely new level of understanding of the depths of end-times prophecy. This study will begin with the first prophecy we find in the Bible, in the earliest parts of Genesis, which declared that one day, the Final Nephilim would be born.

EXCLUSIVE BONUS CONTENT – Scan the QR code below for bonus content.

CHAPTER 2

THE OTHER SEED

> "And the LORD God said unto the serpent, Because thou hast done this, thou art cursed above all cattle, and above every beast of the field; upon thy belly shalt thou go, and dust shalt thou eat all the days of thy life: And I will put enmity between thee and the woman, **and between thy seed and her seed**; it shall bruise thy head, and thou shalt bruise his heel." – Genesis 3:14–15

> "And as it was in the days of Noe, so shall it be also in the days of the Son of man." – Luke 17:26

Jesus Christ is the central figure of the universe, the Bible, and human history and Genesis 3:15, which first proclaimed Him, is one of the most amazing verses in the Bible. In this one passage, God announced the birth of the Messiah, the Savior who would one day conquer Satan and redeem humanity. This also served as a warning to Satan that his defeat would come at the hands of a human child—albeit one with the power of God.

Thus, Satan set out to prevent the birth of this Messiah, whether by violence or by corrupting the entire human race. The Nephilim—the half-human, half-angelic hybrid offspring of fallen angels and human women—were one of the main weapons in the Devil's arsenal to drag humanity into utter genetic and spiritual ruin. However, one aspect of this prophecy is rarely discussed—namely, God said that, in addition to the Seed of the Woman, *there would also be another seed*: the Seed of Satan.

SATAN WILL HAVE HIS OWN "SEED": ANTICHRIST, A LITERAL CHILD OF THE DEVIL

> "Their name, as it is given in the Old Testament is 'Nephilim'... As it was in the Days of Noah so shall it be in the coming of the Son of Man... "I do mean," he replied, "that I am firmly convinced that so far has demonology increased-the door being opened by modern spiritualism-that I believe this poor old world of ours is beginning to experience a return of this association between [fallen angels] and the daughters of men...let me register my firm conviction that I believe from some such demoniacal association there will spring 'the Man of Sin' – The Antichrist." – *The Mark of the Beast*, Sydney Watson, 1918, p. 20–21

As hard as it may be to fathom, God, in Genesis 3:15, clearly points to the revealing of two children: the Messiah and the seed of the Devil, who is Antichrist. With near universal consensus, Bible scholars, theologians, and pastors agree that the "Seed of the Woman" refers to a literal person, Jesus Christ. In other words, this is not a metaphor or an allusion. In His earthly incarnation, Jesus Christ was supernaturally conceived in the womb of a woman and was physically born. We read of the angel explaining to Mary these coming strange but miraculous events in the following:

> "And the angel said unto her, Fear not, Mary: for thou hast found favour with God. And, behold, thou shalt conceive in thy womb, and bring forth a son, and shalt call his name Jesus. He shall be great, and shall be called the Son of the Highest: and the Lord God shall give unto him the throne of his father David: And he shall reign over the house of Jacob for ever; and of his kingdom there shall be no end. Then said Mary unto the angel, How shall this be, seeing I know not a man? And the angel answered and said unto her, The Holy Ghost shall come upon thee, and the power of the

> Highest shall overshadow thee: **therefore also that holy thing which shall be born of thee shall be called the Son of God**." – Luke 1:30–35

Jesus descended from Heaven, voluntarily lowering Himself from purely divine to superpositioned as both divine and mortal by taking the form of a human baby in the womb and being delivered into the world through the body of Mary. The writer of the book of Hebrews confirms this:

> "But we see Jesus, who was made a little lower than the angels for the suffering of death, crowned with glory and honour; that he by the grace of God should taste death for every man.... For verily he took not on him the nature of angels; but he took on him the seed of Abraham." – Hebrews 2:9, 16

By the same interpretation, we should read "thy seed" in Genesis 3:15—referring to the seed of the Devil—**as denoting a literal person who will one day be conceived and born of a woman as well**. Renowned twentieth-century theologian A. W. Pink arrived at this very conclusion:

> "Second, two 'seeds' are here referred to—another item which is generally overlooked—'thy seed' and 'her seed'—Satan's seed and the woman's Seed—the Antichrist and the Christ. In these two persons all prophecy converges. In the former of these expressions—'thy seed' (Satan's seed) we have more than a hint of the supernatural and satanic nature and character of the Antichrist. From the beginning the Devil has been an imitator, and the climax will not be reached until he daringly travesties the hypostatic union of the two natures in our blessed Lord—His humanity and His Deity. The Antichrist will be the Man of Sin and yet the Son of Perdition—literally the seed of the serpent—just as our Lord was the Son of Man and the Son of God in one person.

> This is the only logical conclusion. If 'her seed' ultimates in a single personality—the Christ—**then by every principle of sound interpretation 'thy seed' must also ultimate in a single person—the Antichrist.**" – *Gleanings in Genesis,* A. W. Pink, Moody Press, 1922, p. 43

THE ANTICHRIST WILL BE A NEPHILIM

As A.W. Pink stated in the excerpt above, the Devil is an imitator of God. And as the Lord brought a Son into this world to redeem humanity from the curse of sin and death, so too will the Devil conceive a son, one who will seek to bring all people into damnation and perdition. Thus, the Antichrist by nature will be a Nephilim—a half-human, half-fallen, angelic hybrid being.

This will be a repeat of what took place in Genesis 6, when the Devil instigated a rebellion among his angels to enter the human realm and take women as wives:

> "And it came to pass, when men began to multiply on the face of the earth, and daughters were born unto them, That the sons of God saw the daughters of men that they were fair; and they took them wives of all which they chose. And the LORD said, My spirit shall not always strive with man, for that he also is flesh: yet his days shall be an hundred and twenty years. There were giants in the earth in those days; and also after that, when the sons of God came in unto the daughters of men, and they bare children to them, the same became mighty men which were of old, men of renown." – Genesis 6:1–4

Many commentaries, articles, and podcasts point to the Antichrist as a charismatic figure who will dazzle the world with his knowledge and leadership abilities. However, the Bible goes much further in explaining the reason for his powerful persona; it states that he is literally the seed of the Devil. This has been the understanding of the Church for centuries:

> "There is a statement in Genesis 3:15, that seems to throw considerable light on the subject we are discussing. It reads—'I will put enmity between thee (Satan) and the woman (Eve) and between thy seed (Anti-Christ) and her seed (Christ). It (Christ) shall bruise thy head and thou shalt bruise His heel.' From this it seems clear that Satan has the power of procreation, and that he will beget a son—'THE ANTICHRIST,' called in 2 Thessalonians 2:3 the 'SON OF PERDITION.'
>
> While Perdition is a place (Revelation 17:8–11) and also a 'condition' into which men may fall (1 Timothy 6:9; Hebrews 10:39), the author of it is Satan and Antichrist in the above passage is called the 'Son of Perdition' because he is the son of the author of Perdition, or Satan. As Christ was born of a virgin by the Holy Spirit without the instrumentality of a human father, so it would appear that Antichrist, in imitation of the birth of Christ, is to be born of a woman (not necessarily a virgin) with Satan as his father. This is no new view, but, has been held by many of God's spiritually minded children since the days of the Apostle John.... If Satan then has the power of procreation why not his and other Fallen Angels."
> – *The Spirit World*, Clarence Larkin, 1921, p. 34

We know from Scripture that one-third of the angels rebelled in allegiance to the Devil:

> "And there appeared another wonder in heaven; and behold a great red dragon, having seven heads and ten horns, and seven crowns upon his heads. And his tail drew the third part of the stars of

> heaven, and did cast them to the earth: and the dragon stood before the woman which was ready to be delivered, for to devour her child as soon as it was born. And she brought forth a man child, who was to rule all nations with a rod of iron: and her child was caught up unto God, and to his throne.
>
> And the woman fled into the wilderness, where she hath a place prepared of God, that they should feed her there a thousand two hundred and threescore days. And there was war in heaven: Michael and his angels fought against the dragon; **and the dragon fought and his angels**, And prevailed not; neither was their place found any more in heaven. And the great dragon was cast out, that old serpent, called the Devil, and Satan, which deceiveth the whole world: **he was cast out into the earth, and his angels were cast out with him.**" – Revelation 12:3–9

A faction of these apostate angels took part in one of the most forbidden and heinous sins in biblical history: fornication with human women. Understanding the sins of this era is the key to uncovering the true identity and nature of the Antichrist, and it all goes back to Genesis chapter 6.

INVASION OF FALLEN ANGELS AND BIRTH OF THE NEPHILIM: ANCIENT EVENTS THAT WILL REPEAT IN THE END TIMES

> "For as in the days that were before the flood they were eating and drinking, marrying and giving in marriage, until the day that Noe entered into the ark, And knew not until the flood came, and took them all away; so shall also the coming of the Son of man be." – Matthew 24:38–39

Twice in Scripture, Jesus Christ prophesied that the end times—the final years before His return to Earth as detailed in Revelation—would be a repetition of the era of Noah. What made the antediluvian age so unique that the Savior pointed to the "days of Noah" as the preview of what the end of the world would look like? That ancient era was when the fallen angels attempted to contaminate the human race genetically and spiritually via fornication. "They" were eating, drinking, and marrying human women until the Flood swept them away in a judgment of God so severe that only eight humans survived.

THE SUPERNATURAL INTERPRETATION OF GENESIS 6

> "And it came to pass, when men began to multiply on the face of the earth, and daughters were born unto them, That the sons of God saw the daughters of men that they were fair; and they took them wives of all which they chose. And the LORD said, My spirit shall not always strive with man, for that he also is flesh: yet his days shall be an hundred and twenty years. There were giants in the earth in those days; and also after that, when the sons of God came in unto the daughters of men, and they bare children to them, the same became mighty men which were of old, men of renown." – Genesis 6:1–4

Much of my first book, *Judgment of the Nephilim*, was devoted to making the biblical case for the above passage presenting the history of a time when angels married human women and produced offspring. (For a detailed analysis on this subject, please refer to that book). However, in order to grasp the significance of the "days of Noah," this study requires some examination of that era as well.

The "Sons of God" in Genesis 6 Were Angels

> "The angels of [Genesis 6:2] were instigated by Satan to the commission of their sin, in order that he might thus be enabled to effect what we may, not inappropriately, term the adulteration of the Adamite race—that the race, for the salvation of which the promised seed of the woman should come, should be no longer purely Adam's, but a race imputed and mixed—partly of demonic origin—attempting thus to overthrow the counsel, and defeat the purpose of God." – *The Fallen Angels and Heroes of Mythology*, Reverend John Fleming, Dublin: Hodges, Foster and Figgis, 1879, p. 132

The term "sons of God" (Hebrew: *b'nai ha Elohim*) in Genesis 6:2 exclusively refers to angels in the Old Testament. When the Devil was sentenced by God in Genesis 3:15, he was informed that his conquest would come at the hands of the Seed of the Woman:

> "And I will put enmity between thee and the woman, and between thy seed and her seed; it shall bruise thy head, and thou shalt bruise his heel." – Genesis 3:15

This human child would one day "bruise," or crush, the head of the Serpent, putting the Devil on notice that his conqueror would be a child born from a human woman. This divine proclamation would set the course of human history for the next six thousand years. Satan knew where his defeat would come from and thus targeted this prophesied human Messiah for destruction. No clearer picture of this is given than in Revelation 12:

> "And there appeared a great wonder in heaven; a woman clothed with the sun, and the moon under her feet, and upon her head a

> crown of twelve stars: And she being with child cried, travailing in birth, and pained to be delivered. And there appeared another wonder in heaven; and behold a great red dragon, having seven heads and ten horns, and seven crowns upon his heads. And his tail drew the third part of the stars of heaven, and did cast them to the earth: and the dragon stood before the woman which was ready to be delivered, for to devour her child as soon as it was born." – Revelation 12:1–4

The "woman" in the above passage is the nation of Israel, from which the Savior Jesus Christ would be born. This symbolism is confirmed in Genesis chapter 37, where we read about the faithful Joseph sharing his dream with his father, Jacob, and his brothers, who—along with him—were the patriarchs of the twelve tribes of Israel. Right after the woman is described in the Revelation passage noted here, we see the dragon (Satan) ready to "devour her child as it was born."

Satan's great mission has been to thwart God's plan to redeem mankind through the Promised Messiah, the Seed of the Woman. By preventing this birth or stopping the Messiah, the Devil could demonstrate to the angelic realm that God's Word was not always true—that a prophecy failed. We see the brazen attempts throughout biblical history. Cain, the first son of Adam and Eve, could have been the Messiah. After all, he was the first "seed" of the woman. Eve clearly recognized this possibility when she named him, proclaiming, "I have gotten a man from the LORD" (Genesis 4:1). Cain was the first potential son sent from God to fulfill Genesis 3:15.

In response to this threat, the Devil sprang into action via sinful temptation (the same tactic he used on Cain's parents). The first son was quickly seduced into apostasy from faithful service to God and then into homicidal jealousy of his brother Abel, whom he murdered. In *Judgment of the Nephilim*, I explained:

> "Again, consider this situation in light of the Prophecy. Satan had succeeded in luring Cain into sinful rebellion, thus removing one potential threat to his reign. With the older brother corrupted and effectively out of the picture, perhaps his younger twin, Abel, was the Messiah? By corrupting Cain so effectively that he would murder his own brother in spite and jealousy, Satan was in effect killing two threats with one deception. Scripture confirms that Cain was under satanic influence:
>
> > 'For this is the message that ye heard from the beginning, that we should love one another. Not as Cain, who was of that wicked one, and slew his brother. And wherefore slew he him? Because his own works were evil, and his brother's righteous.' – 1 John 3:11–12
>
> The devil led the very lineage God ordained to redeem the world into sin. This is a recurring theme throughout biblical history. Cain was so depraved he was 'of that wicked one'—a spiritual seed of Satan—and this fueled his hatred of Abel to the point of homicide."
> – *Judgment of the Nephilim*, Ryan Pitterson, 2018, p. 27

But as the human population expanded in the generations after Cain and Abel, the Devil needed a more large-scale attack to bring humanity into ruin. Thus, he provoked some of the fallen angels to violate God's genetic order and fornicate with human women.

THE DEVIL HIDES BEHIND PROXIES TO CARRY OUT HIS WICKED AGENDA

> "Lest Satan should get an advantage of us: for we are not ignorant of his devices." – 2 Corinthians 2:11

It should be no surprise that Satan would enlist *other angels* to attempt the illicit relations with humans first, *before he did.* In fact, Satan often conceals himself or uses proxies to do his bidding. For example, in the Garden of Eden, he appeared to Eve as the Serpent (Hebrew: *nachash*)—a luminous serpentine being. In Job chapters 1 and 2, a large group of angels stands before the throne of God and Satan appears "among them" (Job 1:6, 2:1). And, during the days of Moses, Satan used a wicked Pharaoh to try to exterminate a generation of newborn male Israelites in an attempt to destroy the prophesied Seed:

> "And the king of Egypt spake to the Hebrew midwives, of which the name of the one was Shiphrah, and the name of the other Puah: And he said, When ye do the office of a midwife to the Hebrew women, and see them upon the stools; if it be a son, then ye shall kill him: but if it be a daughter, then she shall live. But the midwives feared God, and did not as the king of Egypt commanded them, but saved the men children alive.... And Pharaoh charged all his people, saying, Every son that is born ye shall cast into the river, and every daughter ye shall save alive." – Exodus 1:15–17, 22

Even after the Flood, the Nephilim reemerged on Earth and the Devil set his hybrid minions in the heart of the Promised Land, which the postdiluvian giants named after their progenitor, calling it "the land of Canaan." It was three giants—Ahiman, Sheshai, and Talmai, the sons of Anak—who frightened the Israelites so badly they doubted that God could even deliver them to the Promised Land:

> "But the men that went up with him said, We be not able to go up against the people; for they are stronger than we. And they brought up an evil report of the land which they had searched unto the children of Israel, saying, The land, through which we have gone to search it, is a land that eateth up the inhabitants thereof; and all the people that we saw in it are men of a great stature. And there we saw the giants [*Nephilim*], the sons of Anak, which come of the giants: and we were in our own sight as grasshoppers, and so we were in their sight." – Numbers 13:31–33

This blatant lack of faith in God's might, power, and Word was the result of seeing just three Nephilim in the Promised Land. This was only a short time after God had delivered Israel from slavery in Egypt via ten supernatural plagues and the parting of the Red Sea that destroyed Pharaoh and the most powerful army on Earth at that time. Even after all that, the twelve tribes cowered in fear at the sight of the three giants. Their refusal to enter the Promised Land led to the wilderness judgment, in which an entire generation of Israelites died in the desert on the outskirts of the land of Canaan.

In the days when the Lord Jesus Christ was incarnated in the form of a human child, as recorded in the New Testament, the Devil again used a despot to try to "devour the child as soon it was born"—this time using King Herod. When the tetrarch learned that a Jewish Messiah had been born who could potentially usurp him, Herod issued a similar genocidal decree to Pharaoh specifically aimed at killing all male children born from Israel:

> "Then Herod, when he saw that he was mocked of the wise men, was exceeding wroth, and sent forth, and slew all the children that were in Bethlehem, and in all the coasts thereof, from two years old and under, according to the time which he had diligently inquired of the wise men." – Matthew 2:16

It is critical to understand that Satan is not merely a "force for evil," "evil personified," or an idea. He is an intelligent being, created millennia before humanity came into existence. He was originally one of the highest-ranking angels who stood close to the throne of God itself:

> "Thou hast been in Eden the garden of God; every precious stone was thy covering, the sardius, topaz, and the diamond, the beryl, the onyx, and the jasper, the sapphire, the emerald, and the carbuncle, and gold: the workmanship of thy tabrets and of thy pipes was prepared in thee in the day that thou wast created. Thou art the anointed cherub that covereth; and I have set thee so: thou wast upon the holy mountain of God; thou hast walked up and down in the midst of the stones of fire. Thou wast perfect in thy ways from the day that thou wast created, till iniquity was found in thee." – Ezekiel 28:13–15

In the Septuagint (the oldest extant version of the Old Testament and the one most quoted by Jesus Christ and the apostles), we are told that Satan was "with the cherub," indicating his proximity to God, as the cherubim surround God's throne in Heaven (see 2 Samuel 6:2, Psalm 99:1, and Ezekiel 10:9–22).

So, as we've seen, using unwitting proxies and minions has long been a part of Satan's schemes. He conceals his appearance as long as he can, letting his servants enter the fray. And when necessary, he can mask his appearance as well as that of those in his charge. The Bible warns: "For Satan himself is transformed into an angel of light. Therefore, it is no great thing if his ministers also be transformed as the ministers of righteousness; whose end shall be according to their works" (2 Corinthians 11:14–15). And in the days of Noah, those satanic ministers were a group of fallen angels known as the *b'nai ha Elohim*—the sons of God.

SCRIPTURE CONFIRMS THAT "SONS OF GOD" WERE ANGELS

The Bible is self-confirming, and one passage of Scripture can always be explained by another. The book of Job verifies that the term "sons of God" refers to angels:

> "Now there was a day when the sons of God came to present themselves before the Lord, and Satan came also among them. And the Lord said unto Satan, Whence comest thou? Then Satan answered the Lord, and said, From going to and fro in the earth, and from walking up and down in it." – Job 1:6–7

This passage details God's literal meeting with the sons of God in Heaven. This was a "Divine Council" in which God presides over an assembly of holy and fallen angels to discuss worldly affairs, grants permission to carry out certain actions in the human realm, or assigns various tasks.

Job 2 describes another Divine Council:

> "Again there was a day when the sons of God [*b'nai ha elohim*] came to present themselves before the Lord, and Satan came also among them to present himself before the Lord." – Job 2:1

From the clear reading of the text, the "sons of God" are not human, but are in fact angels who were meeting with the Lord in Heaven. The third reference to the "sons of God" in the Old Testament is also in the book of Job, in chapter 38. When God was posing questions to Job about the creation of the universe (to show Job how little understanding and knowledge he had compared to the Lord), He proclaimed:

> "Where wast thou when I laid the foundations of the earth? declare, if thou hast understanding. Who hath laid the measures thereof, if thou knowest? or who hath stretched the line upon it? Whereupon are the foundations thereof fastened? or who laid the corner stone thereof; When the morning stars sang together, and all the sons of God [*b'nai ha Elohim*] shouted for joy?" – Job 38:4–7

Thus, the sons of God were not only in the presence of the Lord, but they existed even before the Earth itself was created. Every use of the term *b'nai ha Elohim* in the Old Testament refers to angelic beings. This has been the understanding of the Church for millennia. Irenaeus (early second century, ca. AD 202) was the bishop or pastor of the church in what is now Lyons, France. He was a disciple of Polycarp, who was a disciple of the Apostle John. His treatise, *Against Heresies,* was a landmark work that challenged the heretical Gnostic Christianity that threatened the true faith at that time. On Genesis 6:2, he wrote:

> "And for a very long while wickedness extended and spread, and reached and laid hold upon the whole race of mankind, until a very small seed of righteousness remained among them and illicit unions took place upon the earth, since angels were united with the daughters of the race of mankind; and they bore to them sons who for their exceeding greatness were called giants." – *A Discourse in the Demonstration of Apostolic Preaching,* 18

(Again, for a detailed examination and study of the Nephilim, their origin, and the abundance of biblical evidence for their existence and their threat to humanity, please see my previous book, *Judgment of the Nephilim,* which is a comprehensive biblical study of the Nephilim giants and their angelic forefathers.)

We see further confirmation of this illicit relationship in the two principal passages on the angelic incursion and the birth of the Nephilim:

> "And the angels which kept not their first estate, but left their own habitation, he hath reserved in everlasting chains under darkness unto the judgment of the great day. Even as Sodom and Gomorrah, and the cities about them in like manner, giving themselves over to fornication, and going after strange flesh, are set forth for an example, suffering the vengeance of eternal fire." – Jude 1:6–7

This passage explains that certain angels "left their own habitation" and, just like what happened in the account of Sodom and Gomorrah, they gave "themselves over to fornication, going after strange flesh"—in this case, human women. Further confirmation is found in 2 Peter:

> "For if God spared not the angels that sinned, but cast them down to hell, and delivered them into chains of darkness, to be reserved unto judgment; And spared not the old world, but saved Noah the eighth person, a preacher of righteousness, bringing in the flood upon the world of the ungodly; And turning the cities of Sodom and Gomorrah into ashes condemned them with an overthrow, making them an ensample unto those that after should live ungodly." – 2 Peter 2:4–6

The purpose behind these illicit relationships was to corrupt human genetics so that a human Messiah could not be born, thwarting the Lord's prophecy. Satan aimed to make humanity something other than image-bearers of God in order to disqualify us from salvation. To counter this assault on His creation, God ushered in the Flood judgment to wipe out the Nephilim, punish the apostate angels, and restart the human race through Noah and his family.

Theologians of the past concurred with this interpretation of Genesis 6:

"'The earth was filled with violence.' 'All flesh had corrupted *his way* upon the earth.' Here, the corruption of the Divine Way, or principle on which, and purpose for which the creation was brought into existence, seems to have been the production of a monstrous violent race outside the limits of creation prescribed by the Creator. Therefore, the necessity for the destruction of this mongrel brood, in order to preserve the original race of Adam from entire contamination." - "Angels That Kept Not Their First Estate," H. Goodwin, as printed in *The Rainbow, A Magazine of Christian Literature*, Vol. 18, 1882, p. 314–315

THE END TIMES: SATAN'S FINAL ATTEMPT TO UNDO THE GENESIS 3:15 PROPHECY

"And therefore these words of the psalmist must belong to times of the Messiah, by whom this promise was fulfilled to the true Israel of God, who were delivered from that most dreadful of all captivities the captivity of sin and Satan as is declared Luke 1:68–75; 4:18; Eph 4:8. And they shall be literally accomplished to the natural seed of Jacob, or Israel, according to the expectation and belief of all the Jews in their several ages, and of most Christian writers. *The Redeemer shall come to Zion* by his Word and Spirit, by his gospel and his grace, as he before came in the flesh and shall turn away all ungodliness from Jacob.

For this time of universal reformation the psalmist longs and prays now in the time of universal corruption; as if he had said, Those will be glorious times, as the present are melancholy ones, for *then Jacob,* that is the seed of Jacob, shall rejoice and Israel shall be glad. The triumphs of the king of Zion will be the joy of Zion's children.

> **And at the second coming of Christ finally to extinguish the dominion of sin and Satan, this salvation will be completed, which as it is the hope, so will it be the joy of every true Israelite.**" – *The Holy Bible, with Critical, Practical and Explanatory Notes, Volume II, The First Book of Kings to Proverbs,* Reverend Joseph Benson, 1846, p. 694

> "And he came to Nazareth, where he had been brought up: and, as his custom was, he went into the synagogue on the sabbath day, and stood up for to read. And there was delivered unto him the book of the prophet Esaias. And when he had opened the book, he found the place where it was written, The Spirit of the Lord is upon me, because he hath anointed me to preach the gospel to the poor; he hath sent me to heal the brokenhearted, to preach deliverance to the captives, and recovering of sight to the blind, to set at liberty them that are bruised, To preach the acceptable year of the Lord. **And he closed the book, and he gave it again to the minister, and sat down.** And the eyes of all them that were in the synagogue were fastened on him. And he began to say unto them, This day is this scripture fulfilled in your ears." – Luke 4:16–21

The incarnation of Jesus Christ on Earth as the Messiah and Seed of the Woman was fulfilled two thousand years ago. During that time, Jesus came as the "Lamb of God"—the Suffering Servant who would give His life "as a ransom for many" (Matthew 20:28). This is what the Lord was referring to when He read from the book of Isaiah in the synagogue as cited above in Luke 4. It was the time for the Messiah to bring healing and redemption and to free the captives—all humanity, as we are all born in sin—from the bondage of our guilt before God through His atoning sacrifice on the cross.

However, that was only a partial fulfillment of Genesis 3:15. The verse also prophesied that Satan would have his head "bruised" (*shuwph,* or שׁוּף in Hebrew, which means "to crush") by the Messiah. This will be fulfilled at the

Second Coming of the Seed of the Woman. This was why the Lord *Yeshua* "closed the book" after only reading the first half of the prophecy from Isaiah 61. Here is the remainder:

> "...**and the day of vengeance of our God**; to comfort all that mourn; **To appoint unto them that mourn in Zion, to give unto them beauty for ashes**, the oil of joy for mourning, the garment of praise for the spirit of heaviness; that they might be called trees of righteousness, the planting of the LORD, that he might be glorified." – Isaiah 61:2–3

BEAUTY FOR ASHES: THE RETURN OF JESUS CHRIST TO CONQUER SATAN IS INEXTRICABLY LINKED TO THE END-TIMES GATHERING AND REDEMPTION OF ISRAEL

> "For Zion's sake will I not hold my peace, and for Jerusalem's sake I will not rest, until the righteousness thereof go forth as brightness, and the salvation thereof as a lamp that burneth. And the Gentiles shall see thy righteousness, and all kings thy glory: and thou shalt be called by a new name, which the mouth of the LORD shall name. Thou shalt also be a crown of glory in the hand of the LORD, and a royal diadem in the hand of thy God. Thou shalt no more be termed Forsaken; neither shall thy land any more be termed Desolate: but thou shalt be called Hephzibah, and thy land Beulah: for the LORD delighteth in thee, and thy land shall be married." – Isaiah 62:1–4

Time and time again in the Old Testament, God prophesied a redemption of Israel linked to His return to earth, again giving Satan advanced notice of his impending defeat. Having failed in the first half of the prophecy (preventing the birth of the Messiah), the Devil then turned his sights to the second half: trying to destroy Israel outright, prevent its redemption, or corrupt it beyond repair. This is a critical part of the Devil's end-times machinations to "prove God wrong" before the heavenly host and let a divine prophecy fail.

It could also prevent or delay the return of the Savior, as the two events are connected repeatedly in Bible prophecy:

> "Behold, the LORD hath proclaimed unto the end of the world, Say ye to the daughter of Zion, Behold, **thy salvation cometh; behold, his reward is with him**, and his work before him. And they shall call them, **The holy people, The redeemed of the LORD**: and thou shalt be called, Sought out, A city not forsaken." – Isaiah 62:11–12

The Lord, in His infinite wisdom, once again put His Holy Name on the line by linking the prophesied return of Messiah to the redemption of Israel. Satan attempted to stop the Messiah the first time and failed. And during the final years before the Second Coming of the Seed of the Woman, the Devil will empower his own seed—Antichrist—to try to topple God's prophetic proclamation.

As will be shown, the Antichrist, who is the Final Nephilim, will have a satanic obsession with corrupting and destroying Israel. That mission will be the centerpiece of his reign of terror. But he will not be alone. The fallen angels will return to the human realm once again. In the days of Noah, Satan enlisted a faction of fallen angels to assist his schemes. In the end times, they will return.

"The angels that sinned" were the *b'nai ha Elohim* of Genesis 6. The principal New Testament passages on the Nephilim describe their present confinement:

> "And the angels which kept not their first estate, but left their own

> habitation, he hath reserved in everlasting chains under darkness unto the judgment of the great day. Even as Sodom and Gomorrah, and the cities about them in like manner, giving themselves over to fornication, and going after strange flesh, are set forth for an example, suffering the vengeance of eternal fire." – Jude 1:6–7
>
> "For if God spared not the angels that sinned, but cast them down to hell, and delivered them into chains of darkness, to be reserved unto judgment; And spared not the old world, but saved Noah the eighth person, a preacher of righteousness, bringing in the flood upon the world of the ungodly." – 2 Peter 2:4–5

Notice both passages include references to their punishment: being sentenced to imprisonment in the Abyss—the bottomless pit of Hell—where they are chained in darkness until the "judgment of the great day." We will now examine that time—the "judgment of the great day"—and see that the Bible predicts that these same rebel angels will be released from the pit and bring a judgment on mankind so severe that it will be reminiscent of the global Flood.

CHAPTER 3

THE RETURN OF THE SONS OF GOD

The apostate angels who sinned in Genesis 6 were punished with imprisonment in the Abyss. They will eventually be released. For thousands of years, these rebels have remained removed from both the angelic and the human realm, languishing in Hell under a supernatural, thick cloud of darkness. The only solitary break from this bleak existence was when the Lord Jesus Christ, during His three days of death, proclaimed His victory in Crucifixion on the cross:

> "For Christ also hath once suffered for sins, the just for the unjust, that he might bring us to God, being put to death in the flesh, but quickened by the Spirit: **By which also he went and preached unto the spirits in prison; Which sometime were disobedient, when once the longsuffering of God waited in the days of Noah**, while the ark was a preparing, wherein few, that is, eight souls were saved by water." – 1 Peter 3:18–20

But since that time, these angels remain locked in the solitary darkness of the Abyss—one of the compartments of Hell.

"HELL": ABODE FOR THE RIGHTEOUS *AND* THE WICKED

In the Old Testament, *Sheol* is referred to as "hell," "the pit," or "the grave."

Rather than being just an abode for the damned, Hell—or, more accurately, *Sheol* or *Hades*—was the destination for both believers and unbelievers before the Resurrection of Christ.

The Lord Jesus Christ provided the most succinct description of what happened to the souls of all the dead who perished before His First Coming to Earth in His account of the rich man and Lazarus:

> "There was a certain rich man, which was clothed in purple and fine linen, and fared sumptuously every day: And there was a certain beggar named Lazarus, which was laid at his gate, full of sores, And desiring to be fed with the crumbs which fell from the rich man's table: moreover the dogs came and licked his sores. And it came to pass, that the beggar died, and was carried by the angels into Abraham's bosom: the rich man also died, and was buried; ***And in hell*** he lift up his eyes, being in torments, **and seeth Abraham afar off, and Lazarus in his bosom**. And he cried and said, Father Abraham, have mercy on me, and send Lazarus, that he may dip the tip of his finger in water, and cool my tongue; for I am tormented in this flame.
>
> But Abraham said, Son, remember that thou in thy lifetime receivedst thy good things, and likewise Lazarus evil things: but now he is comforted, and thou art tormented. And beside all this, between us and you there is a great gulf fixed: so that they which would pass from hence to you cannot; neither can they pass to us, that would come from thence. Then he said, I pray thee therefore, father, that thou wouldest send him to my father's house: For I have five brethren; that he may testify unto them, lest they also come into this place of torment. Abraham saith unto him, They have Moses and the prophets; let them hear them. And he said, Nay, father Abraham: but if one went unto them from the dead, they will repent. And he said unto him, If they hear not Moses and the

prophets, neither will they be persuaded, though one rose from the dead." – Luke 16:19–31

In *Sheol*, there was a place of comfort for those who had been believers and were saved ("Abraham's Bosom"), as well as a place of punishment that served as a temporary holding cell for the wicked (the "place of torment") until God's final judgment of all unbelievers in the end times when they will be cast into the Lake of Fire (Revelation 20:12–15). (*After* Christ's Resurrection, the souls of born-again believers could rightly and justly access Heaven, emptying Abraham's Bosom permanently; see Psalm 68:18 and Ephesians 4:8).

As we look at the Lord's narrative, note that it is not a parable. Jesus stated that "there was a *certain* rich man," indicating that He was referring to a real person, not sharing an object lesson or presenting a fictional character. He also gave the *name* of the beggar—another detail we never find in a parable.

Jesus explained very clearly that the rich man, who had died as an unbeliever, could see Abraham and the beggar Lazarus in Hell. They were separated, however, by a great gulf. Thus, we have a word picture of the arrangement of *Sheol*. This is especially important for our study because the Nephilim before the Flood are constantly linked to *Sheol* in Scripture.

BOTTOMLESS PIT: THIRD COMPARTMENT OF HELL AND PRISON OF THE GENESIS 6 FALLEN ANGELS

In addition to Jesus' account of Lazarus and the Rich Man, which refers to the two areas of Sheol designated for believers and unbelievers after death, the Bible refers to a *third* compartment of *Sheol*: the Abyss. Also known as the "bottomless pit" in Scripture, this is where the apostate angels of Genesis 6 were dragged by the waters of the Flood, and it's where they remain today until their release in the end times. Abraham's Bosom and the place of torment housed *the human dead*, but the fallen angels, still alive, were taken to the bottomless pit. While the Flood in the days of Noah did indeed exterminate all of the antediluvian Nephilim (though their DNA remained on the ark through the wives of Noah's sons), their angelic forefathers were not killed in the raging floodwaters; instead, they were dragged down into the Abyss alive. As the waters that came from within the Earth returned below surface, the apostate angels were sent to their prison. A nineteenth-century commentary confirms this notion:

> "In accordance with this Jude speaks (verse 6) of 'the angels who kept not their first estate' as being 'kept in perpetual chains beneath darkness' unto the judgment of the great day. The idea is that of confinement in a dark place, and so that they cannot escape from the judgment which finally awaits them. It seems like a temporary imprisonment of an arrested criminal, before his final trial and condemnation.
>
> To the same purpose Peter speaks (2 Peter 2:4): 'If God spared not the angels who sinned, but thrusting them down to the abyss in chains of darkness, assigned them to be kept for judgment.' The phrase 'chains of darkness' seems plainly to mean chains or bonds in a dark place and the participle indicates of course that this place was a deep abyss." –*Bibliotheca Sacra; Or, Tracts and Essays on Topics Connected with Biblical Literature and Theology*, edited by Edward Robinson, 1843, p. 136

During Jesus Christ's ministry on earth, the demons—spirits of the dead Nephilim giants—begged the Lord to not dispatch them to the Abyss:

> "And when he went forth to land, there met him out of the city a certain man, which had devils long time, and ware no clothes, neither abode in any house, but in the tombs. When he saw Jesus,

> he cried out, and fell down before him, and with a loud voice said, What have I to do with thee, Jesus, thou Son of God most high? I beseech thee, torment me not.
>
> (For he had commanded the unclean spirit to come out of the man. For oftentimes it had caught him: and he was kept bound with chains and in fetters; and he brake the bands, and was driven of the devil into the wilderness.) And Jesus asked him, saying, What is thy name? And he said, Legion: because many devils were entered into him. **And they besought him that he would not command them to go out into the deep.**" – Luke 8:27–31

When the demons encountered the incarnate Christ, they immediately recognized Him. They were standing face to face with the "Angel of the Lord" of the Old Testament—the preincarnate presence of Christ—who repeatedly waged war against the Nephilim. During the campaign to recapture the Promised Land from the Canaanite usurpers, the Lord personally engaged the giants in combat, wiping them out and leaving the armies of Israel to clean up the mess of retreating, discomfited soldiers.

Encountering their conqueror again in the New Testament, the demons pleaded for mercy. And notice their request. They begged Jesus not to send them to "the deep." The Greek term for "the deep" is *aboussos*, the same term used in the New Testament for the "bottomless pit." The giants were terrified to be sent to the same place where their fallen angelic ancestors were presently imprisoned. We see affirmation of the distinction between the Abyss and the other compartments of Hell in the excerpt below:

> "'The deep' in [8:31] into which the demons that possessed the Gadarene maniacs besought Jesus not to cast them, is evidently the place of punishment to which they knew they were ultimately to be consigned; for the being sent thither stands in that passage as equivalent to suffering the torment before the time spoken of in

Matt 8:29, which they feared might be at once inflicted on them.

We may say further in view of the evident analogy between these passages and Jude verse 6, that 'abyss' is the place also where other wicked spirits of the same class are already confined awaiting the more complete punishment, which they are to suffer after the judgment of the great day. 'Abyss' is not one of the names actually applied to the state or place of wicked men after death; but we seem to be forbidden by such language as that in Matthew 25:41 to infer that **the condition of lost men and fallen angels is to be essentially different when the last stage of their destiny is reached.**" – *Dr. William Smith's Dictionary of the Bible*, Vol. 1, 1877, p. 579

REBEL SONS OF GOD RELEASED FROM THE ABYSS DURING DAY OF THE LORD

"And I beheld, and heard an angel flying through the midst of heaven, saying with a loud voice, Woe, woe, woe, to the inhabiters of the earth by reason of the other voices of the trumpet of the three angels, which are yet to sound! **And the fifth angel sounded, and I saw a star fall from heaven unto the earth: and to him was given the key of the bottomless pit.** And he opened the bottomless pit; and there arose a smoke out of the pit, as the smoke of a great furnace; and the sun and the air were darkened by reason of the smoke of the pit. And there came out of the smoke locusts upon the earth: and unto them was given power, as the scorpions of the earth have power.

And it was commanded them that they should not hurt the grass of the earth, neither any green thing, neither any tree; but only those

> men which have not the seal of God in their foreheads. And to them it was given that they should not kill them, but that they should be tormented five months: and their torment was as the torment of a scorpion, when he striketh a man. And in those days shall men seek death, and shall not find it; and shall desire to die, and death shall flee from them." – Revelation 8:13, 9:1–6

At the fifth trumpet of Revelation, the bottomless pit—which, as stated earlier, is also known as the Abyss (*aboussos*), is opened. This is when the fallen angels of Genesis 6 are finally unleashed onto the world. This passage warrants a verse-by-verse examination to fully understand the context and timing of when this horrific judgment of God will take place.

DEVIL AND HIS ANGELS RETURN TO EARTH IN THE END TIMES

> "And I beheld, and heard an angel flying through the midst of heaven, saying with a loud voice, Woe, woe, woe, to the inhabiters of the earth by reason of the other voices of the trumpet of the three angels, which are yet to sound!"

This is the turning point of the end times—when Satan and his fallen angels will be evicted from Heaven and Hell and permitted to manifest in the earthly realm. They will once again walk among and interact with humanity in the open, something that has not taken place since the days of Noah. Recall that, in the antediluvian era, open interaction between the angelic realm and humanity was commonplace:

- God spoke to Adam directly. There was no separation between humanity and God before sin entered the picture.

- Adam and Eve were able to see, talk to, and stand next to Satan. Furthermore, Eve was not frightened by the appearance of the talking, shining Serpent (see Genesis 3:1–4).
- After falling into sin, the disgraced Adam and Eve "heard" the voice of the Lord "walking in the Garden," and knew to hide themselves from His presence (Genesis 3:9).
- God addressed Adam, Eve, and the Serpent in person, giving them their respective punishments (Genesis 3:12–15).
- The Lord made coats of animal skins for Adam and Eve to wear (Genesis 3:22).
- After banishing Adam and Eve from the Garden located within Eden, a cherubim and a supernatural sword that could swing on its own were placed at the entrance of the Garden to prevent any reentry.
- In Genesis 6, the sons of God, in rebellion, entered the human realm, took human wives, and conceived hybrid children who would be the Nephilim.

In the postdiluvian world, appearances by angels or God were few and far between. When they did occur, the person visited by the angel was overwhelmed with fear. Eve wasn't scared of the Devil himself, yet the prophet Daniel fainted in shock upon seeing a good, holy angel. Angels often reassure humanity with the greeting of "do not be afraid" when they appear, as their mere presence is overwhelming to the senses for mortals.

However, at the fifth trumpet, the veil between the heavenly and earthly realms will start to recede with an onslaught of fallen angels:

> "And the fifth angel sounded, and I saw a star fall from heaven unto the earth: and to him was given the key of the bottomless pit."

The "star" in this passage refers to the Devil. Notice that the verse says the key to the bottomless pit was given "to him"—indicating that a specific being is in view. This is the moment when Satan is banished from Heaven. We see confirmation of this eviction and the biblical symbolism of angels as stars in Revelation 12:

> "And there appeared another wonder in heaven; and behold a great red dragon, having seven heads and ten horns, and seven crowns upon his heads. And his tail drew the third part of the stars of heaven, and did cast them to the earth: and the dragon stood before the woman which was ready to be delivered, for to devour her child as soon as it was born….
>
> And there was war in heaven: Michael and his angels fought against the dragon; and the dragon fought and his angels, And prevailed not; neither was their place found any more in heaven. And the great dragon was cast out, that old serpent, called the Devil, and Satan, which deceiveth the whole world: he was cast out into the earth, and his angels were cast out with him.
>
> And I heard a loud voice saying in heaven, Now is come salvation, and strength, and the kingdom of our God, and the power of his Christ: for the accuser of our brethren is cast down, which accused them before our God day and night. And they overcame him by the blood of the Lamb, and by the word of their testimony; and they loved not their lives unto the death. Therefore rejoice, ye heavens, and ye that dwell in them. Woe to the inhabiters of the earth and of the sea! for the devil is come down unto you, having great wrath, because he knoweth that he hath but a short time." – Revelation 12:3–12

In John's vision, the "stars" that are dragged down to Earth are the fallen angels who are in league with the Devil. This is confirmed later in the passage, where we see exactly how this eviction takes place. Michael, a righteous archangel assigned to the protection of Israel, enters Heaven to wage war against the Devil.

In *Judgment of the Nephilim*, I discussed in detail that Satan, at present, is permitted access to Heaven. This is clearly established in Job chapters 1 and 2, where we read that, on two separate occasions, the Devil appears before the throne of God:

> "Now there was a day when the sons of God came to present themselves before the LORD, and Satan came also among them. And the LORD said unto Satan, Whence comest thou? Then Satan answered the LORD, and said, From going to and fro in the earth, and from walking up and down in it." – Job 1:6–7
>
> "Again there was a day when the sons of God came to present themselves before the LORD, and Satan came also among them to present himself before the LORD. And the LORD said unto Satan, From whence comest thou? And Satan answered the LORD, and said, From going to and fro in the earth, and from walking up and down in it." – Job 2:1–2

Contrary to popular belief, the Devil doesn't reside in Hell. In fact, there is no biblical reference to Satan even experiencing Hell up to this point in history. God, in His infinite wisdom, has permitted Satan access to Heaven, and Revelation 12 informs us that the Devil uses his time of audience with God to "accuse the brethren," arguing for the guilt and condemnation of the saints of God—people who are born-again believers in the Gospel of Jesus Christ.

But at the fifth trumpet, the angelic battle is waged. Michael and the holy angels of God prevail, and Satan is permanently banished from Heaven. This is when Satan falls from Heaven. Jesus Christ saw a prophetic vision of this during His earthly ministry:

> "And the seventy returned again with joy, saying, Lord, even the devils are subject unto us through thy name. And [Jesus] said unto them, I beheld Satan as lightning fall from heaven. Behold, I give unto you power to tread on serpents and scorpions, and over all the power of the enemy: and nothing shall by any means hurt you. Notwithstanding in this rejoice not, that the spirits are subject unto you; but rather rejoice, because your names are written in heaven."
> – Luke 10:17–20

A nineteenth-century commentary citing the Church Father Tertullian confirms that the "fallen star" of the fifth trumpet is indeed Satan:

> "Here as in [chapter 1:20] the *personal* import of the Star is implied. In the Old Testament conception of 'the host of heaven,' a Star and an Angel are kindred ideas—Job 38:7, Psalm 103:20–21, and some personal agent of the divine justice is evidently intended.... The analogy of Isaiah24:12, Luke 10:18, (Revelation 12:9) suggests that an evil angel is described.... He is Satan himself according to Tertullian." – *The Holy Bible According to the Authorized Version (AD: 1611): With an Explanatory and Critical Commentary, Vol. 4, Hebrews to Revelation*, F. C. Cook, 1890, p. 606

A second commentary also identifies the Devil as the fallen star of Revelation 9:

> "Clearly therefore the star is identified with a person: no doubt a 'fallen angel' in the common sense of the term. For the identification of angels with stars, [Revelation 1:20 and Job 38:7]: and of *fallen* angels in particular, [1 Enoch 18:16, 21:3, and 100]. The fall of this star may legitimately be *illustrated*, as to the image by Isaiah 14:12 and as to the meaning by Luke 10:18 and 21:9 in

> this book: but it is not to be assumed that this passage refers to the same event as either of the two last, still less that the first does." – *The Revelation of St. John the Divine*, William Henry Simcox, 1891, p. 59

Fallen from Heaven, the Devil descends to literally unleash Hell on earth.

"LOCUSTS": THE IMPRISONED ANGELS OF GENESIS 6

> "And he opened the bottomless pit; and there arose a smoke out of the pit, as the smoke of a great furnace; and the sun and the air were darkened by reason of the smoke of the pit." – Revelation 9:2

This "smoke" is so murky and thick that it darkens the sun itself! This is no normal smokestack. This is a part of the supernatural darkness the Lord used to envelop the sinning sons of God, the forefathers of the Nephilim. After they were sucked down to the Abyss when the floodwaters "abated" and returned underground, God surrounded them with heavy blackness for millennia:

> "And the angels which kept not their first estate, but left their own habitation, **he hath reserved in everlasting chains under darkness** unto the judgment of the great day." – Jude 1:6

> "For if God spared not the angels that sinned, but cast them down to hell, **and delivered them into chains of darkness**, to be reserved unto judgment." – 2 Peter 2:4

Scripture confirms that the punishment of the angels of Genesis 6 who committed fornication with human women consisted not just of imprisonment in the Abyss in chains, but also of being enveloped by this heavy gloom. A similar punishment was inflicted upon Egypt during the Exodus:

> "And the LORD said unto Moses, Stretch out thine hand toward heaven, that there may be darkness over the land of Egypt, **even darkness which may be felt**. And Moses stretched forth his hand toward heaven; **and there was a thick darkness in all the land of Egypt three days**: They saw not one another, neither rose any from his place for three days: but all the children of Israel had light in their dwellings." – Exodus 10:21–23

Note that the supernatural darkness could be felt; it was a physical darkness, like smoke. And this is precisely what we see bursting from the bottomless pit at the fifth trumpet.

FALLEN ANGELS CARRY OUT GOD'S JUDGMENT ON THE UNBELIEVING WORLD

This will be a full return to the days of Noah, the period when angelic beings openly interacted with the human realm. But this time, the *b'nai ha Elohim* will be a tool of the wrath of God. Renowned theologian Robert Govett came to the same conclusion about the mission of the locusts when the Abyss is opened:

> "If this be granted, then the answer to the question, 'Who are these thus addressed' and 'what is that which is opened' will be less incredible. For the reply then let us turn to Revelation 9:1. 'And the fifth angel sounded, and I saw a star fall from heaven unto the earth: and to him was given the key of the bottomless pit.' By the

> star we cannot understand a literal star because it is added 'to *him* was given the key of the bottomless pit.'
>
> This star thus falling from heaven to the earth is, it would seem, **Satan who shall be cast out of heaven when 'Michael stands up for the children of the people of the Jews.'** That this war is literal and future.... Thus then, to him and his angels is given a charge to open the bottomless pit. '*Open ye princes"*... In Isaiah these are represented as 'giants' and instead of the agency of Satan in loosing them, which is remarked in Revelation, we are directed to the all-ordaining word of Jehovah in this place as the Mighty One, from whom the design of wrath originally proceeds and of which Satan is but the instrument." – *Isaiah Unfulfilled: Being an Exposition of the Prophet, with New Version and Critical Notes,* Robert Govett, 1841, p. 173–174

The sinning sons of God, once rulers of the planet and viewed as gods in the days of Noah, return as grotesque, hybrid, locust-like creatures in the end times. This degraded state was dubbed "the Reverse Rapture" in *Judgment of the Nephilim.*

REVERSE RAPTURE: APOSTATE ANGELS TURN INTO GROTESQUE CREATURES

> "What? know ye not that he which is joined to an harlot is one body? for two, saith he, shall be one flesh. But he that is joined unto the Lord is one spirit. Flee fornication. Every sin that a man doeth is without the body; but he that committeth fornication sinneth against his own body." – 1 Corinthians 6:16–18

Here we read that fornication is unique from all other sins in that it is a sin against one's own body. A body is defiled by sexual sin, and this is precisely what took place during the era of human-angelic fornication in Genesis 6. Jude 1:6 states that the apostate angels "kept not their first estate, but left their own habitation." The translation of "habitation," *oikētērion* in Greek, occurs only twice in the Bible. The only other instance is in 2 Corinthians 5:

> "For we know that if our earthly house of this tabernacle were dissolved, we have a building of God, an house not made with hands, eternal in the heavens. For in this we groan, earnestly desiring to be clothed upon with our house [*oikētērion*] which is from heaven: If so be that being clothed we shall not be found naked. For we that are in this tabernacle do groan, being burdened: not for that we would be unclothed, but clothed upon, that mortality might be swallowed up of life. Now he that hath wrought us for the selfsame thing is God, who also hath given unto us the earnest of the Spirit. Therefore we are always confident, knowing that, whilst we are at home in the body, we are absent from the Lord." – 2 Corinthians 5:1–6

Oikētērion here metaphorically describes the glorified, heavenly body born-again believers will eventually receive as a "house" we "earnestly" desire to be clothed with. The Apostle Paul, under the Holy Spirit's inspiration, explains that, for Christians, the flesh bodies we're born with pale in comparison to the heavenly bodies we will receive at the Rapture, when all believers are translated. This celestial body will be immortal and will not contain the sin nature that all have inherited from Adam. So, the "house" that Paul desires is the same "habitation," or *oikētērion,* that the angels who sinned chose to desecrate to pursue their sinful schemes. These apostate angels succumbed to evil desires, degraded their habitation in an immortal, heavenly body, and became "flesh"—stained with sin and destined for God's judgment.

All born-again Christians will one day receive a new, glorified body, a body-like substance of angelic beings. The angels who sinned in Genesis 6 went through a "reverse Rapture," in which they descended to Earth and defiled and corrupted their once-glorified bodies by joining themselves sexually to women who possessed a sinful flesh nature. They had thus disqualified themselves from full heavenly realm access. Instead, for thousands of years, they remained imprisoned in the Abyss and will return to Earth as monstrous agents of wrath.

RETURN OF THE APOSTATE ANGELS IN "THE DAY OF THE LORD"

In the majority of commentaries, articles, and videos about the end times, the terms "the Tribulation," "Great Tribulation," or "seven-year Tribulation" are often used to describe the final, end-times period detailed in the book of Revelation that precedes Armageddon and the Second Coming of Christ. However, we find that, in Scripture, a different term is actually used much more frequently to describe the commencement of this final series of judgments: the Day of the Lord. The Day of the Lord and Daniel's seventieth week (as detailed in Daniel chapter 9; the final seven years of the world that commence with a covenant between Israel and the Antichrist) are the proper biblical titles for the period when God will supernaturally judge the world and unleash the events described in the book of Revelation's trumpet and bowl judgments. (Jesus later refers to this entire time as the "Great Tribulation," which is also an appropriate term).

The phrase "the day of the Lord" is used twenty-four times in the Old Testament, and each occurrence falls in an end-times, prophetic context. The "Day of the Lord" is the biblical, Old Testament term used to refer to the end-of-age judgments of the book of Revelation that God will pour out on the world, starting with a massive, global earthquake (Revelation 6:12). This is a period when God will actively intervene in the affairs of humanity with devastating impact.

These judgments will be experienced by the entire world population at a time when society will have been lulled into a false sense of security. The world will think it has achieved "peace and safety," then sudden destruction from God will come. The Day of the Lord will also overlap (as will be shown) with the seventieth week of Daniel, the prophesied final seven years on Earth before the Second Coming of Jesus Christ. But God will at this time, in anger, send catastrophic judgments that will cause everyone's heart to "melt" in fear. Many verses in the New Testament affirm this:

> "For yourselves know perfectly that the day of the Lord so cometh as a thief in the night. For when they shall say, Peace and safety; then sudden destruction cometh upon them, as travail upon a woman with child; and they shall not escape." – 1 Thessalonians 5:2–3

The prophet Joel, who wrote in great detail on the Day of the Lord, described the heavenly signs of its arrival:

> "The sun shall be turned into darkness, and the moon into blood, before the great and terrible day of the LORD come." – Joel 2:31

This once again coincides with the words of Jesus Christ about the end times:

> "Immediately after the tribulation of those days shall the sun be darkened, and the moon shall not give her light, and the stars shall fall from heaven, and the powers of the heavens shall be shaken: And then shall appear the sign of the Son of man in heaven: and then shall all the tribes of the earth mourn, and they shall see the Son of man coming in the clouds of heaven with power and great glory." – Matthew 24:29–30

While the sun "turns dark" several times in the prophecies of Revelation, there is only one place where the darkening coincides with the moon turning blood red: the opening of the sixth seal of Revelation:

> "And I beheld when he had opened the sixth seal, and, lo, there was a great earthquake; **and the sun became black as sackcloth of hair, and the moon became as blood**; And the stars of heaven fell unto the earth, even as a fig tree casteth her untimely figs, when she is shaken of a mighty wind." – Revelation 6:12–13

The red moon combined with the blackened sun will be the ultimate sign that the final wrath of God has commenced. Even the most powerful and wealthy of the unbelieving world will cower in fear, as they will be well aware that the true day of reckoning has arrived:

> "And the kings of the earth, and the great men, and the rich men, and the chief captains, and the mighty men, and every bondman, and every free man, hid themselves in the dens and in the rocks of the mountains; And said to the mountains and rocks, Fall on us, and hide us from the face of him that sitteth on the throne, and from the wrath of the Lamb: **For the great day of his wrath is come**; and who shall be able to stand?" – Revelation 6:15–17

During the Flood, the ark, carrying Noah—the faithful, believer, and his family—rose up on top of the raging waters as unprecedented, torrential rain pounded the earth. Believers ascended while judgment descended. At the Day of the Lord, believers will once again be taken up—in the Rapture—safely protected in Heaven during the judgments that will come down upon the earth. This is what the Apostle Paul meant when he wrote:

> "For God hath not appointed us to wrath, but to obtain salvation

by our Lord Jesus Christ." – 1 Thessalonians 5:9

The Church will be rescued at the very moment of the Lord's vengeance.

GENESIS 6 ANGELS: ARMY OF GOD'S WRATH

> "Blow ye the trumpet in Zion, and sound an alarm in my holy mountain: let all the inhabitants of the land tremble: **for the day of the LORD cometh**, for it is nigh at hand; A day of darkness and of gloominess, a day of clouds and of thick darkness, as the morning spread upon the mountains: **a great people and a strong; there hath not been ever the like, neither shall be any more after it, even to the years of many generations**. – Joel 2:1-2

> "But when the judgement of God shall have come, 'He shall send,' as he himself says, 'his angels with a great trumpet,' and 'they shall gather his elect from the one end of heaven to the other,' he shall inflict punishments on those who are to be punished by hostile Powers as by means of executioners. **He gives commandment to the angels about him to open their prison that they may depart, and execute vengeance on the ungodly**." – *Isaiah Unfulfilled: Being an Exposition of the Prophet; with New Version and Critical Notes. To Which Are Added, Two Dissertations: One on the "Sons of God" and "Giants" of Genesis VI., and the Other*, Reverend Robert Govett, 1841, p. 177

Notice that the passage above from Joel describes an army so powerful and horrific that there has never been anything like it, nor will there ever be. This coincides with how Jesus described the end times to His disciples:

> "For then shall be great tribulation, such as was not since the

> beginning of the world to this time, no, nor ever shall be." – Matthew 24:21

What makes this period of judgment so unique is that the apostate sons of God of Genesis 6, imprisoned for millennia, will be released to serve as an instrument of God's judgment on the unbelieving world:

> "And there came out of the smoke locusts upon the earth: and unto them was given power, as the scorpions of the earth have power.... And the shapes of the locusts were like unto horses prepared unto battle; and on their heads were as it were crowns like gold, and their faces were as the faces of men.
>
> And they had hair as the hair of women, and their teeth were as the teeth of lions. And they had breastplates, as it were breastplates of iron; and the sound of their wings was as the sound of chariots of many horses running to battle. And they had tails like unto scorpions, and there were stings in their tails: and their power was to hurt men five months." – Revelation 9:3, 7–10

Note the bizarre description of these beings who arise from the Abyss. This is directly in line with the prophecy of the Day of the Lord in Joel chapter 2:

> "Blow ye the trumpet in Zion, and sound an alarm in my holy mountain: let all the inhabitants of the land tremble: for the day of the LORD cometh, for it is nigh at hand; A day of darkness and of gloominess, a day of clouds and of thick darkness." – Joel 2:1–2

This passage directly references the Day of the Lord, indicating that this is an end-times prophecy. It then states that "day" will be a "day of darkness and gloominess, a day of clouds and of thick darkness." Recall that when the bottomless pit is unlocked, "thick darkness" emerges from it:

> "And the fifth angel sounded, and I saw a star fall from heaven unto the earth: and to him was given the key of the bottomless pit. And he opened the bottomless pit; and there **arose a smoke out of the pit**, as the smoke of a great furnace; and **the sun and the air were darkened by reason of the smoke of the pit**." – Revelation 9:1–2

This supernatural darkness was predicted in many Old Testament prophetic passages about the Day of the Lord:

> "The great day of the LORD is near, it is near, and hasteth greatly, even the voice of the day of the LORD: the mighty man shall cry there bitterly. That day is a day of wrath, a day of trouble and distress, a day of wasteness and desolation, **a day of darkness and gloominess, a day of clouds and thick darkness.**" – Zephaniah 1:14–15

> "Woe unto you that desire the day of the LORD! to what end is it for you? the day of the LORD is **darkness**, and not light." – Amos 5:18

This darkness is caused by the supernatural smoke from the bottomless pit that surrounded these fallen angels for thousands of years. When they emerge from the pit, the brightness of the sun will be blocked out.

FALLEN ANGELIC LOCUST ARMY FIGHTS LIKE NEPHILIM

> "'Let all the inhabitants of the land tremble for the Day of The Lord

> cometh; for it is nigh at hand. A day of darkness and gloominess a day of clouds and thick darkness as the Morning spread upon the mountains.' To which is appended in following verses **the character of the Antichristian confederacy—the scourge that will be used of God for His purposes of righteous punishment**."
> – *The Substance of Things Hoped for; a Contrast to the Immaterial and Speculative System of Anti-Millenarianism, Expressed in "the End of All Things" [by J. Grant], and Other Kindred Works,* Henry Goodwyn, 1867, p. 19

Joel 2 continues by stating that a people who are "great…and strong" will also emerge with this darkness. This will be an army of unprecedented strength and might.

> "A fire devoureth before them; and behind them a flame burneth: **the land is as the garden of Eden before them,** and behind them a desolate wilderness; yea, and nothing shall escape them. The appearance of them is as the appearance of horses; and as horsemen, so shall they run. Like the noise of chariots on the tops of mountains shall they leap, **like the noise of a flame of fire** that devoureth the stubble, as a strong people set in battle array. Before their face the people shall be much pained: all faces shall gather blackness." – Joel 2:3–6

We're told that God makes His angels a "flame of fire" (Hebrews 1:7). The army in the book of Joel has a fire devouring before them and a flame behind them. They see the Earth as "the Garden of Eden." As we shall see in the coming pages, the sinful sons of God were able to overtake the land of Eden during the Days of Noah.

We then find the next connection between Joel 2 and Revelation 9's locusts. Joel described this army as having "the appearance of horses" and making the "noise of chariots"; this is precisely how the locusts are described in Revelation 9:

> "And they had breastplates, as it were breastplates of iron; and the sound of their wings was as the sound of chariots of many horses running to battle." – Revelation 9:9

Thus, letting Scripture interpret Scripture, the fifth trumpet of Revelation 9 is the fulfillment of Joel chapter 2.

Helen Maclachlan, a prolific nineteenth-century author on end-times subjects, agreed with the interpretation that **the locust army is comprised of fallen angels**:

> "Here the crowned locusts are particularly described, and in so wonderful a manner, faith hesitates to believe implicitly the marvellous things that Jehovah with outstretched arm has said he will do whilst purging his people in the furnace of the great tribulation.
>
> Unlike locusts, these evil spirits have a king over them: and again unlike locusts they are 'to harm no green thing.' These diversities from ordinary locusts, and the prophecy of Joel, bearing a remarkable resemblance to this passage of Scripture, form an apparent connexion between these supernatural locusts and the northern army that has been generally admitted and much commented on.." – *Notes on the Book of the Revelation, Helen Maclachlan*, 1869, p. 128–129

The prophet Joel describes this army as virtually unstoppable:

> "Before their face the people shall be much pained: all faces shall

> gather blackness. They shall run like mighty men [*giborrim*]; they shall climb the wall like men of war; and they shall march every one on his ways, and they shall not break their ranks:" – Joel 2:6–7

The faces of the people "gathering blackness" is a reference to the look of a dead body. People will literally drop dead at the sight of these wicked beings from Hell running roughshod through their countries and homes. This fallen angelic army will conquer the Earth with little resistance. Note that verse 7 states they shall run like "mighty men." The Hebrew term for "mighty men" in verse 7 is *giborrim*——a term also used to refer to the Nephilim:

> "There were giants in the earth in those days; and also after that, when the sons of God came in unto the daughters of men, and they bare children to them, **the same became mighty men** [*giborrim*] which were of old, men of renown." – Genesis 6:4

Gibborim is a term reserved for warriors with superhuman military skill and might. Nimrod, the first postdiluvian emperor and leader of the Tower of Babel rebellion, is described as a *gibborim* in Genesis 10:

> "And Cush begat Nimrod: he began to be a mighty one [*gibborim*] in the earth. He was a mighty [*gibborim*] hunter before the LORD: wherefore it is said, Even as Nimrod the mighty [*gibborim*] hunter before the LORD." – Genesis 10:8–9

In the Septuagint, the oldest extant version of the Old Testament, an even more startling description of Nimrod is given:

> "And Chus begot Nebrod: he began to be a giant upon the earth. He was a giant hunter before the Lord God; therefore they say, As

> Nebrod the giant hunter before the Lord." – Genesis 10:8–9, LXX

The fighting prowess of the locust army will be something not seen since the Nephilim dominated the world. Renowned theologian and Reverend Robert Govett confirmed the superhuman might of this invading horde of fallen angels:

> "The last term is *Gebborim*, or the mighty, and alludes to their strength, as of a degree vastly superior to man's. **This term is used of angels**, [Joel 3:11] 'Thither cause thy mighty ones (*Gebborim*) to come down, O Lord. Let the heathen be wakened, and come up to the valley of Jehoshaphat: for there will I sit to judge all the heathen round about. Put ye in the sickle; for the harvest is ripe: come get you down for the press is full, the fats overflow; for their wickedness is great. Multitudes, multitudes in the valley of decision: for the day of the Lord is near in the valley of decision.' From these characteristics with others which the reader may see on consulting the whole passage, it will appear satisfactorily that the time spoken of is that of Christ's second advent, **and therefore that the descent of 'the mighty ones' is that of his angels**. Another similar place is [Judges 5:13].
>
> Thus the word *Gebborim* relating principally to creatures possessed of power far superior to human might is capable of being applied either to good or evil beings. Hence Nimrod is called a *Gebor* or giant, and by the same title is Antichrist addressed in [Psalm 52] and [Habakkuk 2:5]. **The same term is applied to the host of Antichrist**, whence it appears probable that this is the host of evil spirits mentioned in a former part of the present work." – *Isaiah Unfulfilled: Being an Exposition of the Prophet; with New Version and Critical Notes*, Robert Govett, 1841, p. 362

Joel chapter 2 continues its description of the rampage of this army that will be used as a tool of God's wrath upon the Earth in the end times:

> "Neither shall one thrust another; they shall walk every one in his path: and when they fall upon the sword, they shall not be wounded. They shall run to and fro in the city; they shall run upon the wall, they shall climb up upon the houses; they shall enter in at the windows like a thief. The earth shall quake before them; the heavens shall tremble: the sun and the moon shall be dark, and the stars shall withdraw their shining: And the LORD shall utter his voice before his army: for his camp is very great: for he is strong that executeth his word: for the day of the LORD is great and very terrible; and who can abide it?" – Joel 2:8–11

Isaiah chapter 13 also details the conquest by this avenging army:

> "Lift ye up a banner upon the high mountain, exalt the voice unto them, shake the hand, that they may go into the gates of the nobles. I have commanded my sanctified ones, I have also called my mighty ones for mine anger, even them that rejoice in my highness. The noise of a multitude in the mountains, like as of a great people; a tumultuous noise of the kingdoms of nations gathered together: the LORD of hosts mustereth the host of the battle. They come from a far country, **from the end of heaven, even the LORD, and the weapons of his indignation**, to destroy the whole land. Howl ye; for the day of the LORD is at hand; it shall come as a destruction from the Almighty." – Isaiah 13:2–6

This army that arrives on the Day of the Lord (Isaiah 13:6) has all the characteristics of the locust army. It is specifically chosen by God for vengeance and makes a noise that's noted twice in the above passage. Recall that both the prophet Joel and the Apostle John in the book of Revelation describe the locust army as making a noise like chariots. Isaiah continues by saying that the soldiers making up the army come from "the end of Heaven," indicating that their origin is not of this world.

Once again, the Septuagint links this army back to the days of Noah:

> "Lift up a standard on the mountain of the plain, exalt the voice to them, beckon with the hand, open the gates, ye rulers. I give command, and I bring them: **giants are coming to fulfil my wrath**." – Isaiah 13:2–3, LXX

The understanding that "the deep" contains the fallen angels who fathered the Nephilim giants and endowed them with superhuman might and psychotic sinful passions is alluded to throughout Scripture. Many of the references to dragons or similar creatures are usually linked to the "deep" or the Abyss:

> "Praise the LORD from the earth, ye dragons, and all deeps:" – Psalm 148:7

Reverend Robert Govett, in his exceptional treatise on prophecy and the supernatural aspects of Scripture, affirmed the connection between the "giants" of Isaiah 13, the angels of Genesis 6, and the locust army unleashed from the Abyss:

> "By 'giants' it is probable that we are to understand those whom David [Psalm 79:49] calls 'evil angels', who, from their cruelty, rejoice at seeing us punished, and regard our misery as their enjoyment, who behave with insolence, though they can effect only what God permits. The command to 'lift up the standard on a mountain of the plain,' the prophet put forth as in the person of

> God, who commands the angels about him to open the closed doors and to send forth, exhort, and hasten those within to vengeance on the ungodly. In which words it is probable, that some region appropriated to hostile Powers as their prison is signified. And may not this be that abyss which is filled with dragons, as it is said, 'Ye dragons and all abysses' [Psalm 148:7], whereunto the demons exhorted the Saviour not to send them 'before the time,' as well aware that the time would come?
>
> And these Powers he calls giants, either as possessing the souls of giants, or **as being of the number of those angels that came down from heaven, of whom 'the giants,' were born by their [connection] with the daughters of men**." – Ibid., p. 175–176

SIGNIFICANCE OF FIVE MONTHS OF TORMENT—THE EXACT LENGTH OF TIME GOD TORMENTED THE GENESIS 6 REBELS IN THE DAYS OF NOAH

> "And it was commanded them that they should not hurt the grass of the earth, neither any green thing, neither any tree; but only those men which have not the seal of God in their foreheads. **And to them it was given that they should not kill them, but that they should be tormented five months**: and their torment was as the torment of a scorpion, when he striketh a man. And in those days shall men seek death, and shall not find it; and shall desire to die, and death shall flee from them." – Revelation 9:4–6

Ezekiel 31 is one of the most amazing and unique chapters in Scripture. It chronicles the rise and fall of the Assyrian—the fallen angelic ruler of the Earth in the days before the Flood. He was the preeminent angel among all of the apostate rebels of Genesis 6 who took human women as wives. His empire of fallen-angelic and Nephilim offspring set him as the unparalleled ruler:

> "Behold, the Assyrian was a cedar in Lebanon with fair branches, and with a shadowing shroud, and of an high stature; and his top was among the thick boughs. The waters made him great, the deep set him up on high with her rivers running round about his plants, and sent her little rivers unto all the trees of the field. Therefore his height was exalted above all the trees of the field, and his boughs were multiplied, and his branches became long because of the multitude of waters, when he shot forth. All the fowls of heaven made their nests in his boughs, and under his branches did all the beasts of the field bring forth their young, **and under his shadow dwelt all great nations.**" – Ezekiel 31:3–6

In *Judgment of the Nephilim,* I went into extensive detail to explain that Ezekiel 31 describes not only this fallen angelic king's ascent to power, but his dramatic fall as God ultimately judged the Assyrian for his arrogance and pride. The chapter describes God using the Flood to send the Assyrian to the Abyss, or "the nether parts of the earth":

> "To the end that none of all the trees by the waters exalt themselves for their height, neither shoot up their top among the thick boughs, neither their trees stand up in their height, all that drink water: **for they are all delivered unto death, to the nether parts of the earth, in the midst of the children of men, with them that go down to the pit.** Thus saith the Lord GOD; In the day when he went down to the grave I caused a mourning: I covered the deep for him, and I restrained the floods thereof, and the great waters were stayed: and I caused Lebanon to mourn for him, and all the trees of the field fainted for him. I made the nations to shake at the sound of his fall, when I cast him down to hell with them that descend into the pit:

> and all the trees of Eden, the choice and best of Lebanon, all that drink water, shall be comforted in the nether parts of the earth." – Ezekiel 31:14–16

The Assyrian and all the other fallen angels who fornicated with human women—called "the trees of Eden" in the passage—were sent to the "nether parts of the earth," which is another term for the Abyss. This chapter describes the judgment of the Nephilim and the angels who sinned in greater detail than any other passage of Scripture or extrabiblical text. Equally stunning is that not only does Ezekiel 31 describe how the Assyrian, the fallen angels under him, and the Nephilim were punished, **but it also reveals the exact timing of this judgment**:

> "Thus saith the Lord GOD; **In the day when he went down to the grave** I caused a mourning: I covered the deep for him, **and I restrained the floods thereof, and the great waters were stayed**: and I caused Lebanon to mourn for him, and all the trees of the field fainted for him." – Ezekiel 31:15

This passage reveals that the Assyrian saw his kingdom destroyed by the raging floodwaters. Only when God caused the waters to "abate" were the Assyrian, his fallen angelic followers, and the corpses of his dead Nephilim children dragged down to Hell.

According to the chronology of Genesis 7, the deluge broke forth and the rain fell from the windows of Heaven for 150 days. Then God "restrained" the waters of judgment, supernaturally pulling them back beneath the earth's surface:

> "And God remembered Noah, and every living thing, and all the cattle that was with him in the ark: and God made a wind to pass over the earth, and the waters assuaged; The fountains also of the

> deep and the windows of heaven were stopped, **and the rain from heaven was restrained**; And the waters returned from off the earth continually: **and after the end of the hundred and fifty days the waters were abated**." – Genesis 8:1–3

In the Hebrew calendar, every month is thirty days. The rebel angels were tormented by the floodwaters for 150 days, or five months, and then were sent to the Abyss. In the end times, when the Assyrian and the fallen angels of the Abyss are released from the bottomless pit, they will inflict a judgment upon sinning, unbelieving humanity *for the exact length of time they were punished*:

> "And to them it was given that they should not kill them, **but that they should be tormented five months**: and their torment was as the torment of a scorpion, when he striketh a man. And in those days shall men seek death, and shall not find it; and shall desire to die, and death shall flee from them." – Revelation 9:5–6

For 150 days, Hell will literally be unleashed upon the earth. These passages are just some of numerous affirmations of Jesus Christ's prophecy that the final years of Earth will be "as the days of Noah" (Matthew 24:37). The days of Noah indeed ripple through time in prophetic Scripture.

Unfortunately for the unbelieving world living during the Day of the Lord, the fallen sons of God of Genesis 6 will not emerge from the Abyss alone. They will be accompanied by their king, the Assyrian, who ruled in the days of Noah and will return in the last days as the Antichrist.

CHAPTER 4

THE ASSYRIAN: ANTICHRIST OF THE OLD TESTAMENT

> "Another name we have claimed for [the Antichrist] is 'the Assyrian,' which occurs among other places in three of the chapters of Isaiah, where he is seen with the same prominence involved in what is to be *only* at the coming of the Lord. In the first of these chapters (Isaiah 10:5) he is spoken of as 'the rod of mine anger sent against the people of my wrath, to tread them down like the mire in the streets. Howbeit he meaneth not so, neither does his heart think so,' (that he is but an instrument,) 'but it is in his heart to destroy and cut off nations not a few.'" – *The Development of Antichrist*, Andrew Bonar, 1853, p. 140

The Old Testament contains dozens of prophecies regarding the Antichrist. And though he is referred to with many different titles, the preeminent appellation is "the Assyrian." In the prior chapter, we noted the first purpose of the Day of the Lord: God's personal intervention into the earthly realm to finally judge the unbelievers and God-haters who will pledge their allegiance to the Antichrist in the end times. There is also a second purpose of the Day of the Lord: the final prophesied reconciliation and redemption of the nation of Israel back to God and Jesus Christ.

JESUS CHRIST PROPHESIED END-TIMES DECEPTION AND ISRAEL'S REDEMPTION

During the final days of His earthly ministry, the Lord Jesus Christ, the Seed of the Woman, made several profound prophecies focused on the nation Israel. Having missed the many signs fulfilled by Christ, the Jewish religious leadership not only rejected Jesus as Messiah, but they conspired to have Him executed by the Roman authorities. Knowing that Israel would incur judgment, Jesus nevertheless predicted a time of reconciliation when the nation would acknowledge Him as *Yeshuah Ha Meshiach*, the prophesied Messiah:

> "O Jerusalem, Jerusalem, thou that killest the prophets, and stonest them which are sent unto thee, how often would I have gathered thy children together, even as a hen gathereth her chickens under her wings, and ye would not! Behold, your house is left unto you desolate. For I say unto you, **Ye shall not see me henceforth, till ye shall say, Blessed is he that cometh in the name of the Lord**."
> – Matthew 23:37–39

Before the Second Coming of Jesus Christ, Israel, corporately, will come to a spiritual awakening to realize that He is truly the Messiah. This is a critical end-times prophecy that must come to pass before Jesus returns. As it was in the days of Noah, Satan's plan is to prevent this prophecy from taking place either by deceiving or destroying Israel before it can be redeemed.

This is not to say that individual Jewish people cannot be saved today. Praise God for the many thousands of Messianic Jews who come to trust and believe in the shed blood of Christ for the forgiveness of their sins (and praise Him for the many hard-working ministries and missionaries who witness to them). However, as a nation, Israel still rejects Jesus, as clearly demonstrated by its tiny Christian minority.

However, God will initiate a spiritual revival among Israel in the last days and defend Jerusalem:

> "And it shall come to pass in that day, that I will seek to destroy all the nations that come against Jerusalem. And I will pour upon the house of David, and upon the inhabitants of Jerusalem, the spirit of grace and of supplications: and they shall look upon me whom they have pierced, and they shall mourn for him, as one mourneth for his only son, and shall be in bitterness for him, as one that is in bitterness for his firstborn." – Zechariah 12:9–10

Israel will realize with mourning that their ancestors, in grave sinful error, arranged for the crucifixion of their Messiah. Then they will repent and receive the spirit of grace from God, receiving the same, free forgiveness all born-again Christians receive today.

But the reconciliation process will be a time of severe testing for the Israelites living in the Day of the Lord. First and foremost, they will be judged and punished for their centuries of apostasy. This will be carried out primarily by the Assyrian—which, again, is the chief title for the Antichrist in the Old Testament.

Jesus prophesied that before Israel acknowledged Him as Messiah, they would first believe in the False Messiah:

> "Search the scriptures; for in them ye think ye have eternal life: and they are they which testify of me. And ye will not come to me, that ye might have life. I receive not honour from men. But I know you, that ye have not the love of God in you. I am come in my Father's name, and ye receive me not: **if another shall come in his own name, him ye will receive.**" – John 5:39–43

THE ASSYRIAN WILL DECEIVE AND PERSECUTE ISRAEL

The Old Testament is filled with passages that describe Israel being deceived into following the Assyrian. This is a key counterstrike by Satan to try to dismantle God's prophecy of redeeming Israel before His return. Thus, the Israelites will put their trust in the Assyrian only to have him betray them and attack them. Finally, however, God will deliver them by personally conquering the Assyrian and saving Israel for good. The first reference to this series of events is found in Isaiah 10:

> "Woe unto them that decree unrighteous decrees, and that write grievousness which they have prescribed; To turn aside the needy from judgment, and to take away the right from the poor of my people, that widows may be their prey, and that they may rob the fatherless! And what will ye do in the day of visitation, and in the desolation which shall come from far? to whom will ye flee for help? and where will ye leave your glory?" – Isaiah 10:1–3

At this time, Israel will be engaging in rampant sinful rebellion. The Lord then will challenge them by asking, "What will ye do in the day of visitation?" This is a reference to the final days before His Second Coming. First Peter 2 confirms the interpretation:

> "Dearly beloved, I beseech you as strangers and pilgrims, abstain from fleshly lusts, which war against the soul; Having your conversation honest among the Gentiles: that, whereas they speak against you as evildoers, they may by your good works, which they shall behold, glorify God in the day of visitation. Having your conversation honest among the Gentiles: that, whereas they speak against you as evildoers, they may by your good works, **which they shall behold, glorify God in the day of visitation**." – 1 Peter 2:11–

13

Isaiah 10 continues with God asking Israel: "To whom will ye flee for help?" This is when the deception of the Assyrian will take place. After the blood-red moon and darkened sun trigger the commencement of the Day of the Lord, Israel will initially believe the Assyrian to be their savior. The fallen angelic ruler of the antediluvian world (as described in Ezekiel 31) will return to deceive the twelve tribes to believe he is the Messiah. Having failed at stopping the birth of the Messiah, the Devil will launch one last effort to thwart God's prophecies by deceiving and destroying Israel in order to sabotage their prophesied redemption. The treachery of the Assyrian—the future Antichrist—will be the Adversary's primary weapon.

After deceiving Israel into believing in him as their savior, the Assyrian will betray them and seek their destruction:

> "Without me they shall bow down under the prisoners, and they shall fall under the slain. For all this his anger is not turned away, but his hand is stretched out still. **O Assyrian, the rod of mine anger**, and the staff in their hand is mine indignation. **I will send him against an hypocritical nation, and against the people of my wrath** will I give him a charge, to take the spoil, and to take the prey, and to tread them down like the mire of the streets. Howbeit he meaneth not so, neither doth his heart think so; but it is in his heart to destroy and cut off nations not a few." – Isaiah 10:4–7

As they lose faith in God, Israel will fall for the deception of the Assyrian, and God will use this deception to judge and punish Israel for millennia of rejecting the Messiah. The Bible confirms throughout that the Assyrian is merely a tool of God, and is no god himself (hence the Scripture passage saying "he meaneth not so"; he is unaware of the Lord's use of him). But the Assyrian's ambition is world domination and godhood.

GOD WILL JUDGE THE ASSYRIAN AND RESCUE THE REMNANT OF ISRAEL

> "Wherefore it shall come to pass, that when the Lord hath performed his whole work upon mount Zion and on Jerusalem, I will punish the fruit of the stout heart of the king of Assyria, and the glory of his high looks. For he saith, By the strength of my hand I have done it, and by my wisdom; for I am prudent: and I have removed the bounds of the people, and have robbed their treasures, and I have put down the inhabitants like a valiant man. And my hand hath found as a nest the riches of the people: and as one gathereth eggs that are left, have I gathered all the earth; and there was none that moved the wing, or opened the mouth, or peeped."
> – Isaiah 10:12–14

Through the persecution of the Assyrian, the true, born-again believers in *Yeshua* will be forged and tried. Once God brings the remnant of Israel to a saving faith in the Lord Jesus Christ, He will punish the Assyrian. Note the wicked aspiration and pride of the Antichrist in the passage from Isaiah 10: He will remove "all the bounds of the people," achieving global dominance and a one-world government. He'll control the wealth of the world and defeat all opposition. He will "gather all the earth," and no one will be able to take any significant action without his authorization. The only leader in the Bible to achieve this level of worldwide dominance is the Antichrist, as prophesied in the book of Revelation.

ASSYRIAN BUILDS A GLOBAL KINGDOM AND IS DEFEATED BY GOD

> "Behold, the Assyrian was a cedar in Lebanon with fair branches,

> and with a shadowing shroud, and of an high stature; and his top was among the thick boughs. The waters made him great, the deep set him up on high with her rivers running round about his plants, and sent her little rivers unto all the trees of the field. Therefore his height was exalted above all the trees of the field, and his boughs were multiplied, and his branches became long because of the multitude of waters, when he shot forth. All the fowls of heaven made their nests in his boughs, and under his branches did all the beasts of the field bring forth their young, and under his shadow dwelt all great nations. Thus was he fair in his greatness, in the length of his branches: for his root was by great waters." – Ezekiel 31:3–7

In the antediluvian world, the Assyrian wielded unparalleled power. Strategically situated by the rivers of the Garden of Eden, he ruled all the nations of the pre-Flood world. All the fallen sons of God of Genesis 6 (the "trees of the field") and their Nephilim offspring were under his dominion. Filled with pride and arrogance because of his global kingdom, the Assyrian met swift destruction by God:

> "The cedars in the garden of God could not hide him: the fir trees were not like his boughs, and the chestnut trees were not like his branches; nor any tree in the garden of God was like unto him in his beauty. I have made him fair by the multitude of his branches: so that all the trees of Eden, that were in the garden of God, envied him. Therefore thus saith the Lord GOD; **Because thou hast lifted up thyself in height**, and he hath shot up his top among the thick boughs, **and his heart is lifted up in his height**; I have therefore delivered him into the hand of the mighty one of the heathen; he shall surely deal with him: I have driven him out for his wickedness." – Ezekiel 31:8–11

In the days of Noah, the Assyrian's arrogance and pride in his power and might provoked a judgment from God that led to the destruction of his kingdom and to his imprisonment. During the end of days, when he returns as the Antichrist, he will once again exalt himself in arrogance against God, and he will be judged one final time:

> "**Shall the axe boast itself against him that heweth therewith**? or shall the saw magnify itself against him that shaketh it? as if the rod should shake itself against them that lift it up, or as if the staff should lift up itself, as if it were no wood. Therefore shall the Lord, the Lord of hosts, send among his fat ones leanness; and under his glory he shall kindle a burning like the burning of a fire.
>
> And the light of Israel shall be for a fire, and his Holy One for a flame: and it shall burn and devour his thorns and his briers in one day; And shall consume the glory of his forest, and of his fruitful field, both soul and body: and they shall be as when a standard-bearer fainteth. And the rest of the trees of his forest shall be few, that a child may write them." – Isaiah 10:15–19

The Antichrist is merely an axe in the hands of a mighty God. And the Lord swiftly judges the Assyrian, returning to destroy him and rescue the remnant of believers in Israel:

> "And it shall come to pass in that day, that the remnant of Israel, and such as are escaped of the house of Jacob, **shall no more again stay upon him that smote them**; but shall stay upon the LORD, the Holy One of Israel, in truth. **The remnant shall return, even the remnant of Jacob, unto the mighty God**. For though thy people Israel be as the sand of the sea, yet a remnant of them shall return: the consumption decreed shall overflow with righteousness." – Isaiah 10:20–22

Here we see a direct reference to "the remnant of Israel," the Jewish believers who will come to saving faith in Christ during the Day of the Lord. Isaiah 10 clearly states that once they have had their spiritual awakening, they will no longer trust or worship "him that smote them"—with "him" referring to the Assyrian. The Lord follows this promise with a word of encouragement to the Israelite remnant:

> "For the Lord GOD of hosts shall make a consumption, even determined, in the midst of all the land. Therefore thus saith the Lord GOD of hosts, O my people that dwellest in Zion, be not afraid of the Assyrian: he shall smite thee with a rod, and shall lift up his staff against thee, after the manner of Egypt. For yet a very little while, and the indignation shall cease, and mine anger in their destruction." – Isaiah 10:23–25

God encourages Israel not to fear the Antichrist, comparing him and his rule over them as an end-times repetition of the Exodus from Egypt. The Assyrian will rule and torment the Israelites for a "yet a very little while" before he is destroyed directly by the Lord Himself. All of this is further confirmation that this angelic ruler from the antediluvian age will indeed return again in the end times as the Antichrist.

> "As yet shall he remain at Nob that day: he shall shake his hand against the mount of the daughter of Zion, the hill of Jerusalem. Behold, the Lord, the LORD of hosts, shall lop the bough with terror: and the high ones of stature shall be hewn down, and the haughty shall be humbled. And he shall cut down the thickets of the forest with iron, and Lebanon shall fall by a mighty one." – Isaiah 10:32–34

Ultimately, the Assyrian and all the fallen angels or "high ones of stature" will be defeated by the Lord at His Revelation. Andrew Bonar, a nineteenth-century minister of the Free Church of Scotland who wrote one of the seminal works on the Antichrist, confirmed this interpretation:

> "Another name we have claimed for [the Antichrist] is "the Assyrian," which occurs among other places in three of the chapters of Isaiah, where he is seen with the same prominence involved in what is to be only at the coming of the Lord.... It is then added 'When the Lord hath performed His *whole work* upon Mount Zion and on Jerusalem, I will punish the proud heart of the king of Assyria and the glory of his high looks for he says By my hand have I done it.'
>
> The time at which this happens as we have seen is when God has performed His whole work after which verse 20 '...in that day the remnant of Israel and such as are escaped of the house of Jacob shall no more again stay upon him that smote them but shall stay upon the Lord the Holy One of Israel....' Who can doubt that this is Antichrist, —the wicked one, who is here called 'the Assyrian' destroyed by the brightness of His coming?" – *The Development of Antichrist*, Andrew Bonar, 1853, p. 140, 143

ASSYRIAN'S DEFEAT AT JESUS CHRIST'S RETURN TO EARTH

Isaiah 11 continues the prophecy of chapter 10 with the return of Jesus Christ to conquer the Antichrist and rescue His people:

> "And there shall come forth a rod out of the stem of Jesse, and a Branch shall grow out of his roots: And the spirit of the LORD shall rest upon him, the spirit of wisdom and understanding, the spirit of counsel and might, the spirit of knowledge and of the fear of the

> LORD; And shall make him of quick understanding in the fear of the LORD: and he shall not judge after the sight of his eyes, neither reprove after the hearing of his ears: But with righteousness shall he judge the poor, and reprove with equity for the meek of the earth: and he shall smite the earth: with the rod of his mouth, **and with the breath of his lips shall he slay the wicked**." – Isaiah 11:1–4

When Jesus Christ returns, it will be to judge the whole Earth and formally take rulership of it (which He earned on the cross two thousand years ago). The passage closes by saying that Jesus will "with the breath of his lips…slay the wicked." The next verses give a description of the Earth in the Millennial Kingdom, further confirming the end-times prophetic context:

> "And righteousness shall be the girdle of his loins, and faithfulness the girdle of his reins. The wolf also shall dwell with the lamb, and the leopard shall lie down with the kid; and the calf and the young lion and the fatling together; and a little child shall lead them. And the cow and the bear shall feed; their young ones shall lie down together: and the lion shall eat straw like the ox.
>
> And the sucking child shall play on the hole of the asp, and the weaned child shall put his hand on the cockatrice' den. They shall not hurt nor destroy in all my holy mountain: for the earth shall be full of the knowledge of the LORD, as the waters cover the sea." – Isaiah 11:5–9

Before establishing His Millennial Kingdom, Jesus Christ will defeat all enemies of God and conquer the Assyrian. The Apostle Paul used this very passage to describe Christ's defeat of the Antichrist at Armageddon:

> "Let no man deceive you by any means: for that day shall not come, except there come a falling away first, and that man of sin be

> revealed, the son of perdition; Who opposeth and exalteth himself above all that is called God, or that is worshipped; so that he as God sitteth in the temple of God, shewing himself that he is God. Remember ye not, that, when I was yet with you, I told you these things? And now ye know what withholdeth that he might be revealed in his time. For the mystery of iniquity doth already work: only he who now letteth will let, until he be taken out of the way.
>
> And then shall that Wicked be revealed, whom the Lord shall consume with the spirit [*pneuma*] of his mouth, and shall destroy with the brightness of his coming: Even him, whose coming is after the working of Satan with all power and signs and lying wonders."
> – 2 Thessalonians 2:3–9

When He returns to earth, Jesus Christ, through His Word, Spirit, and presence, will immediately vanquish the Antichrist. The "spirit" in 2 Thessalonians 2 [πνεῦμα, or *pneuma* in Greek] incorporates the notion of breath. The "inspiration" of Scripture literally means "God-breathed" (*theopneustos* in Greek). Thus, the very Spirit of Christ, the breath of the Lord, is powerful enough to destroy the Antichrist.

A pastor writing about the destruction of the Antichrist drew the same conclusion: Isaiah's prophecies of the Assyrian are a direct reference to the Antichrist:

> "That this 'wicked' or 'wicked one' is the Assyrian or antichrist previously alluded to, would seem obvious, from the whole tenor and connection of the passage; but it is placed beyond doubt by the parallel passage in the Second Epistle to the Thessalonians, where (chapter 2:8) we have a precisely similar announcement in reference to 'the Assyrian' or 'the Man of sin' both as to his end and the time when it shall come to pass, —'And then shall that Wicked be revealed whom the Lord shall consume with the breath of His

mouth and shall destroy with the brightness of His coming.'

The parallelism between these passages is perfect, and the identity of the persons alluded to unquestionable; the time is the same in both—*the time of the coming forth of the Lord;* the character of the adversary to be destroyed is the same in both—*the Wicked One;* and the nature and mode of destruction is the same in both—'*the breath of His lips*' or '*spirit of His mouth.*' **Clearly, then, we have, in Isaiah 10:4 a plain prediction of the destruction of antichrist at and by the coming of our Lord.**" – *Israel's Future, Lectures Delivered in the Lock Chapel in Lent*, Capel Molyneux, 1853, p. 164

THE ASSYRIAN'S GOAL: TO RULE HEAVEN AND EARTH AS GOD

In *Judgment of the Nephilim,* I explained that the Bible has several notable chapters that I call esoteric passages:

"Certain sections of the Bible are addressed to a specific person (typically a king) or group but contain a deeper, hidden message and are directed to a heavenly realm or angelic being. The most famous of these passages is Isaiah 14:

That thou shalt take up this proverb against the king of Babylon, and say, How hath the oppressor ceased! the golden city ceased! the Lord hath broken the staff of the wicked, and the sceptre of the rulers. He who smote the people in wrath with a continual stroke, he that ruled the nations in anger, is persecuted, and none hindereth. The whole earth is at rest, and is quiet: they break forth into singing. Yea, the fir trees rejoice at thee, and the cedars of

> Lebanon, saying, Since thou art laid down, no feller is come up against us. Hell from beneath is moved for thee to meet thee at thy coming: it stirreth up the dead [Rephaim] for thee, even all the chief ones of the earth; it hath raised up from their thrones all the kings of the nations.
>
> All they shall speak and say unto thee, Art thou also become weak as we? art thou become like unto us? Thy pomp is brought down to the grave, and the noise of thy viols: the worm is spread under thee, and the worms cover thee. How art thou fallen from heaven, O Lucifer, son of the morning! how art thou cut down to the ground, which didst weaken the nations! For thou hast said in thine heart, I will ascend into heaven, I will exalt my throne above the stars of God: I will sit also upon the mount of the congregation, in the sides of the north: I will ascend above the heights of the clouds; I will be like the most High. – Isaiah 14:4–14

> This passage, while addressed to the king of Babylon, is commonly accepted as also addressing Lucifer, one of the original titles of Satan. [Some Bible scholars believe the passage is addressing the Antichrist, which does not conflict with the former interpretation because Satan and the Antichrist, who is the seed of Satan, will be unified in spirit, power, and purpose in the end times.]" – *Judgment of the Nephilim*, Ryan Pitterson, 2018, p. 168

As stated above, Isaiah 14, which concludes the end-time prophecy that begins in Isaiah chapter 10, is an address to the Antichrist. Here he is now referred to as "the king of Babylon" (the reason for the numerous titles of the Antichrist will be explained in detail in a later chapter).

In context, Isaiah 14 opens by recording what the world will say after the conquest of the Assyrian by Jesus Christ:

> "For the LORD will have mercy on Jacob, and will yet choose Israel, and set them in their own land: and the strangers shall be joined with them, and they shall cleave to the house of Jacob. And the people shall take them, and bring them to their place: and the house of Israel shall possess them in the land of the LORD for servants and handmaids: and they shall take them captives, whose captives they were; and they shall rule over their oppressors. And it shall come to pass in the day that the LORD shall give thee rest from thy sorrow, and from thy fear, and from the hard bondage wherein thou wast made to serve." – Isaiah 14:1–3

The setting is one in which Israel has been restored and reconciled to God, indicating that this will be during the Day of the Lord.

> "That thou shalt take up this proverb against the king of Babylon, and say, How hath the oppressor ceased! the golden city ceased! The LORD hath broken the staff of the wicked, and the sceptre of the rulers. He who smote the people in wrath with a continual stroke, he that ruled the nations in anger, is persecuted, and none hindereth. The whole earth is at rest, and is quiet: they break forth into singing." – Isaiah 14:4–7

There will be great rejoicing and singing in Israel once "the wicked"—the Antichrist—has been conquered. The passage affirms that the Antichrist will have global authority and will mercilessly enforce his rule. But once he is gone, there will be a global celebration.

> "Yea, the fir trees rejoice at thee, and the cedars of Lebanon, saying, Since thou art laid down, no feller is come up against us. Hell from

> beneath is moved for thee to meet thee at thy coming: it stirreth up the dead [*rephaim*] for thee, even all the chief ones of the earth; it hath raised up from their thrones all the kings of the nations. All they shall speak and say unto thee, Art thou also become weak as we? art thou become like unto us?" – Isaiah 14:8–10

When the Assyrian is sent to Hell, the Rephaim, the giants from the days of Noah, will be stirred to greet him. They will be stunned to see their fallen angelic forefather killed and in Hell alongside them.

> "Thy pomp is brought down to the grave, and the noise of thy viols: the worm is spread under thee, and the worms cover thee. How art thou fallen from heaven, O Lucifer, son of the morning! how art thou cut down to the ground, which didst weaken the nations! For thou hast said in thine heart, I will ascend into heaven, I will exalt my throne above the stars of God: I will sit also upon the mount of the congregation, in the sides of the north: I will ascend above the heights of the clouds; I will be like the most High." – Isaiah 14:11–14

And here is one of the most popular passages of Scriptures concerning the Devil. As stated earlier, there is no conflict between seeing these sinful aspirations as applying to both Satan and to the Antichrist, because the Antichrist is described as follows: "Even him, whose coming is after the working of Satan with all power and signs and lying wonders" (2 Thessalonians 2:9). Just as Christ and the Father are one, so too will the counterfeit Christ and his father, Satan, be one in purpose. Revelation 13 confirms this:

> "And the beast which I saw was like unto a leopard, and his feet were as the feet of a bear, and his mouth as the mouth of a lion: and the dragon gave him his power, and his seat, and great

authority." – Revelation 13:2

Everything the Antichrist will do is fulfilling the will of Satan. Thus, the aspirations of the king of Babylon in this passage applies to both wicked figures. The Assyrian will seek to exalt himself as god and be "like the Most High." This is confirmed in the New Testament:

> "Let no man deceive you by any means: for that day shall not come, except there come a falling away first, and that man of sin be revealed, the son of perdition; **Who opposeth and exalteth himself above all that is called God, or that is worshipped**; so that he as God sitteth in the temple of God, shewing himself that he is God."
> – 2 Thessalonians 2:3–4

ASSYRIAN FAILS AND IS SENT TO HELL

> "Yet thou shalt be brought down to hell, to the sides of the pit. They that see thee shall narrowly look upon thee, and consider thee, saying, Is this the man that made the earth to tremble, that did shake kingdoms; That made the world as a wilderness, and destroyed the cities thereof; that opened not the house of his prisoners?" – Isaiah 14:15–17

The Antichrist will be a vicious, satanic tyrant. He will "make the earth tremble" because of his power and might.

> "All the kings of the nations, even all of them, lie in glory, every one in his own house. But thou art cast out of thy grave like an abominable branch, and as the raiment of those that are slain, thrust

> through with a sword, that go down to the stones of the pit; as a carcase trodden under feet. Thou shalt not be joined with them in burial, because thou hast destroyed thy land, and slain thy people: the seed of evildoers shall never be renowned." – Isaiah 14:18–20

Eventually, the Antichrist will be cast out of hell like "an abominable branch" (showing another contrast in title to Jesus, who is called "the branch of righteousness" in Jeremiah 33:15). He will not remain in the grave. A descent into Hell as other evil leaders before him will not be his final judgment. He will be brought back to stand before God once more, and will be punished in the Lake of Fire.

The close of the prophecy confirms that the identity of the king of Babylon is indeed the Assyrian:

> "The LORD of hosts hath sworn, saying, Surely as I have thought, so shall it come to pass; and as I have purposed, so shall it stand: **That I will break the Assyrian in my land, and upon my mountains tread him under foot**: then shall his yoke depart from off them, and his burden depart from off their shoulders. This is the purpose that is purposed upon the whole earth: and this is the hand that is stretched out upon all the nations. For the LORD of hosts hath purposed, and who shall disannul it? and his hand is stretched out, and who shall turn it back?" – Isaiah 14:24–27

The Assyrian will be defeated on the mountains of Israel. His death will lead to the ultimate freedom of Israel and liberation of the world from the reign of the Devil. The following commentary confirms that the title "king of Babylon" is just one of the many esoteric names for the Assyrian:

> "**It is equally evident that the Assyrian and the king of Babylon must be the same individual**, the name being derived from the

locality of Babylon in the land of Chaldea, embraced in Assyria. In one of the chapters just referred to (Isaiah 14) they are distinctly identified, whilst to the king of Babylon there the exact words and characteristics of Antichrist under all the names we have been considering are given." – *The Development of Antichrist*, Andrew Bomar, 1853, p. 143–144

THE SCROLL OF TIME: BIBLICAL HISTORY REPEATS ITSELF

In the pre-Flood era, the Assyrian took control of the entire earth. All the nations dwelt under his authority as he established an empire of fallen angelic and Nephilim minions. At the peak of his power, the Lord judged this evil angel and brought him to utter ruin. He was banished to the bottomless pit and chained in supernatural darkness for millennia. But during the Great Tribulation, that "judgment of the great day," he will again be released to rule over the world for a short time before the Second Coming of the Seed of the Woman—Jesus Christ. Thus, as it was in the days of Noah, so will it be in the days of the coming of the Son of Man.

These two seeds will inevitably clash in one final battle. This, of course, was prophesied in Genesis 3:15:

> "And the LORD God said unto the serpent, Because thou hast done this, thou art cursed above all cattle, and above every beast of the field; upon thy belly shalt thou go, and dust shalt thou eat all the days of thy life: And I will put enmity between thee and the woman, **and between thy seed and her seed**; it shall bruise thy head, and thou shalt bruise his heel." – Genesis 3:14–15

From the first prophecy of Messiah, God also prophesied that there would be "enmity," or conflict, between the Seed of the Woman, Jesus Christ, and the seed of Satan, Antichrist. These two seeds have warred in various forms throughout biblical history. In Genesis 6, we read that Satan attempted a mimicry of the Seed of the Woman by instigating the sons of God to conceive the Nephilim giants, corrupting the entire human race save for Noah and his family. God responded by wiping out that race of monstrosities and restarting humanity.

The postdiluvian giants were time and time again vanquished by "the Angel of the Lord"—the preincarnate Jesus Christ personally waging war against the giants who populated the Promised Land. King David, from whom the Messiah's lineage would come, defeated the Nephilim Goliath, and his mighty men killed the final remnant of giants in the nation.

With the Devil failing to prevent the birth of the Messiah, Jesus Christ then achieved the ultimate victory by taking on human flesh and serving as an atoning sacrifice for humanity. This was a countermove the Devil did not anticipate:

> "But we speak the wisdom of God in a mystery, even the hidden wisdom, which God ordained before the world unto our glory: Which none of the princes of this world knew: for had they known it, they would not have crucified the Lord of glory." – 1 Corinthians 2:7–8

The Devil did not know Jesus would take the punishment for the sins of the human race, allowing us to be freely forgiven and reconciled to God. In response, Satan, in the end times, will employ his final grand tactic, creating his own "Messiah" to deceive and eradicate Israel in an attempt to topple God's plan of redemption. The Antichrist will be far more than a charismatic, ingenious man. He will be a supernaturally endowed, hybrid being—a Nephilim. To understand how this is achieved, we must first look at the powerful foreshadows that have already rippled through biblical history.

CHAPTER 5

FORESHADOWS OF THE BEAST

> "Many and marvellous were the types of the Lord's anointed before the angel of the Lord announced to the shepherds of Bethlehem the birth of Jesus Christ, and scarcely less numerous and marvellous are the foreshadows of the last Antichrist, the man of sin—the Son of Perdition…the mighty being to whom Satan, the god of this world, in the closing days of this dispensation, will give 'his power and his throne, and great authority.'" – "Foreshadows of the Antichrist During the Times of the Gentiles," as printed in *The Rainbow, a Magazine of Christian Literature*, Volume 5, 1868, p. 376

Before His First Advent, Jesus Christ made many appearances throughout the Bible. So, too, does the Antichrist, or his spirit, find himself making infamous manifestations throughout biblical history. Just as God, in His infinite wisdom, permits Satan and his fallen angels to still enter Heaven, stand before His throne, and roam through the earthly realm, the Lord also granted the spirit of Antichrist to make appearances throughout human history. In both types and shadows, **and in literal incarnations**, the Antichrist is foreshadowed throughout the Bible. In studying these examples, we see not only the wicked agenda of the Antichrist, but also early confirmation that he will indeed be a part-human, part-fallen-angelic hybrid.

JUDAS

Judas Iscariot is, without a doubt, one of the most infamous figures from the Bible. On the surface, his "life story" seems straightforward. He was the wicked disciple of Jesus Christ, the one who never believed in the Messiah but pretended to be His follower for personal gain. He habitually stole money from the disciples' treasury, and when offered thirty pieces of silver, he conspired to frame Jesus for a crime that would lead to the Savior's Crucifixion. But why did Judas do this? Looking deeper into the description of this mysterious traitor reveals a sinister spiritual agenda at play in his heart, as he was indeed intricately connected to the Devil.

Possessed by Satan Himself

> "Now the feast of unleavened bread drew nigh, which is called the Passover. And the chief priests and scribes sought how they might kill him; for they feared the people. **Then entered Satan into Judas surnamed Iscariot**, being of the number of the twelve. And he went his way, and communed with the chief priests and captains, how he might betray him unto them. And they were glad, and covenanted to give him money." – Luke 22:1–5

Judas was literally indwelled by the Devil. No other person in the entire Bible bears this tragic distinction. Like the Antichrist's plan for world dominance, Judas' ill-fated scheme to frame Jesus Christ and arrange His execution was "after the workings of Satan."

Called "The Devil"

> "Jesus answered them, Have not I chosen you twelve, and one of you is a devil?" – John 6:70

Another of Judas' dubious distinctions is that he was also the only person aside from Satan himself to be called "devil" in the Bible. The Greek term used for "devil" in this verse is *diabolos*, a word only used to refer to Satan. The term should not be confused with "devils"—the many demons that Jesus cast out of people who were possessed:

> "When the even was come, they brought unto him many that were possessed with devils [*daimonion*]: and he cast out the spirits with his word, and healed all that were sick." – Matthew 8:16
>
> "And certain women, which had been healed of evil spirits and infirmities, Mary called Magdalene, out of whom went seven devils [*daimonion*]." – Luke 8:2
>
> "And when he was come to the other side into the country of the Gergesenes, there met him two possessed with devils [*daimonion*], coming out of the tombs, exceeding fierce, so that no man might pass by that way." – Matthew 8:28

In each of these above and in every other reference in the Bible, the term *daimonion* is used to distinguish demons or "devils"—the spirits of the deceased Nephilim—from *diabolos*, which is a reference to Satan.

Theologians in earlier centuries recognized the distinction between "devil" and "evil spirit" in the Old Testament. The latter was a spirit of the deceased giants:

> "It is unfortunate that our translation makes no distinction between the Devil and a Demon, which can very clearly be distinguished from each other in the originals, both Hebrew and Greek: Satan both in Hebrew and Greek, and διαβάλλω, in Greek is never found in the plural number when applied to the Evil Spirit; δαίμων and δαιμονίζομαι are so frequently. In Jewish theology

> these two classes are distinct Satan, being a pure Spirit of like nature with the angels, while the *Shedim,* or demons, are half human. These last are identified with the Nephilim, or 'Fallen ones,' the giants, the children of the sons of God and the daughters of men (Gen 6:2); half angelic, half human, in many Jewish writings most conspicuously in the Book of Enoch." – *The Christian Remembrancer, a Quarterly Review,* Vol. LI, William Scott, Francis Garden, James Bowling Mosley, 1866, p. 273

Thus, there was something so sinister and evil in Judas' nature that Jesus, early in His ministry, identified him as "the devil." Additionally, Jesus gave Judas a title reserved for the Antichrist.

Called "Son of Perdition"

John chapter 17 contains a beautiful prayer the Lord Jesus Christ offered for His disciples and all future believers. In it, the Lord referenced Judas:

> "And now I am no more in the world, but these are in the world, and I come to thee. Holy Father, keep through thine own name those whom thou hast given me, that they may be one, as we are. While I was with them in the world, I kept them in thy name: those that thou gavest me I have kept, and none of them is lost, **but the son of perdition**; that the scripture might be fulfilled." – John 17:11–12

This term "son of perdition" is the same title the Apostle Paul gave Antichrist:

> "Let no man deceive you by any means: for that day shall not come, except there come a falling away first, and that man of sin be revealed, **the son of perdition**; Who opposeth and exalteth himself above all that is called God, or that is worshipped; so that he as God

> sitteth in the temple of God, shewing himself that he is God." – 2 Thessalonians 2:3–4

Perdition, *apoleia* in Greek, means "destruction." This is in line with the description of the Antichrist when he is released from the bottomless pit:

> "And they had a king over them, which is the angel of the bottomless pit, whose name in the Hebrew tongue is Abaddon, but in the Greek tongue hath his name Apollyon." – Revelation 9:11

"Apollyon" means "destroyer," and "Abaddon" in Hebrew refers to destruction. The word also became synonymous with the pit of Hell itself. Thus, **Judas is linked directly to Satan and the Antichrist twice by The Lord**. This remarkable connection certainly has been noted by theologians of the past:

> "But why was Judas called the 'Son of Perdition'? Was he a child of Satan by some woman, or was he simply indwelt by Satan? Here we must let the Scriptures speak for themselves. In John 6:70–71 we read that Jesus said 'Have not I chosen you Twelve, and one of you is a Devil?' He spake of Judas Iscariot the son of Simon; for he it was that should betray Him being one of the Twelve. In no other passage than this is the word 'Devil' applied to anyone but to Satan himself. Here the word is 'diabolus' the definite article is employed, and it should read—'and one of you is the Devil.' This would make Judas the Devil incarnate, or the 'Mystery of Iniquity,' and explains why Jesus in John 17:12 calls him the 'Son of Perdition.'
>
> This is the only place in the Scriptures where the word 'diabolus' is applied to a human being **and it implies an incarnation**. While Perdition is a place (Rev 17:11) it is also a condition into which men may fall (1 Timothy 6:9; Hebrews 10:39), and while men who

> have committed the 'Unpardonable Sin' are 'sons of perdition' because they are destined to the place of the irrevocably lost, yet Judas and Antichrist are the 'Sons of Perdition' in a special sense for they are the 'sons' of the author of Perdition—the Devil. That is, they are not merely 'obsessed' or controlled by the Devil the Devil has incarnated himself in them and for the time being to all practical purposes they are the very Devil himself." – *Dispensational Truth, or God's Plan and Purpose in the Ages*, Clarence Larkin, 1920, p. 119

Here, Larkin clearly connects the titles given to Judas with the Devil and Antichrist. He notes that it "implies an incarnation," as if Judas were an actual form of Satan or the Antichrist himself. This prophetically previews the Final Nephilim, whose power and spiritual agenda will come directly from the Devil.

DECEIVER AND THIEF

The Antichrist will be a False Messiah (2 Thessalonians 2:1–4). Judas was a false disciple merely pretending to be a true believer in Jesus Christ:

> "And while he yet spake, behold a multitude, and he that was called Judas, one of the twelve, went before them, and drew near unto Jesus to kiss him. But Jesus said unto him, Judas, betrayest thou the Son of man with a kiss?" – Luke 22:47–48

Judas was also a thief:

> "Then took Mary a pound of ointment of spikenard, very costly, and anointed the feet of Jesus, and wiped his feet with her hair: and the house was filled with the odour of the ointment. Then saith one of his disciples, Judas Iscariot, Simon's son, which should betray

> him, Why was not this ointment sold for three hundred pence, and given to the poor? This he said, not that he cared for the poor; but because he was a thief, and had the bag, and bare what was put therein." – John 12:3–6

Judas showed his true character in this passage. Out of pure greed, he tried to deceive everyone in the room by acting as if he wanted to use the expensive ointment to care for the poor. He also disregarded Mary's worship of Jesus. Scripture reveals that Judas was stealing from "the bag"—the collection the disciples took to take care of their needs and to help others.

Jesus Christ referred to Satan as a "thief" as well:

> "The thief cometh not, but for to steal, and to kill, and to destroy: I am come that they might have life, and that they might have it more abundantly. I am the good shepherd: the good shepherd giveth his life for the sheep." – John 10:10–11

Rather than stealing and killing, Jesus came to give life and lay down His own life for the world. Though Judas meant to bring Jesus to an end by conspiring with the Pharisees, he was merely a tool to bring to fruition Jesus' plan to willingly die on the cross. Once his purpose was served, Judas died, falling head first into the ground after hanging himself. Similarly, in the end times, the Antichrist will think he is usurping God, but he in fact will be nothing more than a tool of judgment in the Lord's hand. Antichrist will be dispatched of speedily at Christ's return (and will also suffer a wound to the head like Judas).

Old Testament Connections to Satan and Antichrist

A fascinating passage in the book of Acts tells of the disciples preparing to select a replacement for the recently deceased Judas. The verses describe the traitorous disciple as having a direct connection to Hell:

> "And in those days Peter stood up in the midst of the disciples, and said, (the number of names together were about an hundred and twenty,) Men and brethren, this scripture must needs have been fulfilled, which the Holy Ghost by the mouth of David spake before concerning Judas, which was guide to them that took Jesus. For he was numbered with us, and had obtained part of this ministry.
>
> Now this man purchased a field with the reward of iniquity; and falling headlong, he burst asunder in the midst, and all his bowels gushed out. And it was known unto all the dwellers at Jerusalem; insomuch as that field is called in their proper tongue, Aceldama, that is to say, The field of blood. For it is written in the book of Psalms, Let his habitation be desolate, and let no man dwell therein: and his bishoprick let another take." – Acts 1:15–20

Examining this passage gives us further insight into the life and nature of Judas. With the words, "Men and brethren, this scripture must needs have been fulfilled, which the Holy Ghost by the mouth of David spake before concerning Judas," the Apostle Peter, inspired by the Holy Spirit and knowledgeable of God's Word, declared that King David had written prophetic passages about Judas. Both of these prophecies were included in the book of Psalms.

Also note that Judas arranged to purchase a field with the thirty pieces of silver he was paid by the Sanhedrin to conspire with them in the Crucifixion of the Lord Jesus Christ. Although he threw the money at the Pharisees in a moment of panic after the death of Jesus (Matthew 27:5), the funds were still used to purchase the field he desired. A nineteenth-century commentary affirms this:

> "Three small points have troubled some minds: 1) How to

> reconcile the account in Matthew 27:7, that the priests bought the potter's field, with that in Acts 1:18, that Judas purchased the field? It is not unreasonable to suppose that when Judas (before the Passover, Luke 22:1–6) made his covenant with the priests for thirty pieces of silver, he made another bargain to buy the potter's field, but had not paid its owner the price, and that the priests carried out the agreement. In any case the field was bought with the money of Judas, so it might be considered as bought by him." – *Lessons on the: I. Names and Titles of Our Lord, II. Prophecies Concerning Our Lord, and Their Fulfillment,* Flavel S. Cook, 1888, p. 72

The field was called *Aceldama,* or the "field of blood." It is noteworthy that Judas chose to hang himself from a tree, dying in a similar manner to the Lord, as the Apostle Peter detailed in Acts chapter 5:

> "The God of our fathers raised up Jesus, whom ye slew and hanged on a tree. Him hath God exalted with his right hand to be a Prince and a Saviour, for to give repentance to Israel, and forgiveness of sins." – Acts 5:30–31

Judas also had his body opened at death. But where the connection gets even more profound is in the examination of the two passages from the book of Psalms that prophesy of Judas. We find references to those verses in the following:

> "For it is written in the book of Psalms, Let his habitation be desolate, and let no man dwell therein: and his bishoprick let another take." – Acts 1:20

In this passage, Peter quotes *two different verses from the Psalms* that refer to

Judas. The first is found in Psalm 69:

> "Draw nigh unto my soul, and redeem it: deliver me because of mine enemies. Thou hast known my reproach, and my shame, and my dishonour: mine adversaries are all before thee.... Pour out thine indignation upon them, and let thy wrathful anger take hold of them. **Let their habitation be desolate**; and let none dwell in their tents." – Psalm 69:18–19, 24–25

Through divine inspiration, King David predicted that a part of the punishment of Judas for being an enemy of Christ was that no one would ever dwell in the land that belonged to him.

The second verse Peter pointed to is in Psalm chapter 109, where we see several astounding references:

> "Hold not thy peace, O God of my praise; For the mouth of **the wicked** and the mouth of the deceitful are opened against me: they have spoken against me with a lying tongue. They compassed me about also with words of hatred; and fought against me without a cause. For my love they are my adversaries [*satan*]: but I give myself unto prayer. And they have rewarded me evil for good, and hatred for my love.
>
> **Set thou a wicked man over him: and let Satan stand at his right hand**. When he shall be judged, let him be condemned: and let his prayer become sin. Let his days be few; **and let another take his office**." – Psalm 109:1–8

Note that this passage references "the wicked," a title used for the Antichrist by the Apostle Paul in 2 Thessalonians 2:8. It goes on to say that "the wicked" have spoken against the Lord with a lying tongue; that is precisely what Judas did in framing Jesus for a crime He did not commit. In verse 4, the Hebrew word translated as "adversaries" is *Satan,* making yet another sinister connection. Judas certainly repaid the love of Jesus with hatred.

> "Set thou a wicked man over him: and let Satan stand at his right hand." – Psalm 109:6

Here is where the type and shadow of Antichrist are revealed. This prophecy of Judas portrays Satan standing "at his right hand." Like the final son of perdition, Judas was operating in concert with the Devil.

Joshua William Brooks, a nineteenth-century priest in the Church of England, connected the prophecy of Judas to the Antichrist:

> "From the various names which are given to [Antichrist], his character and the nature of the offices he will assume, may be pretty clearly inferred: but in regard to three of those offices, viz. prophet, priest, and king—in which he more particularly mimics the character of the Lord Jesus, a few observations may be needful; the more especially as some have concluded that he will be altogether void of religious profession. There is no need to show that he is to be a king that is universally concurred in, and the fact that he is described so repeatedly *as a horn* (which is a type of a king and a kingdom,) and 'the head over the wicked,' and 'the king that doeth according to his will,' sufficiently bespeaks it.
>
> That he is to be a priest likewise may be inferred from [Psalm 109] which is applied in [Acts 1:20] to Judas Iscariot, who was a type of Antichrist, and is therefore called 'the son of perdition.' He was clearly an apostle of Christ, though he proved a deceiver and betrayer of his trust; and the words of the Psalm—'and let another take his office' are quoted by St. Peter from the Septuagint, as

> referring to his ministerial office—'and his bishopric let another take'" – *Elements of Prophetical Interpretation*, Joshua William Brooks, 1841, p. 257

In Revelation 13, we are told that the Final Nephilim, called "the Beast" in that chapter, will receive his power directly from the Devil:

> "And I stood upon the sand of the sea, and saw a beast rise up out of the sea, having seven heads and ten horns, and upon his horns ten crowns, and upon his heads the name of blasphemy. And the beast which I saw was like unto a leopard, and his feet were as the feet of a bear, and his mouth as the mouth of a lion: and the dragon gave him his power, and his seat, and great authority." – Revelation 13:1–2

After Satan loses the battle to Michael in Revelation 12, he will fall to Earth and unlock the Abyss. When the Assyrian emerges from the pit, he will then be endowed with power and authority from Satan. The Devil will be "at his right hand" when the Antichrist rules over the planet, just as he was the right hand of Judas during the betrayal of Jesus.

An article in an Oxford University publication notes that Psalm 109 is in fact a double prophecy pointing both to Judas and the end-times Antichrist:

> "The reason alleged for the supposition that Judas was a type of the last Antichrist, and perhaps the only type that occurs in the Christian dispensation is derived from the fact that a portion of [Psalm 109] is applied to Judas in Acts 1:20; whilst it is quite evident that the prophecy contained in that psalm is far too large to be restricted to Judas, and must consequently point, in its ultimate meaning, to the manifestation evil in the person of Antichrist, of whom it is said in the psalm that 'Satan shall stand at

his right hand.'" – *The Retrospect, an Enquiry Into the Fulfilment of Prophecy During the Last 20 Years*, Volume 2, Oxford University, 1845, p. 106–107

From the Abyss?

The search for Judas' replacement soon narrowed down to two men: Barsabas and Matthias. The apostles closed the meeting with a prayer to God for wisdom in the selection. The words of the prayer revealed a mysterious connection between Judas and Hell:

> "And they appointed two, Joseph called Barsabas, who was surnamed Justus, and Matthias. And they prayed, and said, Thou, Lord, which knowest the hearts of all men, shew whether of these two thou hast chosen, That he may take part of this ministry and apostleship, **from which Judas by transgression fell, that he might go to his own place**. And they gave forth their lots; and the lot fell upon Matthias; and he was numbered with the eleven apostles." – Acts 1:23–26

Judas certainly died in his sins and went to Hell. Interestingly, the apostles refer to Judas' death and subsequent entry into Hell as going "to his own place." Throughout Scripture, we are told that the seed of the Serpent, the Final Nephilim, will emerge from Hell:

> "And when they shall have finished their testimony, the beast that **ascendeth out of the bottomless pit** shall make war against them, and shall overcome them, and kill them." – Revelation 11:7

> "The beast that thou sawest was, and is not; and **shall ascend out of the bottomless pit**, and go into perdition: and they that dwell on the earth shall wonder, whose names were not written in the

> book of life from the foundation of the world, when they behold the beast that was, and is not, and yet is." – Revelation 17:8

The Assyrian, who returns as the end-times Antichrist, is "the angel of the bottomless pit." It is clearly "his own place," and it is where he will return:

> "And the beast that was, and is not, even he is the eighth, and is of the seven, and goeth into ***perdition***." – Revelation 17:11

The Archbishop of Canterbury, England, writing in 1838, affirmed this interpretation:

> "Hell was Judas's *own place*. He had sold himself to Satan, whilst apparently in the service of Christ. He had followed the example and lived under the influence of 'the angels that sinned.' Whilst here on earth the society of the good was not his place; this he had shown, pursuing a sinful habit, and proving that he was still of the earth, earthly; still of the world, worldly. And at last he had done an act of wickedness which manifested the hardness of a heart fast held 'in the bond of iniquity.'
>
> Therefore, a place where dwell 'the wicked and the devilish' 'shut out from the presence of the Lord' was his own place. It was the place belonging to his nature, and the place assigned of God to natures like his." – *A Practical Exposition of the Acts of the Apostles*, John Bird Summer, Archbishop of Canterbury, 1838, p. 9

Judas was in many respects a type of the Final Nephilim. The Lord Jesus Christ made references to Judas that were otherwise reserved for the Antichrist and Satan. This was further confirmed when Judas was literally indwelled by the Devil. At the critical moment when he betrayed the Messiah, **Judas was**

both human and fallen angel in one body. He was a hybrid being, just as the Final Nephilim.

The Old Testament contains another foreshadow of the Antichrist, who also for a time lived as a hybrid being: King Nebuchadnezzar.

NEBUCHADNEZZAR

> "Is there any thing whereof it may be said, See, this is new? it hath been already of old time, which was before us." – Proverbs 1:10

One of the most fascinating figures in the Bible, Nebuchadnezzar, king of Babylon, was also a foreshadow of the Final Nephilim. In his notorious career, not only were his actions a prophetic ripple in time of the Antichrist to come, but his supernatural visions and very nature hearkened back to Genesis 6, the fallen angels and the Nephilim.

A Tool of God's Judgment

When the twelve tribes of Israel fell into rampant apostasy by worshiping demons—the spirits of the dead Nephilim giants and their fallen angelic ancestors—God sent His prophets to repeatedly warn that if they did not repent, they would suffer utter ruin and the loss of the Promised Land. Despite these admonitions, they didn't heed the Word of the Lord. Centuries earlier, when Israel had been under the leadership of faithful Joshua, they had waged a string of successful military campaigns against the Nephilim in the land of Canaan, thwarting Satan's plan to usurp God's portion on earth. However, what the Devil could not accomplish through the sheer military might of the Nephilim hybrids, he achieved through their deceased demonic spirits luring the Israelites into idolatry.

In response to the sinful rebellion, God warned the Northern Kingdom of

Israel that if they did not repent, their defeat would come at the hands of Sennacherib, king of the Assyrian Empire (we'll explore this in greater detail in a later chapter). Sadly, this destruction came to pass.

Years later, the same warnings were given to the Southern Kingdom of Judah, who was told that their punishment would come at the hands of King Nebuchadnezzar:

> "In his days Nebuchadnezzar king of Babylon came up, and Jehoiakim became his servant three years: then he turned and rebelled against him. And the LORD sent against him bands of the Chaldees, and bands of the Syrians, and bands of the Moabites, and bands of the children of Ammon, **and sent them against Judah to destroy it, according to the word of the LORD, which he spake by his servants the prophets. Surely at the commandment of the LORD came this upon Judah**, to remove them out of his sight, for the sins of Manasseh, according to all that he did; And also for the innocent blood that he shed: for he filled Jerusalem with innocent blood; which the LORD would not pardon. Now the rest of the acts of Jehoiakim, and all that he did, are they not written in the book of the chronicles of the kings of Judah?" – 2 Kings 24:1–5

Nebuchadnezzar was victorious over Israel only because God allowed it as a punishment of the Southern Kingdom for their brazen rebellion in worshiping false gods. In the end times, the Antichrist will play the same role as that ancient king:

> "**O Assyrian, the rod of mine anger, and the staff in their hand is mine indignation**. I will send him against an hypocritical nation, and against the people of my wrath will I give him a charge, to take the spoil, and to take the prey, and to tread them down like the mire of the streets. Howbeit he meaneth not so, neither doth his

heart think so; but it is in his heart to destroy and cut off nations not a few." – Isaiah 10:5–7

The Antichrist, a "rod" and "staff" in God's hand, doesn't even realize that he is merely the Lord's tool of punishment ("Howbeit he meaneth not so"). After he betrays Israel, the Antichrist will destroy Jerusalem.

Desecrates God's Temple

> "Jehoiakim was twenty and five years old when he began to reign, and he reigned eleven years in Jerusalem: and he did that which was evil in the sight of the LORD his God. Against him came up Nebuchadnezzar king of Babylon, and bound him in fetters, to carry him to Babylon. Nebuchadnezzar also carried of the vessels of the house of the LORD to Babylon, and put them in his temple at Babylon....
>
> Jehoiachin was eight years old when he began to reign, and he reigned three months and ten days in Jerusalem: and he did that which was evil in the sight of the LORD. And when the year was expired, king Nebuchadnezzar sent, and brought him to Babylon, with the goodly vessels of the house of the LORD, and made Zedekiah his brother king over Judah and Jerusalem.
>
> Zedekiah was one and twenty years old when he began to reign, and reigned eleven years in Jerusalem. And he did that which was evil in the sight of the LORD his God, and humbled not himself before Jeremiah the prophet speaking from the mouth of the LORD. And he also rebelled against king Nebuchadnezzar, who had made him swear by God: but he stiffened his neck, and hardened his heart from turning unto the LORD God of Israel.
>
> Moreover all the chief of the priests, and the people, transgressed

> very much after all the abominations of the heathen; and polluted the house of the LORD which he had hallowed in Jerusalem. And the LORD God of their fathers sent to them by his messengers, rising up betimes, and sending; because he had compassion on his people, and on his dwelling place:
>
> But they mocked the messengers of God, and despised his words, and misused his prophets, until the wrath of the LORD arose against his people, till there was no remedy. Therefore he brought upon them the king of the Chaldees, who slew their young men with the sword in the house of their sanctuary, and had no compassion upon young man or maiden, old man, or him that stooped for age: he gave them all into his hand.
>
> And all the vessels of the house of God, great and small, and the treasures of the house of the LORD, and the treasures of the king, and of his princes; all these he brought to Babylon. **And they burnt the house of God, and brake down the wall of Jerusalem, and burnt all the palaces thereof with fire, and destroyed all the goodly vessels thereof.**" – 2 Chronicles 36:5–19

The kingdom of Judah refused Yahweh and chose to worship demons instead. This plunged them even deeper into grave, sinful rebellion. They mocked God's prophets and attacked anyone who was delivering a message of repentance. And at each turn, Nebuchadnezzar was sent by the Lord as an instrument of punishment, with the severity of his attacks culminating in the destruction of the First Temple of God.

During the end times, Israel will fall for the Great Delusion—believing that the Antichrist is the Messiah. This deception will lead to judgment for their rejection of God and will culminate with the "abomination of desolation," when the Antichrist enters the Holy Temple proclaiming himself as God:

> "Let no man deceive you by any means: for that day shall not come, except there come a falling away first, and that man of sin be revealed, the son of perdition; Who opposeth and exalteth himself above all that is called God, or that is worshipped; so that he as God sitteth in the temple of God, shewing himself that he is God." – 2 Thessalonians 2:3–4

Theologians through the centuries have recognized Nebuchadnezzar as a type and shadow of the Antichrist:

> "Nebuchadnezzar is a type of the final Antichrist. The points of similarity here are many. Nebuchadnezzar was a proud, haughty monarch. He lifted himself up above others. He boasted of himself and of his own achievements. We read of him: 'At the end of twelve months he walked in the palace of the kingdom of Babylon. The king spake, and said, Is not this great Babylon, that I have built for the house of the kingdom by the might of my power, and for the honor of my majesty?'—Dan 4:29–30. Notice how self-exalting Nebuchadnezzar was. His acts are prophetical of the self-exaltation of Antichrist. Paul in speaking of Antichrist says: 'Who opposeth and exalteth himself above all that is called God, or that is worshipped; so that he as God sitteth in the temple of God, showing himself that he is God.' – 1 Thessalonians 2:4
>
> Every person that lifts himself up in self-exaltation is a forerunner of Antichrist. Spiritual pride is an antichristian spirit. If we would belong to Christ, we must keep humble. Nebuchadnezzar was abased for his pride; and his abasement is prophetical of the eternal overthrow of the final Antichrist." – *The Second Coming of Jesus,* Reverend G. F. Taylor, 1916, p. 152

Prophetic Dream of Antichrist's Kingdom and Its Destruction

As Nebuchadnezzar's most trusted advisor, the prophet Daniel provides enormous personal insight into the life of the king. In Daniel chapter 2, we read that the king had a nightmare that frightened him so severely he called for all of the occult practitioners in his royal court not only to provide an interpretation, but to tell him what the dream had been—without Nebuchadnezzar revealing anything about it. The "Chaldeans"—a name for the wizard and occult priests—thought this was impossible:

> "The Chaldeans answered before the king, and said, There is not a man upon the earth that can shew the king's matter: therefore there is no king, lord, nor ruler, that asked such things at any magician, or astrologer, or Chaldean. And it is a rare thing that the king requireth, and there is none other that can shew it before the king, except the gods, whose dwelling is not with flesh." – Daniel 2:10–11

This is a dynamic picture of the limitless power of God versus the limited abilities of Satan, the fallen angels, and demons. Satan's power doesn't rival the Lord's. While the Devil was constrained from helping his servants in the king's court, the prophet Daniel, through the power of God, was able to describe the dream and give its meaning.

Nebuchadnezzar had dreamt of a giant statue with a head of gold, torso of silver, midsection of brass, legs of iron, and toes of iron and miry clay. Daniel explained that the imagery was a prophetic revelation of a succession of Gentile kingdoms that would rule the earth, culminating with the kingdom of the Antichrist:

> "Daniel answered in the presence of the king, and said, The secret which the king hath demanded cannot the wise men, the astrologers, the magicians, the soothsayers, shew unto the king; But

> there is a God in heaven that revealeth secrets, and maketh known to the king Nebuchadnezzar what shall be in the latter days. Thy dream, and the visions of thy head upon thy bed, are these; As for thee, O king, thy thoughts came into thy mind upon thy bed, what should come to pass hereafter: and he that revealeth secrets maketh known to thee what shall come to pass....
>
> This is the dream; and we will tell the interpretation thereof before the king. Thou, O king, art a king of kings: for the God of heaven hath given thee a kingdom, power, and strength, and glory. And wheresoever the children of men dwell, the beasts of the field and the fowls of the heaven hath he given into thine hand, and hath made thee ruler over them all. Thou art this head of gold. And after thee shall arise another kingdom inferior to thee, and another third kingdom of brass, which shall bear rule over all the earth." – Daniel 2:27–39

Nebuchadnezzar, like the Antichrist, was a global ruler. His power and might were unmatched. And he was set up for this level of authority by God. In a remarkable testament to its supernatural accuracy, Scripture later confirms that the silver and brass kingdoms would be that of the Medo-Persians (who eventually conquered Babylon) and the Greek Empire, which succeeded the Medo-Persians as the dominant empire of the world (Daniel 8:20–21). But it is the fourth kingdom that represented the final world kingdom before the Second Coming of Jesus Christ:

> "And the fourth kingdom shall be strong as iron: forasmuch as iron breaketh in pieces and subdueth all things: and as iron that breaketh all these, shall it break in pieces and bruise. And whereas thou sawest the feet and toes, part of potters' clay, and part of iron, the kingdom shall be divided; but there shall be in it of the strength of the iron, forasmuch as thou sawest the iron mixed with miry clay. And as the toes of the feet were part of iron, and part of clay, so the

> kingdom shall be partly strong, and partly broken.
>
> And whereas thou sawest iron mixed with miry clay, they shall mingle themselves with the seed of men: but they shall not cleave one to another, even as iron is not mixed with clay." – Daniel 2:40–43

The iron kingdom is the end-times empire of Antichrist and his fallen angelic minions. A great deal of the prophecy in the book of Daniel is devoted to detailing this kingdom—and repeatedly, iron is symbolically connected:

> "After this I saw in the night visions, and behold a fourth beast, dreadful and terrible, and strong exceedingly; *and it had great iron teeth*: it devoured and brake in pieces, and stamped the residue with the feet of it: and it was diverse from all the beasts that were before it; and it had ten horns. I considered the horns, and, behold, there came up among them another little horn, before whom there were three of the first horns plucked up by the roots: and, behold, in this horn were eyes like the eyes of man, and a mouth speaking great things." – Daniel 7:7–8

The beast representing the Antichrist kingdom in this vision was also seen by the Apostle John, who wrote the book of Revelation:

> "And I stood upon the sand of the sea, and saw a beast rise up out of the sea, having seven heads and ten horns, and upon his horns ten crowns, and upon his heads the name of blasphemy. And the beast which I saw was like unto a leopard, and his feet were as the feet of a bear, and his mouth as the mouth of a lion: and the dragon gave him his power, and his seat, and great authority." – Revelation 13:1–2

The beast of Daniel 7 is not just the Antichrist; it represents his supernatural kingdom of fallen angels and human subjects. This is explained in Revelation 17:

> "And the angel said unto me, Wherefore didst thou marvel? I will tell thee the mystery of the woman, and of the beast that carrieth her, which hath the seven heads and ten horns. The beast that thou sawest was, and is not; and shall ascend out of the bottomless pit, and go into perdition: and they that dwell on the earth shall wonder, whose names were not written in the book of life from the foundation of the world, when they behold the beast that was, and is not, and yet is.... And the ten horns which thou sawest are ten kings, which have received no kingdom as yet; but receive power as kings one hour with the beast.... These have one mind, and shall give their power and strength unto the beast." – Revelation 17:7–8; 12–13

The end-times kingdom of Antichrist *will be a fallen angelic one*, which makes it "diverse" from any other kingdom that has ruled the earth. Recall that when the apostate angels of Genesis 6 are released from the Abyss, they are wearing iron:

> "And they had breastplates, as it were breastplates of iron; and the sound of their wings was as the sound of chariots of many horses running to battle." – Revelation 9:9

The iron kingdom will be a repetition of the days of Noah, when the Assyrian, along with the apostate sons of God and their Nephilim offspring, dominated the antediluvian world. Daniel 2:43 then refers to the return of the illicit relations that led to the birth of the Nephilim giants:

> "And whereas thou sawest iron mixed with miry clay, **they shall mingle themselves with the seed of men**: but they shall not cleave one to another, even as iron is not mixed with clay."

The destruction of the iron and clay kingdom by Jesus Christ, the Stone cut without hands, **confirms that this is an end-times kingdom,** not ancient Rome:

> "**And in the days of these kings shall the God of heaven set up a kingdom, which shall never be destroyed**: and the kingdom shall not be left to other people, but it shall break in pieces and consume all these kingdoms, and it shall stand for ever." – Daniel 2:44

The kingdom God sets up that will "never be destroyed" is established at the Second Coming of Christ. Thus, we can confirm that the final kingdom in Nebuchadnezzar's vision is **one yet to come: the kingdom of Antichrist:**

> "'Smote the image upon his feet'—this respects what is yet to be done when Christ will subdue and destroy the ten kingdoms given to Antichrist, and him himself.... Christ's kingdom from small beginnings has increased and will more and more until the whole earth is subject unto it." – *The Condensed Commentary and Family Exposition of the Holy Bible, with Practical Reflections; and Marginal References, Chronology, Indexes, Etc.*, Reverend Ingram Cobbin, M. A., 1837, p. 907

Demands Worship

In Daniel chapter 3, the king of Babylon erected a golden statue of his likeness and mandated worship of himself as god under penalty of death:

> "Nebuchadnezzar the king made an image of gold, whose height was threescore cubits, and the breadth thereof six cubits: he set it up in the plain of Dura, in the province of Babylon. Then Nebuchadnezzar the king sent to gather together the princes, the governors, and the captains, the judges, the treasurers, the counsellors, the sheriffs, and all the rulers of the provinces, to come to the dedication of the image which Nebuchadnezzar the king had set up. Then the princes, the governors, and captains, the judges, the treasurers, the counsellors, the sheriffs, and all the rulers of the provinces, were gathered together unto the dedication of the image that Nebuchadnezzar the king had set up; and they stood before the image that Nebuchadnezzar had set up.
>
> Then an herald cried aloud, To you it is commanded, O people, nations, and languages, That at what time ye hear the sound of the cornet, flute, harp, sackbut, psaltery, dulcimer, and all kinds of musick, ye fall down and worship the golden image that Nebuchadnezzar the king hath set up: And whoso falleth not down and worshippeth shall the same hour be cast into the midst of a burning fiery furnace. Therefore at that time, when all the people heard the sound of the cornet, flute, harp, sackbut, psaltery, and all kinds of musick, all the people, the nations, and the languages, fell down and worshipped the golden image that Nebuchadnezzar the king had set up." – Daniel 3:1–7

During the Day of the Lord, the Antichrist will institute a similar form of worship of himself via the image of the Beast:

> "And I beheld another beast coming up out of the earth; and he had two horns like a lamb, and he spake as a dragon. And he exerciseth all the power of the first beast before him, and causeth the earth and them which dwell therein to worship the first beast,

> whose deadly wound was healed. And he doeth great wonders, so that he maketh fire come down from heaven on the earth in the sight of men,
>
> And deceiveth them that dwell on the earth by the means of those miracles which he had power to do in the sight of the beast; saying to them that dwell on the earth, that they should make an image to the beast, which had the wound by a sword, and did live. And he had power to give life unto the image of the beast, that the image of the beast should both speak, and cause that as many as would not worship the image of the beast should be killed." – Revelation 13:11–15

An article in a Christian magazine in the early twentieth century affirms the prophetic connection between Daniel 3's statue of gold and the end times:

> "The Image of Gold which Nebuchadnezzar would have everyone in his empire worship. His effort to establish one religion for all by force. He was in this, a type of the Antichrist Beast." – "The Book of Daniel" by William F. Jordan, as printed in *Leaves of Healing, Vol. 50*, Zion Publishing House, 1922, p. 73

The False Prophet, the religious cohort of the Antichrist who serves in the role of "prime minister" in the end-times kingdom, will lead the deceived people of the world to create an "image" of the Beast. This will not be a normal statue, though, as the image will be given "life," will have the ability to speak, and will be able to enforce the death penalty for those who do not worship it. It is the ultimate fulfillment of the mandatory one-world religion Nebuchadnezzar tried to bring about in his day.

Nebuchadnezzar's Statue and the Mark of the Beast

The details of the statue described in Daniel chapter 3—specifically the numbers in those details—suggest prophetic links to the kingdom of the Final Nephilim. The image was sixty cubits high ("threescore cubits") and six cubits wide (Daniel 3:1), and worship was initiated at the sounding of six instruments ("the cornet, flute, harp, sackbut, psaltery, dulcimer"). Thus, we see the number six repeated three times in association with the worship of Nebuchadnezzar as a god.

Turning to Revelation chapter 13, we see there will be a "number of the Beast" to be associated with the worship of and submission to the Antichrist. All people will be required to receive a "mark" in their right hand or forehead that bears this number, which is 666, echoing the three sixes involved in worship of Nebuchadnezzar's statue:

> "And [the False Prophet] causeth all, both small and great, rich and poor, free and bond, to receive a mark in their right hand, or in their foreheads: And that no man might buy or sell, save he that had the mark, or the name of the beast, or the number of his name. Here is wisdom. Let him that hath understanding count the number of the beast: for it is the number of a man; **and his number is Six hundred threescore and six**." – Revelation 13:16–18

Again, we see that both Nebuchadnezzar and the Antichrist incorporate the number 666 into their attempts to be exalted as gods. Letting Scripture interpret Scripture, we see a clear type of the Beast in the ancient king of Babylon, as further supported in the following:

> "The history of Nebuchadnezzar is necessarily related to that of Antichrist. Nebuchadnezzar was the first king of that Gentile dynasty which Antichrist concludes. Antichrist inherits that power which was first committed to Nebuchadnezzar as the golden head

of the image shown to Daniel. Nebuchadnezzar was the first 'treader down' of Israel—Antichrist the last.

Nebuchadnezzar raised an image and caused it to be worshipped destroying those who refused—so will Antichrist. Nebuchadnezzar was the spring of Babylon's energies—so will Antichrist. The offences which Nebuchadnezzar commenced against Israel and Israel's God are said in Jeremiah to be finally punished when the last king of Babylon—Antichrist is smitten." – *Thoughts on the Apocalypse*, Benjamin Wills Newton, 1853, p. 313

A Human-Beast Hybrid

In Daniel chapter 4, we read that Nebuchadnezzar received another prophetic dream that led to one of the most startling and unique events in Scripture. In his dream, the king envisioned a giant tree with towering branches, flourishing leaves and fruits, and many animals dwelling in it:

> "Thus were the visions of mine head in my bed; I saw, and behold a tree in the midst of the earth, and the height thereof was great. The tree grew, and was strong, and the height thereof reached unto heaven, and the sight thereof to the end of all the earth: The leaves thereof were fair, and the fruit thereof much, and in it was meat for all: the beasts of the field had shadow under it, and the fowls of the heaven dwelt in the boughs thereof, and all flesh was fed of it." – Daniel 4:10–12

We know from the interpretation provided by Daniel that this magnificent tree symbolized the king and his global empire:

> "Then Daniel, whose name was Belteshazzar, was astonied for one hour, and his thoughts troubled him. The king spake, and said,

> Belteshazzar, let not the dream, or the interpretation thereof, trouble thee. Belteshazzar answered and said, My lord, the dream be to them that hate thee, and the interpretation thereof to thine enemies. The tree that thou sawest, which grew, and was strong, whose height reached unto the heaven, and the sight thereof to all the earth; Whose leaves were fair, and the fruit thereof much, and in it was meat for all; under which the beasts of the field dwelt, and upon whose branches the fowls of the heaven had their habitation: **It is thou, O king, that art grown and become strong**: for thy greatness is grown, and reacheth unto heaven, and thy dominion to the end of the earth." – Daniel 4:19–22

All of the attributes of the mighty tree represented various aspects of the strength of Nebuchadnezzar's kingdom. In *Judgment of the Nephilim*, I devoted an entire chapter to explaining Ezekiel chapter 31, an esoteric passage that is addressed to "Pharaoh of Egypt," but that is truly directed at the Assyrian, the fallen angel who ruled during the Genesis 6 invasion and will return against in the end times. The description of the Assyrian and Nebuchadnezzar have remarkable parallels:

> "Behold, the Assyrian was a cedar in Lebanon with fair branches, and with a shadowing shroud, and of an high stature; and his top was among the thick boughs. The waters made him great, the deep set him up on high with her rivers running round about his plants, and sent her little rivers unto all the trees of the field. Therefore **his height was exalted above all the trees of the field**, and his boughs were multiplied, and his branches became long because of the multitude of waters, when he shot forth. All the fowls of heaven made their nests in his boughs, and under his branches did all the beasts of the field bring forth their young, **and under his shadow dwelt all great nations**. Thus was he fair in his greatness, in the length of his branches: for his root was by great waters." – Ezekiel

31:3–7

The Assyrian was the first global monarch in human history, and his height or power was greater than all the "trees of the field"—or the other fallen angels who invaded the human realm during the Genesis 6 incursion. This is made abundantly clear, as Ezekiel 31 describes the Assyrian's presence in the Garden of Eden:

> "**The cedars in the garden of God could not hide him**: the fir trees were not like his boughs, and the chestnut trees were not like his branches; **nor any tree in the garden of God** was like unto him in his beauty. I have made him fair by the multitude of his branches: so that **all the trees of Eden**, that were in the garden of God, envied him." – Ezekiel 31:8–9

Ezekiel 31 makes more references to the Garden of Eden than does any other chapter of the Bible. The Assyrian ruled from Eden, with his fallen angelic and Nephilim armies murdering and debasing humanity to the point that "all flesh" was corrupted on the earth save for Noah and his family. Thus, we see a compelling foreshadow in that a giant tree symbolized both Nebuchadnezzar and the Antichrist.

Returning to Daniel's account of Nebuchadnezzar's dream, we see an appearance by the angels known as the Watchers:

> "I saw in the visions of my head upon my bed, and, behold, **a watcher and an holy one came down from heaven**; He cried aloud, and said thus, Hew down the tree, and cut off his branches, shake off his leaves, and scatter his fruit: let the beasts get away from under it, and the fowls from his branches:
>
> Nevertheless leave the stump of his roots in the earth, **even with a**

> **band of iron** and brass, in the tender grass of the field; and let it be wet with the dew of heaven, and let his portion be with the beasts in the grass of the earth." – Daniel 4:13–15

The Watcher angels are at the center of the illicit relations between angels and human women in the apocryphal Book of Enoch. Here they come down to deliver a prophetic admonishment to Nebuchadnezzar of impending doom if he does not repent: The great tree representing the king will be hewn to a stump with a band of iron and brass placed on it (the iron symbolism of the end-times kingdom of Antichrist again being linked to Nebuchadnezzar). In the next verse, the judgment awaiting the Babylonian king grows even more mysterious:

> "Let his heart be changed from man's, and let a beast's heart be given unto him; and let seven times pass over him." – Daniel 4:16

As a result of his sin and refusal to repent, Nebuchadnezzar was literally transformed into a human-animal hybrid:

> "The same hour was the thing fulfilled upon Nebuchadnezzar: and he was driven from men, and did eat grass as oxen, and his body was wet with the dew of heaven, till his hairs were grown like eagles' feathers, and his nails like birds' claws." – Daniel 4:33

Many Bible commentaries and sermons interpret this passage as indicating that Nebuchadnezzar suffered from some type of mental illness. But that is not what the text states. The king of Babylon was *physically changed.* He grew animal claws and had so much hair that he looked like he was covered in feathers! He lived outside and ate grass like an ox. He was a man by nature, but his heart was supernaturally removed and replaced with a "beast's heart."

In Revelation chapter 13, the words about the Antichrist alternate between descriptions of man and of beast:

> "And they worshipped the dragon which gave power unto the beast: and they worshipped the beast, saying, Who is like unto the beast? who is able to make war with him? **And there was given unto him a mouth speaking great things and blasphemies**; and power was given unto him to continue forty and two months. And he opened his mouth in blasphemy against God, to blaspheme his name, and his tabernacle, and them that dwell in heaven. And it was given unto him to make war with the saints, and to overcome them: and power was given him over all kindreds, and tongues, and nations.
>
> And that no man might buy or sell, save he that had the mark, or the name of the beast, or the number of his name. Here is wisdom. Let him that hath understanding **count the number of the beast: for it is the number of a man**; and his number is Six hundred threescore and six." – Revelation 13:4–7, 17–18

The Antichrist is a "beast," but he will be "given a mouth" to speak. Nebuchadnezzar was a man, but he was "given a beast's heart." The Antichrist is a "beast," but he is able to wage war and rule the nations. He has a "number of the beast," which is "the number of a man." Like his prophetic prototype, the Antichrist will be man *and* "beast" (fallen angel)—within one body.

Significance of Seven Years

In Nebuchadnezzar's dream, the Watcher angels announce that his punishment would last "seven times." This is another way of saying it would last seven Hebrew years (each year being 360 days long). This is the same duration of the reign of Antichrist. We see confirmation of this in Daniel chapter 7:

> "And the ten horns out of this kingdom are ten kings that shall arise: and another shall rise after them; and he shall be diverse from the first, and he shall subdue three kings. And he shall speak great words against the most High, and shall wear out the saints of the most High, and think to change times and laws: **and they shall be given into his hand until a time and times and the dividing of time.** But the judgment shall sit, and they shall take away his dominion, to consume and to destroy it unto the end." – Daniel 7:24–26

The reign of Antichrist is divided into two consecutive three and one-half-year periods, or seven years (the duration of the covenant he makes with Israel; see Daniel 9:27). The political rise of the False Messiah takes place in the first half. He is then killed by a "deadly wound" at the midpoint of the seven years and comes back from the dead. This is when the Antichrist transforms into "the Beast," the satanically empowered False Messiah who takes over the world. His global government lasts for "a time" (one year), and "times" (two years), and "the dividing of time" (half of a year)"—or three and a half years. The duration given by Daniel is confirmed in Revelation 13:

> "And they worshipped the dragon which gave power unto the beast: and they worshipped the beast, saying, Who is like unto the beast? who is able to make war with him? And there was given unto him a mouth speaking great things and blasphemies; **and power was given unto him to continue forty and two months.**" – Revelation 13:4–5

Forty-two months is the equivalent of three and a half years. We know from Revelation chapter 11 that the Two Witnesses—supernaturally empowered Jewish witnesses for God—will preach and warn the world to repent for three and a half years before the Antichrist emerges from the Abyss and kills them:

> "And I will give power unto my two witnesses, **and they shall prophesy a thousand two hundred and threescore days**, clothed in sackcloth. These are the two olive trees, and the two candlesticks standing before the God of the earth. And if any man will hurt them, fire proceedeth out of their mouth, and devoureth their enemies: and if any man will hurt them, he must in this manner be killed. These have power to shut heaven, that it rain not in the days of their prophecy: and have power over waters to turn them to blood, and to smite the earth with all plagues, as often as they will. And when they shall have finished their testimony, **the beast that ascendeth out of the bottomless pit shall make war against them**, and shall overcome them, and kill them." – Revelation 11:3–7

"A thousand two hundred and threescore days" is the third biblical measure of expressing three and a half years. After the witnesses preach for this period, the Antichrist becomes "the Beast"—merged with human and fallen angel—and kills the men. He will then reign for three and a half more years before being defeated by the Lord Jesus Christ. Thus, the total time between God sending His witnesses (at the beginning of the Day of the Lord) and the destruction of Antichrist is seven Hebrew years, or "seven times." The seven-year punishment of Nebuchadnezzar was an early ripple through time of the final seven-year punishment of the world that will be led by "rod" of the Lord's anger—the Antichrist.

God's Warning to Israel

Why does Yahweh allow the Antichrist to reign? As a punishment against Israel and the unbelieving world for its apostasy and rebellion. Ultimately, the Beast is a tool the Lord uses to chastise and refine the final believing remnant of Israel who will acknowledge Him as Messiah, fulfilling a prophecy that dates back to the days of Moses:

> "I am the LORD your God, which brought you forth out of the land of Egypt, that ye should not be their bondmen; and I have broken the bands of your yoke, and made you go upright. But if ye will not hearken unto me, and will not do all these commandments; And if ye shall despise my statutes, or if your soul abhor my judgments, so that ye will not do all my commandments, but that ye break my covenant:
>
> I also will do this unto you; I will even appoint over you terror, consumption, and the burning ague, that shall consume the eyes, and cause sorrow of heart: and ye shall sow your seed in vain, for your enemies shall eat it." – Leviticus 26:13–16

When the people of Israel fall for the great delusion, also known as "the lie" in Scripture, and put their faith in the Antichrist, it will be the ultimate rejection of God's commandments. For this reason, the Lord will judge Israel with "terror, consumption and the burning ague." Recall that, in Isaiah 10, in direct reference to the Assyrian, God promised the Israelites that, despite the horrific judgments that awaited, the Antichrist would be defeated and the "consumption" would come to an end:

> "And it shall come to pass in that day, that the remnant of Israel, and such as are escaped of the house of Jacob, shall no more again stay upon him that smote them; but shall stay upon the LORD, the Holy One of Israel, in truth. The remnant shall return, even the remnant of Jacob, unto the mighty God. For though thy people Israel be as the sand of the sea, yet a remnant of them shall return: the consumption decreed shall overflow with righteousness.
>
> **For the Lord GOD of hosts shall make a consumption**, even determined, in the midst of all the land. Therefore thus saith the Lord GOD of hosts, O my people that dwellest in Zion, be not

> afraid of the Assyrian: he shall smite thee with a rod, and shall lift up his staff against thee, after the manner of Egypt. **For yet a very little while, and the indignation shall cease, and mine anger in their destruction**." – Isaiah 10:20–25

The supernatural judgments of the Day of the Lord and the tyrannical, genocidal reign of the Assyrian are part of the "consumption" decreed by God. It is the righteous judgment from a Holy God on people and a world at large who has rejected Him in favor of false gods and the very seed of Satan. However, the consumption will end. The Lord's anger will "cease," and the era of peace, reconciliation, and righteousness will be ushered in.

The prophetic warning of Leviticus 26 closes with a direct connection to the book of Revelation:

> "And I will set my face against you, and ye shall be slain before your enemies: they that hate you shall reign over you; and ye shall flee when none pursueth you. And if ye will not yet for all this hearken unto me, **then I will punish you seven times more for your sins**. And I will break the pride of your power; **and I will make your heaven as iron, and your earth as brass**." – Leviticus 26:17–19

Recall that when Nebuchadnezzar was warned of the judgment to come, the Watchers placed a "band of iron and brass" on the tree stump for "seven times" (Daniel 4:23). Additionally, in the passage above, God told Israel that He would make their "heaven as iron, and your earth as brass." In the end times, the iron kingdom of apostate angels will literally fall from Heaven and terrorize humanity.

The following confirms the dynamic parallel through time between the sentencing of Nebuchadnezzar, the king of Babylon (who was part-man, part beast), with the Antichrist, the final king of Babylon (who is a man and yet also "the Beast"):

> "Another harmony is evolved here in the process of Reversal. The world-empire going back to Babylon, and Nebuchadnezzar being the head of gold, we are brought back to the period of the 'beast's heart,' the 'seven times,' exactly corresponding with the final hebdomad of the covenant between Antichrist and the Jews." – *The Expected Rapture of the Church, or, the Analogy of Prophecy and Established Fact,* G. Warrand Houghton, Elliot Stock 62, Paternoster Row, 1884, p. 239

GOLIATH

Yet another type and shadow of the Final Nephilim in Scripture, and perhaps the starkest, is the Nephilim Goliath.

> "The second, but less type of Antichrist, is the antagonist David, Goliath. David was also a type of Messiah, and hence Goliath is a type of his opponent. The peculiarity of this giant, and son a giant, consist in this, that he completes the prophets in the character of a boasting blaspheming popular orator, representing this form the popularization of the pseudo system." – *The Protestant Theological and Ecclesiastical Encyclopedia, Volume 1,* John Henry Bomberger, 1860, p. 176

Descended from the fallen angels, Goliath embodied their evil and their hatred of the people of God. A brief examination reveals many commonalities between Goliath and the Antichrist:

- Goliath was a hybrid being. The Antichrist will be the seed of Satan and a hybrid being himself.
- Goliath sought to rule over Israel and oppress them:

"And he stood and cried unto the armies of Israel, and said unto them, Why are ye come out to set your battle in array? am not I a Philistine, and ye servants to Saul? choose you a man for you, and let him come down to me. If he be able to fight with me, and to kill me, then will we be your servants: but if I prevail against him, and kill him, then shall ye be our servants, and serve us." – 1 Samuel 17:8–9

The Antichrist will also seek to rule Israel and oppress the Jewish people:

"I am come in my Father's name, and ye receive me not: if another shall come in his own name, him ye will receive." – John 5:43

"And it was given unto him to make war with the saints, and to overcome them: and power was given him over all kindreds, and tongues, and nations." – Revelation 13:7

- Goliath appeared invincible. No solider in the entire army of Israel would dare challenge him in battle:

"And the Philistine said, I defy the armies of Israel this day; give me a man, that we may fight together. When Saul and all Israel heard those words of the Philistine, they were dismayed, and greatly afraid.... And all the men of Israel, when they saw the man, fled from him, and were sore afraid." – 1 Samuel 17:10–11, 24

Likewise, the Antichrist will appear to be so powerful and have such military prowess that the whole world will think he cannot be defeated:

> "And they worshipped the dragon which gave power unto the beast: and they worshipped the beast, saying, Who is like unto the beast? who is able to make war with him?" – Revelation 13:4

- Goliath was a blasphemer who openly defied God with his words:

> "And the Philistine said, I defy the armies of Israel this day." – 1 Samuel 17:10

The Final Nephilim will be a blasphemer as well:

> "And there was given unto him a mouth speaking great things and blasphemies." – Revelation 13:5

Goliath's Connection to the Number of the Beast

The Philistine Nephilim provided further evidence of Yahweh weaving prophetic events and symbolic numbers through time and space. Like Nebuchadnezzar, Goliath has a numeric connection to the Antichrist. In 1 Samuel chapter 17, the description of Goliath reveals curious details:

> "And there went out a champion out of the camp of the Philistines, named Goliath, of Gath, whose height was **six cubits** and a span. And he had an helmet of brass upon his head, and he was armed

> with a coat of mail; and the weight of the coat was five thousand shekels of brass. And he had greaves of brass upon his legs, and a target of brass between his shoulders. And the staff of his spear was like a weaver's beam; and his spear's head weighed **six hundred shekels of iron**: and one bearing a shield went before him." – 1 Samuel 17:4–7

The Nephilim champion of the Philistines was six cubits in height, had a spear's head that weighed six hundred shekels, and wore six pieces of armor. Further, his spear's tip was made from iron—the symbol of the Antichrist kingdom in the prophetic dreams of the book of Daniel we looked at earlier (Daniel 2:42–43; 7:7).

> "This [Mark of the Beast] will be branded or burnt on. It will probably be the Number Of The Beast or 666. The number 666 is the Number of Man and stops short of the perfect number seven. Man was created on the sixth day. Goliath, the opposer of God's people, a type of Satan, was 6 cubits in height, he had 6 pieces of armor and his spearhead weighed 600 shekels. 1 Samuel 17:4. Nebuchadnezzar's Image—a type of the Image of the Beast—was 60 cubits in height 6 cubits wide and 6 instruments of music summoned the worshippers. Daniel 3:17." – *Rightly Dividing the Word*, Clarence Larkin, 1921, p. 107

Opposing the seemingly invincible Goliath was David, through whom God promised would come the Messianic lineage. As detailed in *Judgment of the Nephilim*, David was a foreshadow of Jesus Christ. In fact, in several Old Testament passages, God referred to the Messiah as "David."

Even the means by which Goliath was killed prophetically echoes back to the Garden of Eden:

> "And it came to pass, when the Philistine arose, and came, and drew nigh to meet David, that David hastened, and ran toward the army to meet the Philistine. And David put his hand in his bag, and took thence a stone, and slang it, **and smote the Philistine in his forehead, that the stone sunk into his forehead**; and he fell upon his face to the earth. So David prevailed over the Philistine with a sling and with a stone, and smote the Philistine, and slew him; but there was no sword in the hand of David. Therefore David ran, and stood upon the Philistine, and took his sword, and drew it out of the sheath thereof, and slew him, **and cut off his head therewith**. And when the Philistines saw their champion was dead, they fled." – 1 Samuel 17:48–51

> "And I will put enmity between thee and the woman, and between thy seed and her seed; **it shall bruise thy head**, and thou shalt bruise his heel." – Genesis 3:15

Goliath was killed by a blow from a stone the young David hurled at his head. God told Satan in the first prophecy in Scripture that the Seed of the Woman would one day "bruise," or crush, the head of Satan. In Nebuchadnezzar's dream of the statue of kingdoms through time, the final kingdom of Antichrist is destroyed when it is hit by a stone.

Showing even further waves through time, the Antichrist, when he is first killed, will die from a wound to the head:

> "And I saw one of his heads as it were wounded to death; and his deadly wound was healed: and all the world wondered after the beast." – Revelation 13:3

JUDAS, NEBUCHADNEZZAR, AND GOLIATH: CONFIRMATION THAT ANTICHRIST WILL BE A NEPHILIM

> "Now all these things happened unto them for examples: and they are written for our admonition, upon whom the ends of the world are come." – 1 Corinthians 10:11

As we've seen, Scripture furnishes an enormous number of details about Judas, Nebuchadnezzar, and Goliath, the most prominent foreshadows of the Final Nephilim we find in Scripture. The Antichrist will be the literal seed of Satan (Genesis 3:15). Like Nebuchadnezzar, he will be a hybrid. However, he will suffer a mortal wound:

> "And I stood upon the sand of the sea, and saw a beast rise up out of the sea, having seven heads and ten horns, and upon his horns ten crowns, and upon his heads the name of blasphemy. And the beast which I saw was like unto a leopard, and his feet were as the feet of a bear, and his mouth as the mouth of a lion: and the dragon gave him his power, and his seat, and great authority. **And I saw one of his heads as it were wounded to death; and his deadly wound was healed**: and all the world wondered after the beast." – Revelation 13:1–3

This deadly wound and subsequent satanic healing will take place at the fifth trumpet we read about in Revelation 9. This is when the bottomless pit is opened and the fallen angelic Assyrian will be given one final chance to take over the body of the man who is the Antichrist, in the same fashion that the Devil inhabited Judas. Thus, the Antichrist will be at one time a hybrid seed of Satan and indwelled by a fallen angel.

This won't be first time the fallen angel called the Assyrian entered a human body. The Bible very clearly details that the fallen angelic spirit of the Antichrist has lived within human beings and walked the Earth before.

CHAPTER 6

THE RETURN OF THE ANTICHRIST

> "I am Alpha and Omega, the beginning and the ending, saith the Lord, which is, and which was, and which is to come, the Almighty." – Jesus Christ, Revelation 1:8

When declaring Himself the "beginning and ending" and the One who "is, and which was, and which is to come," the Lord is referring to His eternality. Though He died on the cross, Jesus Christ conquered death and Hell forever:

> "I am he that liveth, and was dead; and, behold, I am alive for evermore, Amen; and have the keys of hell and of death." – Revelation 1:18

Standing outside of time, Jesus demonstrates quantum superposition as the One "that liveth, and was dead; and behold, I am alive evermore." The Antichrist, conversely, is merely a satanic imitation of Christ. He is not fully God and fully man as Jesus Christ is. Instead, he is a Nephilim hybrid who, after dying and being resurrected by the Devil, will ultimately be possessed by a fallen angel.

FALLEN ANGELIC SPIRIT INDWELLING INFAMOUS LEADERS THROUGHOUT BIBLICAL HISTORY

The Antichrist isn't an eternal being sitting outside of time. The Assyrian—the fallen angel who will indwell the Antichrist—was initially banished to the Abyss, where he remained chained under darkness with the rest of the Genesis 6 rebel angels. However, he has been permitted to emerge from the Abyss throughout biblical history and indwell certain notorious figures. This is confirmed in Revelation chapter 17:

> "And the angel said unto me, Wherefore didst thou marvel? I will tell thee the mystery of the woman, and of the beast that carrieth her, which hath the seven heads and ten horns. The beast that thou sawest was, and is not; and shall ascend out of the bottomless pit, and go into perdition: and they that dwell on the earth shall wonder, whose names were not written in the book of life from the foundation of the world, when they behold the beast that was, and is not, and yet is.
>
> And here is the mind which hath wisdom. The seven heads are seven mountains, on which the woman sitteth. And there are seven kings: five are fallen, and one is, and the other is not yet come; and when he cometh, he must continue a short space. And the beast that was, and is not, even he is the eighth, and is of the seven, and goeth into perdition." – Revelation 17:7–11

This mysterious passage describes the Antichrist, symbolized by the seven-headed beast. The seven heads represent seven kings. Many commentaries change the word "kings" to "kingdoms," but the text emphasizes that individuals are in view. The Apostle John clarifies that these seven kings who are a part of the Beast have existed through time:

> "And there are seven kings: five are fallen, and one is, and the other is not yet come; and when he cometh, he must continue a short space. **And the beast that was, and is not, even he is the eighth**, and is of the seven, and goeth into perdition." – Revelation 17:10–11

Scripture establishes Jesus Christ as He that "is, and was, and is to come." The Final Nephilim is he that "was, and is not and shall ascend out of the bottomless pit." Thus, unlike Jesus, who has existed continually, the Antichrist has lived in the past, then died, and will later return to earth. The seven kings represent incarnations of this angelic being throughout biblical history.

Bible researcher and author Peter Goodgame explained this concept in his book *Red Moon Rising*:

> "The seven heads of Satan that are also shown as seven heads of the Beast are explained as being seven kings. They are seven Satanic kings that ruled on the earth during different periods in history, and they have all been enemies of God, each possessing '*a blasphemous name.*'... The seventh king would then be followed by the Antichrist himself, who would be the eight but also of the seven." – *Red Moon Rising, the Rapture and the Timeline of the Apocalypse*, Peter Goodgame, 2005, p. 173–174

John wrote the book of Revelation ca. AD 96. By this time, five of these "Mystery Kings" had died. One of them, the sixth, was alive at the time of the writing of the book. The seventh was "not yet come," but would come only for a "short space." And the Beast, the Antichrist, would be the eighth, but "of the seven," and ultimately going to perdition. What this complex passage is stating is that **the Antichrist has existed before**. The fallen angel known as the Assyrian, Abaddon, and Apollyon has indwelled other people in the past. And during the Day of the Lord, in the days of the Great Tribulation, he will make one final appearance as the end-times Antichrist.

Though this may sound like a bizarre and even unthinkable concept, it was once a common understanding in the Church. One commentary describes this interpretation with precision:

> "These are all to be peculiar characteristics of the beast when he shall exist in his last form as the Antichrist, and belong to that one head, and to that one period of his appearance among men. But the other phraseology…'the beast which was, is not, and yet is,' is clearly applicable to a much more extended period of time, **and to the successive forms in which the beast existed**. For speaking personally to John, then living in Patmos, the angel said, 'The beast *was*, and *is not*, and *shall ascend* out of the abyss.' Rev 17:8.
>
> It appears to me that the grammatical form of this sentence will bear no other construction than that which I have given it at pages 58, 59, of my little work; **namely, that the beast thus described *had lived before* the days of John, *did not live* in John's days, and *should live again* at some day future to John coming up from the abode of the dead for that purpose.** This is a totally different thing to being wounded to death, *as it were,* by a sword in the last stage of his existence, and still continuing to live, though both are to be wondered at." – "The Wounded Head of the Beast," E. G. Lea, as printed in *The Rainbow, a Magazine of Christian Literature*, Volume 2, 1865, p. 234–235

Biblical history has seen the spirit of Antichrist also rippling through time and space, emerging at specific times when God permits as His tool to turn the tide of biblical history.

THE SEVEN SATANIC MYSTERY KINGS

NIMROD: THE FIRST MYSTERY KING

> "Nimrod. This personal type of the Antichrist is deeply interesting and remarkably full in its details. His exploits are recorded in Genesis 10 and 11, and it is most significant that in this person and history are there introduced at the point immediately preceding God's call of Abraham from among the Gentiles and His bringing him into the promised land. Thus will history repeat itself." – *The Antichrist*, Arthur W. Pink, 1923, p. 218–219

Genesis 10 lists the Table of Nations after the world was divided at the events surrounding the construction of the Tower of Babel. The lineages of the sons of Noah are listed to document the successful preservation of the Holy Seed. Alternatively, when Ham's lineage is listed, one name immediately stands out: Nimrod.

> "And the sons of Ham; Cush, and Mizraim, and Phut, and Canaan. And the sons of Cush; Seba, and Havilah, and Sabtah, and Raamah, and Sabtechah: and the sons of Raamah; Sheba, and Dedan. **And Cush begat Nimrod: he began to be a mighty one in the earth. He was a mighty hunter before the LORD: wherefore it is said, Even as Nimrod the mighty hunter before the LORD** And the beginning of his kingdom was Babel, and Erech, and Accad, and Calneh, in the land of Shinar." – Genesis 10:6–10

Just as Lamech, Naamah, and Canaan received special distinction in genealogies, Nimrod is the fourth person in Scripture with an exceptional reference. Several verses record his infamy. He was the first murderer and conqueror in the post-Flood world. He was the founder of the city of Babylon, which became a center of pagan, satanic idolatry, many versions of which featured Nimrod himself being worshiped as a god. His name, which means "to rebel" or "let us rebel," indicated his disposition. He was an enemy of God and Satan's main servant on Earth at that time. He is credited with leading the effort to build the Tower of Babel, a religious temple of worship for false gods and the first attempt to form a global government. The ancient king aspired for man to reach the spiritual realm and "godhood" without the Lord (to which God swiftly responded by destroying the structure, confusing the languages of all the people of the world, and scattering them all over the earth).

WAS NIMROD A NEPHILIM?

It is interesting to note that verse 9 states that Nimrod "began to be a mighty one in the earth." "Mighty one" is translated from the Hebrew *gibbowr* or *gibborim*, which, as we looked at earlier, is also used to describe the Nephilim giants in Genesis 6 who were also "mighty men" (Genesis 6:4) and the giant Goliath (1 Samuel 17:51). *Gibborim* was also used in the Bible to describe human men:

> "So Joshua arose, and all the people of war, to go up against Ai: and Joshua chose out thirty thousand mighty [*gibbowr*] men of valour, and sent them away by night." – Joshua 8:3
>
> "These *be* the names of the mighty men [*gibbowr*] whom David had: The Tachmonite that sat in the seat, chief among the captains; the same *was* Adino the Eznite: ***he lift up his spear*** **against eight hundred, whom he slew at one tim**e." – 2 Samuel 23:8

Rather than designating a giant, *gibbowr* or *gibborim* referred to someone with exceptional, almost superhuman, fighting ability. The description fits Adino the Eznite in 2 Samuel 23:8 above, who singlehandedly killed eight hundred enemies. Nimrod was the first of the post-Flood *gibborim*, far exceeding his contemporaries in combat. Although that would not necessarily mean he was a Nephilim giant, it is clear that he was so imposing and so dominant in warfare that he was the starkest reminder of the giants who once terrified humanity with their weapons of war.

The final interesting hint of evidence to consider is that in the Septuagint, the oldest version of the Old Testament, the same verse from Genesis reads:

> "And [Cush] begot [Nimrod]: **he began to be a giant upon the earth.** He was ***a giant hunter*** before the Lord God; therefore they say, As **[Nimrod] the giant hunter** before the Lord." – Genesis 10:8, 9, LXX

Three times the text uses the word "giant" to describe Nimrod. The following commentary acknowledges the seeming connection between this conqueror and the Nephilim:

> "This principle took its ground in Nimrod, that great monarch and first establisher of idolatry, and the first grand persecutor of God in his select seed, therefore called the mighty hunter before the Lord.... This Nimrod, having the fullness of the Angels nature in him, made him exceeding proud, thinking himself equal with God." – *Truth's Triumph: Or a Witness to the Two Witnesses*, Thomas Tomkinson, Printed by W. Smith, King Street, London, 1690, p. 19–20

By combination of his genetics, fighting prowess, and defiance of God, Nimrod became the first postdiluvian on par with the Rephaim of the ancient world. Could Nimrod have gone through a transformation into a hybrid in the same fashion as King Nebuchadnezzar? Scripture is silent, but there is certainly room to think something on a more supernatural level was taking place with Nimrod.

NIMROD AS INCARNATION OF ANTICHRIST

> "And the whole earth was of one language, and of one speech. And it came to pass, as they journeyed from the east, that they found a plain in the land of Shinar; and they dwelt there. And they said one to another, Go to, let us make brick, and burn them thoroughly. And they had brick for stone, and slime had they for morter. And they said, Go to, let us build us a city and a tower, whose top may reach unto heaven; and let us make us a name, lest we be scattered abroad upon the face of the whole earth." – Genesis 11:1–4

The Tower of Babel rebellion was the earliest corporate assault against the Lord recorded after the Flood. It represented the effort to establish a global governance. The world's population was gathered in the plain of Shinar (in contradiction to God's command that the people should "fill the earth"). Nimrod, the leader of the rebellion, as we know, wanted to erect a tower that could "reach unto Heaven." The structure was to be no normal building; it was an attempt to access the heavenly realm absent God. Just as Adam and Eve had been tempted to do in the Garden, the world was once again trying to "reach unto Heaven" on its own terms. And the leader of this sinful conspiracy was Nimrod.

The materials used to construct the tower were brick and "slime." The slime, *chemar* in Hebrew, was bitumen, the same sealant material God instructed Noah to use in building the ark (referred to as "pitch" in Genesis 6:14). The tower was designed to withstand rising floodwaters; it's important to remember that these events were taking place just 100–150 years after the Flood. Noah, Shem, Japheth, and Ham were all still alive. So, their knowledge of the pre-Flood world and its superhuman angelic and Nephilim rulers, was well-known. Nimrod's perspective would have been informed by his wicked grandfather, Ham. Thus, he would certainly have known of the Flood judgment from the Lord. Second-century historian Herodotus wrote of the construction at Babel:

> "The earth of the trench was first of all laid in heaps, and when a sufficient quantity was obtained, made into square bricks, and baked in a furnace. They used as cement a composition of heated bitumen, which, mixed with the tops of reeds, was placed between every thirtieth course of bricks. Within an eight days journey from Babylon is a city called Is; near which flows a river of the same name, which empties itself into the Euphrates. With the current of this river particles of bitumen descend towards Babylon, by means of which its walls were constructed." – Herodotus, ca. AD 179, as quoted in *The Testimony of the Heathen to the Truths of Holy Writ: A Commentary on the Old and New Testaments*, Reverend Thomas Street Millington, Printed by Seeley, Jackson and Halliday, 1863, p. 80

The Tower of Babel embodied Nimrod's arrogance and mockery of God's Word. The Lord promised never to flood the world again, but Nimrod encouraged his subjects to doubt God and construct the ziggurat so that they could survive a second deluge. Satan needed a human agent to carry out his agenda, and he found it in the grandson of Ham. Rather than spreading out to replenish the planet, Nimrod consolidated the global population in one city dedicated to pagan worship.

Reverend Henry Beamish, writing in 1854, understood Nimrod to be an early incarnation of the Antichrist:

> "The first [organized] confederacy of the serpent's seed, in a direct act of treason against Christ, is found in the building of the tower of Babel, under the headship of Nimrod whose name signifies rebellion: the record of this act of human iniquity is to be found in the eleventh chapter of the book of Genesis. This confederacy was defeated by the miraculous interposition of God, and a seal, as it were stamped upon that enterprise, which was to render it for

> evermore the symbol of that wicked effort of fallen humanity to *enthrone Satan and dethrone Christ* on this earth, which was to be afterwards displayed in the oppression of the Jewish people by the cruel and despotic power of the Babylonish empire under Nebuchadnezzar, and which is yet to have its full display in the final and universal gathering of the hosts of apostate Christendom, in the *mystical* Babylon under the headship of Antichrist in his last and most monstrous development." – *What, Where, and Who Is Antichrist; Being the Substance of Four Lectures,* Henry Hamilton Beamish, 1854, p. 12

NIMROD WANTED TO CREATE A "NAME"

In Scripture, God is often referred to as *Hashem* or "The Name," merging the Hebrew definitive article *Ha* with *Shem*. Thus, in attempting to make "a name" for themselves, the Babel rebels were conspiring to supplant God Himself. Nimrod was leading the people to establish their own name and object of idolatry.

As noted earlier, the Antichrist will also seek to establish a one-world system of worship centered on himself:

> "And deceiveth them that dwell on the earth by the means of those miracles which he had power to do in the sight of the beast; saying to them that dwell on the earth, that they should make an image to the beast, which had the wound by a sword, and did live. And he had power to give life unto the image of the beast, that the image of the beast should both speak, and cause that as many as would not worship the image of the beast should be killed." – Revelation 13:14–15

Furthermore, the Final Nephilim will seek to "oppose" and "exalt himself above all that is called God, or that is worshipped; so that he as God sitteth in the temple of God, shewing himself that he is God" (2 Thessalonians 2:4). Nimrod's ambition at Babel was merely an earlier version of the same wicked desire. Reverend G. F. Taylor, writing about the Antichrist, identified Nimrod as a literal incarnation:

> "Again it is stated of Nimrod, 'He *began* to be a mighty one in the earth.' Genesis 10:8. This seems to intimate that his greatness was only begun, but not finished. All of these things tend to identify Nimrod as the final Antichrist.
>
> As a farther means of the identity of Nimrod and Antichrist, let us notice that each has a mark. Nimrod said, 'Let us make us a name' (Hebrew, '*Sem,*' a token, a mark). – Genesis 11:4. 'He causeth all to receive a mark.' Revelation 13:16. The mark of Antichrist, as we have seen before, is both a mark and a name. Though the outward resemblance between these two marks may be distant, yet their primary purpose is the same. Nimrod's mark was a literal stamp, it was both a mark and a name, an outward profession of religion and a sign of confederation; and the mark of Antichrist is all of these."
> – *The Second Coming of Jesus*, Reverend G. F. Taylor, 1916, p. 138

In *Judgment of the Nephilim,* I noted that, time and time again, wherever the Nephilim were present, the Lord personally intervened to rescue the world from the beings' destructive presence. At the Tower of Babel rebellion, He again directly intervened to thwart the attempted apostasy:

> "**And the LORD came down to see the city and the tower**, which the children of men builded. And the LORD said, Behold, the people is one, and they have all one language; and this they begin to do: **and now nothing will be restrained from them, which they have imagined to do**. Go to, let us go down, and there confound

> their language, that they may not understand one another's speech. So the LORD scattered them abroad from thence upon the face of all the earth: and they left off to build the city. Therefore is the name of it called Babel; because the LORD did there confound the language of all the earth: and from thence did the LORD scatter them abroad upon the face of all the earth." – Genesis 11:5–9

The world was on the verge of unbridled evil in the construction of the tower. Yahweh stated that, had the project been completed, "nothing" would "be restrained" from the people of the world. Would the structure have tapped into the spirit realm? Could it possibly have allowed access to the fallen angels and their powers? It seems most likely that would have been the case. In Daniel chapter 11, speaking of the Antichrist, the prophet wrote:

> "**And the king shall do according to his will** and he shall exalt himself, and magnify himself above every god, and shall speak marvellous things against the God of gods, and shall prosper till the indignation be accomplished: for that that is determined shall be done." – Daniel 11:36

The Antichrist will be unrestrained in achieving his desires. Energized by Satan and the fallen angelic realm accompanying him, he will appear invincible and unstoppable (Revelation 13:4). And, as we can gather from the text of Genesis 11, Nimrod was well on his way to doing the same. Whatever the case, the Babel conspiracy was so serious that God personally came down from Heaven to end the wicked scheme.

Let's not miss the fact that as the Antichrist approaches the zenith of his power, the Lord Jesus Christ will once again say, "Let us go down," and He will descend from Heaven to Earth to destroy the Antichrist and his global kingdom. Immediately following Jesus' victory, the kingdom of Israel will be established. Just as A. W. Pink's words above alluded to, the restoration of

Israel and the Revelation of Jesus Christ to the world are inextricably linked.

MICAH CONNECTS NIMROD TO ANTICHRIST

> "But thou, Bethlehem Ephrathah, though thou be little among the thousands of Judah, yet out of thee shall he come forth unto me that is to be ruler in Israel; whose goings forth have been from of old, from everlasting." – Micah 5:2

This verse is very well known as one of the many Messianic prophecies fulfilled by the life of Jesus Christ. Writing five hundred years before Christ's First Advent, the prophet Micah accurately predicted that the Messiah would be born in Bethlehem Ephrathah. But the prophecy continues through time from Christ's First Coming to His Second, and specifically details His defeat of the Antichrist:

> "Therefore will he give them up, until the time that she which travaileth hath brought forth: **then the remnant of his brethren shall return unto the children of Israel**. And he shall stand and feed in the strength of the LORD, in the majesty of the name of the LORD his God; and they shall abide: for now shall he be great unto the ends of the earth." – Micah 5:3–4

In the time of "travailing," the "remnant" of believing Jews will return to Israel. Jesus Christ described the end-times Day of the Lord by comparing them to a "woman in travail." And, as noted earlier, this is when the believing remnant of Israel will come to a saving faith in Jesus Christ as *Yeshua Ha Mashiach*. Thus, contextually, the passage is referring to the end times.

> "And this man shall be the peace, **when the Assyrian shall come into our land**: and when he shall **tread in our palaces**, then shall

> we raise against him seven shepherds, and eight principal men. And they shall waste the land of Assyria with the sword, **and the land of Nimrod** in the entrances thereof: thus shall he deliver us from the Assyrian, when he cometh into our land, and when he treadeth within our borders." – Micah 5:5–6

Antichrist will invade Israel and set up his palaces in Jerusalem. Jesus Christ will conquer the Assyrian in the entrances of "the land of Nimrod." Twice, the passages proclaim that the Assyrian will "tread," or conquer and rule within the "borders" of Israel. Daniel chapter 7 proclaims that the Antichrist kingdom will "and shall devour the whole earth, and shall **tread** it down, and break it in pieces" (Daniel 7:23).

The prophecy from Micah chapter 5 also refers to God raising "seven shepherds, and eight principal men." When Jesus Christ returns, He will not be alone. As Enoch prophesied, the Lord will return with "ten thousands of his saints" (Jude 1:14). The passage also presents a mystical converse of the Antichrist, who is the eighth "Mystery King," but "is of the seven." In ancient times, God said "let us go down" before He destroyed the one-world government of Nimrod. In the end times, God will once again say "let us go down"—this time, it will be to destroy the one-world government of the Final Nephilim.

The clear connections between Nimrod and Antichrist were apparent to many of the biblical commentators of the early twentieth century. For example:

> "This identity [Nimrod and Antichrist] is further shown by reference to a few points given in connection with the origin of Antichrist in Chapter 18. It is clear that the purpose of Nimrod in building his tower, and of Antichrist in his reign is: 1st—To counteract the religion of Christ; 2nd—To exalt self above all others; 3rd—To establish a government in connection with his religion; 4th—That the religion and governmental center be one

> and be in the land of Shinar; 5th—To heap their means and labor into one place; 6th—To have world-wide authority; and 7th—That the people of their kingdoms be united and known to all by a certain sign badge or mark. **Thus in many ways, Antichrist points us back to Nimrod, and Nimrod points us forward to Antichrist.**" – *The Second Coming of Jesus*, Reverend G. F. Taylor, 1916, p. 138–139

> "We cannot but fail to see that [in Nimrod] we have a wonderfully complete typical picture of the person, the work, and the destruction of the Antichrist." – *The Antichrist*, A. W. Pink, 1923, p. 222

PHARAOH OF EGYPT DURING THE EXODUS: THE SECOND MYSTERY KING

If there was any notorious figure in Scripture whose life and career served as an almost verbatim foreshadow of the Great Tribulation, it is the Pharaoh of Egypt in the book of Exodus. As stated earlier, the end-times judgment of the world and rescue of Israel is a prophetic repeat of the events of the book of Exodus. And Pharaoh certainly embodied the spirit of Antichrist.

PHARAOH AS GENOCIDAL OPPRESSOR OF ISRAEL

> "And there appeared a great wonder in heaven; a woman clothed with the sun, and the moon under her feet, and upon her head a crown of twelve stars: And she being with child cried, travailing in birth, and pained to be delivered. And there appeared another wonder in heaven; and behold a great red dragon, having seven heads and ten horns, and seven crowns upon his heads. And his tail drew the third part of the stars of heaven, and did cast them to the earth: and the dragon stood before the woman which was ready to be delivered, **for to devour her child as soon as it was born.**" –

> Revelation 12:1–4
>
> "And Pharaoh charged all his people, saying, Every [Israelite] son that is born ye shall cast into the river." – Exodus 1:22

Revelation 12 outlines the primary reason for the original incursion of fallen angels and the birth of the Nephilim: to prevent, corrupt, or destroy the prophesied Messiah of Genesis 3:15. Pharaoh was clearly under satanic influence when he issued a decree to order all male Jewish babies born in his kingdom to be murdered in cold blood by drowning them. Such a sadistic, murderous scheme could only originate from the Devil himself.

EXODUS PLAGUES MIRROR THOSE OF GREAT TRIBULATION

> "The attentive Bible student will not fail to discern in all this matchless display of Divine strength and greatness, together with the onslaught and overthrow of Pharaoh and his host, a foreshadowing of the events narrated in Revelation 16 and 19. There is a wonderful similarity between the record of the plagues of Egypt and the pouring out of the vials of the wrath of God upon the earth in the last days. Pharaoh is himself a remarkable type of the antichrist yet to come, and the destruction of the one foreshadows that of the other." – *What Saith the Scripture? An Exposition and Analysis of the Pentateuch and Earlier Historical Books of the Old Testament,* Dr. John Anderson, 1885, p. 121

A comparison of the events of the Exodus with the end-times judgments of the Antichrist kingdom in the book of Revelation leaves little doubt that Pharaoh is one of the most glaring foreshadows and early incarnations of the Assyrian in all of the Bible. This section will take an in-depth look at the numerous parallels in the supernatural judgments God unleashed against both satanic kingdoms as Yahweh declares the end from the beginning.

- WATER TURNING TO BLOOD

> "And Moses and Aaron did so, as the LORD commanded; and he lifted up the rod, and smote the waters that were in the river, in the sight of Pharaoh, and in the sight of his servants; and all the waters that were in the river were turned to blood. And the fish that was in the river died; and the river stank, and the Egyptians could not drink of the water of the river; and there was blood throughout all the land of Egypt." – Exodus 7:20–21

> "And the second angel sounded, and as it were a great mountain burning with fire was cast into the sea: and the third part of the sea became blood." – Revelation 8:8

At the second and third vial judgments, the damage to the waters will be far more severe:

> "And the second angel poured out his vial upon the sea; and it became as the blood of a dead man: and every living soul died in the sea. And the third angel poured out his vial upon the rivers and fountains of waters; and they became blood. And I heard the angel of the waters say, Thou art righteous, O Lord, which art, and wast, and shalt be, because thou hast judged thus. For they have shed the blood of saints and prophets, and thou hast given them blood to drink; for they are worthy." – Revelation 16:3–6

In both the Exodus and the Great Tribulation, all natural sources of water turn to blood and sea life perish.

- FROGS

> "And the LORD spake unto Moses, Go unto Pharaoh, and say unto him, Thus saith the LORD, Let my people go, that they may serve me. And if thou refuse to let them go, behold, I will smite all thy borders with frogs: And the river shall bring forth frogs abundantly, which shall go up and come into thine house, and into thy bedchamber, and upon thy bed, and into the house of thy servants, and upon thy people, and into thine ovens, and into thy kneading troughs:
>
> And the frogs shall come up both on thee, and upon thy people, and upon all thy servants. And the LORD spake unto Moses, Say unto Aaron, Stretch forth thine hand with thy rod over the streams, over the rivers, and over the ponds, and cause frogs to come up upon the land of Egypt. And Aaron stretched out his hand over the waters of Egypt; and the frogs came up, and covered the land of Egypt. And the magicians did so with their enchantments, and brought up frogs upon the land of Egypt." – Exodus 8:1–7

The plague of frogs overran the Egyptian Empire. In the book of Revelation, the Devil, Antichrist, and the False Prophet summon demonic spirits that appear as frogs to recruit the regional rulers under Antichrist to join forces to battle against Jesus Christ at Armageddon:

> "And the sixth angel poured out his vial upon the great river Euphrates; and the water thereof was dried up, that the way of the kings of the east might be prepared. **And I saw three unclean spirits like frogs** come out of the mouth of the dragon, and out of the mouth of the beast, and out of the mouth of the false prophet. For they are the spirits of devils, working miracles, which go forth unto the kings of the earth and of the whole world, to gather them to the battle of that great day of God Almighty." – Revelation

16:12–14

- GRUESOME BOILS AND SUPERNATURAL DARKNESS

Though not as commonly known as some of the more infamous punishments, one of the plagues God inflicted upon the Egyptians was horrific sores and boils that appeared on their skin:

> "And they took ashes of the furnace, and stood before Pharaoh; and Moses sprinkled it up toward heaven; and it became a boil breaking forth with blains upon man, and upon beast. And the magicians could not stand before Moses because of the boils; for the boil was upon the magicians, and upon all the Egyptians." – Exodus 9:10–11

There was also a plague of darkness so thick that it could be "felt":

> "And the LORD said unto Moses, Stretch out thine hand toward heaven, that there may be darkness over the land of Egypt, even darkness which may be felt. And Moses stretched forth his hand toward heaven; and there was a thick darkness in all the land of Egypt three days: They saw not one another, neither rose any from his place for three days: but all the children of Israel had light in their dwellings." – Exodus 10:21–23

This "thick darkness" is the same supernatural smoke that currently envelopes the apostate angels of Genesis 6:

> "And the angels which kept not their first estate, but left their own habitation, he hath reserved **in everlasting chains under darkness**

unto the judgment of the great day." – Jude 1:6

In Revelation, the judgments of supernatural darkness and sores are combined at the pouring of the fifth vial:

> "And the fifth angel poured out his vial upon the seat of the beast; and his kingdom was full of darkness; and they gnawed their tongues for pain, And blasphemed the God of heaven because of their pains and their sores, and repented not of their deeds." – Revelation 16:10–11

- LOCUSTS

This study has already gone into extensive details on the "locusts" that emerge from the bottomless pit at the fifth trumpet of Revelation chapter 9. Real locusts were a judgment against Pharaoh and a prophetic similitude of the end times:

> "And Moses stretched forth his rod over the land of Egypt, and the LORD brought an east wind upon the land all that day, and all that night; and when it was morning, the east wind brought the locusts. And the locust went up over all the land of Egypt, and rested in all the coasts of Egypt: very grievous were they; before them there were no such locusts as they, neither after them shall be such." – Exodus 10:13–14

- HAIL AND FIRE

> "And Moses stretched forth his rod toward heaven: and the LORD

> sent thunder and hail, and the fire ran along upon the ground; and the LORD rained hail upon the land of Egypt. **So there was hail, and fire mingled with the hail**, very grievous, such as there was none like it in all the land of Egypt since it became a nation." – Exodus 9:23–24

The judgment of fire mixed with hail is incredibly unique in Scripture. To no surprise, outside of the Exodus judgments against Pharaoh, the only other time this unusual judgment was poured out by the Lord is during the end times, at the first trumpet of Revelation chapter 8:

> "And the seven angels which had the seven trumpets prepared themselves to sound. The first angel sounded, and **there followed hail and fire mingled with blood**, and they were cast upon the earth: and the third part of trees was burnt up, and all green grass was burnt up." – Revelation 8:6–7

- DEATH OF THE FIRSTBORN

The final event that brought Pharaoh to his knees, allowing the Israelites to leave his control and go to the wilderness to worship Yahweh, was the killing of his firstborn child by supernatural attack:

> "And it came to pass, that at midnight the LORD smote all the firstborn in the land of Egypt, from the firstborn of Pharaoh that sat on his throne unto the firstborn of the captive that was in the dungeon; and all the firstborn of cattle. And Pharaoh rose up in the night, he, and all his servants, and all the Egyptians; and there was a great cry in Egypt; for there was not a house where there was not one dead.
>
> And he called for Moses and Aaron by night, and said, Rise up, and

> get you forth from among my people, both ye and the children of Israel; and go, serve the LORD, as ye have said. Also take your flocks and your herds, as ye have said, and be gone; and bless me also." – Exodus 12:29–32

In the end times, the Antichrist, the firstborn son of Satan, will be conquered and killed by the True *Yeshuah Ha Meshiach* at His Second Coming:

> "And then shall that Wicked be revealed, whom the Lord shall consume with the spirit of his mouth, and shall destroy with the brightness of his coming." – 2 Thessalonians 2:8

A nineteenth-century Baptist minister remarked on the end-times prophetic foreshadowing in this last strike against Pharaoh:

> "Looking, however, at these plagues as a whole, one cannot fail to be struck with their correspondency with those that will be visited upon the world at a later day during the sway of the antichrist. (See Revelation 16:1–14). Pharaoh indeed is no mean adumbration of this last antagonist of God and His Christ. But as God was glorified in His controversy with the one, so will He be in that with the other; for if Pharaoh rushed to his doom, and was whelmed in the waters of the Red Sea, he and all his host, the antichrist rising to a still greater height of daring impiety, will together with the 'beast' whose false prophet he had been, be 'cast alive into a lake of fire burning with brimstone.'" (Revelation 19:20).
>
> Well then might the Psalmist cry, 'Kiss the Son, lest He be angry, and ye perish from the way, when His wrath is kindled but a little.' (Psalm 2:12). It would be folly, indeed, to be deaf to the lessons which God' controversy with Pharaoh so loudly proclaims." – *Typical Teachings of Exodus, Being a Simple Exposition*, Edward

Dennett, 1882, p. 50

ISRAELITES PROTECTED IN THE EXODUS AND IN THE DAY OF THE LORD

During the Exodus plagues, Israel was supernaturally protected in the city of Goshen, their designated place of residence with Egypt:

> "And the LORD said unto Moses, Rise up early in the morning, and stand before Pharaoh; lo, he cometh forth to the water; and say unto him, Thus saith the LORD, Let my people go, that they may serve me. Else, if thou wilt not let my people go, behold, I will send swarms of flies upon thee, and upon thy servants, and upon thy people, and into thy houses: and the houses of the Egyptians shall be full of swarms of flies, and also the ground whereon they are. And I will sever in that day the land of Goshen, in which my people dwell, that no swarms of flies shall be there; to the end thou mayest know that I am the LORD in the midst of the earth. And I will put a division between my people and thy people: tomorrow shall this sign be." – Exodus 8:20–23

Similarly, when God smote the cattle of Egypt, none of the Israelites' livestock was harmed (Exodus 9:4). When the plague of hail struck the Egyptians, there was no hail in Goshen (Exodus 9:26). Over and over, the people of Yahweh were divinely protected from the plagues that tormented those who followed the satanic king. The ultimate sign of this distinction was the Passover, in which the firstborn of all the Egyptians died, while the Israelites remained safe because they had the blood of the lamb on their doors. This was a sign of protection from God and a foreshadowing of the blood Jesus Christ shed on the cross, saving all who believe in Him from the wrath of God.

In the book of Revelation, the believing remnant of Israel will flee Jerusalem and again enter the wilderness, where they will be protected by the Lord:

"And when the dragon saw that he was cast unto the earth, he persecuted the woman which brought forth the man child. And to the woman were given two wings of a great eagle, that she might fly into the wilderness, into her place, where she is nourished for a time, and times, and half a time, from the face of the serpent." – Revelation 12:13–14

CAPITAL CITY OF THE ANTICHRIST CALLED "EGYPT"

One of the clearest evidences of the end times being a "second Exodus" is that "Mystery Babylon"—the headquarters of the Antichrist—is called "Egypt" in the book of Revelation:

"And when they shall have finished their testimony, the beast that ascendeth out of the bottomless pit shall make war against them, and shall overcome them, and kill them. And their dead bodies shall lie in the street of the great city, **which spiritually is called Sodom and Egypt**, where also our Lord was crucified." – Revelation 11:7–8

FAITHFUL MARTYRS SING "SONG OF MOSES" IN HEAVEN

"And I saw another sign in heaven, great and marvellous, seven angels having the seven last plagues; for in them is filled up the wrath of God. And I saw as it were a sea of glass mingled with fire: and them that had gotten the victory over the beast, and over his image, and over his mark, and over the number of his name, stand on the sea of glass, having the harps of God. **And they sing the song of Moses the servant of God**, and the song of the Lamb, saying, Great and marvellous are thy works, Lord God Almighty;

> just and true are thy ways, thou King of saints. Who shall not fear thee, O Lord, and glorify thy name? for thou only art holy: for all nations shall come and worship before thee; for thy judgments are made manifest." – Revelation 15:1–4

This passage details a scene of Antichrist's persecution of all believers during his reign of terror. The people who will have "gotten victory over the beast" will do so by dying as martyrs rather than taking the mark in subservient worship of the Final Nephilim. And, as they stand before the throne of God, they will sing the "song of Moses"—the anthem Moses sang after God's conquest of Pharaoh at the Red Sea.

A popular Bible commentary confirms the connection:

> "With this song of victory over Pharaoh…the Holy Ghost compares the song of those who have gotten the victory over the spiritual Pharaoh, *the beast,* (Antichrist,) when they stand by the sea of glass mingled with fire, (as Israel stood here by the Red Sea,) having the harps of God (as the women here had timbrels, verse 20,): 'and they the song of Moses the servant of God and the of the Lamb the Son of God,' Rev 15:2–4." – *The Holy Bible, Containing the Old and New Testaments, the Text Carefully Printed from the Most Correct Copies of the Present Authorized Translation,* Commentary by Adam Clarke, 1837, p. 372

The Clarke commentary even calls the Antichrist "the spiritual Pharaoh," acknowledging the extraordinary recurrence of God's prophetic Word through time and space.

SCRIPTURE DIRECTLY CONNECTS PHARAOH TO ANTICHRIST

In Isaiah chapter 10, which chronicles Yahweh's use of the Antichrist as a tool of judgment against Israel, the prophet makes a direct connection to the Exodus:

> "For the Lord GOD of hosts shall make a consumption, even determined, in the midst of all the land. Therefore thus saith the Lord GOD of hosts, O my people that dwellest in Zion, **be not afraid of the Assyrian**: he shall smite thee with a rod, **and shall lift up his staff against thee, after the manner of Egypt**. For yet a very little while, and the indignation shall cease, and mine anger in their destruction." – Isaiah 10:23–25

The persecution of Israel by the Antichrist will be "after the manner of Egypt." Thus, Pharaoh is explicitly confirmed as a forerunner and prototype of the Antichrist. An even more startling and mystical reference is found in the fifty-second chapter of Isaiah:

> "Awake, awake; put on thy strength, O Zion; put on thy beautiful garments, O Jerusalem, the holy city: for henceforth there shall no more come into thee the uncircumcised and the unclean. Shake thyself from the dust; arise, and sit down, O Jerusalem: loose thyself from the bands of thy neck, O captive daughter of Zion. For thus saith the LORD, Ye have sold yourselves for nought; and ye shall be redeemed without money. For thus saith the Lord GOD, **My people went down aforetime into Egypt** to sojourn there; **and the Assyrian oppressed them without cause**." – Isaiah 52:1–4

This passage illustrates the spiritual connection, as it identifies the Pharaoh as the Assyrian! A similar dual title of Pharaoh is found in Ezekiel 31—the esoteric passage that details the rise and fall of the Assyrian when he ruled over the pre-Flood world:

> "Son of man, **speak unto Pharaoh king of Egypt**, and to his multitude; Whom art thou like in thy greatness? **Behold, the Assyrian was a cedar in Lebanon** with fair branches, and with a shadowing shroud, and of an high stature; and his top was among the thick boughs." – Ezekiel 31:2–3

Numerous passages confirm that the spirit indwelling Pharaoh was that of the Assyrian.

NEBUCHADNEZZAR, AN INCARNATION OF THE ASSYRIAN: THE THIRD MYSTERY KING

Please refer to the previous chapter for an in-depth analysis of this point.

SENNACHERIB: THE FOURTH MYSTERY KING

Although not as popular as Nimrod or Pharaoh in the teachings of the modern church, Sennacherib, the king of Assyria in the days of the prophet Isaiah, provides a stunning foreshadow of the Beast and is a strong candidate as one of the seven kings indwelled by the spirit of the Assyrian. First, note that Sennacherib actually was an ethnic Assyrian. Among the many titles God gives to the Antichrist in the Old Testament, "the Assyrian" is the most commonly used.

The books of 2 Kings, 2 Chronicles, and Isaiah document the exploits of Sennacherib and his attempt to conquer Israel. Not only do the numerous references to this king emphasize his importance in biblical history, but the accounts also reveal startling similarities to the end-times Beast.

BENT ON CONQUERING JERUSALEM AND THE ISRAELITES

> "Now it came to pass in the fourteenth year of king Hezekiah, that Sennacherib king of Assyria came up against all the defenced cities of Judah, and took them." – Isaiah 36:1

Like the Antichrist to come, Sennacherib was consumed with the conquest of Israel. In this passage, he had already destroyed the Northern Kingdom and turned his sights towards the Southern Kingdom of Judah and the capital city of Jerusalem. In a foolish effort to earn the mercy of this wicked king, Hezekiah, the king of Judah, sent a massive amount of treasure to Sennacherib:

> "And Hezekiah king of Judah sent to the king of Assyria to Lachish, saying, I have offended; return from me: that which thou puttest on me will I bear. And the king of Assyria appointed unto Hezekiah king of Judah three hundred talents of silver and thirty talents of gold. And Hezekiah gave him all the silver that was found in the house of the LORD, and in the treasures of the king's house. At that time did Hezekiah cut off the gold from the doors of the temple of the LORD, and from the pillars which Hezekiah king of Judah had overlaid, and gave it to the king of Assyria." – 2 Kings 18:14–16

Notice the extent to which Hezekiah went to appease the Assyrian king. He emptied all of the silver and gold from the Temple and paid what would no doubt amount to millions of dollars in today's economy. He then had the gold from the very door of the Temple of God scraped off for a gift to present to the pagan tyrant. Rather than going to the house of God in prayer and seeking His protection, Hezekiah foolishly opted to desecrate the Temple to earn the favor of men.

This effort to buy peace from Sennacherib failed miserably, as the Assyrian king immediately violated his peace covenant with the Israelites and threatened war. This is a type and shadow of Israel's future covenant with the Antichrist that will be broken after three and a half years, when the fallen angelic Assyrian spirit indwells the Final Nephilim. Once his full satanic nature is revealed at the midpoint of the seven years, Antichrist will betray Israel and defile the Temple:

> "And one week shall establish the covenant with many: and in the midst of the week my sacrifice and drink-offering shall be taken away: **and on the temple *shall be* the abomination of desolations**." – Daniel 9:26, LXX

Fully energized with satanic power and possessed by a fallen angelic spirit, the Antichrist will ban all forms of Jewish worship and will commit the "abomination of desolations" when he sits in the Temple of God and proclaims himself to be God. This devastating betrayal is clearly prefigured in Sennacherib's actions.

GENERAL RABSHAKEH FORESHADOWS THE FALSE PROPHET

Rather than addressing Hezekiah directly, Sennacherib dispatched Rabshakeh, his general and vizier (chief cupbearer), to essentially intimidate the Southern Kingdom into full surrender:

> "And the king of Assyria sent Tartan and Rabsaris and Rabshakeh from Lachish to king Hezekiah with a great host against Jerusalem. And they went up and came to Jerusalem. And when they were come up, they came and stood by the conduit of the upper pool, which is in the highway of the fuller's field.... And Rabshakeh said unto them, Speak ye now to Hezekiah, Thus saith the great king, the king of Assyria, What confidence is this wherein thou trustest?

> Thou sayest, (but they are but vain words,) I have counsel and strength for the war. Now on whom dost thou trust, that thou rebellest against me?.... But if ye say unto me, We trust in the LORD our God: is not that he, whose high places and whose altars Hezekiah hath taken away, and hath said to Judah and Jerusalem, Ye shall worship before this altar in Jerusalem?" – 2 Kings 18:17–22

Rabshakeh mocked the Israelites repeatedly and made a bold show of force by setting up his military units at Jerusalem's sole source of water. He instigated the people to doubt Hezekiah, their righteous, faithful king, by criticizing him for tearing down the "high places"—locations of pagan worship in Israel—as if this were somehow an offense to God. His aim was to frighten the people of the Southern Kingdom into fearing Sennacherib more than they did God Himself. This is precisely the agenda of the False Prophet.

Continuing in 2 Kings:

> "Now therefore, I pray thee, give pledges to my lord the king of Assyria, and I will deliver thee two thousand horses, if thou be able on thy part to set riders upon them. How then wilt thou turn away the face of one captain of the least of my master's servants, and put thy trust on Egypt for chariots and for horsemen?"

This is another taunt. Rabshakeh was saying, "Even if I gave you two thousand horses, the Jewish people would not even be able to find men brave enough to ride them against the Assyrian Empire." Nor could the Egyptian Empire (upon whom the Northern Empire relied) come to aid Judah against Sennacherib's warriors. They had no chance against the least of the soldiers in the enemy forces. This boasting of Sennacherib's power is a prophetic superposition of the seemingly invincible military might of the Antichrist:

> "And they worshipped the dragon which gave power unto the beast: and they worshipped the beast, saying, Who is like unto the beast? **who is able to make war with him**?" – Revelation 13:4

As Rabshakeh continued his oratory, his sinister *spiritual agenda* was revealed as well:

> "Am I now come up without the LORD against this place to destroy it? The LORD said to me, Go up against this land, and destroy it. Then said Eliakim the son of Hilkiah, and Shebna, and Joah, unto Rabshakeh, Speak, I pray thee, to thy servants in the Syrian language; for we understand it: and talk not with us in the Jews' language in the ears of the people that are on the wall. But Rabshakeh said unto them, Hath my master sent me to thy master, and to thee, to speak these words? hath he not sent me to the men which sit on the wall, that they may eat their own dung, and drink their own piss with you?" – 2 Kings 18:25–27

The vizier lied and stated that God was *working with Assyria and* instructed them to go to Judah to destroy the kingdom. This was shameless blasphemy against God. The frightened representatives of King Hezekiah immediately begged Rabshakeh to speak in the Syrian language so the Israelites within earshot of this meeting wouldn't understand what was being said. The vizier declined, and continued his verbal offense of the True and Living God:

> "Then Rabshakeh stood and **cried with a loud voice in the Jews' language**, and spake, saying, Hear the word of the great king, the king of Assyria: Thus saith the king, Let not Hezekiah deceive you: for he shall not be able to deliver you out of his hand: **Neither let Hezekiah make you trust in the LORD, saying, The LORD will surely deliver us**, and this city shall not be delivered into the hand

> of the king of Assyria.
>
> Hearken not to Hezekiah: for thus saith the king of Assyria, Make an agreement with me by a present, and come out to me, and then eat ye every man of his own vine, and every one of his fig tree, and drink ye every one the waters of his cistern: Until I come and take you away to a land like your own land, a land of corn and wine, a land of bread and vineyards, a land of oil olive and of honey, that ye may live, and not die: and hearken not unto Hezekiah, when he persuadeth you, saying, The LORD will deliver us.
>
> Hath any of the gods of the nations delivered at all his land out of the hand of the king of Assyria? Where are the gods of Hamath, and of Arpad? where are the gods of Sepharvaim, Hena, and Ivah? have they delivered Samaria out of mine hand? Who are they among all the gods of the countries, that have delivered their country out of mine hand, that the LORD should deliver Jerusalem out of mine hand?" – 2 Kings 18:28–35

This is by far an account of one of the most egregious displays of blasphemy in all of Scripture. With vile audacity, Rabshakeh, speaking on behalf of Sennacherib, declared that the Israelites shouldn't listen to Hezekiah or trust in God. Sennacherib was clearly familiar with the culture and faith of the kingdom of Judah and wanted to directly defy their God and blaspheme the Lord right in their ears. His threats were intended to win over the hearts and minds of the Jewish people—to persuade them to abandon the Lord and make a covenant with himself instead. He even offered to take them to a different Promised Land—"like your own land."

This is precisely what the False Prophet will orchestrate on behalf of the Antichrist:

> "And [the False Prophet] exerciseth all the power of the first beast

> before him, **and causeth the earth and them which dwell therein to worship the first beast**, whose deadly wound was healed. And he doeth great wonders, so that he maketh fire come down from heaven on the earth in the sight of men, **And deceiveth them that dwell on the earth** by the means of those miracles which he had power to do in the sight of the beast; saying to them that dwell on the earth, that they should make an image to the beast, which had the wound by a sword, and did live." – Revelation 13:12–14

The False Prophet will trick the world into worshiping the Antichrist and making their covenant with him instead of with the Lord. All this will happen after they hear the Beast repeatedly blaspheming God. A British clergyman recognized the similarities between the wicked Rabshakeh and the end-times False Prophet:

> "Indeed what more graphic account could be given of the pride and arrogance of the false prophet, than the chapter of Isaiah in which the boastfulness of the king of Assyria is described: or how could the watchword employed by him in his attacks upon nations professing Christianity, be more correctly parodied than in the words of Rabshakeh concerning Jerusalem?" – *The Problem, "What Is the Church?" Solved. Or the Counter Theory*, Edmond Salusbury Ffolkes, 1853, p. 67

One of the hallmarks of the Antichrist will be his blasphemy directly against God:

> "And there was given unto him a mouth speaking great things and blasphemies; and power was given unto him to continue forty and two months. And he opened his mouth in blasphemy against God, to blaspheme his name, and his tabernacle, and them that dwell in heaven. And it was given unto him to make war with the saints,

> and to overcome them: and power was given him over all kindreds, and tongues, and nations." – Revelation 13:5–7

Daniel chapter 11 also prophesies of the Beast's outrageous blasphemy against the Lord:

> "And the king shall do according to his will; and he shall exalt himself, and magnify himself above every god, and shall speak marvellous things against the God of gods, and shall prosper till the indignation be accomplished: for that that is determined shall be done. Neither shall he regard the God of his fathers, nor the desire of women, nor regard any god: for he shall magnify himself above all." – Daniel 11:36–37

Sennacherib repeatedly exalted himself above God. He mocked God's ability to save Israel and used his servant to deliver a message to the Southern Kingdom to show he had absolutely no regard for the God of their fathers. He also boasted about himself over all other gods—the fallen angels who have dominion over the pagan nations:

> "Hath any of the gods of the nations delivered his land out of the hand of the king of Assyria?" – Isaiah 36:18

Theologians through the centuries have acknowledged this spiritual connection:

> "So nearly, indeed, do the times and destinies of the Man of Sin accord therewith that prophecies which speak of the final overthrow of the last 'destroyer of the Gentiles,' have been supposed to be fulfilled in the destruction of Sennacherib. Let us then endeavour to gather up and present in one view those parts of the

history before us which have a predictive force, in which Sennacherib and Rabshakeh and Hezekiah stand only in the light of type. **First, then, Sennacherib, king of Assyria, is the type of the Great Assyrian whom the Lord shall tread under foot on the mountains of Israel.**...The next feature of strong resemblance is the boasting and blasphemous message to Hezekiah. Multitudes of passages attest that proud blasphemy shall be the peculiar characteristic of the last ages and especially of Antichrist." – *Isaiah Unfulfilled, Being an Exposition of the Prophet; with New Versions and Critical Notes*, Robert Govett, 1841, p. 268–269

SUPERNATURALLY DESTROYED BY GOD

The prophetic foreshadowing continues in the defeat of Sennacherib. In this instance, God personally intervened to vanquish his entire army:

"When Isaiah the son of Amoz sent unto Hezekiah, saying, Thus saith the LORD God of Israel, Whereas thou hast prayed to me against Sennacherib king of Assyria: This is the word which the LORD hath spoken concerning him; The virgin, the daughter of Zion, hath despised thee, and laughed thee to scorn; the daughter of Jerusalem hath shaken her head at thee. Whom hast thou reproached and blasphemed? and against whom hast thou exalted thy voice, and lifted up thine eyes on high? even against the Holy One of Israel.

By thy servants hast thou reproached the Lord, and hast said, By the multitude of my chariots am I come up to the height of the mountains, to the sides of Lebanon; and I will cut down the tall cedars thereof, and the choice fir trees thereof: and I will enter into the height of his border, and the forest of his Carmel. I have digged, and drunk water; and with the sole of my feet have I dried up all

> the rivers of the besieged places."– Isaiah 37:21–25

Instances of direct addresses from God are extremely rare throughout Scripture; when they do occur, almost all of the encounters involve one of the seven Mystery Kings of Revelation 17. As the Lord continued His one-on-one rebuke of Sennacherib, the context transitions into the supernatural realm:

> "**Hast thou not heard long ago, how I have done it; and of ancient times**, that I have formed it? Now have I brought it to pass, that thou shouldest be to lay waste defenced cities into ruinous heaps." – Isaiah 37:26

Would there have been any chance that the king of Assyria would have "long ago" heard of the work of God in "ancient times"? Doubtful. So, who was God addressing here? Rather than speaking to the human vessel, He was speaking to the spirit of the fallen angel: the Assyrian who *indwelled* the human king. The Lord, in His amazing wisdom, revealed that the limited military victories Sennacherib had up to that point **were a part of His plan**. Like the Final Nephilim, Sennacherib was merely a tool in His hand.

> "Therefore their inhabitants were of small power, they were dismayed and confounded: they were as the grass of the field, and as the green herb, as the grass on the housetops, and as corn blasted before it be grown up. But I know thy abode, and thy going out, and thy coming in, **and thy rage against me**. Because thy rage against me, and thy tumult, is come up into mine ears, **therefore will I put my hook in thy nose, and my bridle in thy lips**, and I will turn thee back by the way by which thou camest." – Isaiah 37:27–29

Here God was announcing that, although many people cowered in fear of Sennacherib, the Lord knew the king's "abode," and his "going out, and…coming in." This wicked king was making no moves that God wasn't fully observing. The Lord also discerns the heart, so He knew that Sennacherib was "raging" against Him—more evidence of the satanic spirit that had taken up residence in this man. Take note of the reference to the "hook" and "bridle" God used as metaphors for making Sennacherib do His bidding (this same illustrative language will be used prophetically in reference to another Mystery King).

> "Therefore thus saith the LORD concerning the king of Assyria, He shall not come into this city, nor shoot an arrow there, nor come before it with shields, nor cast a bank against it. By the way that he came, by the same shall he return, and shall not come into this city, saith the LORD. For I will defend this city to save it for mine own sake, and for my servant David's sake. **Then the angel of the LORD went forth, and smote in the camp of the Assyrians a hundred and fourscore and five thousand**: and when they arose early in the morning, behold, they were all dead corpses.
>
> So Sennacherib king of Assyria departed, and went and returned, and dwelt at Nineveh. And it came to pass, as he was worshipping in the house of Nisroch his god, that Adrammelech and Sharezer his sons smote him with the sword; and they escaped into the land of Armenia: and Esarhaddon his son reigned in his stead." – Isaiah 37:33–38

In *Judgment of the Nephilim*, I explained that the "Angel of the Lord" in the Old Testament was Jesus Christ manifesting on Earth in His preincarnate form. We see confirmation of this in the book of Exodus:

> "Behold, I send an Angel before thee, to keep thee in the way, and

> to bring thee into the place which I have prepared. Beware of him, and obey his voice, provoke him not; for he will not pardon your transgressions: for my name is in him." – Exodus 23:20–21

"This 'Angel,' the preincarnate Jesus Christ, literally waged wars against the Nephilim kingdoms. No 'normal' angel could 'pardon…transgressions,' but the Messiah, as the Angel of the Lord, certainly could.

In the following passage, we see further verification that Jesus was the 'Angel of the Lord' of the Old Testament:

> 'And the angel of the LORD appeared unto him in a flame of fire out of the midst of a bush: and he looked, and, behold, the bush burned with fire, and the bush was not consumed. And Moses said, I will now turn aside, and see this great sight, why the bush is not burnt. And when the LORD saw that he turned aside to see, God called unto him out of the midst of the bush, and said, Moses, Moses. And he said, Here am I. And he said, Draw not nigh hither: put off thy shoes from off thy feet, for the place whereon thou standest is holy ground. Moreover he said, I am the God of thy father, the God of Abraham, the God of Isaac, and the God of Jacob. And Moses hid his face; for he was afraid to look upon God.' – Exodus 3:2–6

The Angel of the Lord was the bodily manifestation of God on Earth in the Old Testament. Only Jesus Christ can fulfill this role, 'for in him dwelleth all the fulness of the Godhead bodily' (Colossians 2:9). In the New Testament, Jesus Himself stated: 'Not that any man hath seen the Father, save he which is of God, he hath

> seen the Father' (John 6:46), further confirming that no person in history saw God the Father. It was God the Son—Jesus Christ—making the in-person visitations to Earth and fighting before the people of Israel." – *Judgment of the Nephilim*, Ryan Pitterson, 2018, p. 340–341

Frequently, when the Nephilim were threatening the Israelites, Jesus Christ personally intervened to wage war and conquer the giants. Here against Sennacherib, the Lord interceded once again to lay waste to the Assyrian armies. Commentator Robert Govett confirms this interpretation in the following:

> "The last point of evident and especial resemblance [to Antichrist] is the sudden destruction of the Assyrian's host by night to the amount of 185,000 men. This was effected, we are told, by 'The Angel' (or messenger) of the Lord, a name referring so evidently to Christ in many passages, that no proof is here attempted. In like manner shall take place the slaughter of the armies of Antichrist so often noticed above: the Lord shall go forth and suddenly destroy them coming upon them 'as a thief in the night.'" – *Isaiah Unfulfilled, Being an Exposition of the Prophet; with New Versions and Critical Notes*, Robert Govett, 1841, p. 271

ANTIOCHUS EPIPHANES – THE FIFTH MYSTERY KING

One of the fiercest enemies of God and His people was Antiochus IV, who would be later known as Antiochus Epiphanes, king of the Seleucid Empire from 175–164 BC. Although fewer verses of Scripture are devoted to his career than to the activities of his predecessors, his actions were equally blasphemous and prophetic in foreshadowing the reign of the Final Nephilim.

DANIEL 11: STUNNING SIMILARITIES TO ANTICHRIST

Daniel chapter 11 is a particularly challenging passage of Scripture. In rapid fashion, the prophet outlines the history of the various leaders who would rule the divided Greek Empire following the death of Alexander the Great. Several centuries of history are packed into one chapter with such incredible accuracy that many Bible skeptics incorrectly theorize that it was written centuries after the life of Daniel. In the division of the empire, Judea was under Antiochus' rule.

It is important to note that, in addition to chronicling a great deal of prophecy regarding the Antichrist, it was the prophet Daniel who was also charged by God to outline the predictions of the future Gentile kingdoms that would dominate the Earth and the land of Israel until the end times. Chapter 11 is just one of several chapters on the "time of the Gentiles," and the portion devoted to Antiochus Epiphanes starts at verse 21:

> "And in his estate shall stand up a vile person, to whom they shall not give the honour of the kingdom: but he shall come in peaceably, and obtain the kingdom by flatteries. And with the arms of a flood shall they be overflown from before him, and shall be broken; yea, also the prince of the covenant. And after the league made with him he shall work deceitfully: for he shall come up, and shall become strong with a small people. He shall enter peaceably even upon the fattest places of the province; and he shall do that which his fathers have not done, nor his fathers' fathers; he shall scatter among them the prey, and spoil, and riches: yea, and he shall forecast his devices against the strong holds, even for a time." – Daniel 11:21–24

This passage warrants close examination:

> "And in his estate shall stand up a vile person, to whom they shall

> not give the honour of the kingdom: but he shall come in peaceably, and obtain the kingdom by flatteries."

The history of Jerusalem in this era is recorded in the book 2 Maccabees, one of the most noteworthy apocryphal Jewish texts written during the period between the conclusion of events recorded in the Old Testament and the beginning of the events recorded in the New Testament. These books were not a part of the canon of divinely inspired Scripture, but were maintained alongside the Old Testament for their historical value (and, unlike other apocryphal books like the Book of Enoch or Book of Jasher that depict numerous supernatural events not recorded in Scripture, they do not describe actions of God or angels—instead detailing Jewish history). The books of 1 and 2 Maccabees focus on the reign of Antiochus Epiphanes and his vicious attacks on Jerusalem and the Jewish people. And, as Scripture confirms, the tyrant came into power through political intrigue.

> "Now when the holy city was inhabited with all peace, and the laws were kept very well, because of the godliness of Onias the high priest, and his hatred of wickedness, It came to pass that even the kings themselves did honour the place, and magnify the temple with their best gifts; Insomuch that Seleucus of Asia of his own revenues bare all the costs belonging to the service of the sacrifices."
> – 2 Maccabees 3:1–3

At the time of Antiochus' emergence, the Jewish people in Israel were at peace and enjoyed good relations with the various leaders of the Seleucid Empire who ruled over them, King Seleucus in particular. As the passage above states, Seleucus even gave gifts for the Temple. However, after his murder, there was much jockeying for the throne. Demetrius, the son of Seleucus, was the rightful heir, but Antiochus IV negotiated with the Roman Empire to keep Demetrius as a hostage in Rome in exchange for a portion of the kingdom. This opened the door for Antiochus IV to seize power.

> "And with the arms of a flood shall they be overflown from before him, and shall be broken; yea, also the prince of the covenant. And after the league made with him he shall work deceitfully: for he shall come up, and shall become strong with a small people. He shall enter peaceably even upon the fattest places of the province; and he shall do that which his fathers have not done, nor his fathers' fathers; he shall scatter among them the prey, and spoil, and riches: yea, and he shall forecast his devices against the strong holds, even for a time." – Daniel 11:22–24

Antiochus made a pact, or was "in league" with, Ptolemy Philometer, the teenage ruler of Egypt (and son of Queen Cleopatra). He dispatched Apollonius to attend Ptolemy's *anaklētēria*, an ancient coronation ceremony, to curry favor by distributing treasure and giving favors to the political elite.

> "And he shall stir up his power and his courage against the king of the south with a great army; and the king of the south shall be stirred up to battle with a very great and mighty army; but he shall not stand: for they shall forecast devices against him. Yea, they that feed of the portion of his meat shall destroy him, and his army shall overflow: and many shall fall down slain." – Daniel 11:26

Ptolemy Philometer, the "king of the south" in this passage, was attacked by Antiochus IV. The "flatteries" ended and the treachery commenced as Antiochus IV used a false-flag event to storm Egypt with his armies and take almost all territories outside of Alexandria. However, he ordered his men not to kill the Egyptians, but to capture them alive. He then visited King Ptolemy and blamed the war on a misunderstanding due to Ptolemy's governor. This led to the two kings meeting for a "peace talk."

> "And both of these kings' hearts shall be to do mischief, and they

> shall speak lies at one table; but it shall not prosper: for yet the end shall be at the time appointed." – Daniel 11:27

Having thus intimidated his rival, Antiochus IV then maneuvered his way into control over the king of the south. He and Ptolemy Philometer agreed that Antiochus IV would serve as a mentor to the boy king. With minimal bloodshed, Antiochus vastly expanded his empire. And it was during this peace talk that he and the boy king turned their attention towards a common enemy: the Jewish people in Judea. This was the "mischief" Daniel references in the verse above.

BETRAYER OF THE JEWS AND A GREAT DESTROYER OF JERUSALEM

> "Then shall he return into his land with great riches; **and his heart shall be against the holy covenant**; and he shall do exploits, and return to his own land." – Daniel 11:28

This is when the persecution of the Jewish people truly began for Antiochus IV. During his military campaign against Egypt, a rumor spread back in Judea that he had died in battle. Incensed at this, and supposing that the Jewish people would revolt because they thought him dead, Antiochus IV returned to Jerusalem and instigated a slaughter of God's people:

> "And after that Antiochus had smitten Egypt, he returned again in the hundred forty and third year, and went up against Israel and Jerusalem with a great multitude, And entered proudly into the sanctuary, and took away the golden altar, and the candlestick of light, and all the vessels thereof, And the table of the shewbread, and the pouring vessels, and the vials. and the censers of gold, and the veil, and the crown, and the golden ornaments that were before

> the temple, all which he pulled off. He took also the silver and the gold, and the precious vessels: also he took the hidden treasures which he found.
>
> And when he had taken all away, he went into his own land, having made a great massacre, and spoken very proudly. Therefore there was a great mourning in Israel, in every place where they were; So that the princes and elders mourned, the virgins and young men were made feeble, and the beauty of women was changed. Every bridegroom took up lamentation, and she that sat in the marriage chamber was in heaviness, The land also was moved for the inhabitants thereof, and all the house of Jacob was covered with confusion." – 1 Maccabees 1:20–28

The vile king killed forty thousand Jews, sold thousands more into slavery, and raided the Temple of God for all of the gold and silver ornaments that adorned it.

> "At the time appointed he shall return, and come toward the south; but it shall not be as the former, or as the latter. For the ships of Chittim shall come against him: therefore he shall be grieved, and return, and have indignation against the holy covenant: so shall he do; he shall even return, and have intelligence with them that forsake the holy covenant." – Daniel 11:29–30

Continuing his treachery, Antiochus IV once again led a campaign against Egypt in 168 BC. On his way to conquest, the Roman armies (the "ships of Chittim") sent assistance to the Egyptians, and together they defeated Antiochus. Stung by this slight defeat, the wicked Greek king returned to Judea and again vented his anger and rage towards the Israelites.

INITIATED A GREAT "FALLING AWAY" FROM THE JEWISH FAITH

Antiochus IV had "indignation against the holy covenant," as he developed an irrational hatred towards Judaism. He brokered "intelligence"—giving bribes and political favor towards any Jews who were willing to give up their faith in God to follow him. They would then work to persuade other Israelites to turn away from the faith. This is described in detail in the book of 1 Maccabees:

> "In those days went there out of Israel wicked men, who persuaded many, saying, Let us go and make a covenant with the heathen that are round about us: for since we departed from them we have had much sorrow. So this device pleased them well. Then certain of the people were so forward herein, that they went to the king, who gave them license to do after the ordinances of the heathen: Whereupon they built a place of exercise at Jerusalem according to the customs of the heathen: And made themselves uncircumcised, **and forsook the holy covenant**, and joined themselves to the heathen, and were sold to do mischief....
>
> And after two years fully expired the king sent his chief collector of tribute unto the cities of Juda, who came unto Jerusalem with a great multitude, And spake peaceable words unto them, but all was deceit: for when they had given him credence, he fell suddenly upon the city, and smote it very sore, and destroyed much people of Israel. And when he had taken the spoils of the city, he set it on fire, and pulled down the houses and walls thereof on every side. But the women and children took they captive, and possessed the cattle.
>
> Then builded they the city of David with a great and strong wall, and with mighty towers, and made it a strong hold for them. And they put therein a sinful nation, wicked men, and fortified

> themselves therein. They stored it also with armour and victuals, and when they had gathered together the spoils of Jerusalem, they laid them up there, and so they became a sore snare: For it was a place to lie in wait against the sanctuary, and an evil adversary to Israel.
>
> Thus they shed innocent blood on every side of the sanctuary, and defiled it: Insomuch that the inhabitants of Jerusalem fled because of them: whereupon the city was made an habitation of strangers, and became strange to those that were born in her; and her own children left her. Her sanctuary was laid waste like a wilderness, her feasts were turned into mourning, her sabbaths into reproach her honour into contempt. As had been her glory, so was her dishonour increased, and her excellency was turned into mourning." – 1 Maccabees 1:11-15; 29–40

Once again, like the Antichrist to come, Antiochus lured the Israelites into a pact with him only to betray and viciously attack them afterwards. The book of 2 Thessalonians details that a similar apostasy or "falling away" from true faith in God will take place before the arrival of Antichrist:

> "Let no man deceive you by any means: for that day shall not come, except there come a falling away first, and that man of sin be revealed, the son of perdition." – 2 Thessalonians 2:3

The "falling away," *apostasia* in Greek, is another term for the apostasy—when believers abandon the faith. In a remarkable foreshadow, this is precisely what many Jewish people did: fall for the bribery to abandon God right up to the point that Antiochus betrayed them and ordered their slaughter. Renowned first-century Jewish historian Josephus also recorded this devastating persecution of the Israelites:

"Now it came to pass, after two years, in the hundred forty and fifth year, on the twenty-fifth day of that month which is by us called Chasleu, and by the Macedonians Apelleus, in the hundred and fifty-third olympiad, that the king [Antiochus IV] came up to Jerusalem, and, pretending peace, he got possession of the city by treachery; at which time he spared not so much as those that admitted him into it, on account of the riches that lay in the temple... And when he had pillaged the whole city, some of the inhabitants he slew, and some he carried captive, together with their wives and children, so that the multitude of those captives that were taken alive amounted to about ten thousand. He also burnt down the finest buildings; and when he had overthrown the city walls, he built a citadel in the lower part of the city, for the place was high, and overlooked the temple; on which account he fortified it with high walls and towers, and put into it a garrison of Macedonians.

....And when the king had built an idol altar upon God's altar, he slew swine upon it, and so offered a sacrifice neither according to the law, nor the Jewish religious worship in that country. He also compelled them to forsake the worship which they paid their own God, and to adore those whom he took to be gods; and made them build temples, and raise idol altars in every city and village, and offer swine upon them every day. He also commanded them not to circumcise their sons, and threatened to punish any that should be found to have transgressed his injunction. He also appointed overseers, who should compel them to do what he commanded.

And indeed many Jews there were who complied with the king's commands, either voluntarily, or out of fear of the penalty that was denounced. But the best men, and those of the noblest souls, did not regard him, but did pay a greater respect to the customs of their country than concern as to the punishment which he threatened to the disobedient; on which account they every day underwent great

> miseries and bitter torments; for they were whipped with rods, and their bodies were torn to pieces, and were crucified, while they were still alive, and breathed. They also strangled those women and their sons whom they had circumcised, as the king had appointed, hanging their sons about their necks as they were upon the crosses. And if there were any sacred book of the law found, it was destroyed, and those with whom they were found miserably perished also." – *Antiquities of the Jews*, Book 12, Chapter 5, as reprinted in *The Complete Works of Flavius Josephus, the Celebrated Jewish Historian*, William Whiston, 1901, p. 207–209

Antiochus' sadistic, psychotic obsession with destroying the Jewish people was reminiscent of Pharaoh in the days of the Exodus and a preview of the coming persecution of the Antichrist. Also note his hatred of God's Word; he destroyed any copy of Scripture that was found, and he killed those who dared to possess any. Would it be any surprise to see owning copies of the Bible outlawed in the future, during the Great Tribulation?

The fallen angelic spirit of Apollyon indwelled this wicked Greek king for a time, making him literally hell-bent on destroying the Jewish nation. Dr. Andrew Bonar, in his remarkable commentary on the Antichrist, identified Antiochus as one of the spiritual foreshadows of the Beast to come:

> "The many antichrists are thus forerunners of the Antichrist himself, **and must of necessity therefore exhibit in some degree his characteristics**; not the least remarkable of which (as attempted to be shown) are his personality and also his rising out of an apostacy. In fact, many individuals have actually, from time to time, presented themselves to the notice of the world answering in various particulars the description we have of him in [Daniel 11:36–40 and Revelation 13:5–8]. **One of the most remarkable of these to begin with was Antiochus Epiphanes about 160 years before Christ**, whose history is given by Josephus, and also in the

> uninspired book of Maccabees, 1st chapter, which although apocryphal, is of good repute as a history and as such respected by the Jews themselves.
>
> This antichrist Antiochus was the savage persecutor of the Jews in their latter times, as the Antichrist himself will be of both Jews and Christians when at the end transgressors shall have come to the full. He followed or rather rose out of an apostacy then, as the Antichrist will be revealed out of the still more 'fearful falling away' of which St Paul speaks in his Second Epistle to the Thessalonians. A few extracts from the chapter of Maccabees referred to will show this and help to give us some idea from what he did of what the Antichrist himself will do in his times." – *The Development of Antichrist*, Andrew Bonar, Esq., 1853 p. 26–27

The early Church clearly understood that Antiochus was indeed an antichrist.

THE ORIGINAL ABOMINATION OF DESOLATION

The reign of terror did not stop with the attack on the Jewish people. Antiochus then mandated the end of Temple worship and sacrifices and went on to commit one of the evilest acts in all of the Bible—desecrating the altar of God:

> "And arms shall stand on his part, and they shall pollute the sanctuary of strength, and shall take away the daily sacrifice, **and they shall place the abomination that maketh desolate.**" – Daniel 11:31

This is where there the connection to the Final Nephilim is clear. Antiochus issued a decree that all Temple sacrifices and worship were to end. Any person caught worshiping God would be sentenced to death:

> "Moreover king Antiochus wrote to his whole kingdom, that all should be one people, And every one should leave his laws: so all the heathen agreed according to the commandment of the king. Yea, many also of the Israelites consented to his religion, and sacrificed unto idols, and profaned the sabbath.
>
> For the king had sent letters by messengers unto Jerusalem and the cities of Juda that they should follow the strange laws of the land, And forbid burnt offerings, and sacrifice, and drink offerings, in the temple; and that they should profane the sabbaths and festival days: **And pollute the sanctuary and holy people: Set up altars, and groves, and chapels of idols, and sacrifice swine's flesh, and unclean beasts**: That they should also leave their children uncircumcised, and make their souls abominable with all manner of uncleanness and profanation: To the end they might forget the law, and change all the ordinances.
>
> **And whosoever would not do according to the commandment of the king, he said, he should die.** In the selfsame manner wrote he to his whole kingdom, and appointed overseers over all the people, commanding the cities of Juda to sacrifice, city by city." – 1 Maccabees 1:41–51

In stunning similarity to the decree of Nebuchadnezzar before him and to that of the Final Nephilim to come, Antiochus outlawed the worship of Yahweh and executed anyone who dared to defy him. Additionally, this satanic tyrant sacrificed a pig—unclean under Mosaic law—on the altar of God in the Temple. He profaned the Most Holy place on Earth in act of worship to the Greek god Zeus.

In the book of Revelation, the Lord Jesus Christ, in His address to the church of Pergamos, made a reference to the "altar of Zeus," an ancient place of worship of the pagan Greek God, which was located in Pergamum:

> "And to the angel of the church in Pergamos write; These things saith he which hath the sharp sword with two edges; I know thy works, **and where thou dwellest, even where Satan's seat is**: and thou holdest fast my name, and hast not denied my faith, even in those days wherein Antipas was my faithful martyr, **who was slain among you, where Satan dwelleth.**" – Revelation 2:12–13

We read in the following about "Satan's seat" indeed referring to the altar of Zeus:

> "The excavations of German scholars at Pergamum, beginning in 1878, resulted in the discovery of some three hundred feet of sculptured figures which once decorated the white marble altar of Zeus on the acropolis of Pergamum. This was perhaps the structure referred to in the New Testament (Revelation 2:13) as 'Satan's throne.' The figures represented a contest between the gods and the giants." – *Ancient History*, Hutton Webster, 1918, p. 287

Even a secular history book makes the same connection between Zeus and Satan:

> "The gigantic figures that decorated the base are now in the Berlin Museum. This is doubtless what in [Revelation 2:13] is called 'Satan's seat.' The early Christians, in their image-breaking zeal, so mutilated the statues that the modern excavators of the ruins found hardly a face unmarred." – *Ancient History, Second Revised Edition*, Philip Van Ness Myers, 1916, p. 275

Thus, in the book of Revelation, **the Lord Jesus Christ identifies "Zeus" as another title for Satan**. And his "seat" or throne in Pergamos depicted ancient wars of the fallen angels and Nephilim. Antiochus, in his profane sacrifice, was honoring the Devil. This was one of the most blasphemous acts recorded in all of Scripture, again proving that Antiochus, in his zealous hatred of Israel and God, was one of the incarnations of the spirit of Antichrist.

A SECOND ABOMINATION OF DESOLATION

Daniel chapter 9 contains the mysterious "seventy weeks" prophecy, which predicts the construction of the Second Temple after the Jews' return to the Promised Land from Babylonian captivity. It then foretells of the destruction of that Second Temple and construction of the Third Temple that will be built in the end times. Each of the seventy "weeks," or *shbua* in Hebrew, is a period of seven years, with the seventieth week in the prophecy representing the final seven years before the return of Jesus Christ. The chapter closes by discussing the Antichrist's prohibition against the worship of God in the Third Temple:

> "And he shall confirm the covenant with many for one week: and in the midst of the week he shall cause the sacrifice and the oblation to cease, and for the overspreading of abominations he shall make it desolate, even until the consummation, and that determined shall be poured upon the desolate." – Daniel 9:27

A great deal of speculation and confusion about this passage centers on who is "confirming a covenant" and whether that covenant is a seven-year peace treaty or some other type of agreement. This study will not go into detail on the interpretation of this text. However, examining it in the Septuagint brings clearer meaning:

> "And one week shall establish the covenant with many: and in the midst of the week my sacrifice and drink-offering shall be taken

> away: **and on the temple *shall be* the abomination of desolations**; and at the end of time an end shall be put to the desolation." – Daniel 9:27

In the final week, "the covenant" will be established; it is the same one Daniel referred to in chapter 11:

> "For the ships of Chittim shall come against him: therefore he shall be grieved, and return, and have indignation against **the holy covenant**: so shall he do; he shall even return, and have intelligence with them that forsake **the holy covenant**." – Daniel 11:30

Throughout the book of Daniel and the entire Old Testament, "the covenant" refers to the Mosaic Law. When Antiochus Epiphanes displayed "indignation against the holy covenant," it was an expression of his hatred towards God's Law that was given to the Jewish people. This is further confirmed in Antiochus' outlawing of Temple sacrifice and worship.

In chapter 9, we read that Daniel said the same prohibition would reoccur during the end times. But this time, it will be the Antichrist who "in the midst of the week"—the midpoint of the final seven years—will ban the "sacrifice and drink-offering." The persecution Antiochus IV carried out in 168 BC was a similitude of the anti-Semitic injustice that will be carried out by the Final Nephilim during the Great Tribulation.

Additionally, Daniel 9:27 states that "on the temple shall be the abomination of desolations." Jesus Christ made a specific reference to this prophecy as a future event:

> "When ye therefore shall see the abomination of desolation, spoken of by Daniel the prophet, stand in the holy place, (whoso readeth, let him understand:) Then let them which be in Judaea flee into

> the mountains: Let him which is on the housetop not come down to take any thing out of his house: Neither let him which is in the field return back to take his clothes." – Matthew 24:15–18

Note that Jesus used the phrase "abomination of desolation," which is only found in the Septuagint version of Daniel, giving major credence to the fact that this was the version the Lord would have quoted from. (Other versions dub the event as "the abomination that maketh desolate," or some other rephrasing). Jesus said these words almost two hundred years after the original abomination of desolation by Antiochus IV.

Antiochus IV, who gave himself the title "Epiphanes," which means "god manifest," was the first Greek ruler to put self-deifying titles on the empire's currency. The Antichrist will commit the second abomination of desolation when he "sits in the temple of God, proclaiming himself God." Just like Antiochus, the Beast will proclaim himself to be "god manifest," placing an image of himself in the Most Holy Place of the temple. This will take place at the opening of the bottomless pit, at the sound of the fifth trumpet, when the spirit of the Assyrian is released one final time to indwell the final Mystery King.

At this point, the believing remnant of Israel will flee to the wilderness, where they will be supernaturally protected by the Lord just as the ancient Israelites were protected in Goshen.

> "And woe unto them that are with child, and to them that give suck in those days!" – Matthew 24:19

Note the use of the term "woe." The is the word used to describe the fifth, sixth and seventh trumpets ("woe, woe, woe"; see Revelation 8:13) that mark the return of the fallen angels and Satan to earth. The Lord also noted that mothers with infant babies will be particularly vulnerable to the end-times persecution of Antichrist (just as they were during the reign of Antiochus, as he forced mothers to carry their murdered babies around their necks – 1 Maccabees 1:60-61).

> "But pray ye that your flight be not in the winter, neither on the sabbath day: For then shall be great tribulation, such as was not since the beginning of the world to this time, no, nor ever shall be."
> – Matthew 24:20–21

This passage provides further confirmation that this is the same time the apostate angels of Genesis 6 will be released from the Abyss:

> "Blow ye the trumpet in Zion, and sound an alarm in my holy mountain: let all the inhabitants of the land tremble: for the day of the LORD cometh, for it is nigh at hand; A day of darkness and of gloominess, a day of clouds and of thick darkness, as the morning spread upon the mountains: **a great people and a strong; there hath not been ever the like, neither shall be any more after it**, even to the years of many generations. A fire devoureth before them; and behind them a flame burneth: the land is as the garden of Eden before them, and behind them a desolate wilderness; yea, and nothing shall escape them." – Joel 2:1–3

The Final Nephilim will betray the Israelites in the middle of the final seven years, proclaiming himself to be God and demanding worship of himself under penalty of death. He will be the ultimate fulfillment of his prior incarnation as Antiochus Epiphanes. This concept was well understood by nineteenth-century theologians, as seen in the following:

> "The third type of Antichrist is the Old Testament theocratic Anti-Messiah himself Antiochus Epiphanes, as he is historically

> described in 1 Maccabees and prophetically in Daniel 8; 9:22; the partial heir of the third universal monarchy, the destroyer of the Jewish temple on Zion, and as such the most powerful type of the last real Anti-Messiah in so far as the same shall appear as a king, whose more definite features, as drawn in Daniel 7:19, 20, agree with those in Dan 12:41." –*The Protestant Theological and Ecclesiastical Encyclopedia, Volume 1,* Reverend John Henry Augustus Bomberger and John Jacob Herzog, 1860, p. 176

Note that Bomberger identifies Antiochus as "the destroyer of the Jewish temple on Zion." When the king of the bottomless pit is revealed in Revelation 9, we learn that his name is "Apollyon" in Greek and "Abaddon" in Hebrew; both mean "destroyer."

DEFEAT OF THE KING AND RESTORATION OF TEMPLE WORSHIP

> "Now Maccabeus and his company, the Lord guiding them, recovered the temple and the city: But the altars which the heathen had built in the open street, and also the chapels, they pulled down. And having cleansed the temple they made another altar, and striking stones they took fire out of them, and offered a sacrifice after two years, and set forth incense, and lights, and shewbread. When that was done, they fell flat down, and besought the Lord that they might come no more into such troubles; but if they sinned any more against him, that he himself would chasten them with mercy, and that they might not be delivered unto the blasphemous and barbarous nations.
>
> Now upon the same day that the strangers profaned the temple, on the very same day it was cleansed again, even the five and twentieth day of the same month, which is Casleu. **And they kept the eight**

> **days with gladness, as in the feast of the tabernacles**, remembering that not long afore they had held the feast of the tabernacles, when as they wandered in the mountains and dens like beasts. Therefore they bare branches, and fair boughs, and palms also, and sang psalms unto him that had given them good success in cleansing his place. They ordained also by a common statute and decree, That every year those days should be kept of the whole nation of the Jews. And this was the end of Antiochus, called Epiphanes." – 2 Maccabees 10:1–9

Interestingly, it was Judah Maccabeus, a member of the tribe of Judah (the human lineage of the Lord Jesus Christ), who led the Jews in their final conquest over Antiochus' forces and recovered the Temple. Their cleansing of the Temple with the candlestick lit for eight days is the origin of the Jewish holiday of Hanukkah. This was a rededication of the Temple back to Yahweh and a time to restore proper worship.

It's important to remember that though they are excellent historical resources and were included in the original 1611 King James Bible, **the books of the Maccabees are not inspired Scripture**. However, the observance of Hanukkah (derived from the Hebrew verb *chanak,* which means "to dedicate"), also called the Feast of the Dedication, is indeed biblical. In fact, the Lord Jesus Christ celebrated it Himself during His First Advent:

> "**And it was at Jerusalem the feast of the dedication, and it was winter**. And Jesus walked in the temple in Solomon's porch. Then came the Jews round about him, and said unto him, How long dost thou make us to doubt? If thou be the Christ, tell us plainly. Jesus answered them, I told you, and ye believed not: the works that I do in my Father's name, they bear witness of me. But ye believe not, because ye are not of my sheep, as I said unto you.
>
> My sheep hear my voice, and I know them, and they follow me:

> And I give unto them eternal life; and they shall never perish, neither shall any man pluck them out of my hand. My Father, which gave them me, is greater than all; and no man is able to pluck them out of my Father's hand. I and my Father are one." – John 10:22–30

So we see that the Lord had attended the celebration of Hanukkah at the Temple, using the occasion to openly declare that He and God the Father "are one." Because of this confirmation that the events that led to implementation of the Feast of Dedication are a part of biblical history, it stands to reason that a similar dedication of the Millennial Temple will take place after the Beast has been defeated by Jesus Christ and Satan is locked away for a thousand years:

> "And from the time that the daily sacrifice shall be taken away, and the abomination that maketh desolate set up, there shall be a thousand two hundred and ninety days. Blessed is he that waiteth, and cometh to the thousand three hundred and five and thirty days." – Daniel 12:11–12

Daniel was told by an angel that the time from the midpoint of the seventieth week (when the daily sacrifice is banned and the abomination of desolation is set up by the Antichrist) until the defeat of the Antichrist shall be 1,290 days. Then, in the next verse, we see a blessing promised to those who "wait" and are still present for 1,335 days from the midpoint. We know from the book of Revelation that the 1,260 days from the midpoint covers the reign of the fully possessed, resurrected Antichrist, culminating with his defeat at the Revelation of Christ. Adding **seventy-five days** from then takes us to 1,335 days. Seventy-five days is the exact time on the Hebrew calendar between Yom Kippur, or the Day of Atonement, and Hanukkah. Thus, the Second Coming of Christ to Jerusalem and the restoration of Israel will occur on Yom Kippur, allowing a time for cleansing the land and dedicating the new Temple from which Christ will rule and reign on the first Hanukkah of the Millennium.

"ONE IS": WAS EMPEROR DOMITIAN THE SIXTH MYSTERY KING?

> "And there are seven kings: five are fallen, **and one is.**" – Revelation 17:10

Perhaps the most challenging Mystery King to identify is the sixth, as it was a king who was alive at the time of the writing of the book of Revelation. The two most common dates assigned to its authorship are AD 68 and AD 96. Almost all theologians agree that the Apostle John wrote the book of Revelation while he was in exile on the isle of Patmos. The specific king in power at that time is the identity of the sixth king, referred to in this passage as "one is." There are several reasons this king might be Domitian, leader of the Roman Empire from AD 81 to AD 96.

REVELATION WRITTEN DURING REIGN OF DOMITIAN

Domitian, as noted, was the emperor of Rome from AD 81 to AD 96. He was the younger brother of Titus Vespasian, his predecessor. Titus conquered Jerusalem in AD 70, destroying the Second Temple of God in the process. A number of early Christian sources confirm that Domitian ruled Rome at the time of John's exile to the island of Patmos:

- **Irenaeus** (early second century – ca. AD 202) was the bishop or pastor of the church in what is now Lyons, France. His treatise, *Against Heresies,* was a landmark work that challenged the heretical Gnostic Christianity that threatened the true faith at that time. He was a student of Polycarp, who was a disciple of the Apostle John, providing a direct connection to the author of the book of Revelation. A collection of his writings detail Irenaeus' identification of Domitian and the date of the writing of Revelation:

> "First comes the decisive testimony of one who certainly knew the true date, Irenaeus, the grand-pupil of John, whom we have already adduced as quoting the words of the personal friends of John whom he knew. In regard to the real name symbolized by 666, he tells us: 'If it were necessary for this name to be at the present time proclaimed it would have been uttered by him who saw the apocalypse for it was not seen a long time ago but almost in our own generation at the end of the reign of Domitian.'" – *Against Heresies*, 5.30.3, Irenaeus, ca. AD 190, as recorded in *Commentary on the New Testament, Intended for Popular Use, Volume V. Titus–Revelation*, D. D. Wheldon, 1880, p. 309

- **Clement of Alexandria** was a Christian bishop in Rome in the first century and a contemporary of the Apostle John. His epistle to the Corinthian church is one of the oldest extant Christian writings outside of the New Testament. A summary of his writings affirms that Clement believed Domitian ruled when John wrote the book of Revelation:

> "Clement of Alexandria says, 'After the tyrant died, John returned from the island of Patmos to Ephesus.' Clement does not in clause mention Domitian by name; but we know from Eusebius, who quotes these words from Clement, that Domitian was the 'tyrant' that Clement meant. For Eusebius introduces the quotation by that John 'addressed the Churches of Asia on his return his banishment to the isle of Patmos after the death of Domitian.'" – Ibid. p. 391

Note that the Christian historian Eusebius also put John's writing of

Revelation at ca. AD 96, right before the end of the reign of Domitian.

- **Victorinus** was a third-century theologian who was bishop of Pettau, or modern-day Germany. He was martyred for his faith by emperor Diocletian. His commentary on Revelation is the second-oldest extant writing on that book today. Thus, Victorinus clearly had a keen interest in the life of the Apostle John. On the timing of the book of Revelation's writing, Victorinus stated:

> "This John saw when he was in the island of Patmos; being condemned to the mines by Domitian Caesar." – Ibid.

LED ANCIENT ROME IN DEVIL WORSHIP

During his reign, Domitian, a passionate worshiper of Jupiter, built the fourth version of the Temple of *Jupiter Capitolinus*, the preeminent temple of the ancient Roman world. He subsequently constructed a second temple to Jupiter called the Temple of *Jupiter Custos*. He minted numerous coins in honor of this deity as well.

In mythology and in the Bible, "Jupiter" was another name for "Zeus." In Acts chapter 11, the apostles Paul and Barnabas, while in the company of pagan worshipers, healed a man who had been crippled from birth. Seeing the miracle, the stunned non-Christian crowd immediately assumed these two apostles were gods:

> "And when the people saw what Paul had done, they lifted up their voices, saying in the speech of Lycaonia, The gods are come down to us in the likeness of men. And they called Barnabas, Jupiter [Ζεύς, or "Zeus," in Greek]; and Paul, Mercurius, because he was the chief speaker." – Acts 14:12

Jupiter was just the Roman appellation for the Greek god Zeus, whom they adopted into their religious beliefs. As shown earlier in this chapter with the description of the altar of Zeus, Domitian, just like Antiochus Epiphanes before him, was worshiping Satan.

PROCLAIMED HIMSELF AND HIS FAMILY TO BE GODS

In type and shadow of the Antichrist, Domitian revived Roman imperial cult worship, in which the ruling family of the empire was deified as gods. He erected numerous statues to himself and put his own image on Roman currency. Reverend Robert Govett aptly summed up the arrogance and desire to "be as god" that burned within Domitian, quoting a secular Roman historian:

> "'[Domitian] did not show all his vices at first," but gave the reins only to his pride and vanity at the commencement of his reign. '*He filled the world as Dion Cassius says, with his statues,* and would suffer none to be erected to him in the capitol that were not of gold, or at least silver, and of a certain weight.' Such quantities of victims were sacrificed to them, that the streets leading to the capitol were often crowded by them.' '*He was so jealous of the respect due to his statues, that he ordered a woman to be put to death for no other crime than having undressed herself before one of them.*' 'The title of "Lord and Master" which both Tiberius and Augustus had rejected with a kind of horror, was too little for Domitian's pride and arrogance, without adding to it that of GOD.
>
> Dictating one day the form to be observed by his attendants, in whatever letters they were to write or publish in his name, he began thus, 'OUR LORD AND GOD COMMANDS AS FOLLOWS.' This impious style was observed during his whole reign!" – *Revelation of Saint John, Literal and Future, Being an Exposition of That Book,*

Rev. Robert Govett, 1843, p. 296–297

Mystery Babylon, the end-times headquarters of the Antichrist, will be the center of worship of the Beast. And, like Domitian, the Final Nephilim will use large amounts of gold and silver. This is confirmed in Revelation chapter 18, which prophesies that the merchants of the world will be saddened once Mystery Babylon is destroyed:

> "And the merchants of the earth shall weep and mourn over her; for no man buyeth their merchandise any more: The merchandise of gold, and silver, and precious stones…" – Revelation 18:11–12

ORDERED JESUS' RELATIVES TO BE KILLED

> "Is not this the carpenter's son? is not his mother called Mary? and his brethren, James, and Joses, and Simon, and Judas [Jude]?" – Matthew 13:55

In the first century AD, the Roman Empire viciously persecuted the Christian faith. Emperor Nero, who infamously started a false-flag fire in the city of Rome and blamed Christians, unleashed sadistic torture on believers (so severe that many believers at the time thought he was the actual Antichrist). Decades later, Domitian resumed the bloodlust of Nero. Still living in paranoia of the worship of Christ, Domitian ordered the execution of any of the relatives of the Messiah, including the grandchildren of the Apostle Jude (the biological brother of the Lord and author of the book of Jude). Domitian was indwelled with the same satanic hatred as his predecessors for God's people.

Hegesippus, a second-century Christian historian, recorded this violence against the faith. Although none of his works are still in existence, he was quoted extensively by the third-century Christian historian Eusebius:

> "But when the same Domitian had issued his orders that the descendants of David should be slain, according to an ancient tradition, some of the heretics accused the descendants of Judas, as the brother of our Saviour, according to the flesh, because they were of the family of David, and as such also were related to Christ. This is declared by Hegesippus as follows.
>
> 'There were yet living of the family of our Lord, the grandchildren of Judas called the brother, of our Lord according to the flesh. These were reported as being of the family of David, and were brought to Domitian by the Evocatus. **For this emperor was as much alarmed at the appearance of Christ as Herod**.'" – *The Ecclesiastical History of Eusebius Pamphillus, Bishop of Caesarea, in Palestine, Translated from the Greek*, Reverend C. F. Cruse, 1851, p. 91–92

Other sources note the Antichrist typology in the reign of Domitian as well, including the following:

> "Domitian was to be a Nero: and so he was. This is, however an imperfect and inadequate fulfilment of the prophecies of Antichrist in this book. Domitian was, it is true, a revival of Nero in his cruelty; he was like Nero a persecutor of the Church, he was also—like Nero, and unlike the predicted Antichrist—foully unclean in life. But he differed from Nero in possessing talents and principles which while to some extent they bring him nearer to the type of spiritual wickedness may also be regarded as giving him the dignity of that power which 'withholdeth' the manifestation of the Lawless One....

Thus it seems necessary to look for a completer fulfilment of the prophecy than any that has yet been seen, while yet it is possible to point to a fulfilment that, to some extent, corresponds with the prediction even in the minutest details.... Just as the 72nd Psalm is recognised as setting forth the greatness of Solomon's 'in type, and in truth of Christ's Kingdom,' so the Revelation may be regarded as a picture of the persecution of the Church, 'in type' by such Emperors as Nero and Domitian, 'in truth' by the Antichrist of the last days, and as a prophecy of Christ's victory over both enemies the type and the antitype." – *The Revelation of St. John the Divine, with Notes and Introduction*, Reverend William Henry Simcox, 1890, p. li–lii

CELEBRATED ROME'S DESTRUCTION OF JERUSALEM AND THE HOLY TEMPLE

Domitian also built the Arch of Titus, one of the most famous monuments of ancient Rome that's still in existence. It was built as a deification of Titus Vespasian and to celebrate his defeat of the Jewish people in AD 70. Before His Crucifixion and Resurrection, Jesus Christ prophesied this specific conquest and the destruction of the Temple:

"Verily I say unto you, **All these things shall come upon this generation**. O Jerusalem, Jerusalem, thou that killest the prophets, and stonest them which are sent unto thee, how often would I have gathered thy children together, even as a hen gathereth her chickens under her wings, and ye would not! **Behold, your house is left unto you desolate**." – Matthew 23:36–38

"**And when ye shall see Jerusalem compassed with armies, then know that the desolation thereof is nigh**. Then let them which are in Judaea flee to the mountains; and let them which are in the

> midst of it depart out; and let not them that are in the countries enter thereinto. For these be the days of vengeance, that all things which are written may be fulfilled. But woe unto them that are with child, and to them that give suck, in those days! for there shall be great distress in the land, and wrath upon this people.
>
> And they shall fall by the edge of the sword, and shall be led away captive into all nations: and Jerusalem shall be trodden down of the Gentiles, until the times of the Gentiles be fulfilled." – Luke 21:20–24

The word "desolation" in Scripture consistently refers to the destruction of the Temple. The above prophecies are some of the most sobering, horrific predictions in the Bible. Jerusalem would once again be conquered, hundreds of thousands would die, and the house of God, the holy Temple where the Lord chose to put His Name, would be destroyed. The remaining Jews who would survive the onslaught would be taken as slaves to the empire, never to see the Promised Land again. And it was this attack on Israel that Domitian chose to celebrate throughout the Roman Empire.

The Arch of Titus, which stands today in Via Sacra in Rome, contains a relief depicting Roman soldiers carrying the golden candlestick and other sacred Temple items back to Rome, where they were placed in the temple of Jupiter. And over the images of the desecration of the Temple is a proclamation of Domitian's brother as a god. It remains a blasphemous memorial of the destruction of the Holy City and the Temple. It is also one of the most replicated monuments in the world, with the most famous copy being the *Arc De Triomphe* in Paris, France.

Domitian continued his blasphemy by minting coins bearing the inscription: *IUDAEA CAPTA* ("Judea has been captured") and *IUDAEA DEVICTA* ("Judea has been defeated"). The maniacal hatred and persecution of the Jewish people, coupled with the exaltation of himself as a god, follows the exact pattern of Pharaoh, Nebuchadnezzar, Antiochus Epiphanes, and other satanically inspired tyrants throughout biblical history. For centuries, theologians have also seen the clear identification of Domitian as the sixth Mystery King of Revelation 17:

> "We have now to notice the sixth of the predecessors of the Wild Beast. If the others have been correctly stated, this was none other than Domitian, by whom the Apostle John was banished to the isle of Patmos." – *The Revelation of St. John Literal and Future: Being an Exposition of That Book*, Reverend Robert Govett, 1843, p. 296

GOG, THE CHIEF PRINCE OF MAGOG: THE SEVENTH MYSTERY KING

> "And the other is not yet come; and when he cometh, he must continue a short space." – Revelation 17:10

Many pastors, theologians, bloggers, and laypersons alike have commented on what is commonly called "the Gog-Magog" war: an event wherein a coalition of nations, led by a mysterious figure named Gog, will wage a war against Israel. These events are recorded in Ezekiel chapters 38 and 39. Gog-Magog has proven to be one of the most challenging prophetic passages in all of the Bible, leading to dozens of theories about the identity of Gog, with many usually including an assortment of modern-day political leaders. But what is *not* often discussed is Gog's direct connection to the end times as the seventh predecessor of the Final Nephilim.

REMARKABLE SIMILARITIES TO THE OTHER SIX MYSTERY KINGS

Like his forerunners, Gog is a leader who will seek to conquer the land of Israel in the end times. This is explained in detail in Ezekiel 38:

> "And the word of the LORD came unto me, saying, Son of man, set thy face against Gog, the land of Magog, the chief prince of Meshach and Tubal, and prophesy against him, And say, Thus saith the Lord GOD; Behold, I am against thee, O Gog, the chief prince of Meshach and Tubal." – Ezekiel 38:1–3

Note that, like He did with the fallen angelic Assyrian (whom Ezekiel had also written of extensively, as recorded just seven chapters earlier), **the Lord addresses Gog directly,** as is the case with many of the other Mystery Kings. Isaiah 14 details the same pattern, as God refers to Satan and the Antichrist as "the king of Babylon" or Satan as the "King of Tyre" (Ezekiel 28). This level of attention is a clear biblical indication that this is no normal human leader in view. It is, rather, a fallen angelic being—or someone possessed by one.

Also note that Gog is referred to as a "chief prince" [*ro'sh naisy'* in Hebrew] twice in three verses. The only other being in Scripture referred to by this title is the archangel Michael:

> "In those days I Daniel was mourning three full weeks. I ate no pleasant bread, neither came flesh nor wine in my mouth, neither did I anoint myself at all, till three whole weeks were fulfilled. And in the four and twentieth day of the first month, as I was by the side of the great river, which is Hiddekel.... And he said unto me, O Daniel, a man greatly beloved, understand the words that I speak unto thee, and stand upright: for unto thee am I now sent. And when he had spoken this word unto me, I stood trembling. Then said he unto me, Fear not, Daniel: for from the first day that thou didst set thine heart to understand, and to chasten thyself before thy God, thy words were heard, and I am come for thy words. But the prince of the kingdom of Persia withstood me one and twenty days: but, lo, **Michael, one of the chief princes** [*ri'shown sar*], came

> to help me; and I remained there with the kings of Persia." – Daniel 10:2–4, 11–13

From the opening verses of Ezekiel 38, it is evident that this is more of an esoteric passage aimed at an angelic being than it is an address to a mortal king.

> "And I will turn thee back, and put hooks into thy jaws, **and I will bring thee forth**, and all thine army, horses and horsemen, all of them clothed with all sorts of armour, even a great company with bucklers and shields, all of them handling swords." – Ezekiel 38:4

Just as is the case with the other incarnations of Apollyon throughout Scripture, the Lord reinforces that this apostate angel is merely an instrument of His judgment. God controls the actions and boundaries of this fallen angel, no matter how many times he is permitted back on earth. Yahweh confirms that it is He who will set the course of events to bring Gog into battle against Israel. The Lord will "put hooks" into the "jaws" of Gog, indicating that, like a farm animal, this fallen being will only move when God permits him to do so. Note the similarity in language to the words used by God in His address to Sennacherib, the king of Assyria who was the fourth incarnation of Apollyon:

> "Then Isaiah the son of Amoz sent unto Hezekiah, saying, Thus saith the LORD God of Israel, Whereas thou hast prayed to me against Sennacherib king of Assyria: This is the word which the LORD hath spoken concerning him; The virgin, the daughter of Zion, hath despised thee, and laughed thee to scorn; the daughter of Jerusalem hath shaken her head at thee. Whom hast thou reproached and blasphemed? and against whom hast thou exalted thy voice, and lifted up thine eyes on high? even against the Holy One of Israel.… But I know thy abode, and thy going out, and thy

> coming in, and thy rage against me. Because thy rage against me, and thy tumult, is come up into mine ears, **therefore will I put my hook in thy nose, and my bridle in thy lips, and I will turn thee back by the way by which thou camest.**" – Isaiah 37:21–23, 28–29

When Sennacherib, possessed by the spirit of Apollyon, taunted the Israelites and told them to doubt the Lord, he was soon rebuked. God foretold the defeat of the Assyrian king by saying that He would put a "hook in the nose" and "bridle in the lips" of Sennacherib and destroy him. The symbolic language is almost identical to that used in the address to Gog, as both are ultimately possessed by the same fallen angelic spirit.

EZEKIEL FORETOLD TWO SEPARATE WARS

> "Be thou prepared, and prepare for thyself, thou, and all thy company that are assembled unto thee, and be thou a guard unto them. After many days thou shalt be visited: in the latter years thou shalt come into the land that is brought back from the sword, and is gathered out of many people, **against the mountains of Israel**, which have been always waste: but it is brought forth out of the nations, **and they shall dwell safely all of them.**... Thus saith the Lord GOD; It shall also come to pass, that at the same time shall things come into thy mind, and thou shalt think an evil thought: And thou shalt say, **I will go up to the land of unwalled villages; I will go to them that are at rest, that dwell safely, all of them dwelling without walls, and having neither bars nor gates**, To take a spoil, and to take a prey; to turn thine hand upon the desolate places that are now inhabited, and upon the people that are gathered out of the nations, which have gotten cattle and goods, that dwell in the midst of the land." – Ezekiel 38:7–8, 10–12

This is where the interpretation of these chapters becomes challenging. It is clear that Gog's intention will be to invade Israel. However, the attack being described here will take place at the end of the Millennial Reign of Jesus Christ—*after* the Great Tribulation, the Second Coming, and Armageddon. Ezekiel chapters 38 and 39 **detail the two battles of Gog and Magog in reverse order**. This is critical to properly understanding this prophecy.

Ezekiel chapter 38 is a prophecy of the second Gog-Magog war. After Jesus Christ returns to earth, defeating the Antichrist and his armies and imprisoning Satan, He will rule here for a thousand years during a period known as the "Millennium" or "Millennial Reign." This is when Israel will "dwell safely," and "without walls." The Bible provides many confirming passages that connect the return of Jesus Christ with Israel dwelling in safety:

> "Behold, the days come, saith the LORD, that I will raise unto David a righteous Branch, and a King shall reign and prosper, and shall execute judgment and justice in the earth. **In his days Judah shall be saved, and Israel shall dwell safely**: and this is his name whereby he shall be called, THE LORD OUR RIGHTEOUSNESS." – Jeremiah 23:5–6

> "Behold, the days come, saith the LORD, that I will perform that good thing which I have promised unto the house of Israel and to the house of Judah. In those days, and at that time, will I cause the Branch of righteousness to grow up unto David; and he shall execute judgment and righteousness in the land. **In those days shall Judah be saved, and Jerusalem shall dwell safely**: and this is the name wherewith she shall be called, The LORD our righteousness." – Jeremiah 33:14–16

> "**And the LORD shall be king over all the earth**: in that day shall there be one LORD, and his name one.... And men shall dwell in it, and there shall be no more utter destruction; **but Jerusalem shall**

> **be safely inhabited.**" – Zechariah 14:9, 11

After his thousand-year sentence, the Devil returns to Earth and recruits rebellious humanity one last time for an attack on Jerusalem, which will have just enjoyed a thousand years of total peace and security (and thus has no defensive walls). This *second battle* is recorded in the book of Revelation:

> "**And when the thousand years are expired**, Satan shall be loosed out of his prison, And shall go out to deceive the nations which are in the four quarters of the earth, **Gog, and Magog, to gather them together to battle**: the number of whom is as the sand of the sea. And they went up on the breadth of the earth, and compassed the camp of the saints about, and the beloved city: and fire came down from God out of heaven, and devoured them." – Revelation 20:7–9

The end of Ezekiel chapter 38 and beginning of Ezekiel 39 **detail the first Gog Magog war, which takes place at the beginning of the Day of the Lord** and is in fact one of the major events that kicks off the end times:

> "Therefore, thou son of man, prophesy against Gog, and say, Thus saith the Lord GOD; Behold, I am against thee, O Gog, the chief prince of Meshech and Tubal: And I will turn thee back, and leave but the sixth part of thee, and will cause thee to come up from the north parts, and will bring thee upon the mountains of Israel: And I will smite thy bow out of thy left hand, and will cause thine arrows to fall out of thy right hand.
>
> Thou shalt fall upon the mountains of Israel, thou, and all thy bands, and the people that is with thee: I will give thee unto the ravenous birds of every sort, and to the beasts of the field to be devoured. Thou shalt fall upon the open field: for I have spoken it,

> saith the Lord GOD." – Ezekiel 39:1–5

Note that in this passage, "a sixth" portion of Gog's forces will be spared from destruction. This is quite distinct from the Revelation 20 battle, when all of Gog's forces will be eradicated by heavenly fire. In fact, the destruction of Gog in the first battle differs greatly from the second:

> "And I will call for a sword against him throughout all my mountains, saith the Lord GOD: **every man's sword shall be against his brother**. And **I will plead against him with pestilence and with blood**; and I will rain upon him, and upon his bands, and upon the many people that are with him, **an overflowing rain, and great hailstones, fire, and brimstone**. Thus will I magnify myself, and sanctify myself; and I will be known in the eyes of many nations, and they shall know that I am the LORD." – Ezekiel 38:21–23

In the first Gog-Magog war, the enemies of Israel will end up fighting against themselves. Yahweh will cause Gog's army to go delirious to the point that they fight against their fellow soldiers. The Lord provided this same type of miraculous military victory to Israel during the reign of King Jehoshaphat, when the Southern Kingdom was under attack from the Ammonites, the Moabites, and the Edomites of Mt. Seir:

> "And he said, Hearken ye, all Judah, and ye inhabitants of Jerusalem, and thou king Jehoshaphat, Thus saith the LORD unto you, Be not afraid nor dismayed by reason of this great multitude; for the battle is not yours, but God's.… And when they began to sing and to praise, the LORD set ambushments against the children of Ammon, Moab, and mount Seir, which were come against Judah; and they were smitten. For the children of Ammon and Moab stood up against the inhabitants of mount Seir, utterly to slay

> and destroy them: and when they had made an end of the inhabitants of Seir, **every one helped to destroy another**." – 2 Chronicles 20:15, 22–23

In prophetic repetition, during the first Gog-Magog battle, Gog and his coalition will fight against themselves. Yahweh will then bombard them with pestilence, blood, and hail of fire and brimstone. The use of fire and brimstone *mixed with blood* is a unique judgment found only one other time in Scripture—at the sounding of the first trumpet judgment of Revelation, the start of the Day of the Lord:

> "And another angel came and stood at the altar, having a golden censer; and there was given unto him much incense, that he should offer it with the prayers of all saints upon the golden altar which was before the throne. And the smoke of the incense, which came with the prayers of the saints, ascended up before God out of the angel's hand. And the angel took the censer, and filled it with fire of the altar, and cast it into the earth: and there were voices, and thunderings, and lightnings, and an earthquake.
>
> And the seven angels which had the seven trumpets prepared themselves to sound. **The first angel sounded, and there followed hail and fire mingled with blood, and they were cast upon the earth**: and the third part of trees was burnt up, and all green grass was burnt up." – Revelation 8:3–7

This is the judgment of the Lord that ends the first Gog-Magog war. There is far greater biblical detail and evidence of this intriguing "reverse order" of the two Gog-Magog wars, but they are not germane to this study. What is relevant is that Gog has the same satanic agenda as the previous Mystery Kings: the destruction of Israel. And, once again, the Lord will directly intervene to thwart those plans.

OLD TESTAMENT PROPHECIES OF GOG: INCARNATION OF APOLLYON

Corroboration that Gog is in fact one of the incarnations of Apollyon is found in Ezekiel 38:

> "Thus saith the Lord GOD; Art thou he of whom I have spoken in old time by my servants the prophets of Israel, which prophesied in those days many years that I would bring thee against them?" – Ezekiel 38:17

In this passage, the Lord poses a fascinating question: Was Gog someone whom the Lord referred to numerous times through the testimony of His prophets? Was this mysterious leader someone whom the Bible repeatedly prophesied would come against Israel? Interestingly, there is no mention of Gog invading Israel anywhere else in Scripture. The name doesn't even appear in any other book of the Bible outside of the aforementioned prophecy of the final Gog-Magog war in Revelation 20. The Septuagint version of this verse gives an even more definitive pronouncement that Gog is mentioned throughout the Bible:

> "Thus saith the Lord God, to Gog; **Thou art he concerning whom I spoke in former times, by the hand of my servants the prophets of Israel**, in those days and years, that I would bring thee up against them." – Ezekiel 38:17, LXX

Gog is indeed mentioned by the prophets of the Lord in other books of the Bible—just not by the name "Gog." This is because Gog is just one of the seven vessels for the fallen angelic spirit of the Assyrian, or Apollyon, who reappears throughout biblical history. This is the same angelic spirit that will indwell the Antichrist at the opening of the Abyss in Revelation chapter 9.

> "Though Gog is only mentioned by name in Ezekiel and the Apocalypse, yet we know that the last enemy of the Jews is he; and that his doom, as the Assyrian, as Pharaoh, and as the dragon, has been announced by almost all the prophets. Not that these appellations do not also characterize the personal Antichrist; but Gog is a personal name, and these appellations characterize him also. The Lord says of Gog, 'Art thou he of whom I have spoken in old time by my servants the prophets of Israel, which prophesied in those days many years that I would bring thee against them?' [Ezekiel 38:17].
>
> **By this authority we assert, that 'the Assyrian' of Isaiah 10:5 includes Gog as well as Antichrist**; and many of the notes of agreement are there—as the fire (16, 17), the return and conversion of Jacob (20, 22), the slaughter of Midian and Oreb (26), and the anointing (27). The same may be said of 'the Assyrian' of [Isaiah 14:25] and of [Isaiah 30:31] and of many other places. In short, the *personal* antagonist of the Lord in the time of Israel's restoration, or the second advent, or the resurrection morn, is either the personal Antichrist or Gog, or both combined into one head of opposition."
> – *The Morning Watch, or Quarterly Journal on Prophecy and Theological Review*, Volume 5, 1832, p. 262–263

The *Morning Watch* writers considered the Assyrian, Gog, and the Antichrist as the same entity. This is because the same fallen angelic spirit indwells all of them. Joseph Tyso, an early-nineteenth-century Baptist pastor who wrote extensively on the end times, also identified Gog as a Mystery King, but put him as the eighth and final incarnation:

> "This same beast [the Antichrist] in the plenitude of his power is the eighth, **and is of the same nature and spirit as the preceding seven**, and will concentrate in himself all the pride, energy and

> diabolical principle of his predecessors, and when he comes he will attempt universal dominion. **His origin is hell, and he shall ascend out of the bottomless pit**, and when he has made his last desperate attack upon the Lamb, he shall be completely conquered and go into perdition, and the ten kings his allies shall perish with him [verse 14]. **I think this eighth head of the beast is the personal Antichrist, prince Gog**, foretold by Ezekiel 38 and 39. The same of whom God saith 'Thou art he of whom I have spoken in old time by my servants the prophets in the days of these years that I would bring thee against them [Ezekiel 38:17].'" – *An Elucidation of the Prophecies Being an Exposition of the Books of Daniel ad Revelation*, Joseph Tyso, 1838, p. 223

Tyso correctly connects Gog to the seven Mystery Kings and then ties all of them to Apollyon, the fallen angel who is released from the bottomless pit. Remember that Revelation 17 says the eighth king is "of the seven," meaning he is in some fashion *a recurrence* of the prior seven Mystery Kings.

ANTICHRIST/ASSYRIAN/FINAL NEPHILIM: THE EIGHTH MYSTERY KING

God, in His unfathomable wisdom, has permitted this fallen angelic being to occupy wicked rulers throughout history, with each serving as an instrument of the Lord's severe judgment on unbelieving Israel. But ultimately, this apostate angel has served as a testimony to God's power, salvation, and prophetic truth. Each Mystery King has been either humbled or destroyed by Yahweh, leading to the rescue and restoration of Israel. In *Judgment of the Nephilim*, I noted the same pattern—that the Nephilim were also used by God as a testimony to His power, salvation, and love. Each time the giants have been on the cusp of destroying God's people or the world, the Lord has personally intervened to defeat them and save humanity.

But the final Mystery King will have unprecedented power and global control.

He will be the ultimate global monarch imbued with supernatural, satanic power. He will be a hybrid king who will seek to dethrone God and wage war against the Lord Jesus Christ. This is the Final Nephilim.

EXCLUSIVE BONUS CONTENT – Scan the QR code below for bonus content.

CHAPTER 7

THE RISE AND FALL OF THE FALSE MESSIAH

> "And the beast that was, and is not, even he is the eighth, and is of the seven, and goeth into perdition." – Revelation 17:11

> "And I will put enmity between thee and the woman, **and between thy seed and her seed**." – Genesis 3:15

> "In Gen 3:15 we find the Redeemer of mankind promised as the seed of the woman, and we also read of the seed of the serpent, and everlasting antagonism existing between them. Now the seed of the woman is confessedly one, our Lord Jesus Christ; and consequently the seed of the serpent must be also an individual, and as all the good are headed up in Christ, the representative Man, so all evil will be headed up, and will find its development, in the seed of the serpent, the Antichrist who shall come." – *Things That Must Be—4 Advent Sermons*, Francis Tilney Bassett, 1873, p. 33

The Antichrist is the fulfillment of "thy seed" that was foretold in Genesis 3:15. After hiding behind proxies and servants for millennia, the Devil will ultimately bring to pass what God prophesied from the beginning of the war of the two bloodlines: Satan would one day have his own "seed." The Antichrist will be the Final Nephilim, the last human-satanic hybrid on earth. We'll now examine the life and career of this being who will rule the world for three and a half years before being conquered by the true Messiah, the

Lord Jesus Christ.

THE DEVIL'S PLAN: REPLACE GOD BY IMITATION

We see from the aspirations of the Devil expressed in Ezekiel 28 and Isaiah 14 a glimpse of Satan's ultimate goal:

> "For thou hast said in thine heart, I will ascend into heaven, I will exalt my throne above the stars of God: I will sit also upon the mount of the congregation, in the sides of the north: I will ascend above the heights of the clouds; **I will be like the most High**." – Isaiah 14:13–14

Satan's endgame is to rule over Heaven and Earth, and copying God is a critical step in this scheme. The Devil even wants to rule "upon the mount of the congregation, in the side of the north," which Psalm 48 informs us is Israel:

> "GREAT IS THE LORD, and greatly to be praised in the city of our God, in the mountain of his holiness. Beautiful for situation, the joy of the whole earth, **is mount Zion, on the sides of the north, the city of the great King**." – Psalm 48:1–2

As we read in the book of Matthew, Jesus Christ used a parable to demonstrate that Satan attempts to copy God:

> "Another parable put he forth unto them, saying, The kingdom of heaven is likened unto a man which sowed good seed in his field: But while men slept, his enemy came and sowed tares among the wheat, and went his way. But when the blade was sprung up, and

> brought forth fruit, then appeared the tares also. So the servants of the householder came and said unto him, Sir, didst not thou sow good seed in thy field? from whence then hath it tares?
>
> He said unto them, An enemy hath done this. The servants said unto him, Wilt thou then that we go and gather them up? But he said, Nay; lest while ye gather up the tares, ye root up also the wheat with them. Let both grow together until the harvest: and in the time of harvest I will say to the reapers, Gather ye together first the tares, and bind them in bundles to burn them: but gather the wheat into my barn." – Matthew 13:24–30

The Lord planted His seed, and the Devil sowed his "tares," or weeds, among the godly believers symbolized by wheat in this passage. This is another example illustrating that Satan will seek to copy God in all that He does.

"JUST LIKE GOD," THE DEVIL SENDS HIS SEED TO THE WORLD

Arthur W. Pink, author of one of the most comprehensive studies of the Antichrist on record, noted that the final step in the Devil's mimicry of Yahweh will be in having his own son—the Antichrist:

> "That Satan will have a son ought not surprise us. The Devil is a consummate imitator and much of his success in deceiving men is due to his marvelous skill in counterfeiting the things of God." – *The Antichrist*, A. W. Pink, 1923, p. 43

In the days of Noah, Satan did not participate in the illicit sexual relations between fallen angels and human women. However, having been told by God that he would eventually have a seed, he certainly knew it was possible. The sexual sins of the apostate angels of Genesis 6 were so heinous and unprecedented that God responded in swift and devastating fashion by sending the global Flood to wipe out the Nephilim and drag their fallen angelic forefathers to the Abyss. Thus, the Devil knew a time would come when the risk of having offspring would be dire, but he will still once again choose sinful rebellion. Satan, in his effort to try again to mimic the plans of God in bearing his own child, will produce a demonic copy of the Lord Jesus Christ.

CONTRASTS BEWEEN JESUS CHRIST AND THE ANTICHRIST

We read in Scripture of many contrasts between Jesus Christ and the Antichrist.

Both Are Sons

In *Judgment of the Nephilim,* I explained the spiritual concept behind the term "begetting":

> "'Wherefore, as by one man sin entered into the world, and death by sin; and so death passed upon all men, for that all have sinned.' – Romans 5:12

> All people are born with a sin nature, which is a corrupted spirit that seeks to fulfill fleshly lusts and sin against God. This is the reason the Bible boldly proclaims 'all have sinned.' Notice in the verse above that death—the byproduct of sin—was 'passed upon all men.' Children inherit their spiritual nature from their parents, specifically their fathers.

In the Garden of Eden, Eve sinned first, as 1 Timothy 2 says: 'For Adam was first formed, then Eve. And Adam was not deceived, but the woman being deceived was in the transgression' (1 Timothy 2:13–14). Eve was not only the first sinner but the only one actually deceived by Satan's lies. Adam did not believe in the false promises of Satan when he chose to sin. Yet, it is through Adam that the corrupted sinful nature of man is passed on. In Scripture this 'spiritual inheritance' from the father to his children is referred to as 'begetting':

> 'And Adam lived an hundred and thirty years, and begat a son in his own likeness, and after his image; and called his name Seth.'
> – Genesis 5:3

Adam begat a son in his own likeness, confirming that the fallen spiritual state of mankind would continue until the promised Messiah redeemed it. Through Adam, all human fathers pass on the corrupt sinful nature to their children. The original breath of life that God breathed into Adam to make him a 'living soul' was corrupted, and it was passed on to his sons and daughters. This is confirmed in the book of Job: 'The spirit of God hath made me, and the breath of the Almighty hath given me life' (Job 33:4). After God made Adam, He never personally breathed life into an individual person again. Instead, they inherited this spirit nature from Adam. Thus, in conception, just as the woman produces the physical body of the child, the man produces the spirit nature. This is also confirmed in Scripture:

> 'For the man is not of the woman: but the woman of the man…. For as the woman is of the man, even so is the man also by the

> woman; but all things of God.' (1 Corinthians 11:8, 12)

> Eve was 'of Adam' in the sense that she was literally made from his body and received the spirit of life once breathed into him. But a male is 'also by the woman' in that the physical body of a baby is formed in a woman's body. In the past decade, scientists have confirmed that the Y chromosome (passed down through males) does not recombine or change through generations. Thus, a Y chromosome of a man today would be the same as his paternal ancestors' 6,000 years ago. The genetic inheritance of sin nature from fathers is why God ordained that the Messiah would come through 'the seed of the woman.' The prophesied Savior would have a human mother but God as His father. Therefore, the corrupted spiritual nature inherited from Adam would not pass on to Him. Jesus Christ did not bear the corrupted flesh all other people in human history possess. He was not begotten of Adam. He was the 'only begotten' Son of God—His spiritual nature was wholly divine.
>
> Suddenly, the term 'only begotten' in John 3:16 takes on much greater meaning. Jesus Christ was obviously not the only baby God formed in a womb. Certain angels hold the title 'sons of God.' But what made Christ different in His incarnation is that His Spirit was wholly 'begotten of God' and thus not subject to the corruption and spiritual wickedness inherited from Adam." – *Judgment of the Nephilim*, Ryan Pitterson, 2018, p. 233–234

The Antichrist will also be a unique "son," as the only being to be born directly from Satan. His spiritual nature will come from the Devil. He will then be endowed with all of Satan's power once he suffers a deadly wound and is healed. He will be a Nephilim who is possessed by Apollyon, one of the most powerful fallen angels in Scripture. This combination will give the

Final Nephilim massive supernatural abilities.

By being wholly begotten of God, Jesus Christ is the Son of God. Conversely, as the spawn of the Devil and possessed with the spirit of Apollyon, the Antichrist is literally the son of perdition.

Both Are Shepherds

Jesus expressed His love and care for humanity by declaring Himself "the Good Shepherd":

> "I am the good shepherd: the good shepherd giveth his life for the sheep." – John 10:11

The Antichrist is the "Idol Shepherd"—a false shepherd who lures the people into idolatry:

> "For, lo, I will raise up a shepherd in the land, which shall not visit those that be cut off, neither shall seek the young one, nor heal that that is broken, nor feed that that standeth still: but he shall eat the flesh of the fat, and tear their claws in pieces. **Woe to the idol shepherd that leaveth the flock**! the sword shall be upon his arm, and upon his right eye: his arm shall be clean dried up, and his right eye shall be utterly darkened." – Zechariah 11:16–17

Both Are Compared to Creatures of Nature

> "O Jerusalem, Jerusalem, thou that killest the prophets, and stonest them which are sent unto thee, how often would I have gathered thy children together, even as a hen gathereth her chickens under

> her wings, and ye would not!" – Matthew 23:37

Note here the love Jesus has for His people. In the final days before He would be arrested and wrongfully sentenced to death on the cross, He wept for the people of Israel. Recounting their rejection and murder of the Old Testament, the Lord nonetheless proclaims that He would've gathered them like a hen gathers her chicks "under her wings." The Creator used the most tender and soft analogy to illustrate His love for the same people who would scream for His execution. It is no different today. Jesus loves all people—even those who deny Him or mock the Christian faith. His deepest desire is to gather all people to Him and save them. The only question is whether we will trust Him or, in stubborn rebellion, tell God we "would not," like Israel did during His First Advent.

Conversely, Antichrist is compared to a treacherous animal:

> "As the partridge sitteth on eggs, and hatcheth them not; so he that getteth riches, and not by right, shall leave them in the midst of his days, and at his end shall be a fool." – Jeremiah 17:11

In ancient Israel, partridges were known for resting on the nest of another mother partridge that is out looking for food and tricking the chicks into thinking it is their real mother. The partridge will even mimic the cry of the true mother bird. This is the precise scheme of the Final Nephilim, who will seek to imitate the True Savior to deceive His children.

Both Are "Mysteries"

The revelation that God became a human being and dwelt with humanity is known as the "Mystery of Godliness":

> "And without controversy great is **the mystery of godliness**: God

> was manifest in the flesh, justified in the Spirit, seen of angels, preached unto the Gentiles, believed on in the world, received up into glory." – 1 Timothy 3:16

The revealing of the Antichrist to the world is known as "the Mystery of Iniquity":

> "And now ye know what withholdeth that he might be revealed in his time. **For the mystery of iniquity doth already work**: only he who now letteth will let, until he be taken out of the way. And then shall that Wicked be revealed, whom the Lord shall consume with the spirit of his mouth, and shall destroy with the brightness of his coming: Even him, whose coming is after the working of Satan with all power and signs and lying wonders." – 2 Thessalonians 2:6–9

Both mysteries were "working," or being developed, throughout the Old Testament. The prophets repeatedly foretold of the coming Messiah, but they also told of the coming anti-Messiah. Jesus Christ was initially revealed two thousand years ago, being born from a virgin in accordance with prophecy. The Antichrist has been "revealed" six times throughout history when God used him as a tool of judgment against Israel in rebellion. But in the end times, both mysteries will be fully revealed to the world—first with Antichrist as the deceiver and then with Jesus Christ as Savior, Conqueror of Evil, and King.

An early twentieth-century commentary confirms this amazing biblical contrast:

> "Now as iniquity is the opposite of Godliness, then the mystery of iniquity must be the opposite of the mystery of Godliness. That is, if Christ is the Mystery of Godliness, Antichrist must be the Mystery of Iniquity, and as Christ was the Son of God then

> Antichrist must be the Son of Perdition, that is of Satan. And as Christ was born of a virgin by the Holy Spirit so Antichrist will be born of a woman, not necessarily a virgin, by Satan. This is no new view, for it has been held by many of God's spiritually minded children since the days of the Apostle John and there is some warrant for it in the Scriptures.
>
> In Genesis 3:15 God said to the Serpent Satan, 'I will put enmity between thee and the woman and between "thy seed" and "her seed."" Now the Woman's seed was Christ then the Serpent's seed must be Antichrist." – *Dispensational Truth: Or, God's Plan and Purpose in the Ages*, Clarence Larkin, p. 119

Both Have Supernatural Arrivals

Although physically born in Bethlehem, Jesus Christ made it clear during His earthly mission that He was from Heaven:

> "If I have told you earthly things, and ye believe not, how shall ye believe, if I tell you of heavenly things? And no man hath ascended up to heaven, but he that came down from heaven, even the Son of man which is in heaven." – John 3:12–13
>
> "Jesus answered and said unto them, This is the work of God, that ye believe on him whom he hath sent. They said therefore unto him, What sign shewest thou then, that we may see, and believe thee? what dost thou work? Our fathers did eat manna in the desert; as it is written, He gave them bread from heaven to eat. Then Jesus said unto them, Verily, verily, I say unto you, Moses gave you not that bread from heaven; but my Father giveth you the true bread from heaven. **For the bread of God is he which cometh down from heaven**, and giveth life unto the world.... **For I came down from heaven**, not to do mine own will, but the will of him that

sent me." – John 6:29–33, 38

> "And this is life eternal, that they might know thee the only true God, and Jesus Christ, whom thou hast sent. I have glorified thee on the earth: I have finished the work which thou gavest me to do. And now, O Father, glorify thou me with thine own self with the glory which I had with thee before the world was." – John 17:3–5

Jesus Christ left His throne in Heaven and, in humility and sacrifice, lowered Himself into human form so that He could offer His life as atonement for the sins of humanity. Scripture is clear that Jesus Christ came from Heaven to earth.

Though he will be born of a human woman, the spirit that indwells the Final Nephilim will come to Earth from Hell:

> "And when they shall have finished their testimony, the beast that ascendeth out of the bottomless pit shall make war against them, and shall overcome them, and kill them." – Revelation 11:7

> "And they had a king over them, which is the angel of the bottomless pit, whose name in the Hebrew tongue is Abaddon, but in the Greek tongue hath his name Apollyon." – Revelation 9:11

> "The beast that thou sawest was, and is not; and shall ascend out of the bottomless pit, and go into perdition: and they that dwell on the earth shall wonder, whose names were not written in the book of life from the foundation of the world, when they behold the beast that was, and is not, and yet is." – Revelation 17:8

The Son of God comes from Heaven. The son of Satan comes from Hell.

Both Receive Opposite Responses from the World

Jesus Christ took on the role of a humble servant in His first incarnation on earth. He had little wealth and no "place to lay his head" (Luke 9:58). He preached and healed the sick, devoting His time to traveling the region of Judea, demonstrating He was the Messiah via miracles, and helping those in need. He sought no political office, earthly status, or wealth. And for this, Jesus was hated, rejected, and wrongly executed:

> "He was in the world, and the world was made by him, and the world knew him not. He came unto his own, and his own received him not." – John 1:10–11
>
> "He is despised and rejected of men; a man of sorrows, and acquainted with grief: and we hid as it were our faces from him; he was despised, and we esteemed him not. Surely he hath borne our griefs, and carried our sorrows: yet we did esteem him stricken, smitten of God, and afflicted." – Isaiah 53:3–4
>
> "The world cannot hate you; **but me it hateth**, because I testify of it, that the works thereof are evil." – Jesus Christ, John 7:7

Conversely, the world will embrace, revere, and literally worship the Antichrist:

> "And I saw one of his heads as it were wounded to death; and his deadly wound was healed: **and all the world wondered after the beast**. And they worshipped the dragon which gave power unto the beast: and they worshipped the beast, saying, Who is like unto the beast? who is able to make war with him?" – Revelation 13:3–4
>
> "**And all that dwell upon the earth shall worship him**, whose names are not written in the book of life of the Lamb slain from

the foundation of the world." – Revelation 13:8

Both Display Opposite Regard for the Lord

"And now, O Father, glorify thou me with thine own self with the glory which I had with thee before the world was. I have manifested thy name unto the men which thou gavest me out of the world: thine they were, and thou gavest them me; and they have kept thy word. Now they have known that all things whatsoever thou hast given me are of thee." – John 17:5–7

"Now is my soul troubled; and what shall I say? Father, save me from this hour: but for this cause came I unto this hour. **Father, glorify thy name. Then came there a voice from heaven, saying, I have both glorified it, and will glorify it again**. The people therefore, that stood by, and heard it, said that it thundered: others said, An angel spake to him. Jesus answered and said, This voice came not because of me, but for your sakes. Now is the judgment of this world: now shall the prince of this world be cast out." – John 12:27–31

"Then answered the Jews, and said unto him, Say we not well that thou art a Samaritan, and hast a devil? Jesus answered, I have not a devil; but I honour my Father, and ye do dishonour me. And I seek not mine own glory: there is one that seeketh and judgeth. Verily, verily, I say unto you, If a man keep my saying, he shall never see death. Then said the Jews unto him, Now we know that thou hast a devil. Abraham is dead, and the prophets; and thou sayest, If a man keep my saying, he shall never taste of death.

Art thou greater than our father Abraham, which is dead? and the prophets are dead: whom makest thou thyself? Jesus answered, If I honour myself, my honour is nothing: it is my Father that

> honoureth me; of whom ye say, that he is your God." – John 8:48–54

Although literally God manifest in human flesh, Jesus Christ temporarily lowered Himself to be the perfect, sinless, human sacrifice. And in this mission, He sought to honor and glorify God the Father in everything He said and did.

In contrast, the Final Nephilim, possessed by the spirit of the fallen angelic Assyrian, will be the ultimate blasphemer. He not only will proclaim himself as god, but he also will renounce Yahweh repeatedly:

> "Thus he said, The fourth beast shall be the fourth kingdom upon earth, which shall be diverse from all kingdoms, and shall devour the whole earth, and shall tread it down, and break it in pieces. And the ten horns out of this kingdom are ten kings that shall arise: and another shall rise after them; and he shall be diverse from the first, and he shall subdue three kings. **And he shall speak great words against the most High**, and shall wear out the saints of the most High." – Daniel 7:23–25

> "And the king shall do according to his will; and he shall exalt himself, and magnify himself above every god, **and shall speak marvellous things against the God of gods**, and shall prosper till the indignation be accomplished: for that that is determined shall be done. Neither shall he regard the God of his fathers, nor the desire of women, nor regard any god: for he shall magnify himself above all." – Daniel 11:36–37

> "And there was given unto him a mouth speaking great things and blasphemies; and power was given unto him to continue forty and two months. **And he opened his mouth in blasphemy against God, to blaspheme his name**, and his tabernacle, and them that

dwell in heaven." – Revelation 13:5–6

The Antichrist will repeatedly attack God and all those who believe in the Lord. With his miraculous power and appeal, he will seek to turn the world against God to the point that, by the end of the Great Tribulation, every nation will marshal its forces to fight against Jesus Christ at Armageddon. Consider the power of persuasion this feat will take. Apollyon not only on some level will convince the unbelieving world that God exists, but he will use a deception so powerful that it will trick the people into thinking Jesus is their enemy—so much so that they await His Second Coming ready to engage God in battle. The world will genuinely believe that the Antichrist is their savior.

ANTICHRIST: JEWISH OR CLAIMS JEWISH ANCESTRY

A casual Internet search of "Who is the Antichrist?" generates a laundry list of candidates—a roster that mostly includes political officials, religious leaders, and despots from all over the globe. However, the Bible states that Antichrist will be a descendant of the tribes of Israel. One of the principal passages confirming this is found in Ezekiel chapter 21:

> "And thou, profane wicked prince of Israel, whose day is come, when iniquity shall have an end, Thus saith the Lord GOD; Remove the diadem, and take off the crown: this shall not be the same: exalt him that is low, and abase him that is high. I will overturn, overturn, overturn, it: and it shall be no more, until he come whose right it is; and I will give it him." – Ezekiel 21:25–27

A great deal of prophetic information is packed into this small passage, which warrants close examination.

> "And thou, profane wicked prince of Israel…"

This is the initial confirmation that the Antichrist will be an Israelite. And, from a practical standpoint, it indeed makes sense. The Jewish people, who do not acknowledge Jesus Christ as Messiah, nevertheless understand and teach that their coming Messiah will be Jewish and a descendant of King David. This is firmly established in the Old Testament. It is extremely difficult to envision a scenario in which Jewish believers would ever acknowledge, much less worship, a man who is not Jewish or even claims to be an Israelite.

> "…whose day is come, when iniquity shall have an end…"

Here is the confirmation that this passage is set in an end-times, prophetic context. Iniquity will "have its end" at the return of Jesus Christ. So, contextually, this "wicked prince of Israel" will be in power during the end times. This, of course, will be the Antichrist ruling over Israel during the Day of the Lord.

> "Thus saith the Lord GOD; Remove the diadem, and take off the crown."

Here, we read further biblical evidence of the Antichrist's ethnicity. In the Old Testament, God separated the roles of royalty and priesthood by tribe. The Levites were the only tribe permitted to serve as priests (who wore the "diadem" or "mitre" as their headdress) in the tabernacle or temple:

> "And the LORD spake unto Aaron, Thou shalt have no inheritance in their land, neither shalt thou have any part among them: I am thy part and thine inheritance among the children of Israel. And,

> behold, I have given the children of Levi all the tenth in Israel for an inheritance, for their service which they serve, even the service of the tabernacle of the congregation. Neither must the children of Israel henceforth come nigh the tabernacle of the congregation, lest they bear sin, and die. But the Levites shall do the service of the tabernacle of the congregation, and they shall bear their iniquity: it shall be a statute for ever throughout your generations, that among the children of Israel they have no inheritance." – Numbers 18:20–23

The tribe of Judah served as the royal tribe, designated to provide the kings of Israel (and thus wear "the crown"):

> "And when thy days be fulfilled, and thou shalt sleep with thy fathers, I will set up thy seed after thee, which shall proceed out of thy bowels, and I will establish his kingdom. He shall build an house for my name, and I will stablish the throne of his kingdom for ever. I will be his father, and he shall be my son. If he commit iniquity, I will chasten him with the rod of men, and with the stripes of the children of men: But my mercy shall not depart away from him, as I took it from Saul, whom I put away before thee. And thine house and thy kingdom shall be established for ever before thee: thy throne shall be established for ever." – 2 Samuel 7:12–16

Whenever a king attempted to serve as both king and priest, it led to severe punishment from God. An extraordinary instance of this occurred in the reign of King Uzziah. Though he performed many righteous acts as king, he wrongfully entered the Temple and attempted to act as high priest:

> "But when [Uzziah] was strong, his heart was lifted up to his destruction: for he transgressed against the LORD his God, and went into the temple of the LORD to burn incense upon the altar

> of incense. And Azariah the priest went in after him, and with him fourscore priests of the LORD, that were valiant men: And they withstood Uzziah the king, and said unto him, It appertaineth not unto thee, Uzziah, to burn incense unto the LORD, but to the priests the sons of Aaron, that are consecrated to burn incense: go out of the sanctuary; for thou hast trespassed; neither shall it be for thine honour from the LORD God.
>
> Then Uzziah was wroth, and had a censer in his hand to burn incense: and while he was wroth with the priests, the leprosy even rose up in his forehead before the priests in the house of the LORD, from beside the incense altar. And Azariah the chief priest, and all the priests, looked upon him, and, behold, he was leprous in his forehead, and they thrust him out from thence; yea, himself hasted also to go out, because the LORD had smitten him." – 2 Chronicles 26:16–20

Uzziah was struck with leprosy—a death sentence in the ancient world—in the very moment when he attempted to burn incense in the Temple.

The Antichrist, however, will wear a diadem and a crown, serving as both god and king of the people. His religion will be based on himself. In this way, he is again an imitation of Jesus Christ, the True King *and* High Priest.

> "**But Christ being come an high priest of good things to come**, by a greater and more perfect tabernacle, not made with hands, that is to say, not of this building; Neither by the blood of goats and calves, but by his own blood he entered in once into the holy place, having obtained eternal redemption for us." – Hebrews 9:11–12

Continuing in the prophecy of Ezekiel 21:

> "This shall not be the same: exalt him that is low, and abase him that is high. I will overturn, overturn, overturn, it: and it shall be no more, **until he come whose right it is; and I will give it him**."

God prophesied for millennia that, ultimately, the Antichrist will be conquered. He is merely an instrument of judgment in the hands of the Creator. At Christ's Revelation, the Final Nephilim will be "overturned," losing his kingdom, power, and authority. And the Earth will be rightfully reclaimed by the Lord Jesus Christ, "whose right it is." An early twentieth-century commentary affirms this reading of the text as a double prophecy extending through time:

> "The Wicked Prince and the Coming One are seen in [Ezekiel 21:25–27]. **Here Christ and Antichrist are contrasted**. There can be no question that Zedekiah is first of all in view as the profane wicked prince of Israel. But the prophecy looks far beyond Zedekiah It is the coming wicked prince the one who comes in his own name, the final Antichrist, the false Messiah, or, as he is also called in Revelation, the false prophet. That verse 25 refers to the time of the end, is seen by the words 'in the time of the iniquity of the end.'...
>
> It is the time of the future great tribulation 'when the transgressors are come to the full,' (Daniel 8:23). **This false Christ will claim priestly and kingly honors**. He is the beast out of the earth (Revelation 13) having two horns like a lamb, but speaking as a dragon. The two horns represent the priesthood and the kingship he assumes. And this we learn from verse 26, is the character of the wicked prince of Israel of whom Ezekiel speaks. Again, we must correct the faulty translation of the authorized version: 'Remove the mitre and take off the crown'; the word 'diadem' is mitre, the head dress of the high priest (Exodus 27:4). He wears the mitre of the

> priest and the crown of the king. He is Satan's final counterfeit (like the pope) of the Priest King." – *The Annotated Bible: The Holy Scriptures Annotated and Analyzed, Volume 4*, Arno Clemens Gaebelein, 1921, p. 296

FINAL NEPHILIM: HAILS FROM TRIBE OF DAN

> "Dan shall judge his people, as one of the tribes of Israel. Dan shall be a serpent by the way, an adder in the path, that biteth the horse heels, so that his rider shall fall backward." – Genesis 49:16–17

This passage contains one of several ominous prophecies regarding the tribe of Dan, indicating that the end-times False Messiah will come from this tribe. In the above prophecy, Jacob announced predictions for each of his twelve sons—the patriarchs of the tribes of Israel. The designation of Dan as "judge" of his people points to a time when Dan will have authority over Israel. The connection to the "serpent by the way" paints a dire connection to Satan, "that old serpent" (Revelation 12:9, 20:2). In the Ultimate Prophecy of Genesis 3:15, the Lord told the Devil that he would "bruise the heel" of the Seed of the Woman. Here, Dan is told that his tribe will "biteth the horse heels." All of the symbolic language points to Dan being the tribe of the wicked prince of Israel—the Antichrist.

Other prophecies regarding Dan provide similar, disturbing imagery—for example, the following passage from Jeremiah:

> "The snorting of his horses was heard from Dan: the whole land trembled at the sound of the neighing of his strong ones; for they are come, and have devoured the land, and all that is in it; the city, and those that dwell therein. For, behold, I will send serpents,

> cockatrices, among you, which will not be charmed, and they shall bite you, saith the LORD." – Jeremiah 8:16–17

During the judgments of the Great Tribulation, a fallen angelic army of horsemen is released from the Abyss riding heavenly realm horses:

> "And thus I saw the horses in the vision, and them that sat on them, having breastplates of fire, and of jacinth, and brimstone: and the heads of the horses were as the heads of lions; and out of their mouths issued fire and smoke and brimstone." – Revelation 9:17

This prophecy from Jeremiah also makes a reference to "serpents" being sent with the army from Dan. Of course, during the Great Tribulation, the Final Nephilim will be accompanied by the armies of fallen angels that are released from the Abyss and that fall from Heaven after the battle described in Revelation 12.

> "And of Dan he said, Dan is a lion's whelp: he shall leap from Bashan." – Deuteronomy 33:22

The Devil is referred to as a "roaring lion" in 1 Peter 5:8. The "whelp," or offspring, of the roaring lion will be the Antichrist. The prophecy also notes that Dan will "leap from Bashan"—a stronghold of the Nephilim in the Old Testament. Bashan was territory of King Og, one of the foremost enemies of Moses and the children of Israel as they marched to the Promised Land:

> "**For only Og king of Bashan remained of the remnant of giants**; behold his bedstead was a bedstead of iron; is it not in Rabbath of the children of Ammon? nine cubits was the length thereof, and four cubits the breadth of it, after the cubit of a man." –

Deuteronomy 3:11

A final troubling sign is that when the 144,000 Jewish witnesses are given the Mark of God at the start of the Day of the Lord, Dan is not included among the twelve tribes:

> "Of the tribe of Judah were sealed twelve thousand. Of the tribe of Reuben were sealed twelve thousand. Of the tribe of Gad were sealed twelve thousand. Of the tribe of Aser were sealed twelve thousand. Of the tribe of Nephthalim were sealed twelve thousand. Of the tribe of Manasses were sealed twelve thousand. Of the tribe of Simeon were sealed twelve thousand. Of the tribe of Levi were sealed twelve thousand. Of the tribe of Issachar were sealed twelve thousand. Of the tribe of Zabulon were sealed twelve thousand. Of the tribe of Joseph were sealed twelve thousand. Of the tribe of Benjamin were sealed twelve thousand." – Revelation 7:5–8

Dan is replaced by "the tribe of Joseph" (who was awarded two half-tribes—Ephraim and Manasseh; see Genesis 48, Joshua 14:4). The Antichrist will be the whelp of the roaring lion, Satan. He will leap from the homeland of the Nephilim and bring an army unlike the world has ever seen. And he will be from the tribe of Dan. This was a common belief from the earliest centuries of the Church:

> "With all this is associated the notion that the Antichrist was expected to come from the tribe of Dan. This is an indication that the apocalyptic tradition in question originated under the influence of the Jewish haggadic (homiletic) interpretation. For the belief itself arose out of the Rabbinical exposition of such passages as Deuteronomy 33:22, Genesis 49:17 and Jeremiah 8:16, and is everywhere in patristic literature supported by reference to these passages.

> This notion is probably of long standing. At least we have in Irenaeus, V 30, 2: 'And for this reason this tribe Dan is not numbered in Revelation amongst those that are saved.' It seems to me that this interpretation especially as it is now a mere link in the chain of a much wider connection, is the only one possessing a certain degree of probability. If so the idea must have already been known to the author of Revelation chapter 7." – *The Antichrist Legend*, William Bousset, 1896, p. 171–172

ANTICHRIST: ABANDONS JEWISH FAITH OF HIS ANCESTORS

Daniel 11 documents the career of the Antichrist and offers further prophetic evidence of the Jewish ethnicity of the Final Nephilim:

> "And the king shall do according to his will; and he shall exalt himself, and magnify himself above every god, and shall speak marvellous things against the God of gods, and shall prosper till the indignation be accomplished: for that that is determined shall be done. **Neither shall he regard the God of his fathers**, nor the desire of women, nor regard any god: for he shall magnify himself above all." – Daniel 11:36–37

It has already been well established that the False Messiah will exalt himself over all other gods. However, the passage above explains that he will also disregard "the God of his fathers." Throughout the Old Testament, the term "his fathers" or "God of his fathers" either refers to Abraham, Isaac, and Jacob—the patriarchs of Israel—or to the kings of Israel:

> "So David slept with his fathers, and was buried in the city of

> David." – 1 Kings 2:10
>
> "And Solomon slept with his fathers, and was buried in the city of David his father: and Rehoboam his son reigned in his stead." – 1 Kings 11:43
>
> "And the days which Jeroboam reigned were two and twenty years: and he slept with his fathers, and Nadab his son reigned in his stead." – 1 Kings 14:20
>
> "Amon was twenty and two years old when he began to reign, and he reigned two years in Jerusalem. And his mother's name was Meshullemeth, the daughter of Haruz of Jotbah. And he did that which was evil in the sight of the LORD, as his father Manasseh did. And he walked in all the way that his father walked in, and served the idols that his father served, and worshipped them: **And he forsook the LORD God of his fathers**, and walked not in the way of the LORD." – 2 Kings 21:19–22

Thus, by letting Scripture interpret Scripture, we have additional evidence of the Antichrist being Jewish through the lineage of his mother. But when he comes into power, he will not worship Yahweh, the God of his fathers. Instead, he will lead much of Israel into apostasy and worship of himself as God. The Lord Jesus Christ foretold this during His earthly ministry:

> "And the Father himself, which hath sent me, hath borne witness of me. Ye have neither heard his voice at any time, nor seen his shape. And ye have not his word abiding in you: for whom he hath sent, him ye believe not. Search the scriptures; for in them ye think ye have eternal life: and they are they which testify of me. And ye will not come to me, that ye might have life. I receive not honour from men. But I know you, that ye have not the love of God in you. **I am come in my Father's name, and ye receive me not: if**

> **another shall come in his own name, him ye will receive.**" – John 5:37–43

Consider the spiritual state of Israel at the time *Yeshua* issued this strong rebuke. Prior to the preaching of John the Baptist, there had been four hundred years of silence from the prophets of God. The nation of Israel had fallen away from true teachings, and the priesthood had been corrupted. The once-sacred role of the high priest of the Temple was now awarded to the political favorites of the Roman-appointed leader: Herod. The Sanhedrin, the religious ruling group of Pharisees and Sadducees, was no longer teaching the Word of God accurately, nor were its members even interested in the more than one hundred prophecies of Messiah that pointed to Jesus Christ. The Lord repeatedly rebuked the Pharisees for their disobedience to God and for their false teachings.

The nation would ultimately reject Jesus, calling for His execution on the cross. When apostasy reaches an extreme level, a nation becomes ripe for the "spirit of antichrist":

> "Beloved, believe not every spirit, but try the spirits whether they are of God: because many false prophets are gone out into the world. Hereby know ye the Spirit of God: Every spirit that confesseth that Jesus Christ is come in the flesh is of God: And every spirit that confesseth not that Jesus Christ is come in the flesh is not of God: and this is that spirit of antichrist, whereof ye have heard that it should come; and even now already is it in the world." – 1 John 4:1–3

FORESHADOW OF THE WORSHIP OF ANTICHRIST

During the rigged "investigation" and crooked trial of Jesus Christ that led to

His Crucifixion, there is a famous account of Pontius Pilate giving the Jewish people a final chance to exonerate the Lord. It was Pilate's custom to release a prisoner at Passover, and he gave the people the opportunity to choose between Jesus and Barabbas:

> "Now at that feast he released unto them one prisoner, whomsoever they desired. And there was one named Barabbas, which lay bound with them that had made insurrection with him, who had committed murder in the insurrection. And the multitude crying aloud began to desire him to do as he had ever done unto them. But Pilate answered them, saying, Will ye that I release unto you the King of the Jews? For he knew that the chief priests had delivered him for envy.
>
> But the chief priests moved the people, that he should rather release Barabbas unto them. And Pilate answered and said again unto them, What will ye then that I shall do unto him whom ye call the King of the Jews?
>
> And they cried out again, Crucify him. Then Pilate said unto them, Why, what evil hath he done? And they cried out the more exceedingly, Crucify him. And so Pilate, willing to content the people, released Barabbas unto them, and delivered Jesus, when he had scourged him, to be crucified." – Mark 15:6–15

Barabbas (Βαραββᾶς in Greek) means "son of the father." He was imprisoned for sedition—stirring up people to rebellion and murder. And the chief priests—appointed to teach and honor the Word of God and uphold righteousness—persuaded the people to choose to free a murderer instead of Jesus Christ, who had committed no crime and harmed no one. Consider the prophetic picture: The Jewish people had the Messiah standing right before them, yet they shouted for His death. Jesus Christ said of the Pharisees:

> "**Ye are of your father the devil**, and the lusts of your father ye will do. **He was a murderer from the beginning**, and abode not in the truth, because there is no truth in him. When he speaketh a lie, he speaketh of his own: for he is a liar, and the father of it." – John 8:44

Barabbas, the "son of the father" and a murderer, was chosen by the nation of Israel and released to them from a prison. In the end times, the son of Satan will be released from imprisonment in the Abyss, and the unbelieving world will choose him and his foolish quest to defeat God. This spiritual repetition was understood by theologians of past centuries:

> "Men, rebellious men, will wax worse and worse. They will cast away the cords and bands of Christ's kingdom. They will have another to reign over them—Barabbas, antichrist, any one rather than the anointed of the Lord. Yes; the day is at hand, when, blinded by Satan, and goaded on by insane folly, they will league together in impious and desperate warfare against him who is enthroned in the heavens, against the King of kings and Lord of lords." – "The Kingly Office of Christ," as recorded in *Sermons*, by Reverend Henry Vaughn, Vicar of Crickhowell, Breckonshire, 1833, p. 56–57

> "Antichrist shall come! And when he comes, the world will receive him, in preference to the Christ of God; even as of old they cried 'Not this man, but Barabbas.'" – *The Scattered Nation: Past, Present and Future*, Volume 5, Reverend C. Schwartz, 1870, p. 199

During the Day of the Lord, the world will once again choose a "son of the father" over the true Messiah, the Son of God.

ANTICHRIST: PRIVATELY WORSHIPS SATAN

> "Neither shall he regard the God of his fathers, nor the desire of women, nor regard any god: for he shall magnify himself above all. **But in his estate shall he honour the God of forces:** and a god whom his fathers knew not shall he honour with gold, and silver, and with precious stones, and pleasant things." – Daniel 11:37–38

While the unsaved population will believe that they are worshiping a kind, benevolent messiah, it is the Devil who will be the true power behind the Antichrist. As stated above, the Final Nephilim will not honor Yahweh, the "God of his fathers," nor will he acknowledge "the desire of women"—a reference to *the* Messiah, whom women of Israel desired to give birth to throughout their nation's history. The importance of childbearing in Scripture goes directly back to the Ultimate Prophecy found in Genesis 3:15. The belief and hope in the birth of the Redeemer was the foundation of ancient Jewish belief. Thus, the Messiah was "the desire of women." Many biblical commentators, including the following, concur with this interpretation:

> "But these words—which are placed between 'God of his fathers' and 'any god'—seem rather to refer to an object of divine worship, and to an object also of female desire. Therefore, they may best be interpreted to signify the Messiah: the 'Seed of the woman' (Genesis 3:15), the 'Desire of all nations' (Haggai 2:7; see the phrase in Ezekiel 24:16), especially of women. 'The desires of becoming a mother to the Messiah were very great in every of the daughters of Jacob.'" – Bishop Taylor, *Life of Christ,* p. 2
>
> "'Every of the daughters of Abraham hoped to have the honour to be His mother or something of His kindred.' (Bishop Taylor, *Marriage Ring,* vol 5, p 249)." – *The Book of Daniel, with Notes and*

Introduction, New Edition, C. H. R. Woodsworth, 1873, p. 57

Rather than honoring Jesus, Antichrist will privately worship the Devil. He may fraudulently present himself as a Messianic figure—or even as a compassionate, humane leader imbued with powers from another dimension or planet. But in his own "estate," he worships the "god of forces" or "fortresses." This "god of war" is none other than Satan fulfilling the Ultimate Prophecy's declaration that both Satan and his seed would have "enmity"—be at war—with the woman and her promised Seed:

> "And I will put enmity between thee and the woman, and between thy seed and her seed; it shall bruise thy head, and thou shalt bruise his heel." – Genesis 3:15

The "woman" who delivered the Holy Seed was the nation of Israel (Revelation 12). And the war has been waged for the entire biblical history, culminating in the events of the book of Revelation, with the seed of the Serpent leading the world into war against Israel and her Messiah.

The writer of an article in a nineteenth-century Bible prophecy magazine also deduced that the Final Nephilim will worship the Devil:

> "Now let us turn to what is said of the 'vile person' in the concluding part of [Daniel chapter 11]. It is expressly declared that he shall not regard the God of his fathers, nor the desire of women, that is, Jesus Christ...nor any god; but yet he shall honour the god of forces, a god whom his fathers knew not; and thus he shall do in the most strong holds with a strange god.
>
> Now who can this strange god be?... Not the gods of the heathen world, for it does not appear from the words of the prophecy that the 'vile person' will honour a plurality of gods; he will only honour

> the god of forces, whosoever this god may be. I conjecture this god of forces must be Satan himself." – "What Is the Abomination of Desolation?" as printed in *The Prophetic News and Israel's Watchman*, New Series, Maramensis, January 1881, p. 181

ANTICHRIST: DEFENDER AND FALSE SAVIOR OF ISRAEL

Daniel chapter 11 provides a description of the Antichrist as **a conqueror on behalf of Israel**. In the years before his deadly wound and resurrection—before he is indwelled with the spirit from the Abyss—he will be a military leader conquering the nations that surround Israel. This is when he will win over and deceive the Israelites into believing he is their promised Messiah:

> "Thus shall he do in the most strong holds with a strange god, whom he shall acknowledge and increase with glory: and he shall cause them to rule over many, and shall divide the land for gain. **And at the time of the end shall the king of the south push at him: and the king of the north shall come against him like a whirlwind**, with chariots, and with horsemen, and with many ships; **and he shall enter into the countries, and shall overflow and pass over**." – Daniel 11:39–40

Here, Scripture confirms that the passage is moving from a near-term prophecy (that of Antiochus Epiphanes) to the time of the end. Antichrist, situated in Israel, will take attacks from "the king of the north" (the leader of Syria throughout the chapter) and the "king of the south" (the leader of Egypt). The king of the north, leading a coalition of Israel's neighbors, will launch a multi-front attack. This will likely be the long-awaited battle of the Islamic world against Israel. It is reasonable to assume that such an assault on the Holy Land would draw participation from many of the Muslim nations that surround Israel.

However, the Islamic confederacy will lose. The Antichrist will "enter the countries," not just repelling the attacks, but taking over the territory of the enemies of Israel. His military victory will be an "overflow"; he will overwhelm and dominate his enemies.

> "He shall enter also into the glorious land, and many countries shall be overthrown."

The Final Nephilim will establish himself in Israel, the "glorious land," and take over "many countries." From the Israelites' perspective, it will appear that the Antichrist is rescuing Israel from their Arab Muslim neighbors, with whom Israel had tense relations and conflict for decades.

> "...but these shall escape out of his hand, **even Edom**, and Moab, and the chief of the children of Ammon."

Edom, Moab, and Ammon comprise modern-day Jordan, which will "escape" from the military conquests of the Antichrist. Keep in mind that this area will not be under the Antichrist's control during his reign.

> "He shall stretch forth his hand also upon the countries: and the land of Egypt shall not escape. But he shall have power over the treasures of gold and of silver, and over all the precious things of Egypt: and the Libyans and the Ethiopians shall be at his steps." – Daniel 11:42–43

With cunning and military genius, the Antichrist will conquer almost all of the nations that surround Israel. Additionally, Egypt, Ethiopia, Libya, and the nations allied with them will also fall to the Beast's armies. This was prophesied in the book of Ezekiel:

> "The word of the LORD came again unto me, saying, Son of man, prophesy and say, Thus saith the Lord GOD; Howl ye, Woe worth the day! **For the day is near, even the day of the LORD is near, a cloudy day; it shall be the time of the heathen**. And the sword shall come upon Egypt, and great pain shall be in Ethiopia, when the slain shall fall in Egypt, and they shall take away her multitude, and her foundations shall be broken down.
>
> Ethiopia, and Libya, and Lydia, and all the mingled people, and Chub, and the men of the land that is in league, shall fall with them by the sword. Thus saith the LORD; They also that uphold Egypt shall fall; and the pride of her power shall come down: from the tower of Syene shall they fall in it by the sword, saith the Lord GOD. And they shall be desolate in the midst of the countries that are desolate, and her cities shall be in the midst of the cities that are wasted. And they shall know that I am the LORD, when I have set a fire in Egypt, and when all her helpers shall be destroyed." – Ezekiel 30:1–8

With a direct reference to the Day of the Lord, we know that this is an end-times context. The Antichrist will punish Egypt, Ethiopia, Libya, and other surrounding nations. After their defeat, they will be "desolate"—a trademark of Abaddon, who is a destroyer and "desolator." The removal of the leaders of these three nations is part of the prophesied rise of the False Messiah:

> "After this I saw in the night visions, and behold a fourth beast, dreadful and terrible, and strong exceedingly; and it had great iron teeth: it devoured and brake in pieces, and stamped the residue with the feet of it: and it was diverse from all the beasts that were before it; and it had ten horns. I considered the horns, and, behold, there

> came up among them another little horn, before whom there were three of the first horns plucked up by the roots: and, behold, in this horn were eyes like the eyes of man, and a mouth speaking great things.... Thus he said, The fourth beast shall be the fourth kingdom upon earth, which shall be diverse from all kingdoms, and shall devour the whole earth, and shall tread it down, and break it in pieces. And the ten horns out of this kingdom are ten kings that shall arise: and another shall rise after them; and he shall be diverse from the first, **and he shall subdue three kings**." – Daniel 7:7–8, 23–24

He will conquer and plunder a large number of nations, leaving Israel with little to no challenge from its Arab Muslim neighbors. Thus, he will easily appear to be the long-awaited Messiah of the Jewish people.

Hippolytus of Rome was one of the most important theologians of the second and third centuries. Early Church historians Eusebius and Jerome referenced his writings in great detail, and many of his works are still in existence. His essay, *On Christ and Antichrist*, which dates to ca. AD 202, is **the oldest extant commentary on the book of Revelation**. This is a seminal writing, as it is by far the closest to the days of the apostles of the Lord Jesus Christ of any writing on end-times prophecy.

Almost two thousand years ago, Hippolytus concurred that the Antichrist would indeed conquer the geographic neighbors of Israel to deceive the nation into believing he was their champion:

> "And thereafter, he will be lifted up in heart, and he who was formerly gentle will become violent, and he who pursued love will become pitiless, and the humble in heart will become haughty and inhuman, and the hater of unrighteousness will persecute the righteous. Then, when he is elevated to his kingdom, he will marshal war; and in his wrath he will smite three mighty kings,

> those namely of Egypt, Libya, and Ethiopia. And after that he will build the temple in Jerusalem, and will restore it again speedily and give it over to the Jews." – *On Christ and Antichrist*, Hippolytus, ca. 202, as printed in *Ante-Nicene Christian Library: Irenaeus, v. 2, Hippolytus, v.2, Fragments of Third Century*, 1869, p. 114–115

CONSTRUCTION OF THIRD TEMPLE AND REVIVAL OF LEVITICAL SACRIFICAL SYSTEM

The emergence of Israel as a military powerhouse will also inaugurate the construction of the Third Temple and a restoration of the sacrificial system administered by the Levitical priesthood. Scripture confirms this in Daniel chapter 9's seventy-weeks prophecy that describes the construction of the Second Temple, built in the days of Zechariah and Haggai after the Jews returned to the Promised Land by a decree of King Cyrus. But it also prophesied that a Third Temple would be built in the end times and that there would be a restoration of the Temple sacrifices:

> "**And one week shall establish the covenant with many**: and in the midst of the week my sacrifice and drink-offering shall be taken away: **and on the temple** shall be the abomination of desolations; and at the end of time an end shall be put to the desolation." – Daniel 9:27, LXX

Many call the "covenant" in this passage a "seven-year peace treaty" that Israel will achieve with the Antichrist or with its geographic neighbors. However, this is not supported by the text. Nowhere is there any indication that a peace treaty is drafted and agreed upon by Israel.

As explained earlier in this study, "the covenant"—meaning the Law given to Israel—will be reinstated in the final "week," or seven years before the Second

Coming of the Lord Jesus Christ. The end-times Temple is confirmed in the New Testament, where the Apostle Paul prophesied the Antichrist would sit "in the temple of God":

> "Let no man deceive you by any means: for that day shall not come, except there come a falling away first, and that man of sin be revealed, the son of perdition; Who opposeth and exalteth himself above all that is called God, or that is worshipped; **so that he as God sitteth in the temple of God**, shewing himself that he is God." – 2 Thessalonians 2:3–4

As mentioned earlier, the Second Temple was destroyed in AD 70 by Titus Vespasian and the Roman Empire. In the future, any leader who not only conquers Israel's enemies, but rebuilds a Third Temple and restores Levitical sacrifices, can easily be viewed as "the Savior." This, of course, will all be a deception—what the Bible calls the "strong delusion":

> "For the mystery of iniquity doth already work: only he who now letteth will let, until he be taken out of the way. And then shall that Wicked be revealed, whom the Lord shall consume with the spirit of his mouth, and shall destroy with the brightness of his coming: Even him, whose coming is after the working of Satan with all power and signs and lying wonders, **And with all deceivableness of unrighteousness in them that perish**; because they received not the love of the truth, that they might be saved. **And for this cause God shall send them strong delusion, that they should believe a lie**: That they all might be damned who believed not the truth, but had pleasure in unrighteousness." – 2 Thessalonians 2:7–12

It shouldn't seem odd that a Satan-worshiping leader like the Final Nephilim would restore Jewish worship. His goal is to deceive. His entire existence is one grand spiritual defrauding of the unbelieving world. Just as Jesus Christ proclaimed that He is "the truth" (John 14:6), the Beast is "the lie," and Satan is his father. The Antichrist is the final spiritual test of the world wherein all people will choose their allegiance—either with God or the Devil.

Theologians and lay believers from the early centuries understood that a key component of the Antichrist's deception will be reestablishing the sacrificial system of the Mosaic Law in a rebuilt Temple. The following article summarizes the notion succinctly:

> "'So that he (as God), sitteth in the temple of God, shewing himself that he is God.' It ought to be a settled question among Christians that this does not mean the Christian Church, and indeed, until the professing church fell into rank Judaism, it never was so held. All the early fathers from Hippolytus downward, who have written upon the antichrist have asserted it to be the Jewish temple yet to be rebuilt, and this answers to [Daniel 9:27] where the Jewish sacrificial worship being again established, the prince, the antichrist, 'causes the sacrifice and oblation to cease, and upon the battlements shall be the idols of the desolator.'" – "Brief Notes on the Second Epistle to the Thessalonians," as printed in *The Evangelist, A Monthly Journal*, Vol. 1, New Series, edited by H. H. Snell, 1864, p. 46

Mystery Babylon the Great's Spiritual "Fornication"

> "And there came one of the seven angels which had the seven vials, and talked with me, saying unto me, Come hither; I will shew unto thee the judgment of the great whore that sitteth upon many waters: With whom the kings of the earth have committed fornication, and the inhabitants of the earth have been made drunk with the wine of her fornication.

> So he carried me away in the spirit into the wilderness: and I saw a woman sit upon a scarlet coloured beast, full of names of blasphemy, having seven heads and ten horns. And the woman was arrayed in purple and scarlet colour, and decked with gold and precious stones and pearls, having a golden cup in her hand full of abominations and filthiness of her fornication: And upon her forehead was a name written, MYSTERY, BABYLON THE GREAT, THE MOTHER OF HARLOTS AND ABOMINATIONS OF THE EARTH." – Revelation 17:1–5

"Mystery Babylon," the end-times capital city of the Antichrist, is Jerusalem. It is the "great city" of Revelation 11, where the Two Witnesses of the Lord are assassinated by Antichrist:

> "And when they shall have finished their testimony, the beast that ascendeth out of the bottomless pit shall make war against them, and shall overcome them, and kill them. And their dead bodies shall lie in the street of the great city, which spiritually is called Sodom and Egypt, **where also our Lord was crucified**." – Revelation 11:7–8

It is without question that the Lord Jesus Christ was crucified outside of Jerusalem. No other city on Earth could possibly fit this description. The second confirmation that this is a reference to Jerusalem is that Mystery Babylon is described as a "whore" who has committed "fornication" with all the nations of the world. On numerous occasions in the Old Testament, God used this harsh, sexualized language to refer to Israel's worship of the false gods (who were in fact demons, the spirits of the dead Nephilim giants):

> "When Jehoram went forth with his princes, and all his chariots with him: and he rose up by night, and smote the Edomites which compassed him in, and the captains of the chariots. So the

> Edomites revolted from under the hand of Judah unto this day. The same time also did Libnah revolt from under his hand; because he had forsaken the LORD God of his fathers.
>
> **Moreover he made high places in the mountains of Judah and caused the inhabitants of Jerusalem to commit fornication**, and compelled Judah thereto. And there came a writing to him from Elijah the prophet, saying, Thus saith the LORD God of David thy father, Because thou hast not walked in the ways of Jehoshaphat thy father, nor in the ways of Asa king of Judah, **But hast walked in the way of the kings of Israel, and hast made Judah and the inhabitants of Jerusalem to go a whoring, like to the whoredoms of the house of Ahab**, and also hast slain thy brethren of thy father's house, which were better than thyself: Behold, with a great plague will the LORD smite thy people, and thy children, and thy wives, and all thy goods." – 2 Chronicles 21:9–14

Jeremiah spent most of his life rebuking the Israelites for forsaking Yahweh and worshiping idols. He prophesied the conquest and destruction of the Southern Kingdom of Judah by the Babylonian armies. In his admonition of Israel's rampant sin, he used the same "harlot" language:

> "Thus saith the LORD, After this manner will I mar the pride of Judah, and the great pride of Jerusalem. This evil people, which refuse to hear my words, which walk in the imagination of their heart, and walk after other gods, to serve them, and to worship them, shall even be as this girdle, which is good for nothing.... **I have seen thine adulteries**, and thy neighings, **the lewdness of thy whoredom**, and thine abominations on the hills in the fields. **Woe unto thee, O Jerusalem**! wilt thou not be made clean? when shall it once be?" – Jeremiah 13:9–10, 27

The prophet Ezekiel made more than twenty references to the "whoredoms" of Israel, indicting the twelve tribes for their rejection of God in favor of pagan deities. However, in Ezekiel 43, a prophecy of the Millennial Temple, Ezekiel was provided a glimpse through time of Israel returning to God once and for all:

> "So the spirit took me up, and brought me into the inner court; and, behold, the glory of the LORD filled the house. And I heard him speaking unto me out of the house; and the man stood by me. And he said unto me, Son of man, the place of my throne, and the place of the soles of my feet, where I will dwell in the midst of the children of Israel for ever, and my holy name, shall the house of Israel no more defile, neither they, nor their kings, by their whoredom, nor by the carcasses of their kings in their high places.
>
> In their setting of their threshold by my thresholds, and their post by my posts, and the wall between me and them, they have even defiled my holy name by their abominations that they have committed: wherefore I have consumed them in mine anger. **Now let them put away their whoredom, and the carcasses of their kings, far from me, and I will dwell in the midst of them for ever.**" – Ezekiel 43:5–9

Ezekiel was given a vision of the future Temple from which Jesus Christ will rule and reign after His Second Coming in Jerusalem. At this time, the "abominations" and "whoredom" of the Israelites will cease and their evil kings will be destroyed. The believing remnant will acknowledge Jesus Christ as the True Messiah and will worship Him in spirit and truth. But this beautiful reconciliation takes place *after* the end-times city of Jerusalem, under control of Antichrist, has been conquered and cleansed.

Satanic Imitation of High Priest of God

> "And the woman was arrayed in purple and scarlet colour, and decked with gold and precious stones and pearls, having a golden cup in her hand full of abominations and filthiness of her fornication: And upon her forehead was a name written, MYSTERY, BABYLON THE GREAT, THE MOTHER OF HARLOTS AND ABOMINATIONS OF THE EARTH." – Revelation 17:4–5

This passage is often linked to modern-day organizations like the Roman Catholic Church. However, on the contrary, the symbolism of Revelation 17 directly connects to the Levitical priesthood and the various precious materials that were used in the construction and decoration of the tabernacle and temples of God. First, consider the colors worn by Mystery Babylon—purple and scarlet. Again, using Scripture to interpret Scripture, we see these colors were selected for the tabernacle:

> "Moreover thou shalt make the tabernacle with ten curtains of fine twined linen, and blue, **and purple, and scarlet**: with cherubims of cunning work shalt thou make them." – Exodus 26:1

> "And thou shalt rear up the tabernacle according to the fashion thereof which was shewed thee in the mount. And thou shalt make a vail of blue, **and purple, and scarlet**, and fine twined linen of cunning work: with cherubims shall it be made: And thou shalt hang it upon four pillars of shittim wood overlaid with gold: their hooks shall be of gold, upon the four sockets of silver." – Exodus 26:30–32

> "And for the gate of the court shall be an hanging of twenty cubits, of blue, **and purple, and scarlet,** and fine twined linen, wrought with needlework: and their pillars shall be four, and their sockets four. All the pillars round about the court shall be filleted with

> silver; their hooks shall be of silver, and their sockets of brass." – Exodus 27:16–17

> "And he made an hanging for the tabernacle door of blue, and **purple, and scarlet**, and fine twined linen, of needlework." – Exodus 36:37

Twenty-six times in Scripture, we read that Moses and Aaron were instructed to use "purple and scarlet" in constructing the Tabernacle and creating the robes and garments for the high priest.

Many theologians, pastors, and Bible students alike have speculated on the enigmatic message appearing on the woman's forehead, but in addition to how the Levitical colors figure into a discussion of Mystery Babylon, we also see that the name on the woman's forehead is a satanic copy of the headdress of the Levitical high priest:

> "And thou shalt make a plate of pure gold, and grave upon it, like the engravings of a signet, HOLINESS TO THE LORD. And thou shalt put it on a blue lace, that it may be upon the mitre; upon the forefront of the mitre it shall be. **And it shall be upon Aaron's forehead**, that Aaron may bear the iniquity of the holy things, which the children of Israel shall hallow in all their holy gifts; **and it shall be always upon his forehead, that they may be accepted before the LORD**." – Exodus 28:36–38

Aaron, the first high priest of Israel, was required to wear a plate on his forehead with the words "HOLINESS TO THE LORD" engraved upon it. It was a declaration of praise to God and part of Aaron's divine authorization to bear the sins of the "holy things"—or items in the Temple. The Woman riding the Beast bears the words "MYSTERY, BABYLON THE GREAT, THE MOTHER OF HARLOTS AND ABOMINATIONS OF THE EARTH" (Revelation 17:5).

Rather than being called "Mystery Babylon," the proclamation is actually "Mystery, Babylon the Great."

This passage indicates that this capital city of Antichrist is not the literal, geographic Babylon, but rather is "Babylon" in a mysterious, esoteric manner. It is the "mother" of harlots and abominations, which makes sense, considering that the Antichrist, the chief blasphemer, will proclaim himself to be God in the very Temple of God in Jerusalem. This will be the ultimate home of satanic worship and deceit.

"Luxury Items" Shipped to Jerusalem Are for Temple Worship

> "And the kings of the earth, who have committed fornication and lived deliciously with her, shall bewail her, and lament for her, when they shall see the smoke of her burning, Standing afar off for the fear of her torment, saying, Alas, alas that great city Babylon, that mighty city! for in one hour is thy judgment come. And the merchants of the earth shall weep and mourn over her; for no man buyeth their merchandise any more: The merchandise of gold, and silver, and precious stones, and of pearls, and fine linen, and purple, and silk, and scarlet, and all thyine wood, and all manner vessels of ivory, and all manner vessels of most precious wood, and of brass, and iron, and marble,
>
> And cinnamon, and odours, and ointments, and frankincense, and wine, and oil, and fine flour, and wheat, and beasts, and sheep, and horses, and chariots, and slaves, and souls of men. And the fruits that thy soul lusted after are departed from thee, and all things which were dainty and goodly are departed from thee, and thou shalt find them no more at all. The merchants of these things, which were made rich by her, shall stand afar off for the fear of her torment, weeping and wailing, And saying, Alas, alas that great city, that was clothed in fine linen, and purple, and scarlet, and decked

> with gold, and precious stones, and pearls!" – Revelation 18:9–16

Many commentaries and sermons interpret the commercial items listed in this passage as symbolic of luxury, high-priced articles that "Mystery Babylon" will possess. But there is a much deeper meaning than this. Babylon the Great (as it is properly called in the Bible), will reinstate Temple worship for the first three and a half years of the Antichrist's career. **All the items listed in this passage**—gold, silver, precious, stones, pearls, linen, among others—were used in the Temple of God for sacrifice.[1]

Though he was not permitted to construct the First Temple of God, King David still made extensive preparations for its construction, gathering materials and financing the building project so that his son, Solomon—whom God did select to build the place of worship—could proceed with the magnificent structure's plans. And notice the materials David stockpiled for the divine project:

> "Furthermore David the king said unto all the congregation, Solomon my son, whom alone God hath chosen, is yet young and tender, and the work is great: for the palace is not for man, but for the LORD God. Now I have prepared with all my might for the house of my God the gold for things to be made **of gold, and the silver for things of silver, and the brass for things of brass, the iron for things of iron, and wood for things of wood; onyx stones, and stones to be set, glistering stones, and of divers colours, and all manner of precious stones, and marble stones in abundance.**
>
> Moreover, because I have set my affection to the house of my God, I have of mine own proper good, of gold and silver, which I have given to the house of my God, over and above all that I have prepared for the holy house. Even three thousand talents of gold, of the gold of Ophir, and seven thousand talents of refined silver,

> to overlay the walls of the houses withal:
>
> The gold for things of gold, and the silver for things of silver, and for all manner of work to be made by the hands of artificers. And who then is willing to consecrate his service this day unto the LORD? Then the chief of the fathers and princes of the tribes of Israel and the captains of thousands and of hundreds, with the rulers of the king's work, offered willingly, And gave for the service of the house of God of gold five thousand talents and ten thousand drams, and of silver ten thousand talents, and of brass eighteen thousand talents, and one hundred thousand talents of iron. And they with whom precious stones were found gave them to the treasure of the house of the LORD, by the hand of Jehiel the Gershonite." – 1 Chronicles 29:1–8

All the goods Babylon the Great will purchase from the nations of the world pertain to Temple worship. Looking at the passage above and the items listed in Revelation 18, we see an almost verbatim copy of the inventory for the temple. Even the mention of "thyine wood" in Revelation 18 is another name for the material used by David and Solomon in constructing the Temple:

> "**And the king made of the almug trees pillars for the house of the LORD**, and for the king's house, harps also and psalteries for singers: there came no such almug trees, nor were seen unto this day." – 1 Kings 10:12

The "almug trees" also known as algum, was another name for thyine wood.

A nineteenth-century commentary confirms this connection:

> "'All thyine wood' harks back to the coniferous timbers of the temple. Thyine wood *Thuya,* is the arbor vitae, a variety of cypress,

> which was one of the timbers commanded by both David and Solomon for the temple construction and for musical instruments. In the Vulgate the doubtful *algum* of Chronicles is rendered as thyine." – *The Ship "Tyre"—A Symbol of the Fate of Conquerors as Prophesied by Isaiah, Ezekiel and John and Fulfilled at Nineveh, Babylon and Rome,* William Harvey Schoff, 1920, p. 100

On another interesting note, we see that much of the Revelation 18 roster also includes items that were used in the Second Temple constructed by Herod.

Josephus, the first-century Jewish historian, was an eyewitness to the destruction of that Temple by the Roman Empire in AD 70. In addition to providing historical documentation of the event, he served as an interpreter to Titus Vespasian, who led the attack on ancient Jerusalem. This put Josephus squarely in the middle of the attack on the Holy City. When the Roman soldiers pillaged the demolished structure, they took many of the items recorded in Revelation 18, articles some of the priests offered them in exchange for safety from Rome:

> "But now at this time it was that one of the priests, the son of Thebuthus, whose name was Jesus, upon his having security given him by the oath of Caesar, that he should be preserved, upon condition that he should deliver to him certain of the precious things that had been reposited in the temple, came out of it, and delivered him from the wall of the holy house two candlesticks, like to those that lay in the holy house, with tables and cisterns and vials, all made of solid gold, and very heavy. He also delivered to him the veils and the garments, with the precious stones and a great number of other precious vessels that belonged to their sacred worship.
>
> The treasurer of the temple also, whose name was Phineas, was

> seized on and shewed Titus the coats and girdles of the priests, **with a great quantity of purple and scarlet**, which were then [reposited] for the uses of the veil, as **also a great deal of cinnamon and cassia, with a large quantity of other sweet spices** which used to be mixed together and offered as incense to God every day. A great many other treasures were also delivered to him, with sacred ornaments of the temple not a few which things thus delivered to Titus obtained of him for this man the same pardon that he had allowed to such as deserted of their own accord." – *Wars of the Jews*, Book V, Chapter VIII, Section 3, Flavius Josephus, ca. AD 75, as printed in *The Whole Genuine Works of Flavius Josephus, The Learned and Celebrated Jewish Historian*, Vol. 4, by William Whiston, 1820, p. 225–226

It should now be abundantly clear that, far from being symbolic of high-tech, expensive consumer goods, **the items shipped to Babylon the Great are all designated for use in Temple worship**. This even applies to what might otherwise seem to be insignificant spices such as cinnamon, cassia (a powder made from the bark of a cinnamon tree used for anointing oil), and others. In practice, each of these substances was specifically designated by Yahweh for use in the Temple:

> "Moreover the LORD spake unto Moses, saying, Take thou also unto thee principal spices, of pure myrrh five hundred shekels, and of sweet cinnamon half so much, even two hundred and fifty shekels, and of sweet calamus two hundred and fifty shekels, And of cassia five hundred shekels, after the shekel of the sanctuary, and of oil olive an hin." – Exodus 30:22–24

During the Day of the Lord, Israel will experience an almost unprecedented religious revival and resurgence. Without a doubt, tremendous spiritual excitement will arise in Israel surrounding the rebuilt Temple and reinstitution of the daily sacrifices and oblations.

This should help make it clear as to how much of Israel and the world will identify the Final Nephilim as Savior. Though he will not worship God himself, the Antichrist will permit Temple worship in Jerusalem on a massive scale. All this will serve as part of the "strong delusion" that will convince the unsaved world to believe that he is their Messiah. But, as his wars reach a peak, the Antichrist will die in battle.

ANTICHRIST WILL ENTER BATTLE ONCE MORE AND BE KILLED, ENDING THE FIRST PHASE OF HIS CAREER

> "But tidings out of the east and out of the north shall trouble him: therefore he shall go forth with great fury to destroy, and utterly to make away many. And he shall plant the tabernacles of his palace between the seas in the glorious holy mountain; **yet he shall come to his end, and none shall help him**." – Daniel 11:44–45

Three and a half years into his rise to power, Antichrist will once again go to war to conquer neighboring countries to the north and east of Israel. We ae told that he will defeat "many." This passage also confirms that his palace will be located "between the seas in the glorious holy mountain," which is a reference to Mt. Zion, providing further evidence that the Antichrist will reside in Jerusalem.

But, at some point during his wars, the Antichrist will be attacked and "come to his end" by suffering a violent and public death:

> "Some critics…press the sequence of the word, 'yet he shall come to his end,' to imply that no interval of time or events is to be

> admitted between the clauses of the verse. The words cannot, in their opinion, apply to Antiochus, but have a further meaning: they point onwards to that end when not only such as Antiochus but Antichrist—the last representative of the world-power against the divine—'shall come to his end and there shall be none to help him.'" – *The Holy Bible According to the Authorized Version (AD 1611): Ezekiel. Daniel and the Minor Prophets,* Vol. VI, edited by Frederic Charles Cook, 1876, p. 390

While it may seem like this is Antichrist's absolute end, it is unfortunately just the beginning of his reign of terror. That's because this is the very point when the spirit of Apollyon—the fallen angelic forefather of the Nephilim—will be released from the Abyss and enter the body of the resurrected Antichrist, unleashing the full satanic power of this False Messiah.

[1]For an excellent and detailed study on the biblical evidence for end-times Jerusalem being Babylon the Great, see *Mystery Babylon—When Jerusalem Embraces the Antichrist: An Exposition of Revelation 17 & 18* by Chris White, CWM Publishing, 2013.)

CHAPTER 8

THE FINAL NEPHILIM

The death and satanic resurrection of the Antichrist will take place at the sounding of the fifth trumpet, the midpoint of the final seven years or "seventieth week" before the Second Coming of Jesus Christ. The Final Nephilim, who will be thought dead and gone, will be revived and indwelt with the spirit of the fallen angel Apollyon, who, as we've well established, is also known as the Assyrian (among many other titles) in the Old Testament. This is the moment of his transformation into the eighth and final Mystery King.

Like Judas and Nebuchadnezzar who have cycled through history before him, the Antichrist will be: 1) a hybrid—both man and fallen angel ("beast"), and 2) a human indwelled by the spirit of a fallen angel. Just as Jesus Christ died and rose from the dead, so too will the satanic False Messiah, mimicking the Savior and performing the ultimate deception on the world.

SATAN RELEASES APOLLYON AND RESSURECTS THE ANTICHRIST

Daniel chapter 11 ends with the death of the Antichrist. Of note, however, is that Daniel chapter 12 is a direct continuation of the narrative of that death **and explains the events that immediately follow**. Chapter and verse numbers were not put in the Bible until the 1599 Geneva translation, so the original texts didn't have the same chapter breaks we enjoy today. Examining the end of Daniel 11 and the beginning of Daniel 12 *as one passage* connects the timing of the death of the Antichrist with the casting of Satan from Heaven:

> "But he shall have power over the treasures of gold and of silver, and over all the precious things of Egypt: and the Libyans and the Ethiopians shall be at his steps. But tidings out of the east and out of the north shall trouble him: therefore he shall go forth with great fury to destroy, and utterly to make away many. And he shall plant the tabernacles of his palace between the seas in the glorious holy mountain; yet he shall come to his end, and none shall help him.
>
> **And at that time** shall Michael stand up, the great prince which standeth for the children of thy people: and there shall be a time of trouble, such as never was since there was a nation even to that same time: and at that time thy people shall be delivered, every one that shall be found written in the book. And many of them that sleep in the dust of the earth shall awake, some to everlasting life, and some to shame and everlasting contempt. And they that be wise shall shine as the brightness of the firmament; and they that turn many to righteousness as the stars for ever and ever. But thou, O Daniel, shut up the words, and seal the book, even to the time of the end: many shall run to and fro, and knowledge shall be increased." – Daniel 11:43–45, 12:1–4

Daniel 12 opens with the critical phrase "and at that time," making it clear that it is directly referring to the prior verse and the death of the Antichrist. His death will coincide with the archangel Michael, the righteous angel and chief prince of Israel, "standing up." This is a reference to Michael leaving his post on Earth as protector of Israel and ascending into Heaven to wage the great heavenly war with Satan, as described in Revelation chapter 12:

> "And there was war in heaven: Michael and his angels fought

> against the dragon; and the dragon fought and his angels, And prevailed not; neither was their place found any more in heaven. And the great dragon was cast out, that old serpent, called the Devil, and Satan, which deceiveth the whole world: he was cast out into the earth, and his angels were cast out with him. And I heard a loud voice saying in heaven, Now is come salvation, and strength, and the kingdom of our God, and the power of his Christ: for the accuser of our brethren is cast down, which accused them before our God day and night.
>
> And they overcame him by the blood of the Lamb, and by the word of their testimony; and they loved not their lives unto the death. Therefore rejoice, ye heavens, and ye that dwell in them. **Woe to the inhabiters of the earth and of the sea! for the devil is come down unto you**, having great wrath, because he knoweth that he hath but a short time." – Revelation 12:7–12

Michael's victory and the subsequent eviction of the Devil brings us to the timing of Satan's fall to earth, which will take place at the sounding of the fifth trumpet of Revelation chapter 9:

> "And the fifth angel sounded, **and I saw a star fall from heaven unto the earth**: and to him was given the key of the bottomless pit. And he opened the bottomless pit; and there arose a smoke out of the pit, as the smoke of a great furnace; and the sun and the air were darkened by reason of the smoke of the pit. And there came out of the smoke locusts upon the earth: and unto them was given power, as the scorpions of the earth have power.
>
> ...And they had a king over them, which is the angel of the bottomless pit, whose name in the Hebrew tongue is Abaddon, but in the Greek tongue hath his name Apollyon. **One woe is past; and, behold, there come two woes more hereafter**." – Revelation

9:1–3; 11

Note that when Satan is cast out of Heaven, a voice announces: "Woe to the inhabiters of the earth." In Revelation 9, when the angel falls from Heaven and opens the bottomless pit, "one woe is past." **This is the same event.** A treatise on Bible prophecy expounds on the connection between these pivotal events:

> "That the war in heaven between Michael and his angels, and the dragon and his angels, and the consequent expulsion of Satan and his angels from heaven to the earth, are to be regarded as literal statements of events which are actually to occur in the future, and not as [symbolized] representations of any events which have taken place in the past, is, or ought to be, conclusively evident. No earthly commander of forces can possibly be [symbolized] by Michael the archangel, no human armies by his angels or by the angels of Satan. The warfare here foreshown to John is literal warfare between the respective parties here mentioned. That, previous to this, there has been warfare such as this between good and evil angels in the heavenly places we have evidence from [Daniel 10:20-21]. **The time of the warfare here foretold is manifestly identical with that of Daniel 12:1—'the time of the end.'**" – "The Symbolism of Revelation 12," as printed in *The Prophetic News and Israel's Watchman*, New Series, 1881, p. 311

Revelation 12 is a parenthetical chapter filling in the details of what took place in Heaven that led to Satan being cast to earth. This is the moment when Satan and his fallen angels fully invade Earth, and Apollyon—also known as Abaddon and the Assyrian—is released from the Abyss one final time.

ANTICHRIST REVIVED FROM DEATH AND POSSESSED BY APOLLYON

> "And there are seven kings: five are fallen, and one is, and the other is not yet come; and when he cometh, he must continue a short space. And the beast that was, and is not, even he is the eighth, and is of the seven, and goeth into perdition." – Revelation 17:10–11

> "And I saw one of his heads as it were wounded to death; and his deadly wound was healed: and all the world wondered after the beast." – Revelation 13:3

> "The resurrection of this false Christ will have power to deceive all the Jews whose names are not written in the Lamb's book of life when they see the beast who after being killed and thus 'was not,' come to life again; perhaps in three days like our blessed Saviour who died for our sins and rose again for our justification." – *Notes on the Book of Revelation*, Helen Maclachlan, 1869, p. 194–195

In the first three and a half years leading to the Antichrist's death, Israel will be the world capital of worship of this False Messiah. In response to this global idolatry, the Lord will send the Destroyer one final time—this time to incarnate in the body of the Antichrist. Satan, now cast from Heaven, will endow his offspring with full power over the earth:

> "And I stood upon the sand of the sea, and saw a beast rise up out of the sea, having seven heads and ten horns, and upon his horns ten crowns, and upon his heads the name of blasphemy. And the beast which I saw was like unto a leopard, and his feet were as the feet of a bear, and his mouth as the mouth of a lion: and the dragon gave him his power, and his seat, and great authority." – Revelation 13:1–2

> "And then shall that Wicked be revealed, whom the Lord shall consume with the spirit of his mouth, and shall destroy with the brightness of his coming: **Even him, whose coming is after the working of Satan with all power and signs and lying wonders,** And with all deceivableness of unrighteousness in them that perish; because they received not the love of the truth, that they might be saved." – 2 Thessalonians 2:8–10

ANTICHRIST RESURRECTED IN THE ULTIMATE DELUSION

> "And I saw one of his heads as it were wounded to death; and his deadly wound was healed: and all the world wondered after the beast. And they worshipped the dragon which gave power unto the beast: and they worshipped the beast, saying, Who is like unto the beast? who is able to make war with him?" – Revelation 13:3–4

The world will watch as the Final Nephilim suffers a mortal wound and then shortly afterwards returns to life. This satanically inspired "resurrection" will win the world over to truly worship this man as God and Savior. This "return to life" will be the ultimate turning point in the career of the Wicked One. This is when Satan will achieve his goal of his own seed being worshiped. No doubt, the unbelieving world, ignorant of God's Word and the many prophecies detailing that this precise series of events would happen, will be awestruck that their False Savior achieves what they always wanted: immortality. Here's an outline of this exact deception:

> "See the mimicry of the truth here. God has given to our glorious Christ his kingdom, his power, and glory: 'All things are delivered unto me of my Father.' But here the devil gives this myrmidon of

his, this monster, whom he evokes for his last struggle, the empire that he is to wield. Further, 'I saw' writes John, 'one of his heads as it were, wounded to death.' A climax of the mimicry this [is]. For as our blessed Lord died and rose again triumphantly, this Antichrist will undergo death and by the power of his patron, the devil, (God permitting it), He will rise again.

And then it is that all his votaries will proclaim, 'Who is like unto the beast? who is able to make war with him?' and men, believing the lie, will worship the beast and receive his mark some in the hand, others more unblushingly in the forehead—all those 'whose names are not written in the Lamb's book of life.' All this information is given to us in this book concerning the future." – "Waiting for the Son of God from Heaven," as printed in *The Rainbow, a Magazine of Christian Literature*, Volume 5, 1868, p. 59

This is the ultimate deception. Even today, millions of unbelievers, in arrogant defiance of God, have demanded proof or visible evidence of the Lord's existence. The Final Nephilim, the seed of the Devil, will give that "proof" to them in abundance. And all it takes is one miracle to bring the world to worship Satan. This is the fulfillment of the prophecy of a "strong delusion" that God will permit as a punishment on the many people who defy, reject, and blaspheme His Holy Name:

"Even him, whose coming is after the working of Satan with all power and signs and lying wonders, And with all deceivableness of unrighteousness in them that perish; because they received not the love of the truth, that they might be saved. **And for this cause God shall send them strong delusion, that they should believe a lie:** That they all might be damned who believed not the truth, but had pleasure in unrighteousness." – 2 Thessalonians 2:9–12

There is a price to pay for living a life of sin and utter rejection of the Word of God. All sin will be punished—and in the end times, the judgment will come in the form of the Antichrist. His "lying wonders" will win the world over when they witness his false miracles and will bow to him in worship after he proclaims himself to be god.

THE JEWISH TEACHING OF TWO MESSIAHS: STARTLING PARALLELS TO SCRIPTURE

The Talmud is a rabbinical commentary most commonly used in modern-day Judaism. It is vastly different from and often contradicts Scripture (including blasphemous passages about the Lord Jesus Christ). Interestingly, the Talmud contains a peculiar end-times prophecy teaching that *two* Jewish Messiahs will actually come to earth: Messiah Ben Joseph (*Mashiach Ben Yosef*) and Messiah Ben David (*Mashiach Ben David*). Messiah Ben Joseph, a descendant of the tribe of Ephraim, will first appear on the global stage and wage wars against Israel's enemies. Here is a summary of the teaching:

> "When Jews typically think of 'the' Messiah (i.e., *ha-mashiach*: יחִשָׁמַה), however, they generally have in mi*nd Mashiach ben D*avid of the tribe of Judah who shall rule in the Messianic ag*e. Mashiach ben Yo*sef is said to be of the tribe of Ephraim (son of Joseph), and is also sometimes called Mashiach ben Ephraim (Bavli Sukah 52b*). Mashiach ben Yo*sef will come first, before the advent *of Mashiach ben Da*vid, to prepare the world for the coming of the kingdom of thE Lord. He will fight God's wars (against 'Edom,' collectively understood as the enemies of Israel) in a time preceding the fulfillment of the Messianic Kingdom (this is sometimes referred to *as Ikvot Mashi*ach, the 'footsteps of the Messiah
>
> However, *Mashiach ben Yosef* will be killed during the war against evil, as described in the prophecy of Zechariah, who says of this

> tragedy that 'they shall mourn him as one mourns for an only child' (Zech. 12:10, Bavli Sukkah 52a). His death would be followed by a period of great calamities and tribulations for Israel, and shortly after this Mashiach ben David would appear to avenge his death and inaugurate the Messianic kingdom on earth (*yemot hamashiach*)." – "Mashiach Ben Yosef—Joseph as a Type of Messiah," John J. Parsons, https://www.hebrew4christians.com/Articles/Mashiach_ben_Yosef/mashiach_ben_yosef.html

This strange, unbiblical prophecy seems like an attempt to reconcile the Bible's prophetic passages that state the Messiah will come as a "suffering servant," yet also as a Conquering King. It was also noted by the Church in earlier centuries:

> "As to the opinions of later Jews relative to the sufferings and death of Messiah, it is necessary to notice the assumption of two Messiahs—one the son of David the other the son of Joseph or Ephraim, who is to lead back the ten tribes, subject them to the son of David and then to fall in battle against Gog and Magog. This opinion about an inferior Messiah did not arise till after the temple's destruction and was never general, so that Menasseh Ben Israel calls it 'an imagination of the ancients.'...
>
> The origin of the fiction of Messiah Ben Joseph is difficult of explanation; some as Glaesener and De Wette supposing it to have arisen from a desire to explain the gathering of the ten tribes out of the whole earth; and their restoration to the land of Canaan; others as Schoettgen, attributing it to the influence of Christianity; others still as Hengstenberg, believing that the Jews were obliged to assume a second Messiah by the passages in the Old Testament supposed to refer to Messiah's death, especially Zechariah 12:10. After Messiah Ben Joseph is raised from the dead along with others,

> by Messiah Ben David and Elias we hear no more of him." – "The Jewish Messiah" as printed in *The Theological Review*, Issue No. XXVIII, Samuel Davidson, 1870, p. 20

In stunning fashion, the rabbinical predictions align with the Antichrist prophecies in the books of Daniel (where the Antichrist dies in battle) and Revelation (where he returns as conqueror and ruler of the whole earth). Could the death and resurrection of the Final Nephilim be viewed as a fulfillment of the nonbiblical prophecies of Messiah Ben Joseph and Messiah Ben David? It is at least a coincidence worth consideration.

ANTICHRIST ENTERS THE TEMPLE AND DEMANDS WORSHIP

> "Let no man deceive you by any means: for that day shall not come, except there come a falling away first, and that man of sin be revealed, the son of perdition; Who opposeth and exalteth himself above all that is called God, or that is worshipped; so that he as God sitteth in the temple of God, shewing himself that he is God." – 2 Thessalonians 2:3–4

It is at this point that the Son of Perdition will enter the rebuilt Third Temple and proclaim that he, in fact, is God. This will no doubt be met with resounding praise and jubilation among much of the world. And many of the Jewish nation will also be caught in the delusion. Helen Maclachlan came to this very conclusion:

> "In the third verse, the Greek stands thus: 'and all the earth wondered after the beast.' The resurrection of this *false Christ* will be Satan's masterpiece to deceive the Jews, who will thus be brought

to worship the dragon; and then they will worship the beast on account of his great power and deceivableness in performing lying wonders to substantiate his resurrection, saying '*I am Christ.*' The miracles will be real, but their purpose *false* to prove *the lie,* which shall deceive, if it were possible, the very elect and will impose upon all those 'whose names are not written in the book of life of the Lamb' (verse 8). There will be no multitudinous sects then in that land; only two distinct parties one for God and one for the beast." – *Notes on the Book of Revelation*, Helen Maclachlan, 1869, p. 162

As he attempted in the days of Noah, the Devil will use a Nephilim to counter the fulfillment of God's prophecy. In this final act of treachery, there will be many apostate Christian churches, pagan religions, and occult practitioners that will be absolutely enthralled by the charms and demonic superpowers of the Antichrist. There will no doubt be countless churches, likely teaching heretical or watered-down versions of the Christian faith, that will turn their affections to the seed of the Devil and lead their churches in the worship and exaltation of the Beast. Jesus Christ warned of this, as recorded in the book of Matthew:

"And as [Jesus] sat upon the mount of Olives, the disciples came unto him privately, saying, Tell us, when shall these things be? **and what shall be the sign of thy coming, and of the end of the world**? And Jesus answered and said unto them, Take heed that no man deceive you. For many shall come in my name, saying, I am Christ; and shall deceive many.... Then if any man shall say unto you, Lo, here is Christ, or there; believe it not. **For there shall arise false Christs, and false prophets, and shall shew great signs and wonders**; insomuch that, if it were possible, they shall deceive the very elect. Behold, I have told you before." – Matthew 24:3–5, 23–25

When asked what would be the signature warning of the end of the world and His return, Jesus Christ's first response was that there would be "deception." Unprecedented global deception would take place as false Christs and false prophets would preach their lies to society. The Antichrist, Jesus said, will be the ultimate fulfillment of this treachery, pulling many—even "former Christians"—under his sway. This is commonly known as the "apostasy"—a turn from sound biblical doctrine toward a false religious system that will hearken the arrival of the Antichrist. The Apostle Paul foretold this in the book of 1 Thessalonians:

> "Now we beseech you, brethren, by the coming of our Lord Jesus Christ, and by our gathering together unto him, That ye be not soon shaken in mind, or be troubled, neither by spirit, nor by word, nor by letter as from us, as that the day of Christ is at hand. Let no man deceive you by any means: for that day shall not come, except there come a falling away [*apostaseia*] first, and that man of sin be revealed, the son of perdition." – 2 Thessalonians 2:1–3

The "lukewarm" churches that teach spurious doctrines like Jesus being "one of many ways to Heaven," that the Bible was not divinely inspired, or some type of works-based salvation will be prime candidates for ushering in the arrival of the Beast. The delusion will be so powerful and compelling that the Lord Jesus Christ warned that, if it were possible, it could deceive the "very elect" of God.

The Antichrist's proclamation of himself as God in the Temple will bring an abrupt end to the sacrifices that had been so abundant for the first three and a half years of his career. This moment will be the abomination of desolation.

THE ABOMINATION OF DESOLATION

> "And one week shall establish the covenant with many: and in the midst of the week my sacrifice and drink-offering shall be taken away: and on the temple *shall be* the abomination of desolations; and at the end of time an end shall be put to the desolation." – Daniel 9:27, LXX

Like his prior incarnation, Antiochus Epiphanes, the Final Nephilim will commit the second abomination of desolation. This will be a desecration of the Temple of God in such a blasphemous way that it becomes "desolate"—emptied of any true worship of Yahweh. Recall that Antiochus Epiphanes (whose name means "God manifest") did this by sacrificing a pig on the altar of God as an offering to Satan (1 Maccabees 1:54). The Antichrist will do so by sitting in the Temple, proclaiming himself to be God and allowing his "image" to receive mandatory global worship.

In the Old Testament, an "abomination" was another name for a pagan idol:

> "Cursed be the man that **maketh any graven or molten image, an abomination unto the LORD,** the work of the hands of the craftsman, and putteth it in a secret place. And all the people shall answer and say, Amen." – Deuteronomy 27:15

> "(For ye know how we have dwelt in the land of Egypt; and how we came through the nations which ye passed by; **And ye have seen their abominations, and their idols**, wood and stone, silver and gold, which were among them)." – Deuteronomy 29:16–17

> "**And Josiah took away all the abominations out of all the countries** that pertained to the children of Israel, and made all that were present in Israel to serve, even to serve the LORD their God.

> And all his days they departed not from following the LORD, the God of their fathers." – 2 Chronicles 34:33

After the Antichrist proclaims himself as god, he will place his image in the Temple to be worshiped. Jesus Christ prophesied this profane event:

> "When ye therefore shall see the abomination of desolation, spoken of by Daniel the prophet, stand in the holy place, (whoso readeth, let him understand:) Then let them which be in Judaea flee into the mountains." – Matthew 24:15–16

The "holy place" is the inner sanctuary of the rebuilt Temple where the image of the Beast will be erected. This ceremony will also bring an end to the Temple sacrifice—precisely what the Antichrist did in his prior manifestation on Earth as Antiochus Epiphanes. In the verse above from Daniel 9, we read that in the "midst of the week," or the midpoint of the seventieth week of Daniel, God's "sacrifice and drink offering shall be taken away." This prohibition against the worship of the Lord will be a key sign of the Antichrist's reign. In place of the daily sacrifice will be the image of the Beast—the one created under the leadership of the False Prophet, the religious cohort of the Antichrist.

FALSE PROPHET ESTABLISHES ONE-WORLD RELIGION OF ANTICHRIST

> "And I beheld another beast coming up out of the earth; and he had two horns like a lamb, and he spake as a dragon. And he exerciseth all the power of the first beast before him, **and causeth the earth and them which dwell therein to worship the first beast**, whose deadly wound was healed. And he doeth great

wonders, so that he maketh fire come down from heaven on the earth in the sight of men, And deceiveth them that dwell on the earth by the means of those miracles which he had power to do in the sight of the beast; saying to them that dwell on the earth, that they should make an image to the beast, which had the wound by a sword, and did live. And he had power to give life unto the image of the beast, that the image of the beast should both speak, and cause that as many as would not worship the image of the beast should be killed." – Revelation 13:12–15

Assisting the Final Nephilim in his conquest of the Earth will be the False Prophet, the religious emissary of the Antichrist who will lead the entire world in the worship of Apollyon. Revelation describes the False Prophet as having "horns like a lamb" and speaking "as a dragon" (Revelation 13:12). This is the ultimate fulfillment of Jesus Christ's prophetic warning recorded in Matthew 7:

"Beware of false prophets, which come to you in sheep's clothing, but inwardly they are ravening wolves." – Matthew 7:15

The False Prophet spiritually will have the appearance of a "lamb," seemingly a kind, loving, and godly religious leader. But his words will be inspired by Satan, hence Scripture's statement that he will speak "as a dragon." Rather than use his charisma and popularity to exalt Yahweh, he will deceive the world into worshiping the Antichrist.

FALSE PROPHET COMPLETES SATANIC "TRINITY"

"For there are three that bear record in heaven, the Father, the Word, and the Holy Ghost: and these three are one." – 1 John 5:7

> "And I saw three unclean spirits like frogs come out of the mouth of the dragon, and out of the mouth of the beast, and out of the mouth of the false prophet." – Revelation 16:13

As part of the establishment of the one-world religion, the Devil will even mimic the concept of the Trinity—God existing as three distinct persons, the Father, the Son, and the Holy Ghost. The verse from 1 John above confirms that all three "are one" in nature at the same time. In Scripture, the Father, the Son, and the Holy Spirit are all referred to as "God" on separate occasions, and only quantum physics can come close to providing an earthly explanation of how the Godhead can exist separately but be the same all at once. Satan will attempt a false mockery of this by endowing the False Prophet with "all the power of the first beast" (Revelation 13:12). They will thus be equal in their dark power and occult spiritual energy.

FALSE PROPHET: BLASPHEMOUS PARODY OF THE HOLY SPIRIT

The Lord Jesus Christ said of the Holy Spirit:

> "And I will pray the Father, and he shall give you another Comforter, that he may abide with you for ever; Even the Spirit of truth; whom the world cannot receive, because it seeth him not, neither knoweth him: but ye know him; for he dwelleth with you, and shall be in you.... But the Comforter, which is the Holy Ghost, whom the Father will send in my name, he shall teach you all things, and bring all things to your remembrance, whatsoever I have said unto you." – John 14:16–17, 26

The Holy Spirit, who is God, indwells a born-again believer when he or she trusts in the saving work of Jesus Christ on the cross. The Holy Spirit then helps Christians learn and understand God's Word and convicts them of their sin, building them up towards their ultimate destiny as the sinless, perfected followers of Christ they will be in the afterlife and eternity.

In a spiritual antithesis, the False Prophet will instruct the world in the worship of Antichrist. He will at first appear to be acting as a righteous leader, but will subtly exalt the Final Nephilim as the Savior. He will use his supernatural power to win the world over from whatever religion, spirituality, or atheism they once held. Writing in the early twentieth century, end-times prophecy researcher Sidney Watson confirmed this parallel:

> "As God had ever had a Trinity of personality and power in Himself, so Satan in his damnable, deceivable, counterfeiting has now *his* trinity. Himself (Satan) the embodiment of evil, the suggester, creator, energizer, he makes a *mock* Christ (Apollyon), the Antichrist, answers to the second Person of the divine Trinity. While Apollyon's chaplain, the false prophet, answers to the third person of the divine Trinity." – *The Mark of the Beast*, Sidney Watson, 1918, p. 171

FALSE PROPHET CALLS FIRE FROM HEAVEN

Revelation 13 states that the False Prophet will have the power to "doeth great wonders, so that he maketh fire come down from heaven on the earth in the sight of men" (Revelation 13:13). There will no doubt be extreme shock and awe when the Antichrist sits in the Temple of God and proclaims himself to be God. However, from the Jewish perspective, that concern could be allayed if the False Prophet calls down fire from Heaven "in the sight" of the people—which, in the Old Testament, was a sign of God's approval of a sacrifice.

It is interesting to note that throughout biblical history, at the specific places where God commanded worship, fire from Heaven always led to an immediate reaction from the people of Israel. The first example occurs in Leviticus chapter 9, when Aaron—having just been consecrated as the first high priest—makes his inaugural sacrifice in the Tabernacle:

> "And Aaron lifted up his hand toward the people, and blessed them, and came down from offering of the sin offering, and the burnt offering, and peace offerings. And Moses and Aaron went into the tabernacle of the congregation, and came out, and blessed the people: and the glory of the LORD appeared unto all the people. **And there came a fire out from before the LORD**, and consumed upon the altar the burnt offering and the fat: which **when all the people saw, they shouted, and fell on their faces**." – Leviticus 9:22–24

After conquering the last of the Nephilim giants in the Promised Land as recorded in 1 Chronicles chapter 20, King David fell into a sin that led to miraculous fire coming from Heaven:

> "And it came to pass after this, that there arose war at Gezer with the Philistines; at which time Sibbechai the Hushathite slew Sippai, that was of the children of the giant: and they were subdued. And there was war again with the Philistines; and Elhanan the son of Jair slew Lahmi the brother of Goliath the Gittite, whose spear staff was like a weaver's beam. And yet again there was war at Gath, where was a man of great stature, whose fingers and toes were four and twenty, six on each hand, and six on each foot and he also was the son of the giant. But when he defied Israel, Jonathan the son of Shimea David's brother slew him. These were born unto the giant in Gath; and they fell by the hand of David, and by the hand of his servants." – 1 Chronicles 20:4–8

In *Judgment of the Nephilim*, I noted that this was a very significant event.

With the last of his postdiluvian hybrids destroyed, the next passage of Scripture documents one of the few, rare instances where Satan takes direct action against a person:

> "And Satan stood up against Israel, and provoked David to number Israel." – 1 Chronicles 21:1

This numbering of the armies of Israel was a grave sin in the eyes of God. Measuring military might was a sign of arrogant self-reliance and belief in human might, rather than trust in God to deliver the nation (which He had done on dozens of occasions in history to that point). The Devil put the idea of a census into David's heart, and the king fell for the deception. Angered by David's action, God strangely gave the king a choice of what judgment he should suffer for his sin:

> "So Gad came to David, and said unto him, Thus saith the LORD, Choose thee Either three years' famine; or three months to be destroyed before thy foes, while that the sword of thine enemies overtaketh thee; or else three days the sword of the LORD, even the pestilence, in the land, and the angel of the LORD destroying throughout all the coasts of Israel. Now therefore advise thyself what word I shall bring again to him that sent me. And David said unto Gad, I am in a great strait: let me fall now into the hand of the LORD; for very great are his mercies: but let me not fall into the hand of man. So the LORD sent pestilence upon Israel: and there fell of Israel seventy thousand men." – 1 Chronicles 21:11–14

This peculiar passage demonstrates God's heart and David's wise understanding and deep relationship with Him. David chose the "third option," because it involved a punishment by God's Hand rather than a chastening at the hands of man. Why? Because David knew that God's mercy was far greater than His anger. While people may mercilessly seek vengeance, the Lord wants to forgive His children. We read in 2 Peter that God is "not willing that any should perish, but that all should come to repentance" (2 Peter 3:9). When David repented at the threshing floor of Ornan, Yahweh had mercy on him. The Lord confirmed His forgiveness with fire from Heaven:

> "So David gave to Ornan for the place six hundred shekels of gold by weight. And David built there an altar unto the LORD, and offered burnt offerings and peace offerings, **and called upon the LORD; and he answered him from heaven by fire upon the altar of burnt offering**. And the LORD commanded the angel; and he put up his sword again into the sheath thereof." – 1 Chronicles 21:25–26

This threshing floor at Ornan was the very location where King Solomon, David's son, would later build the Temple in accordance with the Lord's command. At the celebration of the Temple's completion, Solomon offered the Lord a beautiful, lengthy prayer in which he pleaded that The Lord would "hear from Heaven" and that God would answer the people of Israel when they sinned and repented. See below an excerpt of Solomon's prayer—and God's dramatic response:

> "Yet if they bethink themselves in the land whither they are carried captive, and turn and pray unto thee in the land of their captivity, saying, We have sinned, we have done amiss, and have dealt wickedly; If they return to thee with all their heart and with all their soul in the land of their captivity, whither they have carried them captives, and pray toward their land, which thou gavest unto their fathers, and toward the city which thou hast chosen, and toward the house which I have built for thy name: Then hear thou from the heavens, even from thy dwelling place, their prayer and their supplications, and maintain their cause, and forgive thy people

> which have sinned against thee.
>
> Now when Solomon had made an end of praying, **the fire came down from heaven, and consumed the burnt offering and the sacrifices**; and the glory of the LORD filled the house. And the priests could not enter into the house of the LORD, because the glory of the LORD had filled the LORD's house. **And when all the children of Israel saw how the fire came down, and the glory of the LORD upon the house, they bowed themselves with their faces to the ground upon the pavement, and worshipped**, and praised the LORD, saying, For he is good; for his mercy endureth for ever." – 2 Chronicles 6:37–39, 7:1–3

In each instance, the fire from Heaven was a sign of God's approval that immediately prompted those who witnessed it to fall to worship. As satanic deception reaches its pinnacle during the end times, the False Prophet will mimic this supernatural feat—no doubt, to lure Israel and the world into bowing before the Beast.

SATAN: ALWAYS LIMITED BY GOD'S AUTHORITY

The False Prophet's miracle of calling down fire from Heaven won't be the first time satanic power has been used to accomplish this feat. We find the initial instance of this happening in the book of Job, where we read that the Lord gave the Devil limited authority to inflict pain upon the faithful man of God:

> "Now there was a day when the sons of God came to present themselves before the LORD, and Satan came also among them. And the LORD said unto Satan, Whence comest thou? Then Satan answered the LORD, and said, From going to and fro in the earth, and from walking up and down in it. And the LORD aid unto Satan,

> Hast thou considered my servant Job, that there is none like him in the earth, a perfect and an upright man, one that feareth God, and escheweth evil? hen Satan answered the LORD, and said, Doth Job fear God for nought?
>
> Hast not thou made an hedge about him, and about his house, and about all that he hath on every side? thou hast blessed the work of his hands, and his substance is increased in the land. But put forth thine hand now, and touch all that he hath, and he will curse thee to thy face. And the LORD said unto Satan, Behold, all that he hath is in thy power; only upon himself put not forth thine hand. So Satan went forth from the presence of the LORD." – Job 1:6–12

In this account, Satan (standing in Heaven with the sons of God, or *B'nai Ha Elohim*—the same class of angels that fathered the Nephilim in Genesis 6) confirmed that he had not been able to harm Job because God had put a "hedge" of protection around Job to shield him from his spiritual enemies. However, we read here that God responded to Satan by removing that hedge and permitting the Devil to harm Job's possessions—but not Job personally. With that, Satan set out to wipe out everything Job cherished, giving us a glimpse into the supernatural power he wields:

> "And there was a day when his sons and his daughters were eating and drinking wine in their eldest brother's house: And there came a messenger unto Job, and said, The oxen were plowing, and the asses feeding beside them: And the Sabeans fell upon them, and took them away; yea, they have slain the servants with the edge of the sword; and I only am escaped alone to tell thee. While he was yet speaking, there came also another, and said, **The fire of God is fallen from heaven**, and hath burned up the sheep, and the servants, and consumed them; and I only am escaped alone to tell thee." – Job 1:13–16

Note that the first thing the Devil did was murder Job's children. This should drive home the heart and intent of the Adversary. Satan despises humanity—specifically, those who trust and believe in Jesus Christ. If not for God's restraining presence, Satan would wipe out the entire race. This is precisely why God intervened in the days of Noah, saving humanity with the Flood. There were only eight purely human people left on Earth who feared God.

During the Great Tribulation, the Lord will intervene once again, because, absent Christ's Second Coming, "there should be no flesh saved" (Matthew 24:22). The account from Job reveals that the Devil has the ability to call fire from Heaven—so much so that the messenger who spoke to Job *assumed it had come from God*. It was a "lying wonder." However, it's important to remember that nothing is done outside of the Lord's authority. When the prophet Elijah was in a contest with the prophets of Baal to see who worshiped the true God of the universe, the Devil was unable to call fire from Heaven because, on this occasion, God had not given His permission:

> "And Elijah said unto the prophets of Baal, Choose you one bullock for yourselves, and dress it first; for ye are many; and call on the name of your gods, but put no fire under. And they took the bullock which was given them, and they dressed it, and called on the name of Baal from morning even until noon, saying, O Baal, hear us. **But there was no voice, nor any that answered**. And they leaped upon the altar which was made. And it came to pass at noon, that Elijah mocked them, and said, Cry aloud: for he is a god; either he is talking, or he is pursuing, or he is in a journey, or peradventure he sleepeth, and must be awaked.
>
> And they cried aloud, and cut themselves after their manner with knives and lancets, till the blood gushed out upon them. And it came to pass, when midday was past, and they prophesied until the time of the offering of the evening sacrifice, **that there was neither voice, nor any to answer, nor any that regarded**." – 1 Kings

18:25–29

Never doubt God's control over all events. Even when the world is descending into abject wickedness and rejection of the Gospel, He is still on the throne and controlling what the fallen angels can do. During the Day of the Lord, Satan will again be permitted to grant his False Prophet authority over fire, as it will serve as part of the strong delusion that will usher in the worship of the Final Nephilim. Helen Maclachlan arrived at the same conclusion:

> "This is the Jewish false prophet, who with the beast and the great red dragon will complete a *blasphemous* parody of the Holy Trinity. He is the chief of the false prophets predicted by the Lord (coming up out of the *earth* or land of Israel—verse 11) and will be the very worst false shepherd whom Jesus said to his people, 'Beware of false prophets which come to you in sheep's clothing but inwardly they are ravening wolves'.... It is supposed the fire which the false prophet will really bring down from heaven, as Satan did in days of Job, will be used for the daily services of the desecrated temple, and be esteemed *sacred* by the deceived antichristian Jews." – *The Apocalyptic Jesus—Priest and Prince, Being Notes on the Book of Revelation*, Helen Maclachlan, 1885, p. 165–166

FALSE PROPHET FORESHADOWED THROUGOUT THE BIBLE

The first clear types and shadows of the False Prophet were Jannes and Jambres, Pharaoh's chief magicians during the Exodus:

> "And Moses was fourscore years old, and Aaron fourscore and three years old, when they spake unto Pharaoh. And the LORD spake

unto Moses and unto Aaron, saying, When Pharaoh shall speak unto you, saying, Shew a miracle for you: then thou shalt say unto Aaron, Take thy rod, and cast it before Pharaoh, and it shall become a serpent. And Moses and Aaron went in unto Pharaoh, and they did so as the LORD had commanded: and Aaron cast down his rod before Pharaoh, and before his servants, and it became a serpent.

Then Pharaoh also called the wise men and the sorcerers: now the magicians of Egypt, **they also did in like manner with their enchantments**. For they cast down every man his rod, and they became serpents: but Aaron's rod swallowed up their rods. And he hardened Pharaoh's heart, that he hearkened not unto them; as the LORD had said." – Exodus 7:7–13

"And Moses and Aaron did so, as the LORD commanded; and he lifted up the rod, and smote the waters that were in the river, in the sight of Pharaoh, and in the sight of his servants; and all the waters that were in the river were turned to blood. And the fish that was in the river died; and the river stank, and the Egyptians could not drink of the water of the river; and there was blood throughout all the land of Egypt. **And the magicians of Egypt did so with their enchantments**: and Pharaoh's heart was hardened, neither did he hearken unto them; as the LORD had said." – Exodus 7:20–22

"Now as Jannes and Jambres withstood Moses, so do these also resist the truth: men of corrupt minds, reprobate concerning the faith." – 2 Timothy 3:8

These two occult practitioners were able to copy the miraculous acts performed by Moses and Aaron. It is critical to understand that these were actual, literal miracles. They were not merely tricks or sleight-of-hand; these men were able to tap into satanic power to copy the first three wonders that God's servants performed. And each time, the false wonder served as a way to lure Pharaoh away from listening to God. In like manner, the False Prophet will perform actual supernatural feats to turn the hearts and minds of society away from Yahweh and towards worship of the Final Nephilim.

> "Indeed it would seem that Moses and Aaron were signal types of these Witnesses, and Jannes and Jambres of antichrist and the false prophet; the analogy is remarkable and precise—Moses and Aaron witnessed for the Lord and wrought genuine and astounding miracles; Jannes and Jambres witnessed for Pharaoh, and sought to counteract the Lord s servants by magical illusions and lying wonders!" – *Israel's Future, Lectures Delivered in the Lock Chapel, in Lent*, Capel Molyneux, 1853, p. 101

Referencing the power of the False Prophet to "give life" to the image of the Beast, a seventeenth-century commentary also identified the prophetic pattern connecting this future event back to the Exodus:

> "The False Prophet has power to give life to the Image, as Jannes and Jambres imitated the wonders that Moses wrought." – *The Holy Bible Containing New and Old Testament, with Commentary*, Theodorus Beza, 1679, p. 240

FALSE PROPHET: JUDAS RESURRECTED?

In the early Church, one theory held that the False Prophet was to be a resurrected Judas:

> "The considerations offered by this writer as favoring this opinion are that the characteristics of 'The false Prophet,' as here offered to our notice, were typified in the former life of Judas. Does this beast exercise all the power of the first or kingly beast? In his betrayal of

Jesus, Judas appears as leader of the band that took Jesus. He acts out the plans of the wicked [Sanhedrin]. They hated Christ, and he sold himself to them. Is the false prophet partly like a lamb, and partly like a dragon? Judas meets Jesus with a kiss, and the salutation, 'Hail Master;' while he says to His enemies, 'Hold Him fast.'

He furthers the wish of the rulers of apostate Israel. He counsels them. He leads the way. He accomplishes their end for them. He professed great love for the poor yet was influenced by thievish avarice The false prophet presides over the worship of the empire of Antichrist Judas was ordained an apostle of the Christian faith Satan enters him and he is made an apostle of the Devil's son....

There is something peculiar in the description of what became of Judas after death. He went 'to his own place,' as if reserved for some future time and work on the side of evil, as the Two Witnesses, Enoch and Elijah, on the side of good. He and the Man of Sin are the only two to whom the title of 'Son of Perdition' is applied. This is not distinctive of them as going into perdition, for that is the common lot of multitudes of others. A son of perdition is rather one begotten and born of perdition, one that comes forth from hell, **which would be most eminently true if they both are Satanically resurrected men, after having been in hell**." – *The Apocalypse, a Series of Special Lectures on the Resurrection of Jesus Christ, with Revised Text*, Vol. 2, Eighth Edition, Joseph Augustus Seiss, 1865, p. 424

FALSE PROPHET PERSUADES THE WORLD TO WORSHIP ANTICHRIST

With literal supernatural powers at his disposal, the False Prophet will emerge as the ultimate, enlightened "guru" that so much of the unsaved world is already awaiting. How effortlessly could the masses be won over when the False Prophet convinces people of all spiritual backgrounds that he is "their prophet"? As word and images of his miracles go viral, the unbelieving world will view him as an emissary from Heaven or another planet. With his "horns as a lamb," the False Prophet will have a kind demeanor and will speak the peace-loving language of much New Age and occult philosophy today—promoting the notion of "love" (with no recognition of humanity's sin) and "peace" (with open hostility towards God) on a regular basis.

The False Prophet will woo the unsaved world with a message that "all roads lead to the Savior." He'll direct people of all religions to form spiritual "oneness" and "unity" via worship of the Final Nephilim.

> "In other words, [the False Prophet] claims to be the bearer of the sum total of the Universal Wisdom, in which all reason and all revelation are fused into one great system, claimed to be the ultimatum of all truth; the sublime and absolute *Universeology*. And professing to have everything natural and supernatural thus solved and crystallized as the one eternal and perfect Wisdom, he must necessarily present himself as the one absolute apostle and teacher of all that ought to command the thought, faith, and obedience of man. The possession and exercise of the two horns of religious power certainly can mean nothing less than this." – *The Apocalypse. A Series of Special Lectures on the Revelation of Jesus Christ with Revised Text*, Vol. 2, Eighth edition, J. A. Seiss, D. D., 1865, p. 427

The False Prophet will also inspire the unsaved population to create the image of the Beast—a statue or figure of the Antichrist that will be the object of worship. This will be the final repetition of the golden statue of Nebuchadnezzar, who, as we discussed at length earlier, was a prior incarnation of the Antichrist.

Through his satanic energy, the False Prophet will "give life" to the image so that it will actually speak and demand the execution of the few souls who refuse to worship it. The setting up of this image in the Temple is the abomination of desolation. The world will also accept this leader's message as being divinely inspired, even as he paints the God of the Bible as the world's enemy.

FALLEN ANGELS: SATANIC APOSTLES OF ANTICHRIST

> "And the great dragon was cast out, that old serpent, called the Devil, and Satan, which deceiveth the whole world: he was cast out into the earth, **and his angels were cast out with him**." – Revelation 12:9

In the days of Noah, the waters came from the deep and the windows of Heaven. The end times will see a similar angelic flood completed by the rebel angels who are cast from Heaven to Earth, as detailed in Revelation 12. The reality of the Day of the Lord will be that it will truly mirror the days of Noah, when fallen angels openly manifested among humanity, took human wives, and ruled over the earth. At the head of the end-times fallen angelic government will be ten angelic kings who will be the last heads of state on Earth before they turn over their power and authority to the Final Nephilim. Although they're often described as human politicians, there is significant biblical evidence that these rulers are from the angelic realm:

> "And the ten horns which thou sawest are ten kings, which have received no kingdom as yet; but receive power as kings one hour with the beast. These have one mind, and shall give their power and strength unto the beast. These shall make war with the Lamb, and the Lamb shall overcome them: for he is Lord of lords, and King of

> kings: and they that are with him are called, and chosen, and faithful." – Revelation 17:12–14

All parts of the apocalyptic beasts in Scripture are heavenly realm beings, not humans. Thus, the horns that comprise the ten kings are fallen angels who will serve as emissaries of the Antichrist. This is the fulfillment of the ten toes of iron and miry clay that King Nebuchadnezzar (a foreshadow of the Antichrist) dreamt of, as recorded in Daniel chapter 2:

> "And the fourth kingdom shall be strong as iron: forasmuch as iron breaketh in pieces and subdueth all things: and as iron that breaketh all these, shall it break in pieces and bruise. And whereas thou sawest the feet and toes, part of potters' clay, and part of iron, the kingdom shall be divided; but there shall be in it of the strength of the iron, forasmuch as thou sawest the iron mixed with miry clay. And as the toes of the feet were part of iron, and part of clay, so the kingdom shall be partly strong, and partly broken.
>
> **And whereas thou sawest iron mixed with miry clay, they shall mingle themselves with the seed of men**: but they shall not cleave one to another, even as iron is not mixed with clay. And in the days of these kings shall the God of heaven set up a kingdom, which shall never be destroyed: and the kingdom shall not be left to other people, but it shall break in pieces and consume all these kingdoms, and it shall stand for ever." – Daniel 2:40–44

Notice that as Daniel proceeded through the description of the statue in Nebuchadnezzar's dream, he distinguished the fourth kingdom from the ten toes, which represent the final kingdom in the end times. This is where we see the infamous prophecy that "they shall mingle themselves with the seed of men" (Daniel 2:43). The pronoun "they" in the passage refers to something other than humanity—namely, the angelic realm.

This was certainly the understanding in the early Church. Hippolytus, writing in the second century, understood that fallen angels will be a major part of the deception, as they will also inspire the world to worship the Antichrist:

> "Behold the deceit of the enemy, know the machinations of the beguiler, how he seeks to darken the mind of men utterly. For [the Antichrist] will show forth his demons brilliant like angels, and he will bring in hosts of the incorporeal without number. And in the presence of all he exhibits himself as taken up into heaven with trumpets and sounds, and the mighty shouting of those who hail him with indescribable hymns; the heir of darkness himself shining like light, and at one time soaring to the heavens, and at another descending to the earth, with great glory and again, charging the demons, like angels, to execute his behests with much fear and trembling.
>
> Then will he send the cohorts of the demons among mountains and caves and dens of the earth, to track out those who have been concealed from his eyes and to bring them forward to worship him. And those who yield to him he will seal with his seal; but those who refuse to submit to him he will consume with incomparable pains and bitterest torments and machinations, such as never have been, nor have reached the ear of man, nor have been seen by the eye of mortals." – *Appendix to Part II of the Works of Hippolytus*, ca. AD 202, as printed in *Ante-Nicene Christian Library: Irenaeus, v.2, Hippolytus, v.2, Fragments of the Third Century*, Translated by Reverend Alexander Roberts, 1869, p. 118

Imagine the shock society will experience upon seeing hundreds of thousands of angels floating in the air, filling the skies with beautiful heavenly music, and singing to coronate the Antichrist. Picture the Final Nephilim, glowing with supernatural light as he descends from the sky, his angelic servants bowing before him. And finally, envision the False Prophet, the greatest spiritual leader on earth, calling fire from Heaven and proclaiming the Antichrist as God. This would certainly fit the description of a "strong delusion." The biblical narrative makes it clear that, with the small exception of the remnant of believers living as fugitives, the entire world—the whole global population of billions of people—will worship the Antichrist. It will take a monumental deception to achieve this. And, with his fallen angelic army at his disposal, the Final Nephilim will have the means to pull off this trickery.

UFO PHENOMENA POSSIBILY PART OF FALLEN ANGELS' DECEPTION

> "Men's hearts failing them for fear, and for looking after those things which are coming on the earth: for the powers of heaven shall be shaken." – Luke 21:26

It seems that more and more official sources are confirming that the government is investigating and searching for extraterrestrial life. A recent article discloses that a classified program for locating UFOs—a program thought to have been canceled—is still in operation:

> "The *New York Times* has recently reported that a supposedly canceled Pentagon project to investigate strange aerial phenomena is still showing a pulse. The clandestine effort, originally known as the Advanced Aerospace Threat Identification Program, was said to have ended in 2012. But, apparently, it's still doing its thing under the auspices of the U.S. Office of Naval Intelligence, and with a new name: the Unidentified Aerial Phenomenon Task Force." – "Pentagon Admits UFO Program Still Exists. But Navy's Alien Sightings Don't Quite Add Up," https://www.nbcnews.com/think/opinion/pentagon-admits-ufo-

program-still-exists-navy-s-alien-sightings-ncna1235395

In Israel, a former Defense Ministry leader made the shocking proclamation that aliens not only existed, but that government leaders were aware and in communication with them:

> "A former Israeli space security chief has sent eyebrows shooting heavenward by saying that earthlings have been in contact with extraterrestrials from a 'galactic federation.'
>
> 'The Unidentified Flying Objects have asked not to publish that they are here, humanity is not ready yet,' Haim Eshed, former head of Israel's Defense Ministry's space directorate, told Israel's *Yediot Aharonot* newspaper. The interview in Hebrew ran on Friday, and gained traction after parts were published in English by the *Jerusalem Post* on Tuesday.
>
> A respected professor and retired general, Eshed said the aliens were equally curious about humanity and were seeking to understand 'the fabric of the universe.'
>
> Eshed said cooperation agreements had been signed between species, including an 'underground base in the depths of Mars' where there are American astronauts and alien representatives." – "Former Israeli Space Security Chief Says Extraterrestrials Exist, and Trump Knows about It," https://www.nbcnews.com/news/weird-news/former-israeli-space-security-chief-says-extraterrestrials-exist-trump-knows-n1250333

The British Royal Air Force has also released fifty years' worth of correspondence about and inquiries into unidentified aerial vehicles on a public website. All this leads to the question of how the UFO phenomenon fits in with the end times. Will the fallen angels, once on earth, present themselves as beings from another planet? Will they masquerade as benevolent aliens who have come to save humanity or even who created us to begin with?

John Keel, a legendary "ufologist" (although he grew to dislike this term and preferred to be called a "Fortean"), was a Korean War veteran, foreign radio correspondent, Army staffer, and successful Hollywood writer. He coined the term "men in black" and is the author of the book, *The Mothman Prophecies*, about a small town in West Virginia where citizens repeatedly reported sightings of a winged "alien" with red eyes. Keel, who died in 2009, spent years interviewing hundreds of people all over the country who claimed to have had encounters with aliens or UFOs. Having studied tens of thousands of reports on UFO sightings, not only is he considered one of the foremost UFO/alien researchers in history, but he and his work have also been the subject of several films. His research into aliens and UFOs formed the basis for much of the plot of the TV show *The X-Files,* and many science-fiction writers speculate that the main character, Fox Mulder, was based on Keel.

After decades of research, Keel concluded that the UFO/alien abduction phenomenon was *spiritual* in nature:

> "Did ancient man misinterpret UFO manifestations by placing them in religious context? Apparently not. The literature indicates that the phenomenon carefully cultivated the religious frame of reference in early times, just as the modern manifestations have carefully supported the extraterrestrial frame of reference. Operation Trojan Horse is merely the same old game in a new, updated guise. The Devil's emissaries of yesteryear have been replaced by mysterious 'men in black.' The quasi-angels of Biblical times have become magnificent spacemen. The demons, devils, and false angels were recognized as liars and plunderers by early man. The same imposters now appear as long-haired Venusians." – *Operation Trojan Horse*, Jonathan Keel, p. 215–216

Could fallen angels or demons present themselves as beings from another planet? Will they explain the Rapture of the Church as a "removal" of the "undesirable population" who were going to stop humanity's next step in evolution? The Bible says that "Satan himself is transformed into an angel of light" (2 Corinthians 11:14). Thus, it stands to reason that we shouldn't marvel if his servants masquerade as "ministers of light" as well.

ANCIENT CHURCH'S UNDERSTANDING OF THE TEN KINGS

Hippolytus interpreted the ten kings as fallen angels who will serve as the end-times government officials before Antichrist:

> "Then the lawless one, being lifted up in heart, **will gather together his demons in man's form** and will abominate those who call him to the kingdom, and will pollute many souls. **For he will appoint princes over them from among the demons.** And he will no longer seem to be pious, but altogether and in all things he will be harsh, severe, passionate, wrathful, terrible, inconstant, dread, morose, hateful, abominable, Savage, vengeful, iniquitous. And, bent on casting the whole race of men into the pit of perdition, he will multiply false signs. For when all the people greet him with their acclamations at his displays, he will shout with a strong voice, so that the place shall be shaken in which the multitudes stand by him:
>
> 'Ye peoples, and tribes, and nations, acquaint yourselves with my mighty authority and power, and the strength of my kingdom. What prince is there so great as I am? What great God is there but I? Who will stand up against my authority? Under the eye of the spectators he will remove mountains from their places, he will walk on the sea with dry feet, he will bring down fire from heaven, he

> will turn the day into darkness and the night into day, he will turn the sun about wheresoever he pleases; and in short in presence of those who behold him, he will show all the elements of earth and sea to be subject to him in the power of his specious manifestation.
>
> For if, while as yet he does not exhibit himself as the son of perdition, he raises and excites against us open war even to battles and slaughters, at that time when he shall come in his own proper person and men shall see him as he is in reality, what machinations and deceits and delusions will he not bring into play with the purpose of seducing all men, and leading them off from the way of truth, and from the gate of the Kingdom?'" – Appendix to Part II of *The Works of Hippolytus*, ca. AD 202, as printed in *Ante-Nicene Christian Library: Irenaeus, v.2, Hippolytus, v.2, Fragments of the Third Century*, Translated by Reverend Alexander Roberts, 1869, p. 116

The arrogance of the Antichrist mirrors the same heinous ambition he possessed in the days of Noah, when the fallen angel Apollyon, or the Assyrian, ruled the antediluvian world:

> "The waters made [the Assyrian] great, the deep set him up on high with her rivers running round about his plants, and sent her little rivers unto all the trees of the field. Therefore his height was exalted above all the trees of the field, and his boughs were multiplied, and his branches became long because of the multitude of waters, when he shot forth. All the fowls of heaven made their nests in his boughs, and under his branches did all the beasts of the field bring forth their young, and under his shadow dwelt all great nations. Thus was he fair in his greatness, in the length of his branches: for his root was by great waters." – Ezekiel 31:4–7

After he plants his tabernacles "between the seas in the glorious holy mountain" in Jerusalem, the Antichrist will believe he has fully achieved his goal of becoming ruler over the earth. He will delude himself into thinking he has achieved these wicked aspirations prophesied in Isaiah 14:

> "For thou hast said in thine heart, I will ascend into heaven, I will exalt my throne above the stars of God: I will sit also upon the mount of the congregation, in the sides of the north: I will ascend above the heights of the clouds; I will be like the most High." – Isaiah 14:13-16

ANTICHRIST WILL BLASPHEME GOD AND LEAD WAR AGAINST JESUS CHRIST AND ALL BELIEVERS

The Antichrist will not deny the existence of the God of the Bible. On the contrary, he will acknowledge God's presence and even that of the righteous angels and saints in Heaven. But he will blaspheme all God-fearing beings to convince the unbelieving world that Yahweh is their enemy. One of the first acts after his satanic resurrection will be to kill the Two Witnesses appointed by God to preach to the world from Jerusalem. We looked at these men earlier in the book, but let's revisit the topic, this time a little more closely. Details of the witnesses are given in Revelation chapter 11, where we read:

> "And when they shall have finished their testimony, **the beast that ascendeth out of the bottomless pit shall make war against them, and shall overcome them, and kill them**. And their dead bodies shall lie in the street of the great city, which spiritually is called Sodom and Egypt, where also our Lord was crucified. And they of the people and kindreds and tongues and nations shall see their dead bodies three days and an half, and shall not suffer their dead bodies to be put in graves.

> And they that dwell upon the earth shall rejoice over them, and make merry, and shall send gifts one to another; because these two prophets tormented them that dwelt on the earth. And after three days and an half the spirit of life from God entered into them, and they stood upon their feet; and great fear fell upon them which saw them. And they heard a great voice from heaven saying unto them, Come up hither. And they ascended up to heaven in a cloud; and their enemies beheld them." – Revelation 11:7–12

During the rise of the Antichrist to global preeminence, the Lord will endow the pair with supernatural powers to preach the gospel boldly to the world. They will be known throughout the world—and they will be despised. Anyone who attempts to hurt them will either be destroyed by fire that comes from their mouths or by drought they have the power to inflict on an entire nation.

The ministry of these intriguing personalities was foreshadowed in the Old Testament. When the Lord wanted to free Israel from bondage to Egypt, He sent two witnesses to Pharaoh: Moses and Aaron (Exodus 4). When Joshua was preparing his first battle in the conquest of the Nephilim-infested land of Canaan, he sent two witnesses to scout Jericho (Numbers 13). And in the end times, when God prepares to return to Earth, He will again appoint two men to go to Jerusalem to exhort people to repent and turn to God, supernaturally empowering them to defend themselves from any person or government seeking to do them harm. It is only at the resurrection of the Final Nephilim that the time of their testimony will have expired and the Lord will permit the Antichrist to assassinate them.

FINAL NEPHILIM EXHIBITS UNPRECEDENTED LEVELS OF EVIL

The Antichrist, being the seed of Satan and possessed by one of the most powerful fallen angels, will have the most hyper-depraved sin nature of all time. His hatred for anyone who preaches the Gospel or worships God will be unparalleled. He will assassinate the Two Witnesses in cold blood and leave their corpses in the streets of Jerusalem so that the entire world can livestream their deaths from their computers and mobile devices. The unsaved populace will be so relieved that these two "evil preachers" have been murdered that they will send gifts to each other in celebration. Imagine how twisted the minds and hearts of the world must be at this point to essentially create a holiday over the deaths of two people.

And this will just be the beginning of the reign of terror of Apollyon. In his global addresses, he will utter more blasphemy against the name of the Lord than any other leader in history. Scripture repeatedly emphasizes that a key component of his leadership will be denigrating God in order to turn the world away from salvation and into the wicked clutches of Satan:

> "**And he shall speak great words against the most High**, and shall wear out the saints of the most High, and think to change times and laws: and they shall be given into his hand until a time and times and the dividing of time." – Daniel 7:5
>
> "And the king shall do according to his will; and he shall exalt himself, and magnify himself above every god, **and shall speak marvellous things against the God of gods**, and shall prosper till the indignation be accomplished: for that that is determined shall be done." – Daniel 11:36

The prophet Daniel, in writing extensively on the Antichrist, emphasized that the evil leader will use his power of persuasive speech to slander the Lord and exalt himself above Jesus Christ. The Apostle John, in both his epistles and the book of Revelation, repeatedly identified brazen blasphemy as central trait of the Final Nephilim:

> "Little children, it is the last time: and as ye have heard that antichrist shall come, even now are there many antichrists; whereby we know that it is the last time. They went out from us, but they were not of us; for if they had been of us, they would no doubt have continued with us: but they went out, that they might be made manifest that they were not all of us. But ye have an unction from the Holy One, and ye know all things. I have not written unto you because ye know not the truth, but because ye know it, and that no lie is of the truth. **Who is a liar but he that denieth that Jesus is the Christ? He is antichrist, that denieth the Father and the Son.**" – 1 John 2:18–22

A nineteenth-century treatise on end-times prophecy emphatically supports this interpretation:

> "Antichrist is a blasphemer. The greatest blasphemy is to put oneself in the place of God, and this Antichrist does. What words can be stronger than those of [Daniel 9:36]: 'The king shall do according to his will; and he shall exalt himself; and magnify himself above every god, and shall speak marvellous things against the God of gods.' To this the testimony of St Paul remarkably agrees (2 Thessalonians 2:4), 'Who opposeth and exalteth himself above all that is called God, or that is worshipped, so he as God sitteth in the temple of God, showing himself that he is God.'
>
> He allows nothing, whether true or false, to detract from his own greatness or to stand in the way of his own glory. His object is the exaltation of himself and his own cause, and he makes every thing give way to this. 'He opened his mouth,' says St John (Revelation 13:6), 'in blasphemy against God, to blaspheme His name, and His tabernacle, and them that dwell in heaven.'" – "The Portrait of Antichrist," as printed in *The Armoury, a Magazine of Weapons of*

Christian Warfare, Volume 5, Reverend H. S. Warleigh, 1879, p. 188

Looking at society today, the notion that "Bible thumpers," or Bible-believing Christians, are bigoted, ignorant, and outdated people who should be silenced or not taken seriously is already acceptable discourse. During the Day of the Lord, with the Church removed and supernaturally empowered Nephilim and fallen angels roaming the earth, it will be easy to lure humanity into believing that not only are Christians and Messianic Jews wicked, but they need to be exterminated.

ANTICHRIST HUNTS DOWN AND KILLS BELIEVERS

"Then shall they deliver you up to be afflicted, and shall kill you: and ye shall be hated of all nations for my name's sake. And then shall many be offended, and shall betray one another, and shall hate one another. And many false prophets shall rise, and shall deceive many. And because iniquity shall abound, the love of many shall wax cold. But he that shall endure unto the end, the same shall be saved." – Jesus Christ, Matthew 24:9–13

"Declare ye in Judah, and publish in Jerusalem; and say, Blow ye the trumpet in the land: cry, gather together, and say, Assemble yourselves, and let us go into the defenced cities. Set up the standard toward Zion: retire, stay not: **for I will bring evil from the north, and a great destruction. The lion is come up from his thicket, and the destroyer of the Gentiles is on his way**; he is gone forth from his place to make thy land desolate; and thy cities shall be laid waste, without an inhabitant." – Jeremiah 4:5–7

"Now however Satan will endow with 'his power and his seat and great authority,' the beast *in its eighth head existence....* The same

> marvellous being here, called the beast, is in [Revelation 9:11] called in Hebrew, Abaddon, but in Greek, Apollyon; in Jeremiah 4:7 he is spoken of as 'the destroyer of the Gentiles,' 'the lion of the thicket,' as also by Nahum 2:1." – *The Revelation Unraveled: An Outline Exposition on a New Plan*, Reverend Winston Chester, 1867, p. 44–45

The born-again Christians who come to a saving faith in Jesus Christ during the Day of the Lord will be branded as enemies of the state who are to be hunted and killed. They will no doubt be outcasts who are despised by the non-believing members of society who have been deceived by the Final Nephilim. This persecution is confirmed frequently in Scripture:

> "And of the ten horns that were in his head, and of the other which came up, and before whom three fell; even of that horn that had eyes, and a mouth that spake very great things, whose look was more stout than his fellows. **I beheld, and the same horn made war with the saints, and prevailed against them**." – Daniel 7:20–21

> "And his power shall be mighty, but not by his own power: and he shall destroy wonderfully, and shall prosper, and practise, **and shall destroy the mighty and the holy people**." – Daniel 8:24

> "And it was given unto him to **make war with the saints, and to overcome them**." – Revelation 13:7

Through the image of the Beast, which will have the power to determine who is giving proper worship, Antichrist will enforce his self-deification under penalty of death. Anyone refusing to bow down to the image will be captured by Antichrist's hybrid army of fallen angels and deceived humans, then will be executed by beheading. And, as Hippolytus predicted in his writings, it could very well be that the multitude of fallen angels serving the Antichrist will act as the "enforcers" all over the globe, gathering "rebels" to be killed by the one-world government. That such a gruesome and primitive form of capital punishment will be acceptable by society is further evidence of how deep into rebellion the world will have fallen.

GOD RESCUES ISRAEL BY LEADING THEM TO THE WILDERNESS

> "And when the dragon saw that he was cast unto the earth, he persecuted the woman which brought forth the man child. And to the woman were given two wings of a great eagle, **that she might fly into the wilderness**, into her place, where she is nourished for a time, and times, and half a time, from the face of the serpent. And the serpent cast out of his mouth water as a flood after the woman, that he might cause her to be carried away of the flood. And the earth helped the woman, and the earth opened her mouth, and swallowed up the flood which the dragon cast out of his mouth. And the dragon was wroth with the woman, and went to make war with the remnant of her seed, which keep the commandments of God, and have the testimony of Jesus Christ." – Revelation 12:13–17

> "At the same time, saith the LORD, will I be the God of all the families of Israel, and they shall be my people. Thus saith the LORD, **The people which were left of the sword found grace in the wilderness**; even Israel, when I went to cause him to rest. The LORD hath appeared of old unto me, saying, Yea, I have loved thee with an everlasting love: therefore with lovingkindness have I drawn thee. Again I will build thee, and thou shalt be built, O virgin of Israel: thou shalt again be adorned with thy tabrets, and shalt go forth in the dances of them that make merry. Thou shalt

> yet plant vines upon the mountains of Samaria: the planters shall plant, and shall eat them as common things. For there shall be a day, that the watchmen upon the mount Ephraim shall cry, Arise ye, and let us go up to Zion unto the LORD our God." – Jeremiah 31:1–6

One of the lesser-known end-time prophecies describes Jesus Christ leading a portion of the nation of Israel into the wilderness to be supernaturally protected during the reign of the Antichrist. There, God will directly communicate with the remnant and teach them until they come to a full saving faith in the Lord Jesus Christ. With stunning clarity, the Lord proclaims that day when He will personally take away the twelve tribes to protect and preserve them during the Great Tribulation:

> "As I live, saith the Lord GOD, surely with a mighty hand, and with a stretched out arm, and with fury poured out, will I rule over you: And I will bring you out from the people, and will gather you out of the countries wherein ye are scattered, with a mighty hand, and with a stretched out arm, and with fury poured out. **And I will bring you into the wilderness of the people, and there will I plead with you face to face. Like as I pleaded with your fathers in the wilderness of the land of Egypt, so will I plead with you, saith the Lord GOD.**
>
> And I will cause you to pass under the rod, and I will bring you into the bond of the covenant: And I will purge out from among you the rebels, and them that transgress against me: I will bring them forth out of the country where they sojourn, and they shall not enter into the land of Israel: and ye shall know that I am the LORD. As for you, O house of Israel, thus saith the Lord GOD; Go ye, serve ye every one his idols, and hereafter also, if ye will not hearken unto me: but pollute ye my holy name no more with your gifts, and with your idols.

> For in mine holy mountain, in the mountain of the height of Israel, saith the Lord GOD, there shall all the house of Israel, all of them in the land, serve me: there will I accept them, and there will I require your offerings, and the firstfruits of your oblations, with all your holy things. I will accept you with your sweet savour, when I bring you out from the people, and gather you out of the countries wherein ye have been scattered; and I will be sanctified in you before the heathen. And ye shall know that I am the LORD, when I shall bring you into the land of Israel, into the country for the which I lifted up mine hand to give it to your fathers.
>
> And there shall ye remember your ways, and all your doings, wherein ye have been defiled; and ye shall loathe yourselves in your own sight for all your evils that ye have committed. And ye shall know that I am the LORD when I have wrought with you for my name's sake, not according to your wicked ways, nor according to your corrupt doings, O ye house of Israel, saith the Lord GOD." – Ezekiel 20:33–44

This amazing prophecy explains what much of Israel (the Northern ten tribes, predominately; as will be shown, the Southern tribes will remain near Jerusalem) will be doing for the final three and a half years before the official Revelation of Christ to earth. This passage merits close examination:

> "As I live, saith the Lord GOD, surely with a mighty hand, and with a stretched out arm, and with fury poured out, will I rule over you: And I will bring you out from the people, and will gather you out of the countries wherein ye are scattered, with a mighty hand, and with a stretched out arm, and with fury poured out." – Ezekiel 20:33–34

Here God speaks of the end-times gathering of Israel, which will be accomplished by the Lord Himself. God will achieve this "with a mighty hand, and a with a stretched out arm." This is the same illustrative language used by Moses when the Lord gave him the Law to present to Israel after the Exodus:

> "And Moses called all Israel, and said unto them, Hear, O Israel, the statutes and judgments which I speak in your ears this day, that ye may learn them, and keep, and do them.... And remember that thou wast a servant in the land of Egypt, **and that the LORD thy God brought thee out thence through a mighty hand and by a stretched out arm**." – Deuteronomy 5:1, 15

This is clearly a repetition of the events of the Exodus, and the Lord used the original event as a prototype through time and space for how He would fulfill His great prophecy of Israel's reconciliation in the last days.

> "And I will bring you into the wilderness of the people, and there will I plead with you face to face. Like as I pleaded with your fathers in the wilderness of the land of Egypt, so will I plead with you, saith the Lord GOD." – Ezekiel 20:35–36

These verses give full confirmation that the Exodus is a similitude of the end-times redemption of Israel. But recall that the wilderness time was not easy for the twelve tribes. It was a time to receive God's Word and to endure a period of severe testing. Continuing in Ezekiel 20:

> "And I will cause you to pass under the rod, and I will bring you into the bond of the covenant: **And I will purge out from among you the rebels, and them that transgress against me:** I will bring them forth out of the country where they sojourn, and they shall not enter into the land of Israel: and ye shall know that I am the

LORD." – Ezekiel 20:37–38

In the first wilderness journey of the Exodus, God used the forty years of wandering as a punishment of an entire generation of Israelites who had no faith that God could defeat the Nephilim populating the Promised Land:

> "And they told him, and said, We came unto the land whither thou sentest us, and surely it floweth with milk and honey; and this is the fruit of it. Nevertheless the people be strong that dwell in the land, and the cities are walled, and very great: and moreover we saw the children of Anak there. The Amalekites dwell in the land of the south: and the Hittites, and the Jebusites, and the Amorites, dwell in the mountains: and the Canaanites dwell by the sea, and by the coast of Jordan. And Caleb stilled the people before Moses, and said, Let us go up at once, and possess it; for we are well able to overcome it.
>
> But the men that went up with him said, We be not able to go up against the people; for they are stronger than we. And they brought up an evil report of the land which they had searched unto the children of Israel, saying, The land, through which we have gone to search it, is a land that eateth up the inhabitants thereof; and all the people that we saw in it are men of a great stature. **And there we saw the giants [*Nephilim*], the sons of Anak, which come of the giants:** and we were in our own sight as grasshoppers, and so we were in their sight." – Numbers 13:27–33

This event, known as "the provocation" in the book of Hebrews (chapter 4), was a pivotal moment in Israel's history. Just two to three weeks after the Exodus miracle—in which the people of Israel witnessed God unleashing supernatural judgments on Egypt and destroying Pharaoh and the Egyptian army in the Red Sea—most of the nation doubted that God could conquer three Nephilim. This not only speaks to how supernaturally large the Nephilim were, but also to the lack of faith in the hearts of the people. God was so outraged by this failure to believe that He was prepared to destroy the entire nation:

> "And the LORD said unto Moses, How long will this people provoke me? and how long will it be ere they believe me, for all the signs which I have shewed among them? I will smite them with the pestilence, and disinherit them, and will make of thee a greater nation and mightier than they. And Moses said unto the LORD, Then the Egyptians shall hear it, (for thou broughtest up this people in thy might from among them;) And they will tell it to the inhabitants of this land: for they have heard that thou LORD art among this people, that thou LORD art seen face to face, and that thy cloud standeth over them, and that thou goest before them, by day time in a pillar of a cloud, and in a pillar of fire by night.
>
> Now if thou shalt kill all this people as one man, then the nations which have heard the fame of thee will speak, saying, Because the LORD was not able to bring this people into the land which he sware unto them, therefore he hath slain them in the wilderness. And now, I beseech thee, let the power of my lord be great, according as thou hast spoken, saying, The LORD is longsuffering, and of great mercy, forgiving iniquity and transgression, and by no means clearing the guilty, visiting the iniquity of the fathers upon the children unto the third and fourth generation. Pardon, I beseech thee, the iniquity of this people according unto the greatness of thy mercy, and as thou hast forgiven this people, from Egypt even until now." – Numbers 14:11–19

The Lord was actually prepared to create an entirely new nation, with Moses being the patriarch! But Moses, a true type and shadow of Jesus Christ the Messiah, pleaded for mercy on behalf of the people, reminding God of His nature: "longsuffering, and of great mercy, forgiving iniquity and transgression." This was a picture of the work Jesus Christ does for all born-again believers in Heaven:

> "Who is he that condemneth? It is Christ that died, yea rather, that is risen again, who is even at the right hand of God, who also maketh intercession for us." (Romans 8:34)

True to His nature, God did indeed have mercy and spared much of Israel:

> "And the LORD said, I have pardoned according to thy word: But as truly as I live, all the earth shall be filled with the glory of the LORD. Because all those men which have seen my glory, and my miracles, which I did in Egypt and in the wilderness, and have tempted me now these ten times, and have not hearkened to my voice; **Surely they shall not see the land which I sware unto their fathers, neither shall any of them that provoked me see it.**" – Numbers 14:21–23

The generation that was older during the rebellion of the ten spies would die in the wilderness and not see the Promised Land. They were purged from those who would receive the blessing; this is a type and shadow of the end-times purging in Edom.

THE REMANT OF THE NORTHERN TRIBES WILL COME TO SAVING FAITH BEFORE MARCHING WITH CHRIST TO JERUSALEM

With the understanding of the Exodus wilderness journey as a foreshadow of the end times, the prophecy of Ezekiel 20 takes on greater clarity:

> "And I will cause you to pass under the rod, and I will bring you into the bond of the covenant: **And I will purge out from among you the rebels, and them that transgress against me:** I will bring them forth out of the country where they sojourn, and they shall not enter into the land of Israel: and ye shall know that I am the LORD." – Ezekiel 20:37–38

It will be in the wilderness where a large number of the end-times Israelites will be "purged," preventing them from entering the "Promised Land" of the Revelation of Christ. But a third of the nation—the faithful—will receive redemption:

> "As for you, O house of Israel, thus saith the Lord GOD; Go ye, serve ye every one his idols, and hereafter also, if ye will not hearken unto me: but pollute ye my holy name no more with your gifts, and with your idols. For in mine holy mountain, in the mountain of the height of Israel, saith the Lord GOD, there shall all the house of Israel, all of them in the land, serve me: there will I accept them, and there will I require your offerings, and the firstfruits of your oblations, with all your holy things. **I will accept you with your sweet savour, when I bring you out from the people, and gather you out of the countries wherein ye have been scattered; and I will be sanctified in you before the heathen.**
>
> And ye shall know that I am the LORD, when I shall bring you into the land of Israel, into the country for the which I lifted up mine hand to give it to your fathers. And there shall ye remember your ways, and all your doings, wherein ye have been defiled; and ye shall loathe yourselves in your own sight for all your evils that ye have committed. And ye shall know that I am the LORD when I have wrought with you for my name's sake, not according to your wicked ways, nor according to your corrupt doings, O ye house of

> Israel, saith the Lord GOD." – Ezekiel 20:39–44

This beautiful, redemptive work by God will involve a supernatural testimony to Israel. Just as Jesus spoke to the Apostle Paul (then going by the name of Saul) on the road to Damascus, converting him in moments, so too will the believing remnant of the twelve tribes receive a divine impartation of God's Spirit moving them to fervent faith in Jesus Christ. These newly redeemed servants of Christ will reject the Final Nephilim, the Mark of the Beast, and all the devices of the Devil:

> "And I will pour upon the house of David, and upon the inhabitants of Jerusalem, the spirit of grace and of supplications: and they shall look upon me whom they have pierced, and they shall mourn for him, as one mourneth for his only son, and shall be in bitterness for him, as one that is in bitterness for his firstborn. In that day shall there be a great mourning in Jerusalem, as the mourning of Hadadrimmon in the valley of Megiddo." – Zechariah 12:10–11

The "mourning in Hadadrimmon" Zechariah alluded to had taken place during the reign of King Josiah, who led the Southern Kingdom in the greatest spiritual revival of ancient Israelite history. During that time, he recited the Law to the entire nation, something that had not been done in decades. He didn't even have the Mosaic Law in his possession, and had to order priests to search the decrepit Temple to find a lone copy. Josiah also tore down all of the statues, altars, and occult objects of worship to Baal and fallen angels. Even in the Northern Kingdom, troops from Judah removed idols and returned the Ark of the Covenant to the Holy Temple of God. Occult priests and sorcerers were expelled from the kingdom, and Josiah burned the horses and chariots being used for sun worship right in front of the Temple of God.

The most stunning evidence of how far into apostasy the Israelites had fallen is that the king reestablished the Passover. This was the first observance of that sacred holiday since the days of the Judges—almost five hundred years earlier. Sadly, Josiah died in battle (**near Megiddo**) during an attempt to reunify the Northern and Southern Kingdoms. The mourning of his death among the children of Israel was so profound that the prophet Zechariah referenced it as a preview of Israel's remorse during the Great Tribulation, when they will realize that the One they rejected at His First Coming is, in fact, their Redeemer, *Yeshua.*

> "The resumed outpouring of the Spirit upon the Jewish remnant in the last days will cause them to abhor all the abominations done in the land, and make their mourning for national sin deep as for an only son; households apart; men and their wives apart; exactly as foretold here having reference to the Jewish custom, according to which, not only did the females dwell in separate apartments from the males, but also worshipped separately. This mourning is compared with the greatest ever known among the Jews; that for King Josiah, wounded at Hadadrimmon, a place in the great plain of Esdraelon near Megiddo." – *Notes on the Prophecies of Zechariah*, Helen Maclachlan, 1880, p. 67

THE FORTY-TWO MONTHS OF THE ANTICHRIST'S REIGN ARE A PROPHETIC CONNECTION THROUGH TIME BACK TO THE ORIGINAL WILDERNESS JOURNEY

As if there was a need for further confirmation, the Holy Scriptures provide another amazing correlation through time and space between the Final Nephilim and the early events of biblical history. After declaring himself to be god of the world, **the Antichrist will rule for forty-two months before**

the Revelation and Return of Jesus Christ. During this time, the Israelites (particularly, those of the Northern ten tribes) will be in the wilderness of Edom being taught and "purged" by Jesus. In the original wilderness journey recorded in the book of Exodus, we read that Jesus led Israel in a "pillar of cloud" by day and a "pillar of fire" by night to various locations through Edom. **In total, the Lord led Israel to forty-two different locations before entering the Promised Land.** These "forty-two stations of the Exodus," as they are commonly known, are listed in Numbers 33 (with additional details in Exodus and other chapters of Numbers).

This astounding quantum connection between the original Exodus and the end-times departure has been noted by many Christian commentators through the centuries. See the following, for example:

> "As Israel was in the wilderness forty years, and had forty-two stages in her journey, so the Church for *forty-two* months, three and a half years or times, literal seasons used for years in Hellenistic Greek (*Kairous*, Daniel 7:25; 12:7) or 1260 days (v 6) between the overthrow of Jerusalem and the coming again of Christ, shall be a wilderness-sojourner before she reaches her millennial rest (answering to Canaan of old)." – *A Commentary, Critical and Explanatory, on the Old and New Testaments*, Reverends Robert Jamieson, A. R. Fausset, David Brown, 1878, p. 581

PETRA: STRONGHOLD FOR END-TIMES ISRAEL?

One of the main buildings in the Ancient city of Petra

Many theologians and Bible prophecy researchers have speculated that the city of Petra, an ancient stone fortress caved out of the side of a mountain in the region of Edom, could be the place where the Israelites will live for the final forty-two months of the Antichrist's reign (one of the buildings in the complex is pictured above):

> "While the 'place prepared' therein may very probably be Petra in the wilderness of Edom, where a 'city of habitations,' cut out of the solid rock and ready for immediate occupation, has not long since been discovered. Be this, however, as it may, it is specially worthy of notice that the time for which the woman is to be thus sheltered in the wilderness, 'a thousand two hundred and threescore days' (verse 6), or 'time, times, and half a time' (verse 14) is identical with that of the exercise of the power of the last Antichrist, 'forty and two months' (Revelation 13:5) and 'of the treading under foot of the holy city' by the Gentiles 'forty and two months' and 'the prophesying of the two witnesses a thousand two hundred and threescore days' (Revelation 11:2–3)—all so many modes of expressing the one definite period of three years and a half." – "The Symbolism of Revelation XII," as printed in, *The Prophetic News and Israel's Watchman, New Series,* Reverend Richard Chester, 1861, p. 381

Psalm 60 hints at Petra being the "strong city" in Edom to where Jesus will lead the Northern tribes:

> "Who will bring me into the strong city? who will lead me into Edom? Wilt not thou, O God, which hadst cast us off? and thou, O God, which didst not go out with our armies? Give us help from trouble: for vain is the help of man. Through God we shall do

> valiantly: for he it is that shall tread down our enemies." – Psalm 60:9–12

Also recall that in Daniel 11:41, which foretells the military campaigns of the Antichrist, Edom is listed as one of 3 areas The Final Nephilim **never conquers**, making it a safe haven for the remnant. Not up for debate is that this is *when* the fulfillment of Israel's reconciliation will take place. Hosea chapter 2 contains a beautiful prophecy of Jesus reuniting with the believing remnant in Edom:

> "**Therefore, behold, I will allure her, and bring her into the wilderness**, and speak comfortably unto her. And I will give her her vineyards from thence, and the valley of Achor for a door of hope: and she shall sing there, as in the days of her youth, and as in the day when she came up out of the land of Egypt. And it shall be at that day, saith the LORD, that thou shalt call me Ishi; and shalt call me no more Baali. For I will take away the names of Baalim out of her mouth, and they shall no more be remembered by their name."
> – Hosea 2:14–17

With loving, marital language, this expresses that God will bless the believing remnant while they're in the wilderness of Edom, exactly where Jesus led them thousands of years earlier. And, once again, prophecy loops back through time to the Exodus, as the text states that Israel will sing "as in the day when she came up out of the land of Egypt." Jesus will then remove all of the idolatry from the nation. Continuing in Hosea 2:

> "And in that day will I make a covenant for them with the beasts of the field and with the fowls of heaven, and with the creeping things of the ground: **and I will break the bow and the sword and the battle out of the earth, and will make them to lie down safely. And I will betroth thee unto me for ever;** yea, I will betroth thee

> unto me in righteousness, and in judgment, and in lovingkindness, and in mercies. I will even betroth thee unto me in faithfulness: and thou shalt know the LORD." – Hosea 2:18–20

As previously noted, the time when animals will be at peace with humanity is during the Millennial Reign of Christ. It will also be a period when weapons will be destroyed or turned into tools. Israel will "dwell safely" in her own land without a need for defensive walls. God will have completed His mission of reinstalling faith, forgiveness, and salvation in the hearts of the once wayward nation of Israel.

> "And it shall come to pass in that day, I will hear, saith the LORD, I will hear the heavens, and they shall hear the earth; And the earth shall hear the corn, and the wine, and the oil; and they shall hear Jezreel. And I will sow her unto me in the earth; and I will have mercy upon her that had not obtained mercy; and I will say to them which were not my people, Thou art my people; and they shall say, Thou art my God." – Hosea 2:21–23

THE 144,000 AND REMAINING JEWISH BELIEVERS SUFFER PERSECUTION

> "And the dragon was wroth with the woman, and went to make war with the remnant of her seed, which keep the commandments of God, and have the testimony of Jesus Christ." – Revelation 12:17

We must not forget that thwarting God's final plan of salvation of Israel is a paramount goal of the Devil and his False Messiah. Therefore, no Israelite will be spared from the murderous bloodlust of the Final Nephilim. The nation that Satan has tried to exterminate throughout human history will finally be in the palms of his hands, with two-thirds of the population being deceived into thinking that Antichrist is their Savior. Instead, following the abomination of desolation, the evil tyrant will betray Israel and seek to destroy the entire nation altogether. This was prophesied throughout the Old Testament with references to the "Assyrian"—one of the ancient titles for Antichrist.

God warned Israel through the prophets that the Assyrian would be a cruel, murderous leader in their midst. This was God's punishment for His nation's rampant disobedience.

The ten tribes comprising the Northern Kingdom will be "nourished in the wilderness." In the antediluvian age, Noah and his family were safe inside the ark while the rest of the world was completely wiped out by the supernatural Flood judgment of God. Sodom and Gomorrah could not be destroyed until Lot and his family safely escaped. In the end times, the Devil will mimic God with his own "flood" of fallen angels (both falling from Heaven and ascending from the deep like the waters of the Flood) in an attempt to destroy Israel. But the believing third of the population, the remnant of the Northern Kingdom, will be kept safe in "the wilderness."

Once the remnant is safely in hiding, the Devil will no doubt target the 144,000 witnesses designated by God in Revelation 7:

> "And I saw another angel ascending from the east, having the seal of the living God: and he cried with a loud voice to the four angels, to whom it was given to hurt the earth and the sea, Saying, Hurt not the earth, neither the sea, nor the trees, till we have sealed the servants of our God in their foreheads. And I heard the number of them which were sealed: and there were sealed an hundred and forty and four thousand of all the tribes of the children of Israel." – Revelation 7:2–4

The witnesses, selected from the twelve tribes of Israel, will proclaim the Gospel of the Kingdom—the message that the Kingdom of God is at hand and Messiah will soon arrive, in the first half of the Antichrist's career. Like the Two Witnesses of Jerusalem, this throng of witnesses will certainly be a thorn in the side of the unsaved world. Their deaths are confirmed in Revelation 14, where we find them in Heaven:

> "And I looked, and, lo, a Lamb stood on the mount Sion, and with him an hundred forty and four thousand, having his Father's name written in their foreheads. And I heard a voice from heaven, as the voice of many waters, and as the voice of a great thunder: and I heard the voice of harpers harping with their harps: And they sung as it were a new song before the throne, and before the four beasts, and the elders: and no man could learn that song but the hundred and forty and four thousand, which were redeemed from the earth.
>
> These are they which were not defiled with women; for they are virgins. These are they which follow the Lamb whithersoever he goeth. These were redeemed from among men, being the firstfruits unto God and to the Lamb. And in their mouth was found no guile: for they are without fault before the throne of God." – Revelation 14:1–5

It is important to note that "**Mt. Sion" is in Heaven,** and the Mt. Zion on Earth is a mere reflection of it. Along with this attack, Antichrist will initiate his mandatory system of worship under penalty of death, wherein all the born-again Christians who come to saving faith in Jesus Christ during the Day of the Lord will be executed for their faith. God even makes a special proclamation for all of the martyrs of this era:

> "And the third angel followed them, saying with a loud voice, If any man worship the beast and his image, and receive his mark in

> his forehead, or in his hand, The same shall drink of the wine of the wrath of God, which is poured out without mixture into the cup of his indignation; and he shall be tormented with fire and brimstone in the presence of the holy angels, and in the presence of the Lamb: And the smoke of their torment ascendeth up for ever and ever: and they have no rest day nor night, who worship the beast and his image, and whosoever receiveth the mark of his name.
>
> Here is the patience of the saints: here are they that keep the commandments of God, and the faith of Jesus. And I heard a voice from heaven saying unto me, Write, Blessed are the dead which die in the Lord from henceforth: Yea, saith the Spirit, that they may rest from their labours; and their works do follow them." – Revelation 14:9–13

This time of Great Tribulation will be marked by the ultimate choice of the end times: risking one's life by having faith in Christ or taking the Mark of the Beast. The Devil and his offspring will force all people on Earth to make this fateful decision in order to initiate the genetic destruction of humanity, just as they did in the days of Noah.

EXCLUSIVE BONUS CONTENT – Scan the QR code below for bonus content.

CHAPTER 9

THE MARK OF THE BEAST: MINGLING OURSELVES WITH THE SEED OF ANGELS

> "And he causeth all, both small and great, rich and poor, free and bond, to receive a mark in their right hand, or in their foreheads: And that no man might buy or sell, save he that had the mark, or the name of the beast, or the number of his name. Here is wisdom. Let him that hath understanding count the number of the beast: for it is the number of a man; and his number is Six hundred threescore and six." – Revelation 13:16–18

One of the most controversial and debated aspects of the book of Revelation is the prophecy concerning the Mark of the Beast—the identifier that will be placed in the right hand or forehead of all the duped, unsaved people who are victimized by the deceptions of the Antichrist and False Prophet. Accepting the Mark will be the final step in pledging one's allegiance to the Final Nephilim, but it will come at a steep price: eternal damnation. Scripture makes it clear that all who take it will be sentenced to the Lake of Fire.

What is it about the Mark that makes receiving it an unpardonable sin?

It is the satanic power transforming the genetics of the recipient to merge with the DNA of the Final Nephilim.

SATANIC IMITATION OF GOD'S MARK

Throughout the Bible, we read that God designated His salvation and His believers through two common symbols: His "right hand" and "marks." The first time we read of a "mark" in Scripture is in the account of Adam and Eve's sons Cain and Abel. After Cain was banished from Eden for murdering his brother Abel, he complained to the Lord that one day, someone might seek to kill him to avenge his brother's death. God, in His mercy and grace, placed a special mark on Cain as a means of protection:

> "And Cain said unto the LORD, My punishment is greater than I can bear. Behold, thou hast driven me out this day from the face of the earth; and from thy face shall I be hid; and I shall be a fugitive and a vagabond in the earth; and it shall come to pass, that every one that findeth me shall slay me. And the LORD said unto him, Therefore whosoever slayeth Cain, vengeance shall be taken on him sevenfold. And the LORD set a mark upon Cain, lest any finding him should kill him." – Genesis 4:13–15

SIGNIFICANCE OF THE FOREHEAD

As seen in many instances in the biblical narratives, the forehead symbolizes one's allegiance and connection to God. For example, when giving the instructions concerning the garb of the high priest, Yahweh told Moses to adorn Aaron's forehead with a proclamation:

> "And thou shalt make a plate of pure gold, and grave upon it, like the engravings of a signet, HOLINESS TO THE LORD. And thou shalt put it on a blue lace, that it may be upon the mitre; upon the forefront of the mitre it shall be. And it shall be upon Aaron's forehead, that Aaron may bear the iniquity of the holy things,

> which the children of Israel shall hallow in all their holy gifts; and it shall be always upon his forehead, that they may be accepted before the LORD." – Exodus 28:36–38

And in the book of Ezekiel, we read that the prophet has a vision of angelic beings coming to punish the Israelites for their brazen worship of idols. God divided the wicked from the righteous by having His holy angels put a mark on those who were faithful:

> "He cried also in mine ears with a loud voice, saying, Cause them that have charge over the city to draw near, even every man with his destroying weapon in his hand. And, behold, six men came from the way of the higher gate, which lieth toward the north, and every man a slaughter weapon in his hand; and one man among them was clothed with linen, with a writer's inkhorn by his side: and they went in, and stood beside the brasen altar. And the glory of the God of Israel was gone up from the cherub, whereupon he was, to the threshold of the house. And he called to the man clothed with linen, which had the writer's inkhorn by his side;
>
> And the LORD said unto him, Go through the midst of the city, through the midst of Jerusalem, **and set a mark upon the foreheads of the men that sigh and that cry for all the abominations that be done in the midst thereof**. And to the others he said in mine hearing, Go ye after him through the city, and smite: let not your eye spare, neither have ye pity: Slay utterly old and young, both maids, and little children, and women: but come not near any man upon whom is the mark; and begin at my sanctuary. Then they began at the ancient men which were before the house." – Ezekiel 9:1–6

The faithful Israelites who cried out in dismay over the rampant idolatry in the land were given a mark as a sign of their faith in Yahweh and His mercy in sparing them from His wrath.

In yet another example, in Revelation 7, a similar "sealing" is bestowed upon the 144,000 Jewish witnesses:

> "And after these things I saw four angels standing on the four corners of the earth, holding the four winds of the earth, that the wind should not blow on the earth, nor on the sea, nor on any tree. And I saw another angel ascending from the east, having the seal of the living God: and he cried with a loud voice to the four angels, to whom it was given to hurt the earth and the sea, Saying, Hurt not the earth, neither the sea, nor the trees, **till we have sealed the servants of our God in their foreheads**. And I heard the number of them which were sealed: and there were sealed an hundred and forty and four thousand of all the tribes of the children of Israel." – Revelation 7:1–4

Ultimately, all believers saved by faith in Jesus Christ will receive a mark of God for eternity in the new Earth:

> "And they shall see his face; and his name shall be in their foreheads." – Revelation 22:4

The mark is a sign of unity with God and of His salvation.

> "Thus the name of God is said to be in the foreheads of the redeemed, (Apocalypse 22:4), to signify that their ruling love is heavenly, and that they are consequently led by the Lord. The same is involved in what the prophet says respecting 'the man with a writer's inkhorn who was commanded to go through the midst of

> Jerusalem and to set a mark upon the foreheads of the men that sigh and cry for all the abominations that are done in the midst thereof.' [Ezekiel 9:4]. This mark indicated that they were in states of good originating in love to the Lord and were consequently holy in their lives. Hence it was that they escaped the impending judgment. (Verses 5, 6, 7). In the opposite sense, when the governing love is evil, the forehead is said to have 'the mark of the beast upon it.' [Revelation 9:9]." – "Physiology and Theology," as printed in *The Intellectual Repository, and New Jerusalem Magazine*, Vol. XIX – New Series, 1853, p. 44

In stark contrast to these examples of God's people having a mark on their forehead as a sign of His protection and salvation, the Mark of the Beast will be a pledge to the Antichrist. It will permanently align the unsaved soul with the Devil himself, serving as both an emblem of worship of the False Messiah and as a blasphemous mockery of Jesus Christ, who is symbolically referred to as the "Right Hand" of God in Scripture.

The first example of Christ being called this is in the Song of Moses, which the Israelites recited in worship of Yahweh after He delivered them from the Egyptians at the Red Sea:

> "Then sang Moses and the children of Israel this song unto the LORD, and spake, saying, I will sing unto the LORD, for he hath triumphed gloriously: the horse and his rider hath he thrown into the sea. The LORD is my strength and song, and he is become my salvation: he is my God, and I will prepare him an habitation; my father's God, and I will exalt him. The LORD is a man of war: the LORD is his name. Pharaoh's chariots and his host hath he cast into the sea: his chosen captains also are drowned in the Red Sea. The depths have covered them: they sank into the bottom as a stone. **Thy right hand, O LORD, is become glorious in power: thy right hand, O LORD, hath dashed in pieces the enemy.**" – Exodus

15:1–6

On several other occasions, when Jesus appeared to humanity, He was referred to as "Right Hand." For example:

> "And [Moses] said, The LORD came from Sinai, and rose up from Seir unto them; he shined forth from mount Paran, and he came with ten thousands of saints: **from his right hand went a fiery law for them**." – Deuteronomy 33:2
>
> "And he led them on safely, so that they feared not: but the sea overwhelmed their enemies. **And he brought them to the border of his sanctuary, even to this mountain, which his right hand had purchased**. He cast out the heathen also before them, and divided them an inheritance by line, and made the tribes of Israel to dwell in their tents." – Psalm 78:53–55

Rather than rely on the Messiah, the true Right Hand of God, the Antichrist and False Prophet induce the world to rely on their own right hands—a sign of "works-based righteousness." Self-reliance for salvation is a common spiritual error of humanity throughout history.

666: NUMBER OF THE HYBRID

As mentioned in prior chapters, 666, the number of the Beast, which is also mysteriously connected to his name, is identified as a "number of man" in the book of Revelation:

> "Here is wisdom. Let him that hath understanding count **the number of the beast: for it is the number of a man**; and his

> number is Six hundred threescore and six." – Revelation 13:18

Going back to the first chapter of the Bible, we see that man was created on the sixth day:

> "And God said, Let us make man in our image, after our likeness: and let them have dominion over the fish of the sea, and over the fowl of the air, and over the cattle, and over all the earth, and over every creeping thing that creepeth upon the earth. So God created man in his own image, in the image of God created he him; male and female created he them.... And the evening and the morning were the sixth day." – Genesis 1:26–28, 31

In establishing the Sabbath, Yahweh reminded the Israelites about the day of the creation of humanity:

> "But the seventh day is the sabbath of the LORD thy God: in it thou shalt not do any work, thou, nor thy son, nor thy daughter, thy manservant, nor thy maidservant, nor thy cattle, nor thy stranger that is within thy gates: For in six days the LORD made heaven and earth, the sea, and all that in them is, and rested the seventh day: wherefore the LORD blessed the sabbath day, and hallowed it." – Exodus 20:10–11

Once sinful rebellion entered the world, people started relying on their own "power" rather than trusting in the loving hand of God. The number six came to represent the achievement of man without God. We even see this goal of achieving eternal life in the transhumanist movement today.

TECH BILLIONAIRES AND SCIENTISTS SEEK IMMORTALITY THROUGH TECHNOLOGY

> "February saw the announcement in Silicon Valley by X Prize founder, serial entrepreneur, and all-round gee-whiz future-technology promoter Peter Diamandis that he had cofounded a new company called Celularity.
>
> He did so together with Dr. Bob Hariri, a renowned biomedical entrepreneur known for innovations in harvesting placental stem cells. Hariri had previously founded Celgene Cellular Therapeutics.
>
> Here's the new company's aim, as expressed on its website: **'Celularity seeks to make 100 years old the new 60, and to provide people with maximal aesthetics, mobility, and cognition as they age.'**
>
> According to Diamandis, Celularity 'is being born above the line of super credibility, with $250 million (€203 million) in funding from Celgene, United Therapeutics Corporation, Sorrento Therapeutics, Human Longevity, and a group of venture capitalists.'" – *What if Billionaires Could Live Forever?*, https://www.dw.com/en/what-if-billionaires-could-live-forever/a-42840013
>
> "There shall be no more thence an infant of days, nor an old man that hath not filled his days: for the child shall die an hundred years old; but the sinner being an hundred years old shall be accursed." – Isaiah 65:20

In the past decade, a number of Silicon Valley tech billionaires have launched companies and studies on "life-extension technologies," essentially hunting for a means to extend the human life span and achieve eternal life either in the physical body or by transferring the human consciousness into a computer. In arrogance and pride, the most powerful moguls on the planet are attempting to defy death itself by seeking to "play god" rather than worship the Creator. Consider the following:

- Google cofounder Larry Paige used $1.5 billion to launch Calico (or the California Life Company), a biotech firm that seeks to stop aging and "solve the problem of death." The company keeps many of its research projects shrouded in mystery, but did reveal that it invested $250 million into a joint venture with pharmaceutical giant AbbieVie to research cures to "diseases associated with aging."

  Ray Kurzweil, a world-renowned engineer, inventor, and outspoken futurist, was hired to be one of the lead engineers at Calico. Kurzweil is prophet-like in his promotion of the "singularity"—the moment when advanced computers will be able to merge with humanity, leading to a chance at immortality. He was one of the lead organizers of the Global Future 2045 Conference in Russia, a gathering of some of the top scientists and researchers in biology and technology, to focus on ways humanity can leverage technology to solve the "death problem." Here is a statement from the conference:

> "The social movement Russia 2045 was conceived of as a means of promoting the idea of humanity attaining cybernetic immortality. As the founders of the movement, we believe that these technologies in particular will provide the impulse that is so necessary right now to accelerate technological progress. It is cybernetic immortality in particular that will be able to grant people real freedom, including freedom from influence by the environment and the opportunity to explore the far reaches of space. Moreover, it's possible that this scenario will become a reality sooner than other such possibilities for extending life span all the

way to immortality." – "The Singularity: Man's Quest for Immortality and Satan's Deception," https://beginningandend.com/the-singularity-sciences-quest-for-immortality-and-satans-deception/

- Peter Thiel, billionaire cofounder of PayPal and one of the initial seed investors in Facebook, has poured millions of his money into life-extension technologies:

"He has invested heavily to try to fight death for the last several years. Back in 2006, he pledged $3.5 million to the Methuselah Foundation, which is a non-profit group working on life extension by advancing tissue engineering and regenerative medicine.

Thiel has also heavily invested in biotech companies. Most of his investments in the space are made via his Thiel Foundation. But at least five investments—including the DNA laser printing company Cambrian Genomics and cancer drug developer Stem CentRx—via his venture capital firm Founder Fund. He has also invested $17 million in Counsyl since 2011, which is a company that offers DNA screening." – "6 Billionaires Who Want to Live Forever," https://www.businessinsider.com/billionaires-who-want-to-live-forever-2015-9

- Facebook founder Mark Zuckerberg was quite candid about his goals for the future in a Q & A with the late physicist Stephen Hawking. When asked about what "big questions" are on his mind, Zuckerberg replied:

"'I'm most interested in questions about people. What will enable us to live forever? How do we cure all diseases? How does the brain work? How does learning work and how we can empower humans to learn a million times more?… One day, I believe we'll be able to send full rich thoughts to each other directly using technology,' he wrote. 'You'll just be able to think of something and your friends will immediately be able to experience it too if you'd like. This would be the ultimate communication technology." – "Mark Zuckerberg Wants to Answer These Big Questions," https://www.businessinsider.com/mark-zuckerberg-wants-answers-to-these-big-questions-2015-6

- Russian "life extensionist" Alexy Turchin recently completed a paper in Popular Mechanics magazine outlining a technological path to resurrection:

  "Turchin and fellow transhumanist Maxim Chernyakov outlined several future paths toward immortality in a paper they recently self-published. The paper, which comes via *Popular Mechanics,* is titled "Classification of Approaches to Technological Resurrection," and offers several ways people could theoretically not only defy death, but more fantastically, come back from the dead." – "Dyson Sphere May Be The Key To Human Immortality," https://www.yahoo.com/lifestyle/dyson-sphere-may-key-human-134924660.html
- In 2018, Chinese scientist and professor, He Jiankui, claimed to have "created" the "first genetically-edited babies" whose genes were manipulated to make them immune from contracting HIV ("Je Jiankui Defends "World's First Gene-Edited Babies," https://www.bbc.com/news/world-asia-china-46368731).
- In 2019, the Japanese government approved a stem-cell lab to bring a human-animal embryo to full term, with the hope of using the creatures' organs to help patients awaiting transplants ("Japan Approves Groundbreaking Experiment Bringing Human-Animal Hybrids to Term, https://www.sciencealert.com/japan-just-gave-

approval-for-scientists-to-work-on-human-animal-embryo-experiments).

And many futurists are already promoting the idea of "designer babies"— infants genetically designed with a preselected physical appearance and traits, freed from pesky diseases, and potentially enhanced when spliced with DNA from other creatures. Scientists have already created embryos and full-term babies who were given the DNA of three parents, using the third "donor" to provide genetic benefits the other two parents lacked ("Designer Babies: Playing God in the Womb," https://beginningandend.com/designer-babies-playing-god-in-the-womb/).

- Netcome is a research company dedicated to "advancing the science of memory." Its founders, MIT graduates Robert McIntyre and Michael McCanna, claim to have already successfully preserved an animal's brain's connectomes—the neural maps that play a vital role in memory storage—and are researching the possibility of extending the technique to human brains. Netcome offers a service where customers can pay to have their brain embalmed with proprietary chemicals (and also kill the user), which will allow Netcome's artificial intelligence machines to preserve the user's consciousness forever. Some clients have already signed up for the service:

"The method is '100 percent fatal,' claims the company.

'The user experience will be identical to physician-assisted suicide,' Netcome's co-founder Robert McIntyre revealed to the publication.

'Our mission is to preserve your brain well enough to keep all its memories intact: from that great chapter of your favorite book to

> the feeling of cold winter air, baking an apple pie, or having dinner with your friends and family,' writes Nectome on its site.
>
> 'We believe that within the current century it will be feasible to digitize this information and use it to recreate your consciousness'" ("Billionaire Signs Up to Be Killed, Have Brain Digitally Preserved," https://nypost.com/2018/03/14/billionaire-signs-up-to-be-killed-have-brain-digitally-preserved/).

The financial and political elite of the world are racing and spending large amounts of their wealth to secure the one thing humanity has not yet attained: eternal life. In the Great Tribulation, the Antichrist will make this offer a reality by merging human DNA with his. Just as God wants to be one with His people, so too will the Devil seek to "be one" with his followers through the Mark.

MARK OF THE BEAST GRANTS TEMPORARY "IMMORTALITY"

Those who accept this identifier during the last days not only will have access to buy and sell in the marketplace, but also to unify with the Antichrist by becoming "one" with him. Just as God uses "signs" to memorialize His covenants, so too will the Mark of the Beast indicate entering into a "covenant with death and hell" through the Final Nephilim (Isaiah 28:15). It appears from Scripture that this includes a provision of immortality. This would explain the mysterious condition of the populace at the sounding of the fifth trumpet:

> "And the fifth angel sounded, and I saw a star fall from heaven unto the earth: and to him was given the key of the bottomless pit. And he opened the bottomless pit; and there arose a smoke out of the pit, as the smoke of a great furnace; and the sun and the air were

> darkened by reason of the smoke of the pit.... **And in those days shall men seek death, and shall not find it; and shall desire to die, and death shall flee from them**." – Revelation 9:1–6

This is the trumpet that signals the Antichrist's return to life after his deadly wound, as the spirit of Apollyon indwells his formerly lifeless body. It will also be the point when humanity will achieve an inability to die once they receive the Mark. A nineteenth-century commentator remarked on this amazing phenomenon:

> "And the very expression: 'who worship the beast and his image,' seems to refer to the earthly conduct and condition of idolatrous people. **The passage proves an earthly immortality**, if it proves any; and the same may be said of the similar passage in [Revelation 9:6] sometimes adduced in this argument: 'And in those days shall men seek death and shall not find it; and shall desire to die, and death shall flee from them.'" – *Debt and Grace—As Related to the Doctrine of a Future Life*, Charles Frederic Hudson, 1861, p. 212

Hebrews 2:14 confirms that Jesus became flesh in order to: "destroy him that had **the power of death**, that is, the devil." If Satan at present retains the power of death, it is quite logical that he could suspend death for a time to enhance the supernatural benefits of taking the Mark of the Beast. The writer of following excerpt arrived at the same conclusion:

> "It seems as if He who has the power of death will for a season take from the ordinary causes of death their accustomed efficacy, and render man immortal so far as the scorpion power of the locusts can affect them—making their life unattackable and impregnable. For 'in those days shall men seek death' (that is, purposely and perhaps by violent means and attempts at self-destruction) and 'shall not find it; and shall desire to die' (in order to escape the torturing

> power of these indescribable agents of evil), and 'death shall flee from them.' No explanation can be offered of this singular restriction that will not lower its meaning." – "The First Woe" as printed in *The Local Preacher's Magazine and Christian Family Record*, Volume 14, 1864, p. 265

IMMORTALITY ACHIEVED BY BECOMING "ONE" WITH THE ANTICHRIST

As mentioned earlier, the turning point in the Final Nephilim's career is when he returns from the dead fully energized by Satan and possessed by Apollyon. This is what causes the world to marvel at him and worship him as God. He can then make the enticing offer: "You too can live forever, just like me, if you take on my heavenly DNA and become one with me." This will hearken back to Satan's original deception of Eve:

> "And the serpent said unto the woman, **Ye shall not surely die**: For God doth know that in the day ye eat thereof, then your eyes shall be opened, and ye shall be as gods, knowing good and evil." – Genesis 3:4–5

This is when the "mingling with the seed of men" of Daniel 2:43 will be initiated. By taking on the DNA of the Antichrist, humanity will finally achieve earthly immortality, but it will come at the most severe and devastating price: People will corrupt themselves to the point that they will no longer be fully human, thus they will no longer be image-bearers of Yahweh. The ensuing corruption will disqualify them from salvation, and this is precisely what brought human civilization to the brink of extinction in the days of Noah:

> "And God saw that the wickedness of man was great in the earth,

> and that every imagination of the thoughts of his heart was only evil continually. And it repented the LORD that he had made man on the earth, and it grieved him at his heart. And the LORD said, I will destroy man whom I have created from the face of the earth; both man, and beast, and the creeping thing, and the fowls of the air; for it repenteth me that I have made them." – Genesis 6:5–7

Irenaeus directly connected the Mark of the Beast with the original birth of the Nephilim:

> "And therefore, in the Beast when he cometh, there ensues a summing up of all iniquity and all deceit; that in him all the power of rebellion, running into one, and shut up in one may slip down the furnace of fire. Suitably then will his name also have the number 666: **he summing up in himself all the wickedness which was before the Flood, the commixture caused by the Angels revolt.**" – *Against Heresies*, Book V, 2, Irenaeus, translated by Rev. John Keble, as printed in *A Library of Fathers of the Holy Catholic Church, Anterior to the Division of East and West*, Volume 42, 1872, p. 518

Lactantius was a North African Christian apologist who lived in the fourth century AD. His work, *Divine Institutes,* is the oldest extant Christian writing in Latin. He devoted much of his writing to defending the Christian faith against those who favored pagan and polytheistic religions. In discussing the genetic corruption of humanity during the Day of the Lord, he wrote:

> "[The Antichrist] shall harass the world with an intolerable rule; **shall mingle things divine and human;** shall contrive things impious to relate and detestable; shall meditate new designs in his breast, that he may establish the government for himself: he will change the laws, and appoint his own; he will contaminate, plunder, spoil, and put to death. And at length, the name being

> changed and the seat of government being transferred, confusion and the disturbance of mankind will follow." – *The Divine Institutes*, Chapter XVI, as printed in *Ante-Nicene Christian Library: Writings of the Fathers Down to A.D. 325*, Vol. XXI, edited by Rev. Alex Roberts, 1871, p. 465

It is the "mingling of the divine and human" that will be the ultimate death sentence for the unsaved world. Taking the Mark will make a person literally a "seed of Satan"—fully corrupted in mind and body. It is a decision of such extreme consequence that God will dispatch angels to warn the entire world to avoid taking it at all costs:

> "And the third angel followed them, saying with a loud voice, If any man worship the beast and his image, and receive his mark in his forehead, or in his hand, The same shall drink of the wine of the wrath of God, which is poured out without mixture into the cup of his indignation; and he shall be tormented with fire and brimstone in the presence of the holy angels, and in the presence of the Lamb: And the smoke of their torment ascendeth up for ever and ever: and they have no rest day nor night, who worship the beast and his image, and whosoever receiveth the mark of his name. Here is the patience of the saints: here are they that keep the commandments of God, and the faith of Jesus." – Revelation 14:9–12

In the Garden of Eden, the Lord gave Adam and Eve one rule: "Do not eat one specific fruit, because you will certainly die." Their disobedience in taking the fruit corrupted and changed them. This was why God banished Adam and Eve from the Garden. In their corrupted states, had they eaten from the Tree of Life, which granted immortality, they would have permanently remained in their fallen, irredeemable condition (Genesis 3:22):

> "When man had sinned an earthly immortality would have been a curse and not a blessing an endless continuance in this world of sin and sorrow would have been an intolerable existence." – "The Trees of Paradise," as printed in *The Primitive Methodist Magazine*, Rev. A. Beanland, 1871, p. 530

Thus the end times will be in quantum entanglement with the earliest events of biblical history. Like God's one rule in the Garden of Eden, in the Great Tribulation, humanity will face a prophetically similar binary decision: Take the Mark and suffer God's wrath, or refuse it and live.

During the antediluvian era, humanity was so defiled that the Lord wiped out 99 percent of the global population with the Flood. But their corruption wasn't just one of sin; it was the degradation of the human genetic code. Note the final, decisive factor in bringing cataclysmic judgment from Yahweh:

> "And God said unto Noah, **The end of all flesh is come before me**; for the earth is filled with violence through them; and, behold, I will destroy them with the earth." – Genesis 6:13

This was the Devil's strategy. By corrupting human "flesh" or genetics, thus making humans something other than image-bearers of the Lord, Satan wanted to prevent the birth of the Messiah—whom God had said would be born of a woman. Nephilim corruption was the gravest threat yet to the survival of the human race and the prophecy of the Seed of the Woman. If there were no people left on earth, how could the Savior be born? If human beings were no longer human, where could their redemption come from? This is why God's reaction to this violation of His genetic order was so harsh.

As it was in the days of Noah, so it will be again at the coming of the Son of Man. The Mark of the Beast will be the final attempt at genetic corruption, as the fallen angelic realm will once again attempt to merge with humanity.

Thus, Jesus' proclamation that if He did not shorten the days during the reign of Antichrist, no flesh would be saved (Matthew 24:22).

> "Concerning which iron and clay, the prophet points to some attempt, when Satan and his angels shall be upon the earth, to mingle themselves with the seed of men; an additional reason, not only for admiring the forbearance of God, which defers the stroke of unmitigated wrath till thus provoked, but also for desiring the destruction of the human statue.
>
> In frustration of such attempt the blow is struck by the stone of Israel—the Redeemer not the destroyer of mankind; and although, at first sight, the blow deals nothing less than destruction to the human image, on a closer view, this very destruction **is that which preserves, the human race from deeper defilement; namely, from an attempted commixture or impregnation**, which would issue in a more confirmed antagonism to God." – *The Ultimate and Proximate Results of Redemption: Chiefly Deduced from the Oath Sworn to Abraham*, Henry Erskine Head, 1854, p. 175–176

Even Hippolytus speculated that the meaning of the name of the Beast might be connected to the Nephilim:

> "With respect to his name it is not in our power to explain it exactly, as the blessed John understood it and was instructed about it, but only to give a conjectural account of it; for when he appears, the blessed one will show us what we seek to know. Yet as far as our doubtful apprehension of the matter goes, we may speak. Many names indeed we find, the letters of which are the equivalent of this number: **such as, for instance, the word Titan**, an ancient and notable name." *Treatise on Christ and Antichrist*, 50, Hippolytus, ca. AD 202, as printed in *Ante-Nicene Christian Library: Irenaeus,*

> *v. 2, Hippolytus, v. 2, Fragments of the Third Century*, Translated by Reverend Alexander Roberts, 1869, p. 30

The ancient titans were the demigods, offspring of the ancient "gods" (fallen angels) and human woman—Nephilim.

In *Judgment of the Nephilim*, I explained that God established strict genetic rules whereby the DNA of humans, animals, and even plant life were not to be tampered with. The Genesis 6 rebels suffered swift and devastating punishment for violating this code. With the Mark of the Beast, this grave iniquity will be committed by the Antichrist.

Bible researcher Doug Hamp gave a powerful illustration of this very concept:

> "Presumably some point after the rapture, humanity, in an effort to not be removed from the planet (like those taken) and to be able to evolve to be like the Beast (the supposed leader of the 'aliens'), will allow their DNA to be rewritten thus altering their image—that image that was in God's image (though fallen) will therefore become genetically like the Beast and of course Satan and his angels. The mark then would simply be the proof (or perhaps the means by which) one has undergone the genetic transformation. This action of taking the mark will condemn them to hell forever because they will no longer be in the image of God. How sad it is to realize that what man will trade his soul for, God was willing to give for free....
>
> It is reasonable and probable that the mark of the Beast will also be an imitation of what the Lord wants to do for believers. He will restore us spiritually and genetically: we will be like Him, we will be in His image, we will be conformed to His glorious body, we will have God's seed in us. By Satan giving his genetic material to the Beast (who 'replaces' Jesus) and the Beast offering (forcing) all

> to take his altered genetic material, Satan will be perfectly imitating our salvation." – *Corrupting the Image—Angels, Aliens, and the Antichrist Revealed*, Douglas Hamp, Defender Publishing, LLC, 2011, p. 246–247

But this earthly immortality will only last for a brief moment. After the five months have completed, death will return to the unsaved world. And the punishment following the sounding of the sixth trumpet of God will be led by four powerful, fallen angels who have been imprisoned since the days of Noah.

CHAPTER 10

THE MYSTERY OF THE FOUR ANGELS OF THE EUPHRATES

> "And the sixth angel sounded, and I heard a voice from the four horns of the golden altar which is before God, Saying to the sixth angel which had the trumpet, Loose the four angels which are bound in the great river Euphrates. And the four angels were loosed, which were prepared for an hour, and a day, and a month, and a year, for to slay the third part of men." – Revelation 9:13–15

> "These are four evil angels really imprisoned in the Euphrates. Jerusalem's first enemies came from that quarter, and so will the last. The Lord will certainly use evil angels again with regard to the Jewish nation as he did formerly: 'He cast upon them the fierceness of his anger wrath and indignation and trouble by sending evil angels among them.'" – *Notes on the Book of the Revelation,* Helen Maclachlan, James Nisbet & Co., 1869, p. 131

The four angels bound in the Euphrates are part of one of the most mysterious verses in the Bible. Scripture tells us they were "prepared for an hour, and a day, and a month, and a year, for to slay the third part of men." What does this time frame mean? Many commentaries either omit or overlook this subject, but upon close examination, we can see a direct connection to the days of Noah.

ESOTERIC TIMELINE FROM DAYS OF NOAH TO THE DAYS OF LOT

In my previous book, I explained the connection between the fifth trumpet of Revelation and the days of Noah. This, of course, is when the angels who sinned as recorded in Genesis chapter 6 are finally released from imprisonment in the Abyss, where they will have been for millennia. The key linking theme is that when they are unleashed to torment the unsaved world, they attack for five months.

BIBLICAL TIMING OF THE ASSYRIAN'S DESCENT INTO HELL

Ezekiel 31 also provides the timing of the destruction of the Assyrian's kingdom:

> "Thus saith the Lord GOD; In the day when he went down to the grave I caused a mourning: I covered the deep for him, and I restrained the floods thereof, and the great waters were stayed: and I caused Lebanon to mourn for him, and all the trees of the field fainted for him." – Ezekiel 31:15

After day 150 of the Flood, the waters finally started to "abate":

> "And God remembered Noah, and every living thing, and all the cattle that was with him in the ark: and God made a wind to pass over the earth, and the waters assuaged; The fountains also of the deep and the windows of heaven were stopped, and the rain from heaven was restrained; And the waters returned from off the earth continually: and after the end of the hundred and fifty days the

> waters were abated." – Genesis 8:1–3

Both passages point to the same time in the Flood, the moment when God "restrained," or held back, the rain showers from above and "stayed" the massive subterranean waters shooting up from "the deep." The divine force pushing water through the earth's surface ceased, and the waters of the deep returned to beneath the earth's crust. The Assyrian was forced to fight for his survival in his ruined kingdom among the raging floodwaters for 150 days. He watched his kingdom crumble and all his wives and Nephilim children perish. Once God stopped the deluge, the waters of the deep returned underground ("And the waters returned from off the earth continually"), sucking the Assyrian and the other sinning angels down into the Abyss alive.

In Revelation chapter 9, the apostate angels are finally released from the bottomless pit and they torment the unsaved world for five months:

> "And to them it was given that they should not kill them, but that they should be tormented five months: and their torment was as the torment of a scorpion, when he striketh a man." – Revelation 9:5

A month on the Hebrew calendar is thirty days. Thus, just as the Assyrian and his fallen angelic subjects were tormented by the Flood judgment for 150 days before being swallowed into the Abyss, so too will they return and torment unbelieving humanity for the same length of time.

SIXTH TRUMPET CONTINUES THE PATTERN OF CONNECTING DAYS OF NOAH AND LOT WITH GREAT TRIBULATION

"And as it was in the days of Noe, so shall it be also in the days

> **of the Son of man**. They did eat, they drank, they married wives, they were given in marriage, until the day that Noah entered into the ark, and the flood came, and destroyed them all. **Likewise also as it was in the days of Lot**; they did eat, they drank, they bought, they sold, they planted, they builded; But the same day that Lot went out of Sodom it rained fire and brimstone from heaven, and destroyed them all. Even thus shall it be in the day when the Son of man is revealed." – Luke 17:26–30

The Bible includes a series of passages that connect the days of Noah and the days of Lot; the verses above where Jesus linked His own return to those eras are just one example. At the fifth and sixth seals, a similar pattern is revealed.

In the Hebrew calendar, a year (360 days), plus a month (30 days), plus a day (1 day) equals 391 days. Adding an hour brings us to the 392nd day. Examining the lineage of the patriarchs from the time of the Flood (the days of Noah) until the judgment of Sodom and Gomorrah (days of Lot) reveals an astonishing association.

We can establish the timeline from the days of Noah, as Scripture confirms that the first person born after the Flood was Arphaxad:

> "These are the generations of Shem: Shem was an hundred years old, **and begat Arphaxad two years after the flood**:
>
> And Shem lived after he begat Arphaxad five hundred years, and begat sons and daughters. [2 years]
>
> And Arphaxad lived five and thirty years, and begat Salah: [35 years]
>
> And Salah lived thirty years, and begat Eber: [30 years]
>
> And Eber lived four and thirty years, and begat Peleg: [43 years]

And Peleg lived thirty years, and begat Reu: [30 years]

And Reu lived two and thirty years, and begat Serug: [32 years]

And Serug lived thirty years, and begat Nahor: [30 years]

And Nahor lived nine and twenty years, and begat Terah: [29 years]

And Terah lived seventy years, and begat Abram, Nahor, and Haran [70 years]." – Genesis 11:10–26

"**And when Abram was ninety years old and nine**, the LORD appeared to Abram, and said unto him, I am the Almighty God; walk before me, and be thou perfect." – Genesis 17:1

The period between the end of the Flood and the day God appeared to Abraham (at ninety-nine years old) and pronounced the judgment of Sodom and Gomorrah was 392 years. This was the day before the judgment of Sodom and Gomorrah:

"And the men rose up from thence, and looked toward Sodom: and Abraham went with them to bring them on the way. And the LORD said, Shall I hide from Abraham that thing which I do; Seeing that Abraham shall surely become a great and mighty nation, and all the nations of the earth shall be blessed in him? For I know him, that he will command his children and his household after him, and they shall keep the way of the LORD, to do justice and judgment; that the LORD may bring upon Abraham that which he hath spoken of him. And the LORD said, Because the cry of Sodom and Gomorrah is great, and because their sin is very grievous; I will go down now, and see whether they have done altogether according to the cry of it, which is come unto me; and if not, I will know. **And the men turned their faces from thence, and went toward Sodom**: but Abraham stood yet before the LORD" [99 years]. –

> Genesis 18:16–22

The two angels escorting the Lord went to Sodom that same day. In the evening they stayed at Lot's house and warned him to flee.

> "And there **came two angels to Sodom at even**; and Lot sat in the gate of Sodom: and Lot seeing them rose up to meet them; and he bowed himself with his face toward the ground." – Genesis 19:1

The angels came to Sodom the same evening and spent the night in his home. We're even given the detail that takes us to the morning of the 392nd year after the Flood:

> "**The sun was risen upon the earth** when Lot entered into Zoar. Then the LORD rained upon Sodom and upon Gomorrah brimstone and fire from the LORD out of heaven." – Genesis 19:23–24

At the sound of the fifth trumpet, the fallen angels will be released from the Abyss to torment for 150 days, the same length of time they were tormented by the Flood. But at the sounding of the sixth trumpet, the four angels bound beneath the Euphrates will be released to destroy a third of humanity for "an hour, and a day, and a month, and a year"—392 days, symbolically matching the time between the destruction by the Flood during the days of Noah and the destruction of Sodom and Gomorrah during the days of Lot.

"A DAY FOR A YEAR" – GOD USES TEMPORAL SYMBOLISM FOR PROPHECY

This would not be the only instance in which God used a single day to symbolically represent a year. When Joshua sent twelve spies to scout the Promised Land in the Book of Numbers, ten returned and told the Israelites they could not enter the land of Canaan because of the three Nephilim they encountered (Numbers 13:32). I explained this account, later called "the Provocation" in Scripture, in *Judgment of the Nephilim*. It was one of the worst acts of rebellion against the Lord in all of the Bible as the Israelites refused to enter the land God has promised to them and wanted to return to Egypt instead. In punishing Israel, the Lord assigned a year of punishment based on the forty days the scouts were on their mission:

> "But as for you, your carcases, they shall fall in this wilderness. And your children shall wander in the wilderness forty years, and bear your whoredoms, until your carcases be wasted in the wilderness. **After the number of the days in which ye searched the land, even forty days, each day for a year, shall ye bear your iniquities, even forty years, and ye shall know my breach of promise**. I the LORD have said, I will surely do it unto all this evil congregation, that are gathered together against me: in this wilderness they shall be consumed, and there they shall die." – Numbers 14:32–35

In the book of Ezekiel, the Lord instructed the prophet to predict the coming judgment upon the Northern Kingdom of Israel for their idolatry.

> "Moreover take thou unto thee an iron pan, and set it for a wall of iron between thee and the city: and set thy face against it, and it shall be besieged, and thou shalt lay siege against it. This shall be a sign to the house of Israel. Lie thou also upon thy left side, and lay the iniquity of the house of Israel upon it: according to the number of the days that thou shalt lie upon it thou shalt bear their iniquity. For I have laid upon thee the years of their iniquity, **according to the number of the days, three hundred and ninety days**: so shalt thou bear the iniquity of the house of Israel.... **I have appointed**

> **thee each day for a year.**" – Ezekiel 4:3–6

In order to prophetically proclaim the judgment to come upon Israel, Ezekiel was to lay on his side for 390 days—each day representing a year of the Northern Kingdom's spiritual rebellion. And what would be the punishment? The invasion and conquest of the nation at the hands of Sennacherib, the king of Assyria and preincarnation of the Antichrist. At the fifth trumpet, the Assyrian will be released from the Abyss, and at the sixth trumpet, his fallen angelic hordes will attack humanity for 392 days, each day representing a year from the Flood to the judgment of Sodom and Gomorrah.

DAYS OF NOAH AND LOT LINKED THROUGHOUT SCRIPTURE

> "**And the angels which kept not their first estate**, but left their own habitation, he hath reserved in everlasting chains under darkness unto the judgment of the great day. **Even as Sodom and Gomorrah**, and the cities about them in like manner, giving themselves over to fornication, and going after strange flesh, are set forth for an example, suffering the vengeance of eternal fire." – Jude 1:6–7

Many passages link the punishment of the Flood to the judgment of Sodom and Gomorrah, giving credence to the fifth and sixth trumpets being typological repetitions of those ancient supernatural punishments from God. Both accounts involve the sin of fornication with angels. The homosexual lust of the men of Sodom is well chronicled. However, not as often discussed is that the "men" the people of Sodom wanted to sexually assault were angels. Recall that Lot, upon seeing the two angels, recognized that they were not human beings:

> "And there came two angels to Sodom at even; and Lot sat in the gate of Sodom: and Lot seeing them rose up to meet them; and he bowed himself with his face toward the ground." – Genesis 19:1

Thus, the men of Sodom were attempting to go "after strange flesh"—that of angels. And, just as Yahweh did in the days of Noah, as well as in any instance involving the Nephilim, He personally intervened to end the sinful rebellion.

If this association between the sixth trumpet and the days of Lot still seems like a stretch, consider the punishments delivered by the Lord in each account. Sodom and Gomorrah were destroyed by fire and brimstone 392 years after the Flood:

> "The sun was risen upon the earth when Lot entered into Zoar. **Then the LORD rained upon Sodom and upon Gomorrah brimstone and fire from the LORD out of heaven**; And he overthrew those cities, and all the plain, and all the inhabitants of the cities, and that which grew upon the ground. But his wife looked back from behind him, and she became a pillar of salt. And Abraham gat up early in the morning to the place where he stood before the LORD: And he looked toward Sodom and Gomorrah, and toward all the land of the plain, and beheld, and, lo, the smoke of the country went up **as the smoke of a furnace.**" – Genesis 19:23–28

When the four angels are released from beneath the Euphrates River, they will unleash the exact same punishment on humanity for a duration of 392 days:

> "And the four angels were loosed, which were prepared for an hour, and a day, and a month, and a year, for to slay the third part of men. And the number of the army of the horsemen were two

> hundred thousand thousand: and I heard the number of them. And thus I saw the horses in the vision, and them that sat on them, **having breastplates of fire, and of jacinth, and brimstone**: and the heads of the horses were as the heads of lions; **and out of their mouths issued fire and smoke and brimstone**. By these three was the third part of men killed, by the fire, and by the smoke, and by the brimstone, which issued out of their mouths." – Revelation 9:15–18

At Sodom and Gomorrah and at the sounding of the sixth trumpet, the Lord punishes unbelievers with fire, brimstone, and smoke, giving further biblical confirmation that the meaning of the mystery of the four angels was foreshadowed in the days of Lot. A nineteenth-century Irish attorney, writing on this mysterious connection, arrived at the same conclusion:

> "We are led, then, by the date introduced at the opening of the imagery of the sixth trumpet, to fix on this event as typical of that divine visitation, and which (as in the case of Sodom and Gomorrah) is to be rained down, as an exterminating judgment, on 'the third part of (the) men,' in the shape of 'fire, smoke, and brimstone.' And this connection that we have thus traced, by means of the foregoing date, between the portents of the fifth and sixth trumpets, is corroborated by the Scripture connection that exists between the two typical events (viz. the Flood and the destruction of Sodom), in the description that is recorded by St Luke as having been given by our Saviour, of the occurrences that are immediately to precede the approach of the kingdom of heaven, or the day in which the Son of Man is to be revealed; and which, according to our interpretation, is the very period of the progressing sanctification of the Jewish remnant, that is now under our consideration: And as it was in the *days of Noe* so also shall it be in the *days of the Son of Man.*

> They did eat, they drank, they married wives, they were given in marriage, until the day that Noe entered into the ark, and the flood came and destroyed them all. Likewise also as it was in the *days of Lot* they did eat, they drank, they bought, they sold, they planted, they builded; but the same day that Lot went out of Sodom, it rained fire and brimstone from heaven, and destroyed them all. Even thus shall it be in the day that the Son of Man is revealed." – *The Latter Days of the Jewish Church and Nation, as Revealed in the Apocalypse*, Dominick, McCausland, Esq., William Curry, June and Co., 1841, p. 224–225

We also read in 2 Peter 2 of a link between the angels who are bound in the Abyss and Noah and Lot:

> "For if God spared not the angels that sinned, but cast them down to hell, and delivered them into chains of darkness, **to be reserved unto judgment**; And spared not the old world, but saved Noah the eighth person, a preacher of righteousness, bringing in the flood upon the world of the ungodly; **And turning the cities of Sodom and Gomorrah into ashes condemned them with an overthrow, making them an ensample unto those that after should live ungodly**; And delivered just Lot, vexed with the filthy conversation of the wicked: (For that righteous man dwelling among them, in seeing and hearing, vexed his righteous soul from day to day with their unlawful deeds)." – 2 Peter 2:4–8

A close examination of the Greek in Revelation 9:15 reveals that the original Greek detailing "an hour [ὥρα or *hora*], and a day, and a month, and a year" was intended to mean the duration of the judgment of God by these four angels:

> "'*for an hour*'—Should be 'for *the* hour.' The article is not repeated,

> but plainly the one article belongs to all the nouns: they are 'prepared for the hour, and day, and month, and year,' when God has decreed to execute the vengeance here foretold." –*The Revelation of St. John the Divine, with Notes and Introduction*, Reverend William Henry Simcox, 1902, p. 62

The fifth and sixth trumpets will be a repetition of two of the most severe judgments of God in all of Scripture: 150 days of punishment by the sons of God of Genesis chapter 6, followed by 392 days of fire and brimstone from the four angels of the Euphrates and their armies.

EUPHRATES RIVER: BORDER OF PROMISED LAND AND DIVIDING LINE OF BATTLE BETWEEN GOD AND EVIL FORCES

> "And a river went out of Eden to water the garden; and from thence it was parted, and became into four heads. The name of the first is Pison: that is it which compasseth the whole land of Havilah, where there is gold; And the gold of that land is good: there is bdellium and the onyx stone. And the name of the second river is Gihon: the same is it that compasseth the whole land of Ethiopia. And the name of the third river is Hiddekel: that is it which goeth toward the east of Assyria. And the fourth river is Euphrates." – Genesis 2:10–14

> "In the same day the LORD made a covenant with Abram, saying, Unto thy seed have I given this land, from the river of Egypt unto the great river, the river Euphrates." – Genesis 15:18

When God originally designated the geographic location of the Promised Land, its borders were two rivers: the Nile ("the river of Egypt") on the west, all the way east to the Euphrates River. This is a much larger territory than modern-day Israel, as it stretches from northern Egypt, through parts of Saudi Arabia, and all the way to central Iraq and Syria. In ancient times, the Euphrates was the border between Israel and Babylon and Assyria—the nations that would conquer the Northern and Southern Kingdoms. In those times, both the Babylonians and Assyrians were used as instruments of God's judgment. Thus, the Euphrates, from a heavenly standpoint, has always been the true border of Yahweh's territory on earth.

In *Judgment of the Nephilim*, I explained that the nations of the world were divided between God and the fallen angels, based on Deuteronomy 32:

> "When the Most High divided the nations, when he separated the sons of Adam, **he set the bounds of the nations according to the number of the angels of God**. And his people Jacob became the portion of the Lord, Israel was the line of his inheritance." – Deuteronomy 32:8, LXX

The nations were given over to the rebellious "angels of God" to rule over the Gentiles, but God kept Israel as the "line of his inheritance." Yahweh reminded Israel of this once more when He warned them about worshiping the rebel angels:

> "And lest thou lift up thine eyes unto heaven, and when thou seest the sun, and the moon, and the stars, **even all the host of heaven**, shouldest be driven to worship them, and serve them, **which the LORD thy God hath divided unto all nations under the whole heaven**." – Deuteronomy 4:19

The angels who have dominion over the nations even wage combat against each other. One example highlighted in *Judgment of the Nephilim* was from Daniel chapter 10:

> "And he said unto me, O Daniel, a man greatly beloved, understand the words that I speak unto thee, and stand upright: for unto thee am I now sent. And when he had spoken this word unto me, I stood trembling. Then said he unto me, Fear not, Daniel: for from the first day that thou didst set thine heart to understand, and to chasten thyself before thy God, thy words were heard, and I am come for thy words. But the prince of the kingdom of Persia withstood me one and twenty days: but, lo, Michael, one of the chief princes, came to help me; and I remained there with the kings of Persia." – Daniel 10:11–13

Daniel persisted in prayer for the deliverance of the Southern Kingdom captives in Babylon for twenty-one days straight. And when the angel who came to answer his prayer arrived, he informed the prophet that the reason for the delay was that he had "withstood" (or "had been fighting") "the prince of Persia"—the evil angel overseeing that kingdom—for three weeks. Not until the archangel Michael, "one of the chief princes," assisted him had he been able to end the battle.

The angel then announced that he would return to the battle, and afterwards, another fallen angel would arrive:

> "Then said he, Knowest thou wherefore I come unto thee? and now will I return to fight with the prince of Persia: and when I am gone forth, lo, the prince of Grecia shall come. But I will shew thee that which is noted in the scripture of truth: and there is none that holdeth with me in these things, but Michael your prince." – Daniel 10:20–21

In stunning fashion, Scripture weaves in the prophecy that the Greek Empire would succeed the Persians (which happened after Alexander the Great conquered the Persians in 334 BC), while again confirming that the heavenly realm has its own "territorial map" of the Earth that it abides by.

We read confirmation of the concept of the geographical assignments of angels in the following:

> "Indeed the idea was familiar to the Jewish mind that every nation had its representative angel. Thus, in the Septuagint, which was principally used by the Jews of apostolic times, the passage in [Deuteronomy 32:8], is translated, He 'set the bounds of the nations according to the number of the angels of God;' and, in Daniel, a book to which the Apocalypse, in its symbolic phraseology, bears many points of resemblance, the angel Michael is set forth as the prince of Daniel, or of the Hebrews, and Grecia and Persia are represented by their respective princes or angels (Daniel 10:13–20 and 21)." – "The Government of the Primitive Church," George Sidney Camp, Esq., as printed in *The American Presbyterian and Theological Review*, New Series, Vol. III, edited by Henry B. Smith and J. M. Sherwood, 1865, p. 251

Thus, the Euphrates is where God marked off His boundary for the Promised Land. The angels being bound there serve as testimony to the punishment for an assault on God's territory.

HEAVENLY REALM WARHORSES

Angels have armies and wage war (see Revelation 12:7–8). The four angels of the Euphrates were likely some of the Devil's most distinguished military leaders before their imprisonment, hence their special location of punishment. Once they are unleashed, they will command the armies that will slay one-third of the human population:

> "And the number of the army of the horsemen were two hundred thousand thousand: and I heard the number of them. And thus I saw the horses in the vision, and them that sat on them, having breastplates of fire, and of jacinth, and brimstone: and the heads of the horses were as the heads of lions; and out of their mouths issued fire and smoke and brimstone. By these three was the third part of men killed, by the fire, and by the smoke, and by the brimstone, which issued out of their mouths." – Revelation 9:16–18

This massive fallen angelic army (the Greek translation of "horsemen" above is ἱππικός or *hippikos* which means calvary) will overwhelm all those who still refuse to believe and trust in Jesus Christ. Mystical fire and brimstone will adorn their breastplates (providing another allusion to the judgment of Sodom and Gomorrah). That their army was so large—two hundred million men, according to the book of Revelation—shouldn't be surprising, since the Bible informs us that there is "an innumerable company of angels" (Hebrews 12:22). In Revelation 5, we read that just around the throne of Yahweh alone, we find more than a hundred million angels:

> "And I beheld, and I heard the voice of many angels round about the throne and the beasts and the elders: and the number of them was ten thousand times ten thousand, and thousands of thousands." – Revelation 5:11

The fact that these angelic beings are described as "horsemen" makes sense in light of other passages that refer to righteous angels of God using the same heavenly creatures for warfare. An example of this is found in 2 Kings 6, where we read that the prophet Elisha and his servant are surrounded by the enemy armies of Syria:

> "And when the servant of [Elisha] was risen early, and gone forth,

> behold, an host compassed the city both with horses and chariots. And his servant said unto him, Alas, my master! how shall we do? And he answered, Fear not: for they that be with us are more than they that be with them. And Elisha prayed, and said, LORD, I pray thee, open his eyes, that he may see. And the LORD opened the eyes of the young man; and he saw: and, behold, **the mountain was full of horses and chariots of fire round about Elisha**." – 2 Kings 6:15–17

As the current human population approaches eight billion, it will probably rival the hundreds of millions of fallen angels in Satan's armies. The hope, jubilation, and spiritual excitement generated by the Antichrist will quickly disappear when the world is under siege by grotesque, sinister angelic beings from the Abyss executing the wrath of God. This invading army of the sixth trumpet was foretold in the book of Jeremiah:

> "For this is **the day of the Lord** GOD of hosts, a day of vengeance, that he may avenge him of his adversaries: and the sword shall devour, and it shall be satiate and made drunk with their blood: for **the Lord GOD of hosts hath a sacrifice in the north country by the river Euphrates**." – Jeremiah 46:10

The time of God's mercy will run out for those who take the Mark of the Beast. And humanity will stand no chance, as billions will fall to this unstoppable horde. The author of a commentary on Revelation agreed that God will indeed use these fallen angels as his rod of judgment upon the world:

> "Loose the four angels—four evil spirits. God suffers wicked beings to execute his judgments upon evildoers. In [Psalm 17:13] we read, 'Deliver my soul from the wicked, which is Thy sword.' God permitted the Babylonians to punish the Israelites for their sins during seventy years of exile. But these demons from the Euphrates

> had only a year, month, and day to slay the third part of men." – *Church History*, Reverend H. T. Besse, 1908, p. 392

The third portion of the global population that will perish at the sixth trumpet serves as a prophetic type of the fallen angels.

ONE-THIRD OR THIRTY-THREE: ANGELIC REBELLION

> "And there appeared a great wonder in heaven; a woman clothed with the sun, and the moon under her feet, and upon her head a crown of twelve stars: And she being with child cried, travailing in birth, and pained to be delivered. And there appeared another wonder in heaven; and behold a great red dragon, having seven heads and ten horns, and seven crowns upon his heads. **And his tail drew the third part of the stars of heaven**, and did cast them to the earth: and the dragon stood before the woman which was ready to be delivered, for to devour her child as soon as it was born." – Revelation 12:1–4

The fraction "one-third" is associated with the angelic rebellion throughout Scripture:

> "The dragon who stood ready to devour him, is Satan. His tail draws a third part of the stars of heaven, and casts them down, in allusion to his seducing great numbers of angels to their fall." – *The Biblical Repertory and Princeton Review*, James A. Peabody, Volume 26, 1854, p. 291

Other examples of the significance of thirty-three or one-third indicating

God's judgment of rebellion include the following:

- **Joseph**, a foreshadow of Jesus Christ, was imprisoned with two other men. Through prophetic dreams, he and one of the other men were set free, while the third (who was a criminal) died.
- **Noah** had three sons who helped to restart the human population after the Flood. Two of the men were righteous, while the third—Ham—was wicked. Ham's son, Canaan, was the forefather of all the postdiluvian Nephilim.
- **Three Nephilim giants**—descendants of the fallen angels who married human women in Genesis 6—caused the Israelites to refuse to enter the Promised Land (see Numbers 13:33).
- **Joshua and Moses** defeated a combined number of thirty-three kings in the wars against the Nephilim giants (see Joshua 12:1–6, 12:24). The thirty-three kingdoms in the land of Canaan were symbolic of their fallen angelic forefathers.
- **The Crucifixion**, in which two men (Jesus Christ and the thief on another cross who believed in Him) entered Paradise after death while the third man (one-third of those being crucified that day) went to eternal punishment.
- **The Lord Jesus Christ** took on the sins of the world, sacrificing His life on the cross at age thirty-three.

Time and time again, the number thirty-three or one-third relates to rebellion, the righteous judgment of Yahweh, and the legacy of the fallen angels. During the end times, when God unleashes the supernatural judgments of the Day of the Lord (Great Tribulation) as described in Revelation, both the unsaved world and the angels will be judged. We see this repeated in the trumpet judgments of Revelation 8:

> "The first angel sounded, and there followed hail and fire mingled with blood, and they were cast upon the earth: **and the third part of trees was burnt up**, and all green grass was burnt up.

> And the second angel sounded, and as it were a great mountain burning with fire was cast into the sea: and **the third part of the sea became blood; And the third part of the creatures which were in the sea**, and had life, died; and **the third part** of the ships were destroyed.
>
> And the third angel sounded, and there fell a great star from heaven, burning as it were a lamp, **and it fell upon the third part of the rivers**, and upon the fountains of waters; And the name of the star is called Wormwood: **and the third part of the waters** became wormwood; and many men died of the waters, because they were made bitter. And the fourth angel sounded, and **the third part of the sun was smitten**, and **the third part of the moon, and the third part of the stars**; so **as the third part of them was darkened**, and the day shone not **for a third part of it**, and the night likewise." – Revelation 8:8–12

The Lord announced that His judgments in the Great Tribulation would be on humanity and the rebel angelic realm:

> "For the day of the LORD of hosts shall be upon every one that is proud and lofty, and upon every one that is lifted up; and he shall be brought low: And upon all the cedars of Lebanon, that are high and lifted up, and upon all the oaks of Bashan." – Isaiah 2:12–13

Ezekiel 31 details that the "cedars of Lebanon" were a reference to the fallen angels and a specific reference to the Antichrist in the days of Noah:

> "Behold, the Assyrian was a cedar in Lebanon with fair branches, and with a shadowing shroud, and of an high stature; and his top was among the thick boughs.... **The cedars in the garden of God** could not hide him: the fir trees were not like his boughs, and the

> chestnut trees were not like his branches; nor any tree in the garden of God was like unto him in his beauty." – Ezekiel 31:3, 8

The Antichrist and the fallen angels are going to be judged by God, with the destruction by the Lord of one-third of the various parts of the world they once had unjust dominion over. Yahweh pronounced a similar angelic judgment at the Exodus:

> "For I will pass through the land of Egypt this night, and will smite all the firstborn in the land of Egypt, both man and beast; **and against all the gods of Egypt I will execute judgment**: I am the LORD." – Exodus 12:12

> "For the Egyptians buried all their firstborn, which the LORD had smitten among them: **upon their gods also the LORD executed judgments**." – Numbers 33:4

In the days of Noah, God punished angels:

> "**For if God spared not the angels that sinned, but cast them down to hell**, and delivered them into chains of darkness, to be reserved unto judgment; And spared not the old world, but saved Noah the eighth person, a preacher of righteousness, bringing in the flood upon the world of the ungodly; And turning the cities of Sodom and Gomorrah into ashes condemned them with an overthrow, making them an ensample unto those that after should live ungodly." – 2 Peter 2:4–6

God will also redeem a remnant of Jewish believers, and specifically states that He will preserve a third of them:

> "And it shall come to pass, that in all the land, saith the Lord, two parts therein shall be cut off and die; but the third shall be left therein. And I will bring the third part through the fire, and will refine them as silver is refined, and will try them as gold is tried: they shall call on my name, and I will hear them: I will say, It is my people: and they shall say, The Lord is my God." – Zechariah 13:8–9

As one-third of the angels betrayed and abandoned Heaven in ancient times, the third of Israel who believe in the Lord Jesus Christ during the Day of the Lord judgments will symbolically replace them.

UNBELIEVING WORLD CONTINUES TO IGNORE GOD'S WARNINGS

> "And the rest of the men which were not killed by these plagues yet repented not of the works of their hands, that they should not worship devils, and idols of gold, and silver, and brass, and stone, and of wood: which neither can see, nor hear, nor walk: Neither repented they of their murders, nor of their sorceries, nor of their fornication, nor of their thefts." – Revelation 9:20–21

Despite seeing the supernatural works of God in bringing about cataclysmic destruction to much of the Earth and the global population, the unbelieving world, still mired in the strong delusion of the Antichrist, will not repent. Like the days of Noah where "every imagination of the thoughts of his heart was only **evil continually**." (Genesis 6:5), mankind will persist in the abomination of worshiping the seed of Satan and "devils."

As written in *Judgment of the Nephilim*, we can deduce that the demons are a different class of beings than the fallen angels. In fact, they are the spirits of the dead Nephilim. Much of their purpose in death is to promote idolatry—as the giants were the progenitors of almost all of the pagan spirituality in the Bible. In the end times, they will still serve this purpose. In the same passage from Isaiah 2 in which the Lord prophesied that He would punish the fallen angels in the end times, we see that it will greatly be in response to the rampant idolatry that will take place:

> "O house of Jacob, come ye, and let us walk in the light of the LORD. Therefore thou hast forsaken thy people the house of Jacob, because they be replenished from the east, and are soothsayers like the Philistines, and they please themselves in the children of strangers. Their land also is full of silver and gold, neither is there any end of their treasures; their land is also full of horses, neither is there any end of their chariots: **Their land also is full of idols; they worship the work of their own hands, that which their own fingers have made**: And the mean man boweth down, and the great man humbleth himself: therefore forgive them not.
>
> Enter into the rock, and hide thee in the dust, for fear of the LORD, and for the glory of his majesty. The lofty looks of man shall be humbled, and the haughtiness of men shall be bowed down, and the LORD alone shall be exalted in that day. For the day of the LORD of hosts shall be upon every one that is proud and lofty, and upon every one that is lifted up; and he shall be brought low: And upon all the cedars of Lebanon, that are high and lifted up, and upon all the oaks of Bashan." – Isaiah 2:5–13

With seared consciences and demonically altered genetics, the Antichrist loyalists will continue to seek idols for their salvation over Christ. An exposition on Revelation expands on this passage and the irrational refusal by the world to worship God:

"Reference is made here to the *deeds* and the *doctrines* of these sinners, who in vain will be called to repentance. Under strong delusion to believe the lie of the false Christ they will continue to worship the image of the beast: they will even worship the devil, and senseless idols for it is written, 'their land also is full of idols; they worship the work of their hands that which their own fingers have made.'" – *Notes on the Book of Revelation*, Helen Maclachlan, 1869, p. 133

SEVENTH TRUMPET: MYSTERY OF GOD COMPLETE

"And I saw another mighty angel come down from heaven, clothed with a cloud: and a rainbow was upon his head, and his face was as it were the sun, and his feet as pillars of fire: And he had in his hand a little book open: and he set his right foot upon the sea, and his left foot on the earth, And cried with a loud voice, as when a lion roareth: and when he had cried, seven thunders uttered their voices. And when the seven thunders had uttered their voices, I was about to write: and I heard a voice from heaven saying unto me, Seal up those things which the seven thunders uttered, and write them not.

And the angel which I saw stand upon the sea and upon the earth lifted up his hand to heaven, And sware by him that liveth for ever and ever, who created heaven, and the things that therein are, and the earth, and the things that therein are, and the sea, and the things which are therein, that there should be time no longer: But in the days of the voice of the seventh angel, when he shall begin to sound, the mystery of God should be finished, as he hath declared to his servants the prophets." – Revelation 10:1–7

Revelation chapters 10 through 15 are "parenthetical chapters" that provide greater context to the events of the seven trumpet judgments. The seventh and final trumpet is critical, because this is the moment the Lord proclaims that the mystery of God is complete. With all prophecy regarding this "mystery" fulfilled, the Lord can usher in the destruction of the Antichrist kingdom.

JESUS CHRIST DELIVERS THE MESSAGE TO JOHN

> "And I saw another mighty angel come down from heaven, clothed with a cloud: and a rainbow was upon his head, and his face was as it were the sun, and his feet as pillars of fire." – Revelation 10:1

The events of Revelation 10 through Revelation 11:14 are connected to the timing of the sixth trumpet judgment. The Lord Jesus Christ is the "mighty angel" of Revelation 10 as He was in Revelation 8. As one-third of the global population is being wiped out by the four angels of the Euphrates and their fallen angelic armies, the Messiah delivers a prophetic message to the Apostle John.

A number of features about this "angel" lead to no other conclusion than that this is Jesus:

- **He is clothed in a cloud.** When Jesus Christ ascended to Heaven as recorded in Acts chapter 1, He was "taken up; and a cloud received him out of their sight" (Acts 1:9). When Jesus appeared to Moses at Mt. Sinai, He appeared in a "thick cloud" (Exodus 19:9).
- **The rainbow is a symbol of God's salvation.**

> "And God said, This is the token of the covenant which I make between me and you and every living creature that is with you, for

> perpetual generations: I do set my bow in the cloud, and it shall be for a token of a covenant between me and the earth. And it shall come to pass, when I bring a cloud over the earth, that the bow shall be seen in the cloud: And I will remember my covenant, which is between me and you and every living creature of all flesh; and the waters shall no more become a flood to destroy all flesh. And the bow shall be in the cloud; and I will look upon it, that I may remember the everlasting covenant between God and every living creature of all flesh that is upon the earth." – Genesis 9:12–16

The prophet Ezekiel made a similar observation of God's presence resembling the rainbow:

> "As the appearance of the bow that is in the cloud in the day of rain, so was the appearance of the brightness round about. This was the appearance of the likeness of the glory of the **LORD**. And when I saw it, I fell upon my face." – Ezekiel 1:28

- **Jesus' face was "as the sun."** When the select group of disciples saw Jesus in a glorified, divine form on the Mount of Transfiguration, Scripture tells us that "his face did shine as the sun, and his raiment was white as the light" (Matthew 17:2).
- **Jesus' feet were as "pillars of fire."** During the Exodus, Jesus led the Israelites with a "pillar of fire by night" (Exodus 13:21; 13:22; 14:24).
- **Jesus roars like a lion**. One of the most well-known titles of Jesus is "the Lion of the tribe of Judah" (Revelation 5:5).

A treatise by the rector in Albury, England, identified the "angel" as the Lord Jesus Christ:

> "And for this end, [Jesus] is represented as descending to the earth

in a cloud with a rainbow upon His head. His face also resplendent as the sun, and His feet as pillars of fire, aptly represent the purpose He is coming to accomplish. The 'rainbow,' as we have seen in another place, is the symbol of the covenant, and as there is no bow ever seen in the heavens without a cloud giving forth its refreshing water, so is the cloud in this vision used as a symbol of that ministration of the Church of Christ, through which He gives the refreshing rain of the Holy Spirit; and by which His covenant is revived in the hearts of His people. For He comes to revive in their hope, and to present to their faith that inheritance which He has prepared for them." – *The Revelation of Jesus Christ Explained Agreeably to the Analogy of Holy Scripture and the Interpretation of Its Symbols*, John Hooper, 1850, p. 375

SEVEN THUNDERS REVEAL FULFILLMENT OF THE MYSTERY OF GOD

"And when the seven thunders had uttered their voices, I was about to write: and I heard a voice from heaven saying unto me, Seal up those things which the seven thunders uttered, and write them not. And the angel which I saw stand upon the sea and upon the earth lifted up his hand to heaven, And sware by him that liveth for ever and ever, who created heaven, and the things that therein are, and the earth, and the things that therein are, and the sea, and the things which are therein, that there should be time no longer: **But in the days of the voice of the seventh angel, when he shall begin to sound, the mystery of God should be finished, as he hath declared to his servants the prophets.**" – Revelation 10:4–7

The "mystery of God" declared to the Old Testament prophets is that the

Lord would use the nation of Israel to bring His Word and the Messiah to the whole world. However, **it would be the Gentiles who would receive the prophetic promises of salvation first**. And in the end times, the believing remnant of Israel will return, uniting with the Church and making the plan of salvation complete. The passage above makes it clear that the mystery the seven thunders were proclaiming has been "declared to his servants the prophets," thus it is something that can be discovered in Scripture.

"MYSTERY OF GOD" REFERRED TO SEVEN TIMES

We see a direct reference to the "mystery of God" in seven instances in Scripture:

> "And when he was alone, they that were about him with the twelve asked of him the parable. And he said unto them, **Unto you it is given to know the mystery of the kingdom of God**: but unto them that are without, all these things are done in parables: That seeing they may see, and not perceive; and hearing they may hear, and not understand; lest at any time they should be converted, and their sins should be forgiven them." – Mark 4:10–12

> "**But we speak the wisdom of God in a mystery, even the hidden wisdom**, which God ordained before the world unto our glory: Which none of the princes of this world knew: for had they known it, they would not have crucified the Lord of glory." – 1 Corinthians 2:7–8

The Apostle Paul explains the mystery in Ephesians 3:

> "How that by revelation he made **known unto me the mystery**; (as I wrote afore in few words, Whereby, when ye read, **ye may**

> **understand my knowledge in the mystery of Christ**) Which in other ages was not made known unto the sons of men, as it is now revealed unto his holy apostles and prophets by the Spirit; **That the Gentiles should be fellow heirs, and of the same body, and partakers of his promise in Christ by the gospel**:
>
> Whereof I was made a minister, according to the gift of the grace of God given unto me by the effectual working of his power. Unto me, who am less than the least of all saints, is this grace given, that I should preach among the Gentiles the unsearchable riches of Christ; And to make all men see what is the fellowship of the mystery, which from the beginning of the world hath been hid in God, who created all things by Jesus Christ: **To the intent that now unto the principalities and powers in heavenly places might be known by the church the manifold wisdom of God**." – Ephesians 3:3–12

This is the redemption of the Gentile nations as part of the Body of Christ, fulfilling all of the promises made to Abraham, Isaac, and Jacob. **The final nation to be won over by the Gospel will be Israel**. This is the meaning of the phrase, "the first shall be last, the last shall be first" (Matthew 20:16). Israel received the prophecy first, but will be the last to experience its fulfillment. The Gentile Church received the promises last (during the ministry of Jesus on Earth and through the apostles), but experienced its fulfillment first (receiving the Holy Spirit at Pentecost, being raptured, etc.). The Apostle Paul explained this in exquisite fashion in Romans 11:

> "**For I speak to you Gentiles, inasmuch as I am the apostle of the Gentiles**, I magnify mine office: If by any means I may provoke to emulation them which are my flesh [the Jewish people], and might save some of them. **For if the casting away of them be the reconciling of the world, what shall the receiving of them be, but life from the dead**? For if the first fruit be holy, the lump is

> also holy: and if the root be holy, so are the branches. And if some of the branches be broken off, and thou, being a wild olive tree, wert grafted in among them, and with them partakest of the root and fatness of the olive tree; Boast not against the branches. But if thou boast, thou bearest not the root, but the root thee. Thou wilt say then, The branches were broken off, that I might be grafted in." – Romans 11:13–19

Israel's rejection of Christ resulted in, them, as the "natural branch," being "broken off" and the Gentile Church, the wild branch or second child, being "grafted in." So Israel, though the firstborn, rejected salvation in Christ as part of God's overall plan of redemption for the world. We, of course, see the similarities of this to the many sibling rivalries in Scripture: Cain was born first, but Abel was the child of faith. Ishmael was born first, but Isaac, the second born, was the child of promise. Esau was born first, but his blessing switched to Jacob. These are just some of the foreshadows of the sibling rivalry between Israel and its "little brother," the Church. But Paul warned the Church not to boast in understanding and believing the Gospel first:

> "Well; because of unbelief they were broken off, and thou standest by faith. Be not high minded, but fear: For if God spared not the natural branches, take heed lest he also spare not thee. Behold therefore the goodness and severity of God: on them which fell, severity; but toward thee, goodness, if thou continue in his goodness: otherwise thou also shalt be cut off. And they also, if they abide not still in unbelief, shall be grafted in: for God is able to graft them in again. For if thou wert cut out of the olive tree which is wild by nature, and wert grafted contrary to nature into a good olive tree: how much more shall these, which be the natural branches, be grafted into their own olive tree?" – Romans 11:20:24.

If the Christian Church gets lax and falls into apostasy, it can be cut off just as Israel was. But God will graft Israel back into the Tree of Life—His salvation. That will occur during the Day of the Lord. This redemption of Israel will complete "the mystery":

> "**For I would not, brethren, that ye should be ignorant of this mystery**, lest ye should be wise in your own conceits; that blindness in part is happened to Israel, until the fullness of the Gentiles be come in. And so all Israel shall be saved: as it is written, There shall come out of Sion the Deliverer, and shall turn away ungodliness from Jacob." – Romans 11:25–26

The mystery is clearly explained: Israel was cut off from God so that the Gentile Church could be born and receive the Gospel blessing of salvation. Once the Church comes to its "fullness" at the Rapture, God will then turn His face back towards Israel to redeem it and complete the plan He has given to the prophets over millennia.

The Lord's design from the beginning of time is to save all of humanity. Knowing the extent to which the Devil would go to bring the entire world into utter ruin, God hid the execution of the plan of redemption in mystery from all—even the fallen angels. This was declared by the prophets through various points in history. The nations that were once under the dominion of the fallen angels would be filled with the Gospel and won over. No longer would Israel alone be God's portion; the entire Earth was being redeemed and reclaimed from the fallen angelic usurpers. The following excerpt confirms this understanding:

> "The seventh trumpet shall be sounded without further delay. The mystery of God—the theme of the 'little book' and so of the remainder of the Apocalypse. What a grand contrast to the 'mystery of iniquity, Babylon.' **The mystery of God's scheme of redemption, once hidden in God's secret counsels and dimly**

> **shadowed forth in types and prophecies**, but now more and more clearly revealed according as the gospel-kingdom develops itself, up to its fullest consummation at the end. Then, finally, His servants shall praise Him most fully for the glorious consummation of the mystery in having taken to Himself and His saints the kingdom so long usurped by Satan and the ungodly.
>
> Thus, this verse is an anticipation of chapter 11:15–18. 'declared to'—'declared the glad tidings to.' **The mystery of God is the gospel [of] glad tidings**. The office of the prophets is to receive the glad tidings from God in order to declare them to others. The final consummation is the great theme of the gospel announced to and by the prophets." – *A Commentary, Critical, Practical and Explanatory, on the Old and New Testaments*, Robert Jamieson, Andrew Robert Faussett, David Brown, 1884, p. 571

SEVENTH TRUMPET SOUNDS; JEWISH REMNANT—LAST BELIEVERS LEFT ON EARTH

With the world under his sway and the Mark of the Beast corrupting most of the global population, the Antichrist's genocidal campaign against remaining believers in God will almost be complete. At the sound of the sixth trumpet, the Two Witnesses are killed:

> "And when they shall have finished their testimony, the beast that ascendeth out of the bottomless pit shall make war against them, and shall overcome them, and kill them. And their dead bodies shall lie in the street of the great city, which spiritually is called Sodom and Egypt, where also our Lord was crucified. And they of the people and kindreds and tongues and nations shall see their dead bodies three days and an half, and shall not suffer their dead bodies

> to be put in graves. And they that dwell upon the earth shall rejoice over them, and make merry, and shall send gifts one to another; because these two prophets tormented them that dwelt on the earth." – Revelation 11:7–10

The 144,000 will also have been killed, because, by the time of Revelation 14, they are in Heaven on Mt. Sion with the Lord Jesus Christ:

> "And I looked, and, lo, a Lamb stood on the mount Sion, and with him an hundred forty and four thousand, having his Father's name written in their foreheads. And I heard a voice from heaven, as the voice of many waters, and as the voice of a great thunder: and I heard the voice of harpers harping with their harps: And they sung as it were a new song before the throne, and before the four beasts, and the elders: and no man could learn that song but the hundred and forty and four thousand, which were redeemed from the earth."
> – Revelation 14:1–3

And in Revelation 15, we see the sprits of the Great Tribulation martyrs—those who came to saving faith during the reign of Antichrist and refused the Mark of the Beast under penalty of death:

> "And I saw another sign in heaven, great and marvellous, seven angels having the seven last plagues; for in them is filled up the wrath of God. And I saw as it were a sea of glass mingled with fire: and them that had gotten the victory over the beast, and over his image, and over his mark, and over the number of his name, stand on the sea of glass, having the harps of God. And they sing the song of Moses the servant of God, and the song of the Lamb, saying, Great and marvellous are thy works, Lord God Almighty; just and true are thy ways, thou King of saints." – Revelation 15:1–3

Notice that the seven angels holding the vials of wrath have not poured them out yet. The Great Tribulation believers are standing before the throne. As previously mentioned, these beloved martyrs triumphantly sing the song of Moses—the one sung by Moses and the Israelites right after the destruction of Pharaoh and the Egyptian armies by God at the Red Sea (interestingly, we find this song in **the fifteenth chapter** of Exodus):

> "Then sang Moses and the children of Israel this song unto the LORD, and spake, saying, I will sing unto the LORD, for he hath triumphed gloriously: the horse and his rider hath he thrown into the sea. The LORD is my strength and song, and he is become my salvation: he is my God, and I will prepare him an habitation; my father's God, and I will exalt him. The LORD is a man of war: the LORD is his name. Pharaoh's chariots and his host hath he cast into the sea: his chosen captains also are drowned in the Red sea. The depths have covered them: they sank into the bottom as a stone." – Exodus 15:1-5

Moses emphasizes that this is a war: God waging war against the forces of evil for the salvation of His people.

> "Thy right hand, O LORD, is become glorious in power: thy right hand, O LORD, hath dashed in pieces the enemy. And in the greatness of thine excellency thou hast overthrown them that rose up against thee: thou sentest forth thy wrath, which consumed them as stubble. And with the blast of thy nostrils the waters were gathered together, the floods stood upright as an heap, and the depths were congealed in the heart of the sea." – Exodus 15:5-8

As we've noted earlier, the "right hand" of God is the Messiah, *Yeshua*. Just as He conquered the Nephilim and the fallen sons of God with the Flood, Jesus drowned Pharaoh and his armies with the waters of the Red Sea. But in this final battle, He will personally come again to conquer the Final Nephilim.

> "The enemy said, I will pursue, I will overtake, I will divide the spoil; my lust shall be satisfied upon them; I will draw my sword, my hand shall destroy them. Thou didst blow with thy wind, the sea covered them: they sank as lead in the mighty waters." - Exodus 15:9-10

In satanic, delusional, arrogance, the Antichrist will have thought he could gain supreme authority by killing all believers and taking control of the earth. But this was only for a brief season as God prepares to show the world He is returning with the vials of wrath.

> **"Who is like unto thee, O LORD, among the gods?** who is like thee, glorious in holiness, fearful in praises, doing wonders?" – Exodus 15:11

Here Moses again confirms that God is punishing the "gods," or fallen angels, in addition to unsaved humanity. This is the consummation of much of the great war.

> "Thou stretchedst out thy right hand, the earth swallowed them. Thou in thy mercy hast led forth the people which thou hast redeemed: thou hast guided them in thy strength unto thy holy habitation. The people shall hear, and be afraid: sorrow shall take hold on the inhabitants of Palestina. Then the dukes of Edom shall be amazed; the mighty men of Moab, trembling shall take hold upon them; all the inhabitants of Canaan shall melt away.
>
> Fear and dread shall fall upon them; by the greatness of thine arm they shall be as still as a stone; **till thy people pass over, O LORD,**

> **till the people pass over, which thou hast purchased**." – Exodus 15:12-16

This is God's plan. Jesus Christ purchased the salvation of all who believe in Him with His blood shed on the cross. God loves humanity, and the record of human history is a testament to His unfolding plan to redeem us—even when we don't deserve it—to sacrifice for people who are guilty, and to lead people who at one time or another reject Him in sinful rebellion.

> "Thou shalt bring them in, and plant them in the mountain of thine inheritance, in the place, O LORD, which thou hast made for thee to dwell in, in the Sanctuary, O LORD, which thy hands have established. The LORD shall reign for ever and ever." – Exodus 15:17-18

And this brings it all back to Mount Zion—the Holy City of Jerusalem. The way for the True King—the Messiah—was being prepared, and the corrupted Jerusalem and its hybrid leader are soon to be destroyed.

SECOND SONG OF MOSES FURTHER CONFIRMS GOD'S ENSUING VICTORY OVER THE FINAL NEPHILIM

There is a second song of Moses in Deuteronomy 32; it is the final prophecy given by this great servant of the Lord before he went to die on Mt. Pisgah. In it, a double prophecy tells of Israel's rejection of the Lord Jesus Christ at His First Coming as well as gives a dreadful picture of the world in the Great Tribulation after the majority of Israel falls prey to the deception of the Antichrist delusion:

> "Give ear, O ye heavens, and I will speak; and hear, O earth, the

> words of my mouth. My doctrine shall drop as the rain, my speech shall distil as the dew, as the small rain upon the tender herb, and as the showers upon the grass: Because I will publish the name of the LORD: ascribe ye greatness unto our God." – Deuteronomy 32:1–3

The message given through Moses is a declaration to the heavens and earth, as both will be judged in the end times. And this is to proclaim the Name of the Lord—Jesus Christ.

> "He is the Rock, his work is perfect: for all his ways are judgment: a God of truth and without iniquity, just and right is he. **They have corrupted themselves, their spot is not the spot of his children: they are a perverse and crooked generation.**" – Deuteronomy 32:4–5

This is precisely what the state of the world will be during the reign of Antichrist. The overwhelming majority of the planet will have taken the Mark of the Beast, pledged their full allegiance to the Final Nephilim, and "corrupted themselves" genetically. The word "spot" [*m'uwm,* or מְאוּם in Hebrew] refers to a physical blemish and is used repeatedly in Scripture in the rules regarding Temple sacrifices

> "This is the ordinance of the law which the LORD hath commanded, saying, Speak unto the children of Israel, that they bring thee a red heifer without spot [*m'uwm*], wherein is no blemish, and upon which never came yoke." – Numbers 19:2

> "Thou shalt not sacrifice unto the LORD thy God any bullock, or sheep, wherein is blemish [*m'uwm*], or any evil favouredness: for that is an abomination unto the LORD thy God." – Numbers 17:1

Recall that in Genesis 6, Noah was described as "perfect in his generations." The term "perfect" [*tamiym* in Hebrew] denotes physical perfection or being "without blemish." Noah was perfect in the sense that his lineage was wholly human. Renowned theologian A. W. Pink arrived at the same conclusion:

> "Second [Noah] was perfect in his generations Here the reference seems to point to Noah and his family having kept themselves separate from the moral evil around them and preserved themselves from contact with the Nephilim. The Hebrew word is *tamiym* and is elsewhere translated in the Old Testament without blemish forty four times It is probably the word from which our English contaminated springs Noah was uncontaminated in his generations." – *Gleanings in Genesis*, A. W. Pink, 1922, p. 83

The second song of Moses is a prophetic portrayal of the end-times world when the unbelieving populace, genetically corrupted by the Antichrist, can no longer be received by God. The verse above states that "their spot is not the spot of his children," giving further evidence of the genetic and physical nature of the verse. Only the children of God, who are redeemed by "the precious blood of Christ, as of a lamb without blemish and without spot" (1 Peter 1:19), retain their standing as image-bearers of God and will be saved in the final judgment. Continuing in Deuteronomy 32:

> "Do ye thus requite the LORD, O foolish people and unwise? is not he thy father that hath bought thee? hath he not made thee, and established thee? Remember the days of old, consider the years of many generations: ask thy father, and he will shew thee; thy elders, and they will tell thee. When the Most High divided to the nations their inheritance, when he separated the sons of Adam, he set the bounds of the people according to the number of the children of Israel. For the LORD's portion is his people; Jacob is the lot of his

inheritance." – Deuteronomy 32:6–9

As discussed earlier, this passage records the division of the world between the "nations"—the Gentile world that was given to dominion of angels—and Israel, which is "the Lord's portion." While that ancient division took place at the Tower of Babel rebellion, it will be repeated in the Day of the Lord, when the whole world will be turned over to the control and authority of the Antichrist:

> "And power was given him over all kindreds, and tongues, and nations." (Revelation 13:17)

Every nation on Earth will be under the control of Satan, a fallen angel, and his Nephilim progeny, who will be indwelled by a fallen angel. The only remaining portion that is faithful to God will be the one-third, believing remnant of Israel, who will be supernaturally protected from the devastating judgments of the trumpets and bowls:

> "He found him in a desert land, and in the waste howling wilderness; he led him about, he instructed him, he kept him as the apple of his eye. **As an eagle stirreth up her nest, fluttereth over her young, spreadeth abroad her wings, taketh them, beareth them on her wings**: So the LORD alone did lead him, and there was no strange god with him. He made him ride on the high places of the earth, that he might eat the increase of the fields; and he made him to suck honey out of the rock, and oil out of the flinty rock; Butter of kine, and milk of sheep, with fat of lambs, and rams of the breed of Bashan, and goats, with the fat of kidneys of wheat; and thou didst drink the pure blood of the grape." – Deuteronomy 32:10–14

This beautiful passage details Yahweh's love and provision for His people in the wilderness, both after the Exodus and in the future wilderness journey in Edom. Its language mirrors the prophecy of Revelation 12, wherein the Israelites escape the Devil's attack during the Great Tribulation:

> "**And to the woman were given two wings of a great eagle**, that she might fly into the wilderness, into her place, where she is nourished for a time, and times, and half a time, from the face of the serpent." – Revelation 12:14

At the point when the believing remnant flees, the remaining two-thirds and the unbelieving Gentile world will worship the Beast. This is also prophesied in Deuteronomy 32:15:

> "But Jeshurun waxed fat, and kicked: thou art waxen fat, thou art grown thick, thou art covered with fatness; then he forsook God which made him, and lightly esteemed the Rock of his salvation."

In taking the Mark, the unsaved portion of Israel will forsake God and Jesus Christ—the Rock of Salvation and True Messiah.

> "They provoked him to jealousy with strange gods, with abominations provoked they him to anger. They sacrificed unto devils, not to God; to gods whom they knew not, to new gods that came newly up, whom your fathers feared not." – Deuteronomy 32:16

As the Abyss is opened at the sound of the fifth trumpet of Revelation, releasing the apostate sons of God, and one-third of the heavenly rebels are cast to earth, there will be an explosion in the worship of the demons and fallen spirits who invade the planet during the Great Tribulation. There will no doubt be many "new gods" who will be worshiped by the unfaithful world in the final years before the Revelation of Christ.

> "Of the Rock that begat thee thou art unmindful, and hast forgotten God that formed thee. And when the LORD saw it, he abhorred them, because of the provoking of his sons, and of his daughters. And he said, I will hide my face from them, I will see what their end shall be: for they are a very froward generation, children in whom is no faith. They have moved me to jealousy with that which is not God; they have provoked me to anger with their vanities: and I will move them to jealousy with those which are not a people; I will provoke them to anger with a foolish nation." – Deuteronomy 32:18–21

The final "foolish nation" will be the fallen angelic, hybrid kingdom of the Antichrist. The worship of Antichrist will provoke God to judge the Earth with supernatural punishments not experienced in millennia.

> "For a fire is kindled in mine anger, and shall burn unto the lowest hell, and shall consume the earth with her increase, and set on fire the foundations of the mountains. I will heap mischiefs upon them; I will spend mine arrows upon them. They shall be burnt with hunger, and devoured with burning heat, and with bitter destruction: I will also send the teeth of beasts upon them, with the poison of serpents of the dust. The sword without, and terror within, shall destroy both the young man and the virgin, the suckling also with the man of gray hairs." – Deuteronomy 32:22–25

This is obviously fulfilled through the punishments of the trumpets and vials. The lowest Hell is literally opened and unleashed on Earth at the fifth trumpet. And many of the judgments described are experienced throughout the seven vials.

> "I said, I would scatter them into corners, I would make the remembrance of them to cease from among men: Were it not that I feared the wrath of the enemy, lest their adversaries should behave themselves strangely, and **lest they should say, Our hand is high, and the LORD hath not done all this**." – Deuteronomy 32:26–27

Breaking the truth of God's prophetic Word is another primary objective of the Enemy, who wants the Lord's promises to fail before all of Earth and Heaven. God spared Israel repeatedly not just for love, but to prevent the Devil and his minions from ever proclaiming victory.

> "For they are a nation void of counsel, neither is there any understanding in them. O that they were wise, that they understood this, that they would consider their latter end! How should one chase a thousand, and two put ten thousand to flight, except their Rock had sold them, and the LORD had shut them up?" – Deuteronomy 32:28–30

The only time the spiritual enemies can attack Israel is when the nation falls so deep into sinful rebellion that God permits their suffering as a punishment for their wickedness. When God puts His hedge of protection around a believer, Satan, the fallen angelic realm, and the Nephilim are powerless. The Devil admitted as much in reference to Job:

> "And the LORD said unto Satan, Hast thou considered my servant Job, that there is none like him in the earth, a perfect and an upright man, one that feareth God, and escheweth evil? Then Satan answered the LORD, and said, Doth Job fear God for nought? Hast not thou made an hedge about him, and about his house, and about

> all that he hath on every side? thou hast blessed the work of his hands, and his substance is increased in the land." – Job 1:8–10

> "**For their rock is not as our Rock**, even our enemies themselves being judges. For their vine is of the vine of Sodom, and of the fields of Gomorrah: their grapes are grapes of gall, their clusters are bitter: Their wine is the poison of dragons, and the cruel venom of asps." – Deuteronomy 32:31–33

In the end times, the unsaved world will trust in "their rock"—the Final Nephilim who is the vine of "Sodom and Gomorrah" and the wine of the "dragon.". The True Rock of Salvation is Jesus Christ—the Seed of the Woman. This will be a conscious decision. Every person on the planet will have to choose between Christ and Antichrist. During the Exodus, God was in open combat against the gods of Egypt. Pharaoh and his armies acknowledged this as God brought judgment against the Egyptians and rendered their ten gods powerless:

> "And the Egyptians pursued, and went in after them to the midst of the sea, even all Pharaoh's horses, his chariots, and his horsemen. And it came to pass, that in the morning watch the LORD looked unto the host of the Egyptians through the pillar of fire and of the cloud, and troubled the host of the Egyptians, And took off their chariot wheels, that they drave them heavily: **so that the Egyptians said, Let us flee from the face of Israel; for the LORD fighteth for them against the Egyptians.**" – Exodus 14:23–25

During the second Exodus, the rebels will again know and acknowledge that it is the Lord who judges them and avenges His people:

> "And the kings of the earth, and the great men, and the rich men, and the chief captains, and the mighty men, and every bondman,

> and every free man, hid themselves in the dens and in the rocks of the mountains; And said to the mountains and rocks, Fall on us, and hide us from the face of him that sitteth on the throne, and from the wrath of the Lamb: For the great day of his wrath is come; and who shall be able to stand?" – Revelation 6:15–17

Continuing the song of Moses:

> "Is not this laid up in store with me, and sealed up among my treasures? To me belongeth vengeance and recompence; their foot shall slide in due time: for the day of their calamity is at hand, and the things that shall come upon them make haste. For the LORD shall judge his people, and repent himself for his servants, when he seeth that their power is gone, and there is none shut up, or left. And he shall say, Where are their gods, their rock in whom they trusted, Which did eat the fat of their sacrifices, and drank the wine of their drink offerings? let them rise up and help you, and be your protection. See now that I, even I, am he, and there is no god with me: I kill, and I make alive; I wound, and I heal: neither is there any that can deliver out of my hand." – Deuteronomy 32:34–39

Vengeance for all the murder, violence, hatred, robbery, rape, perversion, and every other evil carried out in the world belongs to God. The massive persecution of believers in Christ that has been carried out by Satan for millennia will be avenged by the Lord. When this song is sung, the time for the wrath of God to be poured out on the world will have arrived. No fallen angel, Nephilim, or human army can stop it.

When the destructive force of the seven vials of wrath are poured out, the world will see their rock—Antichrist—rendered powerless in the face of God's might. All of their worship and allegiance will achieve nothing when God arises to bring it to an end and usher in the eternal kingdom.

> "For I lift up my hand to heaven, and say, 'I live for ever.' If I whet my glittering sword, and mine hand take hold on judgment; I will render vengeance to mine enemies, and will reward them that hate me. I will make mine arrows drunk with blood, and my sword shall devour flesh; and that with the blood of the slain and of the captives, from the beginning of revenges upon the enemy. Rejoice, O ye nations, with his people: for he will avenge the blood of his servants, and will render vengeance to his adversaries, and will be merciful unto his land, and to his people. And Moses came and spake all the words of this song in the ears of the people, he, and Hoshea the son of Nun." – Deuteronomy 32:40–44

This will mark the end of the reign of Antichrist. At the seventh trumpet, the mystery will be completed. The remnant of Israel will come to saving faith in Christ, and the Lord will supernaturally protect them from the end-times judgments, just as He did during the first Exodus. And, like Pharaoh, the Final Nephilim will once again watch his kingdom crumble by the mighty Right Hand of God. But this will be the final time. The Messiah is on His way to officially take back His Kingdom.

CHAPTER 11

THE SECOND EXODUS

"And the seventh angel sounded; and there were great voices in heaven, saying, The kingdoms of this world are become the kingdoms of our Lord, and of his Christ; and he shall reign for ever and ever. And the four and twenty elders, which sat before God on their seats, fell upon their faces, and worshipped God, Saying, We give thee thanks, O LORD God Almighty, which art, and wast, and art to come; because thou hast taken to thee thy great power, and hast reigned. And the nations were angry, and thy wrath is come, and the time of the dead, that they should be judged, and that thou shouldest give reward unto thy servants the prophets, and to the saints, and them that fear thy name, small and great; and shouldest destroy them which destroy the earth." – Revelation 11:15–18

"The destruction of Pharaoh (the oppressor of Israel) and his host in 'the overflowing' is typical of the destruction of Antichrist and the confederate armies of the ten kingdoms. The plagues with which the Egyptians were visited are typical of the wrath (Rev 15, 16) which will hereafter be poured out on those who will be connected with Antichrist. The plagues recorded in Exodus, and those predicted in Revelation, are similar.

During the plagues of Egypt and at the destruction of Pharaoh and his host, Moses was a type of Christ. At his command the plagues came on the Egyptians. He stretched forth his rod, and the sea became a deliverance to his people, but destruction to Pharaoh and

> his host. So will it be when Antichrist is destroyed—"at that time shall thy people be delivered" (Daniel 12:1)." – *A Comparison of Prophetic Scripture with Reference to Antichrist*, Henry Kelsall, 1846, p. 86–87

Just when Antichrist thinks he has rid himself of his enemies—by exterminating the Great Tribulation believers and running the Jewish remnant out of the Holy Land—he will suffer the utter ruin of his kingdom by the wrath of God. The mystery of God completed, the Lord initiates the destruction of the Final Nephilim's kingdom.

VIAL JUDGMENTS: SECOND FULFILLMENT OF EXODUS PLAGUES

> "These seven last plagues appear to have some reference to the plagues of Egypt, but they are not for this reason to be merely understood literally, as several commentators suggest. They precede the deliverance of the people of God, as the plagues of Egypt preceded the Exodus, but they especially affect the beast and his worshippers his throne and his city not merely natural objects in themselves." – *The Words of the Angels, or, Their Visits to Earth and the Messages They Delivered*, Rudolf Stier, 1877 p. 209

> "And I heard a great voice out of the temple saying to the seven angels, Go your ways, and pour out the vials of the wrath of God upon the earth. And the first went, and poured out his vial upon the earth; and there fell a noisome and grievous sore upon the men which had the mark of the beast, and upon them which worshipped his image." – Revelation 16:1–2

First Vial: Sores

The first vial causes gruesome sores to grow on everyone who will take the Mark of the Beast. Their population already devastated, the remaining survivors of the trumpet judgments will see their quest to become "evolved human beings" or "human 2.0" fail disastrously as they suffer disgusting sores on their body. The word "noisome" [*kak*, or κακός in Greek] means "evil."

During the first Exodus, this was sixth plague, but it was the first plague that targeted Jannes and Jambres, the top sorcerers in Pharaoh's court:

> "And the LORD said unto Moses and unto Aaron, Take to you handfuls of ashes of the furnace, and let Moses sprinkle it toward the heaven in the sight of Pharaoh. And it shall become small dust in all the land of Egypt, and shall be a boil breaking forth with blains upon man, and upon beast, throughout all the land of Egypt. And they took ashes of the furnace, and stood before Pharaoh; and Moses sprinkled it up toward heaven; and it became a boil breaking forth with blains upon man, and upon beast. **And the magicians could not stand before Moses because of the boils; for the boil was upon the magicians, and upon all the Egyptians**." – Exodus 9:8–11

Those who engage in the satanic worship and witchcraft of the Mark of the Beast will suffer judgment by God.

Second and Third Vials: Seas and Rivers Turn to Blood

> "And the second angel poured out his vial upon the sea; and it became as the blood of a dead man: **and every living soul died in the sea**. And the third angel poured out his vial upon the rivers and fountains of waters; and they became blood. And I heard the angel

> of the waters say, Thou art righteous, O Lord, which art, and wast, and shalt be, because thou hast judged thus. For they have shed the blood of saints and prophets, and thou hast given them blood to drink; for they are worthy. And I heard another out of the altar say, Even so, Lord God Almighty, true and righteous are thy judgments." – Revelation 16:3–7

Imagine that all aquatic life on Earth dies in a moment. Recall that the *second trumpet* judgment is only unleashed on a third of the seas. At the second vial, all waters are completely destroyed. With no fish or sea vegetation, the earth's entire biosphere will be thrown into disarray. Death and blood are the logical conclusion of fully following the Devil. There is no reward in the end for sin. There is no great "party" awaiting those who live in rebellion against the Lord and reject His offer of free salvation through faith in the atoning work of the Messiah. There is only judgment, despair, and death.

Salvation in Jesus Christ through **His blood** gives life and joy eternally. The blood of the Antichrist is a poison that, once mingled with human DNA, ensures punishment. Biblical scholar Matthew Henry included in his commentary remarks on the blood being "dead":

> "God discovered not only the vanity and falsehood of their religion, but the pernicious and deadly nature of it—that the souls of men were poisoned by that which was pretended to be the sure means of their salvation." – *Exposition of the Old and New Testament*, Volume 3, Matthew Henry, 1828, Revelation XVI

At this point, the world will enter a state of complete ruin and decay, just as in Egypt during the Exodus. This "blood" judgment is one of the most well-known among the plagues that was sent upon Pharaoh's kingdom:

> "Thus saith the LORD, In this thou shalt know that I am the LORD:

> behold, I will smite with the rod that is in mine hand upon the waters which are in the river, and they shall be turned to blood. And the fish that is in the river shall die, and the river shall stink; and the Egyptians shall lothe to drink of the water of the river. And the LORD spake unto Moses, Say unto Aaron, Take thy rod, and stretch out thine hand upon the waters of Egypt, upon their streams, upon their rivers, and upon their ponds, and upon all their pools of water, that they may become blood; and that there may be blood throughout all the land of Egypt, both in vessels of wood, and in vessels of stone. And Moses and Aaron did so, as the LORD commanded; and he lifted up the rod, and smote the waters that were in the river, in the sight of Pharaoh, and in the sight of his servants; and all the waters that were in the river were turned to blood.
>
> And the fish that was in the river died; and the river stank, and the Egyptians could not drink of the water of the river; and there was blood throughout all the land of Egypt. And the magicians of Egypt did so with their enchantments: and Pharaoh's heart was hardened, neither did he hearken unto them; as the LORD had said."

The death and decomposition of hundreds of millions of fish and sea creatures will leave a stench not experienced in thousands of years. At the pouring of the third vial, even the rivers and "fountains"—the many springs that deliver fresh water to the earth's surface—will only produce blood. Water, the most essential part of the entire existence of every creature, will be ruined. People will be forced to drink the blood of the dead for sustenance.

This fulfills a Messianic prophecy from the book of Isaiah that details the judgments meted out by Jesus Christ upon His return to earth:

> "But thus saith the LORD, Even the captives of the mighty shall be taken away, and the prey of the terrible shall be delivered: for I will

> contend with him that contendeth with thee, and I will save thy children.
>
> And I will feed them that oppress thee with their own flesh; **and they shall be drunken with their own blood, as with sweet wine**: and all flesh shall know that I the LORD am thy Saviour and thy Redeemer, the mighty One of Jacob." – Isaiah 49:25–26

A commentary on the book of Revelation includes the following description of this horrific future fate of the world:

> "Here too is a fresh notion introduced in reference to the blood. Not only do the rivers and fountains the natural source of life and health, become vehicles of death and destruction, but the drinking of blood is the natural and just reward of those who have shed blood. This corresponds to the prophecy of Isaiah, 'I will feed them that oppress thee with their own flesh; and they shall be drunken with their own blood, as with sweet wine: and all flesh shall know that I the Lord am thy Saviour and thy Redeemer, the mighty One of Jacob.'" – *The New Testament of Our Lord and Saviour Jesus Christ, According to the Authorized Version, with a Brief Commentary by Various Authors, the Acts, Epistles and Revelation*, 1880, Section 4–7

Angel of the Waters Proclaims God's Justice

After the second and third vials are poured out by two of the seven angels in Heaven, the angel of the waters voices approval of the Lord turning the waters of the Antichrist's kingdom to blood:

> "And I heard the angel of the waters say, Thou art righteous, O Lord, which art, and wast, and shalt be, because thou hast judged

> thus. For they have shed the blood of saints and prophets, and thou hast given them blood to drink; for they are worthy." – Revelation 16:5-6

That an angel is designated over the waters of the Earth shouldn't be a surprise. In *Judgment of the Nephilim*, I detailed that angels often manifest near bodies of water—rivers in particular. This angel is akin to the four angels in Revelation 7 who hold back the four winds that traverse the planet:

> "And after these things I saw four angels standing on the four corners of the earth, holding the four winds of the earth, that the wind should not blow on the earth, nor on the sea, nor on any tree. And I saw another angel ascending from the east, having the seal of the living God: and he cried with a loud voice to the four angels, to whom it was given to hurt the earth and the sea, Saying, Hurt not the earth, neither the sea, nor the trees, till we have sealed the servants of our God in their foreheads." – Revelation 7:1–3

The angel of the waters proclaims that the destruction of the waters of the Earth by turning them into blood is a just and right judgment from a Holy God. Because the unsaved world under the leadership of Satan and His Antichrist will shed the blood of so many believers in God for millennia, it will then be time for them to "drink blood."

The Lord's Response to "Where Is God?"

"If God exists, why is He letting bad things happen?" goes a common objection to the Christian faith; this is what so many unbelievers have asked for millennia. How quickly all people (this author included) can desire justice and punishment for the sins of others, but we readily ignore our own sin in demanding that God act. The unbeliever demands justice out of convenience and mocks anyone who believes in a God who "sits by while so many horrible things happen in the world." So why doesn't God show up whenever something bad takes place? The answer is simple when we begin to understand His vast and immeasurable power. When God executes judgment, it is complete and final. The guilty are unable to stand before Yahweh.

Every day the Lord Jesus Christ does not return provides twenty-four more hours of common grace given to all people—Christians, atheists, and followers of other religions alike—so they might have an opportunity to seek forgiveness and mercy. After Jesus' Resurrection, He could have returned at any point to rightly reclaim the Earth and sit on His throne in Jerusalem. Instead, He has waited more than two thousand years, giving humanity chance after chance to cry out for His grace—the free forgiveness given to all who put their faith and trust in Him. But a day will come when the judgment does come from Heaven; all who are not forgiven will be enemies of the Lord and conquered among those who tortured and murdered the prophets and saints throughout human history.

Consider some of the staggering statistics of recent history:

- More than five hundred million people have been killed in wars since the year 1800.
- More than fifty million babies have been aborted in the United States alone since 1973, when the US Supreme Court legalized abortion.
- Atrocities of "developed nations," such as in the antebellum slavery and Jim Crow, race-based government in the United States; the anti-Semitic regime of the Nazis; apartheid in South Africa; and the murderous regimes of Vladimir Lenin, Joseph Stalin, Mao Tse Tung, and others have led to rampant injustices and hundreds of millions of murders.
- Of the 2.2 billion children in the world, one billion live in poverty and twenty-two thousand die each day due to malnutrition and lack of basic resources.

- An estimated twenty to forty million people are human-trafficking victims today, either for forced labor or sexual exploitation. The human-trafficking industry earns an estimated $150 billion annually.
- An estimated one in seven children in the United States will be victims of child abuse. In fact, the US has one of the worst records of child abuse among industrialized nations, with an average of four to seven children dying per day due to child abuse and neglect.
- From 2019–2020, more than 260 million Christians have lived in nations with extreme levels of persecution: 2,983 Christians have been killed for their faith; 9,488 churches and Christian buildings have been burned to the ground or attacked; and 3,711 believers have been detained without trial and imprisoned for believing in the Lord Jesus Christ.

This doesn't take into account the billions of dollars spent in the illegal drug trade, financial crimes, violent crimes against women and children, and the many other heinous acts of perversion carried out in explicit entertainment and real criminal acts. The world has become overrun with sin and is "filled with violence" (Genesis 6:11).

Thus, the angel of the waters, who no doubt will have witnessed all of the atrocities committed over the course of human history, will rightly declare the God is just in punishing the world for thousands of years of violence against His children. German theologian Rudolf Stier, writing an analysis on the angelic realm, agreed with this notion:

> "More narrowly considered, this angel seems to be one set over the rivers and fountains of water named in verse 4, and hence the plural, *angel of the waters,* in contradistinction to the sea in verse 3. Thus, this usually beneficent ministering spirit, the angel of life-sustaining and salubrious fountains (as representative or director of many other such), bends low in acknowledgment of the justice of

> the Highest, which devastates his originally healthful domain....
>
> 'Righteous art thou, which art and wast, the Holy One (or thou Holy One), that thou hast judged thus.' —Thus the saying of the angel should stand, if correctly rendered. It is not here necessary to add, 'which art to come,' because the time of this coming in the last judgments is here anticipated; the words are spoken, as it were in their very midst. 'Holy' is here the chosen epithet of praise, as elsewhere, but yet in a slightly varied sense and the whole passage may be paraphrased thus: 'Equally righteous in thy fierce judgments art thou, *the same* in all time, thou whose nature and property is first of all to be holy, i.e., gracious.'" – *The Words of the Angels, or, Their Visits to the Earth and the Messages They Delivered*, Rudolf Stier, 1877, p. 211–212

The centuries upon centuries of cries for justice upon the enemies of God's people will finally be answered. Psalm 79 prophetically captures a picture of the Lord responding from Heaven to avenge those who have been persecuted:

> "O god, the heathen are come into thine inheritance; thy holy temple have they defiled; they have laid Jerusalem on heaps. The dead bodies of thy servants have they given to be meat unto the fowls of the heaven, the flesh of thy saints unto the beasts of the earth. **Their blood have they shed like water round about Jerusalem; and there was none to bury them**. We are become a reproach to our neighbours, a scorn and derision to them that are round about us. How long, LORD? wilt thou be angry for ever? shall thy jealousy burn like fire? **Pour out thy wrath upon the heathen that have not known thee**, and upon the kingdoms that have not called upon thy name." – Psalm 79:1–6

The Antichrist and his armies will indeed conquer Jerusalem and defile the

Temple at the abomination of desolation. The dead bodies of the Two Witnesses will disrespectfully be left in the streets for three days (and likely much longer, were they not resurrected and taken to Heaven). The Psalm above records the blood of murdered saints being "shed like water." Now the water of those persecutors will have been turned to blood once God pours out His wrath via the seven vials.

> "And I heard another out of the altar say, Even so, Lord God Almighty, true and righteous are thy judgments." – Revelation 16:7

Immediately following the angel of the waters' announcement on Earth of praise to God, another angel in Heaven, standing before the altar of God, confirms the righteousness of the Lord's judgment. Both Heaven and Earth are witness and confirm that God has indeed fulfilled His Word and His plan and prophesies. At no point is Jesus unjust in His dealings with humanity and angels. The double confirmation creates an eternal record that the witnesses of the unfolding plan of salvation agree.

Fourth Vial: Scorched by the Sun

> "And the fourth angel poured out his vial upon the sun; and **power was given unto him** to scorch men with fire. And men were scorched with great heat, and blasphemed the name of God, which hath power over these plagues: and they repented not to give him glory." – Revelation 16:8–9

Here, another righteous, holy angel is given preeminence as his vial "gives" the sun the power to scorch the followers of the Antichrist with fire. Having already suffered horrific sores and then watched all sources of water turn to blood—killing all of the life in the sea—the last rebels against Yahweh will then be supernaturally burnt. The false dreams and hopes of the utopia promised by the Final Nephilim will seem like a distant memory.

Consistent with all prophecy, this passage highlights the numerical foreshadows of this judgment. The sun was illuminated *on the fourth day* ("And God made two great lights; the greater light to rule the day, and the lesser light to rule the night.... And the evening and the morning were the fourth day." – Genesis 1:17, 19). The sun is then smitten at the fourth trumpet and scorches men with fire at the fourth vial.

Once again, the Beast doesn't retaliate or try to rally his subjects. **He takes no action whatsoever as his people suffer**. This is the response of an "idol shepherd." Just as Pharaoh was powerless against Yahweh during the plagues of the Exodus, so too will the Antichrist be rendered useless before the supernatural judgments of the True and Living God.

Despite the failure of their False Messiah, the worshipers of the Final Nephilim, already genetically and spiritually degraded by the Mark of the Beast, will still direct their anger at God:

> "And men were scorched with great heat, and blasphemed the name of God, which hath power over these plagues: and they repented not to give him glory." – Revelation 16:9

Meanwhile, the remnant of believing Israel will be preserved from this plague of fire, fulfilling the prophecy of Psalm 121:

> "I will lift up mine eyes unto the hills, from whence cometh my help. My help cometh from the LORD, which made heaven and earth. He will not suffer thy foot to be moved: he that keepeth thee will not slumber. **Behold, he that keepeth Israel shall neither slumber nor sleep**. The LORD is thy keeper: the LORD is thy shade upon thy right hand. **The sun shall not smite thee by day**, nor the

moon by night." – Psalm 121:1–6

The believing remnant will be preserved through these plagues. And, in the final three vials, God will focus His just wrath directly at the Final Nephilim.

Fifth Vial: Darkness in the Palace of Antichrist

> "And the fifth angel poured out his vial upon the seat of the beast; and his kingdom was full of darkness; and they gnawed their tongues for pain, And blasphemed the God of heaven because of their pains and their sores, and repented not of their deeds." – Revelation 16:10

The darkness that descends on the seat of the Antichrist is yet another warning sign that the reign of the Beast is coming to an abrupt end. The Lord will remove him from the Holy City with supernatural force. Revelation 13 tells us that it is Satan who gives the Final Nephilim "his power, **and his seat**, and great authority" (Revelation 13:2). The Greek word for "seat" is *thronos,* or θρόνος, the origin of the English word "throne." Now that same "seat" will be struck directly from the angels holding the wrath of God, and the global kingdom of the Antichrist will be covered with supernatural darkness, just as Egypt was during the Exodus:

> "And the LORD said unto Moses, Stretch out thine hand toward heaven, that there may be darkness over the land of Egypt, even darkness which may be felt. And Moses stretched forth his hand toward heaven; and there was a thick darkness in all the land of Egypt three days: They saw not one another, neither rose any from his place for three days: but all the children of Israel had light in their dwellings." – Exodus 10:21–23

Darkness was the ninth plague against Egypt before the first Passover, in which all of the firstborn of Egypt would perish and then Pharaoh and his armies died in the Red Sea. Similarly, the darkness at the fifth vial represents the last judgment before Mystery Babylon's destruction and Armageddon.

It is also a similar punishment that Apollyon experienced after he and the apostate angels of Genesis 6 were dragged down to the Abyss in the Days of Noah:

> "For if God spared not the angels that sinned, but cast them down to hell, **and delivered them into chains of darkness**, to be reserved unto judgment; And spared not the old world, but saved Noah the eighth person, a preacher of righteousness, bringing in the flood upon the world of the ungodly." – 2 Peter 2:4–5

This is a darkness that can be "felt," and we see the resulting affliction, as the Antichrist's followers will "gnaw their tongues" because of the pain of the darkness as well as of the sores they received at the first vial. The two-thirds of the population of Israel that will have been deluded into thinking their Messiah has arrived will now curse the God who, for millennia, offered them salvation. And the Antichrist will continue to blaspheme God and will urge his followers to prepare for war against the Creator.

> "The beast is still in power, though doubtless maddened and hardened as Pharaoh was; without whose example we should be at a loss to imagine how he could escape subjection to the Almighty by his sending forth such fearful proofs of his power and might." – *Notes on the Book of Revelation*, Helen Maclachlan, 1869, p. 185

This also fulfills the prophetic warning Moses gave Israel saying what would happen if they didn't hearken unto the Word of God:

> "**The LORD will smite thee with the botch of Egypt**, and with the emerods, and with the scab, and with the itch, **whereof thou canst not be healed**. The LORD shall smite thee with madness, and blindness, and astonishment of heart: **And thou shalt grope at noonday, as the blind gropeth in darkness,** and thou shalt not prosper in thy ways: and thou shalt be only oppressed and spoiled evermore, and no man shall save thee." – Deuteronomy 28:27–29

With his once-glorious palace ruined and plunged into supernatural darkness, the Antichrist will flee Jerusalem to try to recover from the plagues of the Almighty. The Final Nephilim will know his time is coming to an end. And, rather than submit, in pure satanic rebellion, he will marshal the armies of the unsaved world for a war against Jesus Christ.

Sixth Vial: Euphrates River Dries Up

> "And the sixth angel poured out his vial upon the great river Euphrates; and the water thereof was dried up, that the way of the kings of the east might be prepared. And I saw three unclean spirits like frogs come out of the mouth of the dragon, and out of the mouth of the beast, and out of the mouth of the false prophet. For they are the spirits of devils, working miracles, which go forth unto the kings of the earth and of the whole world, to gather them to the battle of that great day of God Almighty.... And he gathered them together into a place called in the Hebrew tongue Armageddon." – Revelation 16:12–16

Recall that at the sixth trumpet, the four angels bound beneath the Euphrates are loosed. At the pouring out of the sixth vial, the prophetic Word of God continues to ripple through time, this time drying up the Euphrates River altogether in order to allow easy passage for the armies of the ten global kings.

As it was in ancient times, the Euphrates—the great boundary of the original Promised Land—will be an attack point for the enemies of God.

An exposition on Revelation highlights the significance of the drying up of the Euphrates as the sign that fallen humanity is so depraved, so imbued with satanic desire, that they are ready to wage open combat against the Lord Jesus Christ.

> "The symbolical meaning of the Euphrates has been touched upon before.... In the great age-long struggle between the kingdoms of Christ and the world the Euphrates represents the great separating boundary between the two kingdoms, as the literal Euphrates formed the barrier between Israel and the hostile northern and eastern kingdoms. It is the great impediment to war. It is true that there is a great interposed boundary of public opinion, which restrains evil from breaking forth in its ruder and more violent forms. Men may be hostile to spiritual religion, yet they scarcely like to shock public sentiment, or to incur the charge of depraving public morals; but there may come a time, after false principles have been taught, corrupt manners tolerated, and the light of better things darkened, when the public sentiment loses all sense of shame, and the decorums of life, which have acted as a breakwater against the tide of outrageous evil are swept away; then is the Euphrates dried, and then may the hostile powers of evil, unrestrained by any considerations, unchecked by the popular conscience, cross boldly over and invade the whole sacred soil of human life." – *A New Testament Commentary for English Readers: Ephesians – The Revelation of St. John, Volume III*, Various Writers, Edited by Charles John Ellicott, 1897, p. 608

Instigating this call to arms are three demonic spirits that resemble "frogs" emerging from the mouth of the Devil, his seed, and the False Prophet. The satanic trinity acts in one accord to release one final delusion on the wicked, fallen world (not coincidentally, producing frogs was the last act of occult magic Pharaoh's sorcerers performed before their powers were no longer permitted by God). The demons will recruit the armies of the ten kings to battle. To the unsaved, genetically corrupted followers of the Final Nephilim, this may seem like the "hope" they are waiting for.

After suffering for months of torment under the supernatural judgments of God, the river that provides access to Israel will be supernaturally dried up, and demons will incite the final global rulers to believe they can claim victory at Armageddon. The demon frogs that come from the mouth of the satanic trinity will even perform miracles before the people, certainly stirring hope that their rebellion against the Creator may work after all. Just as delusional as Nimrod and the builders at Babel, the ten kings will rally and march towards the dry riverbed. It would be no surprise if the end-times rebels attribute the removal of the waters to the powers of the Antichrist. In the days of wicked King Sennacherib, a prior incarnation of the Antichrist, a similar delusion took place:

> "**By thy servants hast thou reproached the Lord, and hast said,** By the multitude of my chariots am I come up to the height of the mountains, to the sides of Lebanon; and I will cut down the tall cedars thereof, and the choice fir trees thereof: and I will enter into the height of his border, and the forest of his Carmel. I have digged, and drunk water; **and with the sole of my feet have I dried up all the rivers of the besieged places.** Hast thou not heard long ago, how I have done it; and of ancient times, that I have formed it? now have I brought it to pass, that thou shouldest be to lay waste defenced cities into ruinous heaps." – Isaiah 37:24–26

In twisted, satanic pride, Sennacherib thought he had "dried up all the rivers" that helped him conquer the many nations he defeated before attempting to storm Jerusalem. But God revealed that it was the Lord all along who allowed that to happen to bring the Assyrians to their ultimate defeat. Yahweh is always in control of all events through history. Even when the wicked feel they have gained advantage, it is God working out His plan, much to their shock. The Antichrist will likely repeat the same hubris: leading the unsaved populace to believe they finally have a chance at victory amidst the literal destruction of earth.

> "Thence from the banks of the Euphrates came the Assyrian, the rod of the Divine anger, the Chaldean, the destroyer of Jerusalem. But here we observe that God Himself prepares the way for them. He dries up the river, as of old the Red Sea, but not for their deliverance (as in the case of the Israelites), but for their destruction as in the case of Pharaoh and the Egyptians. They hasten forward and know not that it is for their life. The Vision assures God's people, that though His enemies rage furiously together and imagine a vain thing, He is ordering all for their overthrow, for His people's triumph." – *The New Testament of Our Lord and Saviour Jesus Christ, The Acts, Epistles and Revelation*, Society for Promoting Christian Knowledge, 1881, Revelation 16

SPIRITS OF NEPHILIM RECRUIT LEADERS INTO BATTLE

On his last legs, the Final Nephilim will join with the False Prophet and Satan Himself to summon the armies of the ten kings to battle. It will be demons—disembodied spirits of the dead giants—who will go out into the world and seduce the final regional rulers into battle. This will repeat the ultimate fate of the ancient King Ahab, husband of the occult witch Jezebel, who, as recorded in the book of 1 Kings, led the children of Israel into brazen idolatry. Jezebel appointed four hundred prophets of Baal to serve in the royal court. In judgment of her wickedness, God ordered a "lying spirit" to deceive the satanic prophets who served King Ahab by urging the foolish king to enter a battle he would lose. Micaiah, the righteous prophet who advised both kings Ahab and Jehoshaphat, told them plainly of God's design:

> "And [Micaiah] said, Hear thou therefore the word of the LORD: I saw the LORD sitting on his throne, and all the host of heaven standing by him on his right hand and on his left. And the LORD said, Who shall persuade Ahab, that he may go up and fall at Ramoth Gilead? And one said on this manner, and another said on that manner.
>
> **And there came forth a spirit**, and stood before the LORD, and said, I will persuade him. And the LORD said unto him, Wherewith? And he said, I will go forth, and I will be a lying spirit in the mouth of all his prophets. And he said, Thou shalt persuade him, and prevail also: go forth, and do so. Now therefore, behold, the LORD hath put a lying spirit in the mouth of all these thy prophets, and the LORD hath spoken evil concerning thee." – 1 Kings 22:19–23

Although God discussed this matter with His angels, it was an evil spirit who came forth to go and deceive the kings into rushing into a battle they would lose. Eighteenth-century commentator Jonathan Gill attributed this role to the Devil:

> "Not from the heavenly host on the right hand or the left, for they are pure and holy spirits, and impeccable, and cannot lie or deceive; but the evil spirit, Satan, the father of lies, the old deceiver, who came forth from his own place and his own company…evil spirits love to be employed in doing harm to men, they go about seeking whom they may devour." – *John Gill's Exposition of the Holy Bible*, https://www.biblestudytools.com/commentaries/gills-exposition-of-the-bible/1-kings-22-21.html

Like foolish kings before him, the Final Nephilim will assemble the armies of the world to mount one last stand against God Almighty. They will be deluded into thinking they truly have an opportunity to try to conquer the Creator of the universe. But they will finally understand the truth of everything Scripture has taught for millennia. The Ultimate Prophecy's fulfilment will have arrived. When Jesus Christ, *Yeshua Ha Meshiach*, the Seed of the Woman, will at last crush the head of the Serpent.

"ARMAGEDDON": A GATHERING OF MILITARY FORCES

It is important to note that "Armageddon" is not the location of the final battle between the Lord Jesus Christ and the Final Nephilim. It is the "muster point" for the Antichrist and the armies of the ten kings. Although it's often described as meaning "the Mount of Megiddo," there is no "Mount Megiddo" in Scripture. Megiddo, a site of some important victories of Israel in the Old Testament, is a plain, not a mountain:

> "In that day shall there be a great mourning in Jerusalem, as the mourning of Hadadrimmon in the valley of Megiddo." – Zechariah 12:11

Writing in the middle of the nineteenth century, Reverend Alexander Morrison explained how the translation from Hebrew to Greek may have led to a misunderstanding of the term "Armageddon":

> "We are thus thrown upon the meaning of the word to understand the signification of the symbol. The word Armageddon is compounded of two Hebrew words. The first is 'har,' signifying a mountain, as critics have generally agreed. I think, however, the etymology will permit another derivation. In translating the

> Hebrew into Greek there are two letters 'He' and 'Ayin' which are so much alike in sound that the Greek writers have no suitable marks to preserve the distinction; and therefore in words spelt with these as initial letters they are unrepresented. Amos and Ezra for instance, are spelt with *Ayin*. Hosea, on the other hand, has the initial letter 'He' which is left out in the Septuagint translation, and in [Romans 10:25] where the Apostle says 'as he saith also in Osee, I will call them my people which were not my people.'
>
> Hence in rendering Armageddon into Hebrew the first part of the word may be commenced with '*Ayin*' and thus instead of 'har' a mountain, we obtain 'ar' a city. The word is the proper name of Rabbah the chief city of Moab, but is employed in the plural when cities are spoken of, and hence in compound words would probably be used instead of 'ir' the more usual form. The other part of the word 'mageddon' signifies, according to the meaning of its root, 'a place of crowds' as Gesenius says, or, according to others, 'of assembly' which is generically the same." – *The Sixth Vial Poured Out; or, the Present Condition of Europe and the East, in Relation to Coming Events: Being the Substance of Two Letters on Revelation 17:12–16*, Rev. Alexander Morrison, 1848, p. 5

Old Testament scholar and contemporary author Dr. Michael Heiser arrived at a similar conclusion:

> "It is crystal clear that *the final conflict occurs at Jerusalem, not Megiddo*. Megiddo is referenced only to compare the awful mourning that will result." – *The Unseen Realm*, Dr. Michael Heiser, 2014, p. 371

Not coincidentally, the term "Armageddon" occurs nowhere else in the Bible, and the Greek translation of "Armageddon" is not found in the Septuagint.

As will be shown, what is commonly known as "the Battle of Armageddon" is a term that in fact refers to a series of battles that stretches from as far north as Megiddo but that culminates at Jerusalem.

JESUS' FINAL WARNING BEFORE THE GREAT BATTLE

> "Behold, I come as a thief. Blessed is he that watcheth, and keepeth his garments, lest he walk naked, and they see his shame." – Revelation 16:15
>
> "Watch therefore: for ye know not what hour your Lord doth come. **But know this, that if the goodman of the house had known in what watch the thief would come**, he would have watched, and would not have suffered his house to be broken up. Therefore be ye also ready: for in such an hour as ye think not the Son of man cometh." – Matthew 24:42–44

Out of His great love, in yet another plea to the unbelieving world, the Lord Jesus Christ provides one final warning of the end of the world as we know it. Before the seventh vial and the final battle with the Antichrist, the Son of God reminds of the need to look to Him—the Author of Salvation and Provider of Mercy—before He returns as the Conquering King. The Day of the Lord, which comes "as a thief in the night" (1 Peter 4:15), is reaching its culmination. Jesus, who was crucified between two thieves, will return as Lord of All.

> "In *mercy* to sinful men, Jesus waits—waits for the poor wandering sheep to be brought into His fold; waits for the prodigal son to seek his Father's House; puts off for their sake the reward of His faithful servants who, yearning for His coming, cry, 'Lord, how long? how

long? Come quickly, Lord Jesus.' Nevertheless, 'He that shall come, will come, and will not tarry.' When the number of His chosen ones shall have been made up, when the wicked shall have filled up the measure of their iniquity, the trump of the herald Archangel shall sound, and, as the lightning that shineth from one part of Heaven to the other, the Son of Man shall come in the clouds of Heaven, to the joy of those that love His appearing, and to the horror and confusion of an unprepared world." – "The Aspects of Our Lord's Coming," as printed *in Literary Churchman Sermons, A Selection of Plain Sermons From 1879 to 1883*, 1883, J. E. Vernon, p. 26

EXCLUSIVE BONUS CONTENT – Scan the QR code below for bonus content.

CHAPTER 12

DAVID VERSUS GOLIATH: A BATTLE TO RULE HEAVEN AND EARTH

> "The second but less complete type of Antichrist is the antagonist of David, Goliath. David was also a type of Messiah and hence Goliath is a type of his opponent." – *The Protestant Theological and Ecclesiastical Encyclopedia, Volume 1*, John Henry August Bomberger, 1860, p. 176

> "...to gather them to the battle of that great day of God Almighty." – Revelation 16:14

The Battle of the Great Day of God Almighty, more commonly called "Armageddon" today, is the final stand of the Antichrist in his doomed attempt to overthrow God. This is one of the Devil's final deceptive acts—luring the unsaved world to unite and prepare for the arrival of Jesus Christ to wage war against Him. Consider how utterly deluded the inhabitants of the planet will be at this time—to the extent that they will truly desire to fight a supernatural army coming from Heaven. Certainly, the fallen angels and spirits of the dead Nephilim will have had to have run amok within the populace to let people even dare to think they can battle The Lord.

When David fought Goliath, we see in both individuals the bloodlines spoken of in Genesis 3:15. David, from the Seed of the Woman as a progenitor of Jesus Christ, faced off with Goliath, a Nephilim hybrid offspring of the fallen angels. This was no doubt one of the most glorious previews of the final confrontation between Jesus and the Final Nephilim. When they battled in that ancient day in the valley of Elah, the future of the entire nation of Israel was at stake. Goliath's terms of battle required Israel to become his "servants" if he prevailed. Of course, David, whom God promised would be an ancestor of the Messiah, conquered the giant in swift fashion—just as Jesus will do to the Antichrist. Psalm 2 provides another dynamic preview of this concluding battle:

> "Why do the heathen rage, and the people imagine a vain thing? **The kings of the earth set themselves, and the rulers take counsel together, against the LORD**, and against his anointed, saying, Let us break their bands asunder, and cast away their cords from us. He that sitteth in the heavens shall laugh: the LORD shall have them in derision. Then shall he speak unto them in his wrath, and vex them in his sore displeasure. **Yet have I set my king upon my holy hill of Zion**. I will declare the decree: the LORD hath said unto me, Thou art my Son; this day have I begotten thee.
>
> Ask of me, and I shall give thee the heathen for thine inheritance, and the uttermost parts of the earth for thy possession. Thou shalt break them with a rod of iron; thou shalt dash them in pieces like a potter's vessel." – Psalm 2:1–9

SEVENTH VIAL: DESTRUCTION OF MYSTERY BABYLYON THE GREAT

"And the seventh angel poured out his vial into the air; and there came a great voice out of the temple of heaven, from the throne, saying, It is done. And there were voices, and thunders, and lightnings; **and there was a great earthquake, such as was not since men were upon the earth**, so mighty an earthquake, and so

> great. **And the great city was divided into three parts, and the cities of the nations fell**: and great Babylon came in remembrance before God, to give unto her the cup of the wine of the fierceness of his wrath. And every island fled away, and the mountains were not found." – Revelation 16:17–20

At the pouring out of the seventh vial, God, speaking from the Temple, proclaims: "It is done" (Revelation 16:17). Just as noted above with the number 666, in the number 777, we see the Lord's perfection and completion of His plan of redemption of humanity and restoration of judgment, justice and righteousness in Heaven and earth. Each seven in the end-times judgments of Revelation bring us to God:

- At the opening of the seventh seal, there is a "silence in Heaven for the space of a half hour"—a solemn period before the trumpet and vial judgments foreshadowed by the silence of Israel for seven days before the conquest of the Nephilim-infested city of Jericho in the book of Joshua.
- At the sounding of the seventh trumpet, voices in Heaven proclaim: "the kingdoms of this world are become the kingdoms of our Lord, and of his Christ; and he shall reign for ever and ever" (Revelation 11:15).
- And at the pouring of the seventh vial, God Himself proclaims: "it is done."

With that divine proclamation, the prophetic Word regarding Israel's judgment and "scattering" all over the globe will be complete. The time for the restoration of the believing remnant of Israel will have arrived. Jesus made a similar declaration on the cross, and the full prophetic implications are understood when we examine more than one account of His final moments before death:

> "After this, **Jesus knowing that all things were now**

> **accomplished, that the scripture might be fulfilled, saith, I thirst**. Now there was set a vessel full of vinegar: and they filled a spunge with vinegar, and put it upon hyssop, and put it to his mouth. When Jesus therefore had received the vinegar, **he said, It is finished**: and he bowed his head, and gave up the ghost." – John 19:28–30
>
> "Jesus, when he had cried again with a loud voice, yielded up the ghost. And, behold, the veil of the temple was rent in twain from the top to the bottom; **and the earth did quake, and the rocks rent**." – Matthew 27:50–51

In the passage from John, the Lord *Yeshua* reached the moment of fulfilling all the Old Testament prophecies of the Messiah's First Coming. The last remaining prophecy was from Psalm 69, which includes numerous references to the Messiah on the cross:

> "Save me, O God; for the waters are come in unto my soul. I sink in deep mire, where there is no standing: **I am come into deep waters, where the floods overflow me**. I am weary of my crying: my throat is dried: mine eyes fail while I wait for my God. They that hate me without a cause are more than the hairs of mine head: they that would destroy me, being mine enemies wrongfully, are mighty: then I restored that which I took not away. O God, thou knowest my foolishness; and my sins are not hid from thee. Let not them that wait on thee, O Lord GOD of hosts, be ashamed for my sake: let not those that seek thee be confounded for my sake, O God of Israel. Because for thy sake I have borne reproach; shame hath covered my face. I am become a stranger unto my brethren, and an alien unto my mother's children.
>
> For the zeal of thine house hath eaten me up; and the reproaches of them that reproached thee are fallen upon me. When I wept, and

> chastened my soul with fasting, that was to my reproach. I made sackcloth also my garment; and I became a proverb to them.... Reproach hath broken my heart; and I am full of heaviness: and I looked for some to take pity, but there was none; and for comforters, but I found none. **They gave me also gall for my meat; and in my thirst they gave me vinegar to drink.**" – Psalm 69:1–11, 20–21

Behold, the amazing love of Jesus Christ! He willingly lowered Himself to assume a human form and took on the disgrace of the world's sin just so He could receive the punishment we all deserve for our lifetimes of wickedness and rebellion against Him. And in this incredible prophecy, we read that, in His suffering, He would be given "vinegar to drink." Hence, His request in John 29: "I thirst." This was all about the prophetic fulfillment. The rejection and assassination of the Messiah by Israel was complete. The bearing of sin and obedience of the Suffering Servant who would be the Savior also came to pass. The fulfillment of God's promises secured the Devil's defeat at the cross.

Another fascinating aspect of Jesus' proclamation of "It is finished" at the cross and "It is done" at the seventh vial is that both moments of fulfillment result in an earthquake in Jerusalem. At the Crucifixion, the earthquake rocked the city and the veil of the Temple was torn in half. At the seventh vial, the earthquake will be the most powerful in history (or at least in the time since humans have inhabited earth) leaving Jerusalem fractured into three parts. All of the "cities of the nations" fall in the destructive aftermath of this divine judgment.

The ten kings, on the march with their armies towards Jerusalem, hear the news of the destruction of their homelands and will seek vengeance on the Holy City.

TEN KINGS ATTACK AND DESTROY END-TIMES JERUSALEM

> "And the woman was arrayed in purple and scarlet colour, and decked with gold and precious stones and pearls, having a golden cup in her hand full of abominations and filthiness of her fornication: And upon her forehead was a name written, MYSTERY, BABYLON THE GREAT, THE MOTHER OF HARLOTS AND ABOMINATIONS OF THE EARTH. And I saw the woman drunken with the blood of the saints, and with the blood of the martyrs of Jesus: and when I saw her, I wondered with great admiration.... And the ten horns which thou sawest upon the beast, these shall hate the whore, and shall make her desolate and naked, and shall eat her flesh, and burn her with fire. For God hath put in their hearts to fulfil his will, and to agree, and give their kingdom unto the beast, **until the words of God shall be fulfilled**. And the woman which thou sawest is that great city, which reigneth over the kings of the earth." – Revelation 17:4–6, 16–18

Under the rule of the Antichrist, Mystery Babylon, or the end-times city of Jerusalem, will be the global center of persecution of believers in Jesus Christ. As it was with the Temple of Solomon and the Second Temple in the days of Christ on Earth, the city will be destroyed. Jesus Christ prophesied that Jerusalem would be rendered "desolate" for the nation's rejection of Christ as the Son of God. The Roman and Jewish authorities persecuted the early Church until Rome turned on Israel and destroyed Jerusalem in AD 70. Jesus Christ had warned the Israelites this would happen:

> "Wherefore, behold, I send unto you prophets, and wise men, and scribes: and some of them ye shall kill and crucify; and some of them shall ye scourge in your synagogues, and persecute them from city to city: **That upon you may come all the righteous blood**

> **shed upon the earth**, from the blood of righteous Abel unto the blood of Zacharias son of Barachias, whom ye slew between the temple and the altar. Verily I say unto you, All these things shall come upon this generation. **O Jerusalem, Jerusalem, thou that killest the prophets, and stonest them which are sent unto thee**, how often would I have gathered thy children together, even as a hen gathereth her chickens under her wings, and ye would not! Behold, your house is left unto you desolate." – Matthew 23:34–38

The Antichrist will use Jerusalem as a base of operations after he deludes the unsaved people of Israel and confirms the Mosaic covenant and Temple sacrifices for three and a half years. The ten kings will urge their nations to give offerings and worship to the Final Nephilim and effectively make Babylon the Great—end-times Jerusalem—the political, financial, and spiritual capital of the world. In both passages above, we see that God declares it is Jerusalem who has killed the "saints" and "prophets." It is the "bloody city" mentioned in Ezekiel 22:

> "Now, thou son of man, wilt thou judge, wilt thou judge the bloody city? yea, thou shalt shew her all her abominations. Then say thou, Thus saith the Lord GOD, The city sheddeth blood in the midst of it, that her time may come, and maketh idols against herself to defile herself. Thou art become guilty in thy blood that thou hast shed; and hast defiled thyself in thine idols which thou hast made; and thou hast caused thy days to draw near, and art come even unto thy years: therefore have I made thee a reproach unto the heathen, and a mocking to all countries." – Ezekiel 22:2–4

End-times Jerusalem will be the epicenter of idolatry and "abominations" via worship of the Final Nephilim and his father, Satan. The world will be deluded into believing that its wealth and prosperity are a sign of a millennial reign. But once God's prophetic Word about Israel is fulfilled, the infatuation ends. At the pouring of the seventh vial, the ten kings, who will be on the march to Armageddon to gather forces for the war against God, will hear the news that their great cities have all been destroyed in the final end-times earthquake and direct their wrath towards Jerusalem. In their satanic rage against Jesus Christ, they will destroy the very city from which He is prophesied to rule. They will attack the ravaged city and destroy it with fire. The destruction will be swift and devastating.

MYSTERY OF THE NUMBER TEN: GOD'S JUDGMENT

> "It is not possible to assign the cause of this act further than it is revealed by God; but this know, impelled irresistibly by God at the moment 'great Babylon comes in remembrance to give the cup of the wine of the fierceness of his wrath,' these ten kings accomplish his will in her sudden destruction by fire, for strong is the Lord that judgeth her: and then these unconscious agents of God's judgment lament over the fall of this city as Titus did over Jerusalem." – *Notes on the Book of Revelation*, Helen Maclachlan, 1869, p. 199

It shouldn't be surprising that the Lord uses the ten kings to destroy end-times Jerusalem, because the number ten in Scripture is frequently associated with God's judgment. Consider the following examples:

- God gave Moses the Ten Commandments, which were used to judge the sins of the nation of Israel (Exodus chapters 19 and 20).
- During the Exodus, the Lord used ten plagues to punish the Egyptians and their false gods.

- During the tenth plague against Egypt, the Passover lamb that was sacrificed was selected on the tenth day of the month (Exodus 12:3).
- Numerous atonement offerings for sin involve a tenth of an item selected by God (e.g., fine flour, barley meal, etc.; see Leviticus chapters 16, 23, and 27).
- There were ten generations in the godly lineage from Adam to Noah before the judgment of the Flood (Genesis 5).
- When the Lord dragged the Assyrian, his fallen angels, and the Nephilim into the Abyss as a judgment for their fornication, the waters took them to their prison "in the tenth month" (Genesis 8:5).
- When Moses sent twelve spies to scout the land of Canaan following the Exodus, ten returned with "evil reports," doubting God could deliver the land to the Israelites once they saw Ahiman, Sheshai, and Talmai—the three Nephilim giants who were dwelling there. When God rebuked the Israelites for their lack of faith in Him, He specifically referenced the fear of the ten doubting spies:

> "Because all those men which have seen my glory, and my miracles, which I did in Egypt and in the wilderness, **and have tempted me now these ten times**, and have not hearkened to my voice; Surely they shall not see the land which I sware unto their fathers, neither shall any of them that provoked me see it: But my servant Caleb, because he had another spirit with him, and hath followed me fully, him will I bring into the land whereinto he went; and his seed shall possess it." – Numbers 14:22–24

This is what led to the Israelites wandering the wilderness for forty years, wherein an entire generation died before entering the land of Canaan. It was a judgment directly connected to the number ten.

- When the Israelites begged God to give them a king (who would be Saul, a type of the Antichrist), the prophet Samuel warned that their desired king would be wicked and would "take the tenth of your seed" and "the tenth of your sheep: and ye shall be his servants" (1 Samuel 8:15; 17).
- God designated the tenth day of the seventh month as Yom Kippur, or the Day of Atonement (Leviticus 23:27).
- When the Lord punished Israel by permitting Nebuchadnezzar to surround Jerusalem with his armies before conquering it, it was "in the tenth month, in the tenth day of the month" (2 Kings 25:1).

Thus, the final ten kings of the Earth will bring the final judgment against apostate Jerusalem, destroying the city and burning it with fire. By committing the ultimate idolatry—the worship of the Final Nephilim and the Devil—the wrath of God will be kindled and poured out on Mystery Babylon the Great. Revelation 17:16 predicts that the ten kings "shall hate the whore, and shall make her desolate and naked, and shall eat her flesh, and burn her with fire." This is all a fulfillment of the warnings given by the prophets in the Old Testament. In *Judgment of the Nephilim*, I explained that marriage—a gift bestowed by humanity—is a prototype of the plan of salvation. Rather than being the "bride," end-times Jerusalem will be "the harlot" and will suffer betrayal at the hands of the very kings she thinks love her:

> "How weak is thine heart, saith the LORD GOD, seeing thou doest all these things, the work of an imperious whorish woman; In that thou buildest thine eminent place in the head of every way, and makest thine high place in every street; and hast not been as an harlot, in that thou scornest hire; **But as a wife that committeth adultery, which taketh strangers instead of her husband!** They give gifts to all whores: but thou givest thy gifts to all thy lovers, and hirest them, that they may come unto thee on every side for thy whoredom....

> Wherefore, O harlot, hear the word of the LORD: Thus saith the Lord GOD; Because thy filthiness was poured out, and thy nakedness discovered through thy whoredoms with thy lovers, and with all the idols of thy abominations, and by the blood of thy children, which thou didst give unto them; **Behold, therefore I will gather all thy lovers**, with whom thou hast taken pleasure, and all them that thou hast loved, with all them that thou hast hated; **I will even gather them round about against thee, and will discover thy nakedness unto them, that they may see all thy nakedness**.
>
> And I will judge thee, as women that break wedlock and shed blood are judged; and I will give thee blood in fury and jealousy. And I will also give thee into their hand, and they shall throw down thine eminent place, and shall break down thy high places: they shall strip thee also of thy clothes, and shall take thy fair jewels, and leave thee naked and bare. They shall also bring up a company against thee, and they shall stone thee with stones, and thrust thee through with their swords. **And they shall burn thine houses with fire, and execute judgments upon thee in the sight of many women**: and I will cause thee to cease from playing the harlot, and thou also shalt give no hire any more. So will I make my fury toward thee to rest, and my jealousy shall depart from thee, and I will be quiet, and will be no more angry. Because thou hast not remembered the days of thy youth, but hast fretted me in all these things; behold, therefore I also will recompense thy way upon thine head, saith the Lord GOD: and thou shalt not commit this lewdness above all thine abominations. Behold, every one that useth proverbs shall use this proverb against thee, saying, As is the mother, so is her daughter."
> – Ezekiel 16:30–44

In this prophetic rebuke, Ezekiel points out all of the sinful rebellion and judgment of end-times apostate Israel—Babylon the Great. The prophet calls her a whore, an adulteress, and the mother of harlots who will lead the entire world into spiritual adultery. God then specifically says that, as a punishment, He will lead the very kings Israel courted in idolatry to betray her ("I will give thee into their hand"). This is precisely what will happen at the pouring out of the seventh vial, when the ten kings who will have once honored Jerusalem as the center of Antichrist worship decide to destroy the city. Both John (in Revelation) and Ezekiel say the betrayers of Israel will make her "naked," exposing the sin and wickedness of Israel to the world. Finally, Ezekiel predicts that Jerusalem will be "burned with fire," which is exactly what will happen to Jerusalem after the attack by the ten kings.

JEREMIAH 50 AND 51: STUNNING PROPHETIC DESCRIPTIONS OF DESTRUCTION OF BABYLON THE GREAT

Though initially directed at the ancient Babylonian Empire that would conquer the kingdom of Judah, the prophecies of Jeremiah chapters 50 and 51 concerning the destruction of Babylon clearly echo into the end times—specifically, Revelation chapters 17 and 18 and Babylon the Great. Consider some of the many startling similarities:

- Revelation 17:1 states that the: "whore…sitteth upon many waters." Jeremiah 51:13 says Babylon "dwellest upon many waters."
- Babylon the Great is described in Revelation as being one "with whom the kings of the earth have committed fornication, and **the inhabitants of the earth have been made drunk with the wine of her fornication…having a golden cup in her hand** full of abominations and filthiness of her fornication" (Revelation 17:2–4).

  Jeremiah 51:7 states: "**Babylon hath been a golden cup in the LORD's hand**, that made all the earth drunken: **the nations have drunken of her wine**; therefore the nations are mad."

The "wine" of Babylon is the false religious system that upholds the Final Nephilim as Messiah. This is the ultimate abomination that makes the whole world "drunk," or victims of the strong delusion.

- In Revelation 17, Mystery Babylon is said to sit upon "many waters." Verse 15 explains: "The waters which thou sawest, where the whore sitteth, are peoples, and multitudes, and nations, and tongues."

  In Jeremiah 51:13, the prophet proclaims: "**O thou that dwellest upon many waters**, abundant in treasures, thine end is come, and the measure of thy covetousness."

- As discussed above, Revelation 17:16 predicts that apostate Jerusalem will be burned with fire. Jeremiah 51:58 foretells the same fate: "Thus saith the LORD of hosts; The broad walls of Babylon shall be utterly broken, and her high gates shall be burned with fire."
- Revelation 18:4 records the well-known warning of God imploring His people to "come out of her, my people, that ye be not partakers of her sins, and that ye receive not of her plagues." Jeremiah 51:45 states a similar admonition: "My people, go ye out of the midst of her, and deliver ye every man his soul from the fierce anger of the LORD."

  Even more interesting is that in Jeremiah 38, the prophet speaking on behalf of the Lord, told the Israelites that they should surrender to Babylon in order for their lives and Jerusalem to be spared (Jeremiah 38:18). Clearly, the directive to surrender was for ancient Babylon as it is contrary to Yahweh's warning in Jeremiah 51 to "go ye out of the midst of her" - a reference to the *end-times Babylon*, which is confirmed by Revelation's similar admonition.

- Revelation 18:5 highlights the excessive sinful rebellion of Mystery Babylon: "For her sins have reached unto heaven, and God hath remembered her iniquities." Jeremiah 51:9 proclaims that "her judgment reacheth unto heaven, and is lifted up even to the skies."

- Revelation 18:6 states: "Reward her even as she rewarded you, and double unto her double according to her works: in the cup which she hath filled fill to her double." Jeremiah 50:15 reads: "For it is the vengeance of the LORD: take vengeance upon her; as she hath done, do unto her."
- Some of the most powerful imagery is seen in the description of the angel in Revelation 18:21: "And **a mighty angel took up a stone** like a great millstone, and cast it into the sea, saying, **Thus with violence shall that great city Babylon be thrown down**, and shall be found no more at all."Recall that in JeremiahRecall that in Jeremiah 51:63–64, the prophet was instructed: "And it shall be, when thou hast made an end of reading this book, **that thou shalt bind a stone to it**, and cast it into the midst of Euphrates: And thou shalt say, **Thus shall Babylon sink, and shall not rise from the evil that I will bring upon her**: and they shall be weary."Recall that in JeremiahGod told Jeremiah to hurl the written prophecy of end-times Babylon into the Euphrates—the very river that will dry up supernaturally to allow the Antichrist to enter Israel to wage war against the Lord Jesus Christ. The following commentary succinctly explains the spiritual role of Jerusalem as Babylon the Great:

"Compare [Matthew 23:35]. The foregoing pictures the doom of this system of evil combines the prophetic denunciations on ancient Babylon, Tyre and Jerusalem as if all their sins and all their punishments were here accumulated in one." – *The Annotated Paragraph Bible, Arranged in Paragraphs and Parallelism*, The Religious Tract Society, 1868, p. 1463

ANTICHRIST JOINS TEN KINGS TO ERADICATE JERUSALEM

> "Behold, the day of the LORD cometh, and thy spoil shall be divided in the midst of thee. For I will gather all nations against Jerusalem to battle; **and the city shall be taken**, and the houses rifled, and the women ravished; and half of the city shall go forth into captivity, and the residue of the people shall not be cut off from the city." – Zechariah 14:1–2

> "And the ten horns which thou sawest are ten kings, which have received no kingdom as yet; but receive power as kings one hour with the beast. **These have one mind, and shall give their power and strength unto the beast. These shall make war with the Lamb**, and the Lamb shall overcome them." – Revelation 17:12–14

Throughout Scripture, Christians are encouraged to strive to be of "one mind," having a spiritual unity and thoughts that are centered on glorifying the Lord and His Word. The ten fallen angelic kings who will rule the Earth in the last days will have "one mind" for evil; they will be united in their exaltation of the Antichrist and his wicked agenda. They will commit to "war with the Lamb," which will be a fatal error.

With his time running alarmingly short, the Beast will resolve to eradicate the Jewish people. Unable to harm the remnant who are divinely sheltered in Edom, he will launch a final assault on the faithful Jews (mostly comprised of the tribes from the Southern Kingdom of Judah) who remain in Jerusalem, just as Antiochus Epiphanes did before him. Recall that after Pharaoh allowed the Israelites to leave Egypt, he abruptly changed his mind and, in rage, dispatched his entire army to try to destroy them. The same satanic obsession with erasing any reference to the Lord or His people will consume the Final Nephilim as he leads his armada towards the Holy City. Something will let the Antichrist know that this action will bring Jesus to Earth for combat, and he will rush in to be conquered just as he did in his prior incarnations.

This anti-Semitic coalition is a fulfillment of Psalm 83:

> "They have said, Come, and let us cut them off from being a nation; that the name of Israel may be no more in remembrance." – Psalm 83:4

With his time running short, the Antichrist will seek to destroy Jerusalem and Israel entirely as a last-ditch effort to try to thwart the mighty hand and plan of God. With His armies from the place of assembly near the Euphrates, the Final Nephilim will lead an assault on Promised Land, heading to Jerusalem to wipe out the final faithful Jews remaining there.

ANTICHRIST TAKES DIRECT PATH SOUTHWEST FROM THE EUPHRATES TOWARDS JERUSALEM

Isaiah 10, which chronicles the career of the Final Nephilim, also gives the specific details of his final attack plan before he is defeated by Jesus Christ at Jerusalem:

> "Therefore thus saith the Lord GOD of hosts, **O my people that dwellest in Zion, be not afraid of the Assyrian**: he shall smite thee with a rod, and shall lift up his staff against thee, after the manner of Egypt. For yet a very little while, and the indignation shall cease, and mine anger in their destruction. And the LORD of hosts shall stir up a scourge for him according to the slaughter of Midian at the rock of Oreb: and as his rod was upon the sea, so shall he lift it up after the manner of Egypt." – Isaiah 10:24–26

Note here that God is specifically speaking to the believing remnant in Zion (Jerusalem) and encourages them to not fear the Assyrian. The Antichrist will be able to harm and oppress them for a "very little while," but God will rescue them just as He did in Egypt during the Exodus.

> "And it shall come to pass **in that day, that his burden shall be taken away from off thy shoulder, and his yoke from off thy neck**, and the yoke shall be destroyed because of the anointing. He is come to Aiath, he is passed to Migron; at Michmash he hath laid up his carriages: They are gone over the passage: they have taken up their lodging at Geba; Ramah is afraid; Gibeah of Saul is fled. Lift up thy voice, O daughter of Gallim: cause it to be heard unto Laish, O poor Anathoth. Madmenah is removed; the inhabitants of Gebim gather themselves to flee." – Isaiah 10:27–32

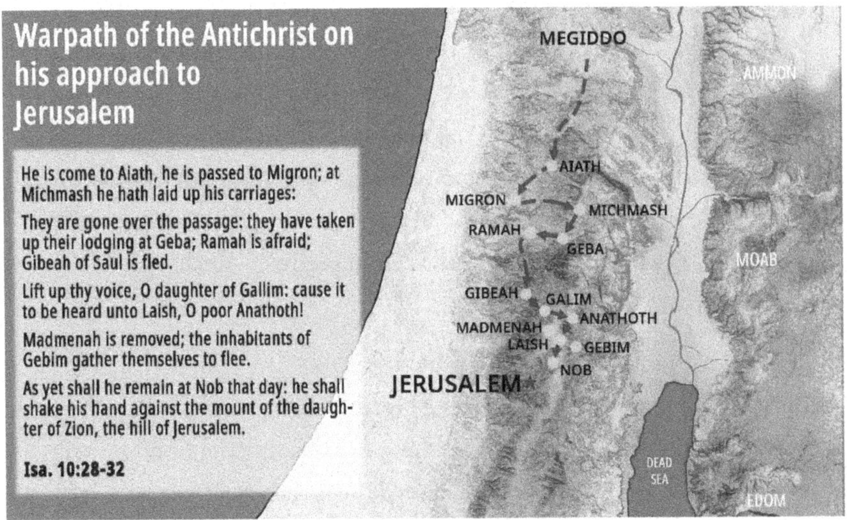

As can be seen from the map above, **all of these cities run in a direct southern line towards Jerusalem**. These cites also belong to the tribe of Benjamin—which, along with Judah and Levi, form the Southern Kingdom of "Judah," giving further confirmation that the tribes are split during this time. The Antichrist, on his final rampage, will gain victory over these cities, sending any survivors fleeing. The passage above clearly says the Israelites will be "afraid." But the tide will turn once the Antichrist is right at the doorstep of Jerusalem.

> "As yet shall he remain at Nob that day: he shall shake his hand against the mount of the daughter of Zion, the hill of Jerusalem."
> – Isaiah 10:32

Again, **note that Nob is just a few miles from Jerusalem**. Once the Destroyer has come this close, his campaign will pause, likely because he knows the Lord is returning to destroy him. This is when he will launch his attack on the Holy City and gain some measure of victory. This is detailed in Zechariah 14:

> "Behold, the day of the LORD cometh, and thy spoil shall be divided in the midst of thee. For I will gather all nations against Jerusalem to battle; and the city shall be taken, and the houses rifled, and the women ravished; and half of the city shall go forth into captivity, and the residue of the people shall not be cut off from the city. Then shall the LORD go forth, and fight against those nations, as when he fought in the day of battle." – Zechariah 14:1–3

As the Antichrist approaches from the North heading towards Jerusalem, the Lord Jesus Christ will approach from the south, leading the Ephraim remnant from Bozrah to fight at Jerusalem. He will hear the cry of the tribe of Judah and come prepared to avenge His people. Isaiah 10 closes with the confirmation of Christ's victory over the Seed of the Serpent:

> "Behold, the Lord, the LORD of hosts, shall lop the bough with terror: and the high ones of stature shall be hewn down, and the

> haughty shall be humbled. And he shall cut down the thickets of the forest with iron, and Lebanon shall fall by a mighty one." – Isaiah 10:33-34

In *Judgment of the Nephilim*, I devoted a chapter to exploring Ezekiel 31, which details the rise of the Assyrian in the days of Noah. The language in that chapter repeatedly refers to the Assyrian and the other fallen angels of that time as trees of a forest. We even read: "Behold, the Assyrian **was a cedar in Lebanon** with fair branches, and with a shadowing shroud, and of an high stature; and his top was among the thick boughs" (Ezekiel 31:3). Now, at the Battle of the Great Day of the Lord Almighty, Jesus Christ will again "lop the bough." The Antichrist and his fallen angelic-human hybrid army will again be chopped down by the might of the Lord.

The following biblical analysis of the Antichrist concurs that the military strategy of the Final Nephilim will be to conquer the cities in the region of Benjamin en route to making war with the Lamb at Jerusalem:

> "These verses describe his last and exterminating attack on the Jewish cities; by the names of the towns here mentioned it is implied that his march towards Jerusalem will be directed from the North or North West: nearly all being known to be cities of the tribe of Benjamin. [Zechariah 14:l 2] describes the same last attack: 'Behold the day of the Lord cometh, and thy spoil shall be divided in the midst of thee; for I will gather ALL NATIONS against Jerusalem to battle; and the city shall be taken, and the houses rifled, and the women ravished, and half of the city shall go forth into captivity, and the residue of the people shall not be cut off from the city.'
>
> ...he shakes his hand against the hill of Jerusalem; that is, he takes the city - his troops rifle the houses, etc., and half of the city goes forth into captivity; but the residue of the people (the remnant) will

> be saved by the Lord Jesus when he appears to fight with those nations as when he fought in the day of battle." – *A Comparison of Prophetic Scripture with Reference to Antichrist, His Person, Actings and Future Manifestations*, Henry Kelsall, 1846, p. 84

JESUS STANDS ON MOUNT OF OLIVES: A DYNAMIC REPEAT OF THE RED SEA PARTING

> "And his feet shall stand in that day upon the mount of Olives, **which is before Jerusalem on the east**, and the mount of Olives shall cleave in the midst thereof toward the east and toward the west, and there shall be a very great valley; and half of the mountain shall remove toward the north, and half of it toward the south. And ye shall flee to the valley of the mountains; for the valley of the mountains shall reach unto Azal: yea, ye shall flee, like as ye fled from before the earthquake in the days of Uzziah king of Judah: and the LORD my God shall come, and all the saints with thee." – Zechariah 14:4–5

As the Antichrist battles against the armies of Judah and ravages the city of Jerusalem, Jesus Christ will come down from the skies after leaving the wilderness of Edom, setting His feet on the Mount of Olives, located east of the city of Jerusalem. This is powerfully prophesied in the book of Isaiah:

> "Who is this that cometh from Edom, with dyed garments from Bozrah? this that is glorious in his apparel, travelling in the greatness of his strength? I that speak in righteousness, mighty to save. Wherefore art thou red in thine apparel, and thy garments like him that treadeth in the wine fat? I have trodden the winepress alone; and of the people there was none with me: for I will tread

> them in mine anger, and trample them in my fury; and their blood shall be sprinkled upon my garments, and I will stain all my raiment. For the day of vengeance is in mine heart, and the year of my redeemed is come." – Isaiah 63:1–4

The one coming from Edom is Jesus Christ. Having removed the ten tribes of the Northern Kingdom from their three-and-a-half-year sanctuary in the wilderness, Jesus will lead them to Jerusalem, annihilating all enemies in His path as He heads northwest to the Holy City. Christ and Antichrist will literally meet in the middle of their respective mustering points for the final confrontation.

Jesus' path from Edom also fulfills a prophecy from Habakkuk:

> "**God came from Teman, and the Holy One from mount Paran**. Selah. His glory covered the heavens, and the earth was full of his praise. And his brightness was as the light; he had horns coming out of his hand: and there was the hiding of his power. Before him went the pestilence, and burning coals went forth at his feet. He stood, and measured the earth: he beheld, and drove asunder the nations; and the everlasting mountains were scattered, the perpetual hills did bow: his ways are everlasting." – Habakkuk 3:3–6

Teman and Mount Paran are in the wilderness of Edom. Scripture again emphasizes the specific route that Jesus will take on His way to reclaim the Holy City. He will conquer all the nations in His path. The True Messiah will "come with clouds" traveling from east to west, fulfilling one of the many prophecies of His return:

> "**For as the lightning cometh out of the east, and shineth even unto the west**; so shall also the coming of the Son of man be. For wheresoever the carcase is, there will the eagles be gathered

> together." – Matthew 24:27–28

There will be many carcasses as Jesus overwhelms the remaining enemy forces with the revealed divine light of His presence on His way to Jerusalem and landing on the Mount of Olives. This is where the Antichrist is finally defeated. Between the Mount of Olives and Jerusalem is the Kidron valley, also known as the valley of Jehoshaphat. **This is where God prophesied the final battle would take place**:

> "For, behold, in those days, and in that time, when I shall bring again the captivity of Judah and Jerusalem, **I will also gather all nations, and will bring them down into the valley of Jehoshaphat**, and will plead with them there for my people and for my heritage Israel, whom they have scattered among the nations, and parted my land.... Proclaim ye this among the Gentiles; Prepare war, wake up the mighty men, let all the men of war draw near; let them come up: Beat your plowshares into swords and your pruninghooks into spears: let the weak say, I am strong. Assemble yourselves, and come, all ye heathen, and gather yourselves together round about: thither cause thy mighty ones to come down, O LORD. **Let the heathen be wakened, and come up to the valley of Jehoshaphat: for there will I sit to judge all the heathen round about.**
>
> Put ye in the sickle, for the harvest is ripe: come, get you down; **for the press is full, the fats overflow; for their wickedness is great**. Multitudes, multitudes in the valley of decision: for the day of the LORD is near in the valley of decision. The sun and the moon shall be darkened, and the stars shall withdraw their shining. The LORD also shall roar out of Zion, and utter his voice from Jerusalem; and the heavens and the earth shall shake: but the LORD will be the hope of his people, and the strength of the children of Israel." – Joel

3:1–2, 9–16

As seen on the map below, when Jesus divides the Mount of Olives, with half splitting northward and half southward, an eastern pathway will be formed by which the faithful remnant of Jews can flee in order to escape the Antichrist and his armies.

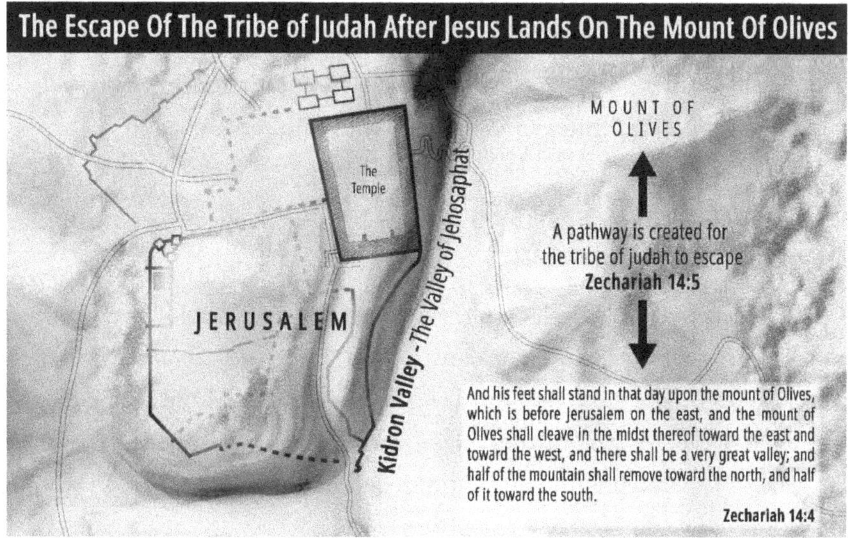

The mere presence of the Lord's feet on the mountain cause an earthquake to divide it and create a new valley in Israel:

> "And ye shall flee to the valley of the mountains; for the valley of the mountains shall reach unto Azal: yea, ye shall flee, like as ye fled from before the earthquake in the days of Uzziah king of Judah." – Zechariah 14:5

FINAL CONQUEST OF ANTICHRIST

> "Then shall the LORD go forth, and fight against those nations, **as when he fought in the day of battle.**" – Zechariah 14:3
>
> "*'Nations'* must include at least a great number of enemies in a confederate attack upon Jerusalem: the city will be taken, and half the inhabitants taken prisoners, and then God will interpose on the behalf of His people in a supernatural manner, as He did at the exodus of the Israelites and in their battles with the Canaanites and other foes." – *What the Prophets Foretold: A Compendium of Scripture Prediction,* John Algernon Clarke, 1862, p. 247

The prophecies of Zechariah emphasize that Armageddon will be a quantum entanglement of ancient campaigns waged by God. Two supernatural conflicts specifically stand out: the day "the sun stood still" and the parting of the Red Sea. The first battle took place when Joshua led the Israelites against the forces of the Nephilim King Adonizedec and his coalition of Canaanite kingdoms:

> "So Joshua ascended from Gilgal, he, and all the people of war with him, and all the mighty men of valour. And the LORD said unto Joshua, Fear them not: for I have delivered them into thine hand; there shall not a man of them stand before thee. Joshua therefore came unto them suddenly, and went up from Gilgal all night. **And the LORD discomfited them before Israel, and slew them with a great slaughter at Gibeon, and chased them along the way that goeth up to Bethhoron, and smote them to Azekah, and unto Makkedah**. And it came to pass, as they fled from before Israel, and were in the going down to Bethhoron, that the LORD cast down great stones from heaven upon them unto Azekah, and they died: they were more which died with hailstones than they whom the

> children of Israel slew with the sword.
>
> Then spake Joshua to the LORD in the day when the LORD delivered up the Amorites before the children of Israel, and he said in the sight of Israel, Sun, stand thou still upon Gibeon; and thou, Moon, in the valley of Ajalon. **And the sun stood still, and the moon stayed, until the people had avenged themselves upon their enemies.** Is not this written in the book of Jasher? So the sun stood still in the midst of heaven, and hasted not to go down about a whole day. **And there was no day like that before it or after it, that the LORD hearkened unto the voice of a man: for the LORD fought for Israel.**" – Joshua 10:7–14

On this historic day, God personally launched the military assault on the forces led by King Adonizedec, launching a frontal assault, followed by a barrage of supernatural hailstones as the enemy frantically retreated. In *Judgment of the Nephilim*, I explained that the Lord Jesus Christ often personally fought against the Nephilim-infested nations in the land of Canaan. Scripture confirms that the Amorites were giants:

> "Yet destroyed I the Amorite before them, whose height was like the height of the cedars, and he was strong as the oaks; yet I destroyed his fruit from above, and his roots from beneath." – Amos 2:9

The battle in Joshua chapter 10 was also an unprecedented day, when the Lord listened to Joshua's request that the "sun stand still." God temporarily halted the earth's rotation until the armies of Israel vanquished the remainder of their defeated enemies.

In Zechariah chapter 14's prophecy of the final battle, we see a similar occurrence:

> "And it shall come to pass in that day, that the light shall not be clear, nor dark: But it shall be one day which shall be known to the LORD, not day, nor night: but it shall come to pass, that at evening time it shall be light." – Zechariah 14:6–7

Will God once again pause the orbit of the earth? Something on such an extreme planetary scale would make it appear to be daytime during the night. As Habakkuk chapter 3 confirms:

> "The sun and moon stood still in their habitation: at the light of thine arrows they went, and at the shining of thy glittering spear. Thou didst march through the land in indignation, thou didst thresh the heathen in anger. Thou wentest forth for the salvation of thy people, even for salvation with thine anointed; thou woundedst the head out of the house of the wicked, by discovering the foundation unto the neck. Selah." – Habakkuk 3:11–13

When Jesus rides His clouds from Mt. Paran and Teman in Edom, the sun and moon will stand still once more. He will then "thresh" the heathen and wound the head of the "house of the wicked"—in fulfillment of the Ultimate Prophecy, as Jesus will crush the head of the Serpent.

> "At this crisis, Messiah is to be revealed from heaven in great pomp and majesty…and, placing himself at the head of his people is to rout with tremendous slaughter the hosts of the enemy, fighting against them in person, 'as when he fought in the day of battle,' that is, in the battle of Joshua with the five kings, when Jehovah cast down great stones from heaven, so that more died with hailstones than were slain by the children of Israel with the sword (Joshua 10:10–11). While the battle is thus raging, and the sword of Messiah is bathed in the blood of his enemies, mighty

> convulsions are to shake the land, rending asunder the Mount of Olives, on which the feet of Christ were first planted in his descent from the skies; before which dread phenomena the saints themselves, while Hushed with so unexpected a victory, are to flee in dismay (ver. 5) as the people fled before the earthquake in the days of Uzziah, king of Judah.
>
> At the time of this visible advent of Christ, and these convulsions of nature, the most eminent of the pious dead, the patriarchs, prophets, apostles, martyrs, and confessors of the past are to come forth from their graves (ver. 5, end) and live again on earth, constituting the court and nobility of the Messianic empire then to commence at Jerusalem." – "Exposition of Zechariah XIV," Professor John Owen, as printed in *Bibliotheca Sacra, Volume 18*, 1861, p. 359–360

The scroll of time in Scripture will also position Armageddon as a repeat of the destruction of Pharaoh in Exodus. The splitting of the Mount of Olives will lure the Final Nephilim to his doom. This is a dynamic reiteration of the parting of the Red Sea. Just as they did during the Exodus, Israel will escape, leaving Pharaoh (the Final Nephilim) to die in pursuit of God's people:

> "And Moses said unto the people, Fear ye not, stand still, and see the salvation of the LORD, which he will shew to you to day: for the Egyptians whom ye have seen to day, ye shall see them again no more for ever. The LORD shall fight for you, and ye shall hold your peace. And the LORD said unto Moses, Wherefore criest thou unto me? speak unto the children of Israel, that they go forward: But lift thou up thy rod, and stretch out thine hand over the sea, and divide it: and the children of Israel shall go on dry ground through the midst of the sea. And I, behold, I will harden the hearts of the Egyptians, and they shall follow them: and I will get me honour upon Pharaoh, and upon all his host, upon his chariots, and upon

> his horsemen.
>
> And the Egyptians shall know that I am the LORD, when I have gotten me honour upon Pharaoh, upon his chariots, and upon his horsemen. And the angel of God, which went before the camp of Israel, removed and went behind them; and the pillar of the cloud went from before their face, and stood behind them: And it came between the camp of the Egyptians and the camp of Israel; and it was a cloud and darkness to them, but it gave light by night to these: so that the one came not near the other all the night. And Moses stretched out his hand over the sea; and the LORD caused the sea to go back by a strong east wind all that night, and made the sea dry land, and the waters were divided. And the children of Israel went into the midst of the sea upon the dry ground: and the waters were a wall unto them on their right hand, and on their left."
> – Exodus 14:13–22

When the Israelites crossed the Red Sea, *heading east*, God used a supernatural wind to part the waters—dividing the sea to the north and the south. The children of Israel were able to cross on dry ground, and when the Egyptians pursued, the waters returned, drowning Pharaoh and his entire army. At the final battle of that great day of God Almighty, Jesus will divide the Mount of Olives (splitting, as mentioned earlier, half to the north and half to the south), providing an escape route for the believing remnant. Here, the Revealed Messiah will complete the destruction of the final enemies of His people. The angels of God and the Church will all be assembled for battle as well.

> "And I saw heaven opened, and behold a white horse; and he that sat upon him was called Faithful and True, and in righteousness he doth judge and make war. His eyes were as a flame of fire, and on his head were many crowns; and he had a name written, that no man knew, but he himself. **And he was clothed with a vesture dipped in blood: and his name is called The Word of God**. And

> the armies which were in heaven followed him upon white horses, clothed in fine linen, white and clean. And out of his mouth goeth a sharp sword, that with it he should smite the nations: and he shall rule them with a rod of iron: and he treadeth the winepress of the fierceness and wrath of Almighty God." – Revelation 19:11–15

This is Jesus' approach to the Mount of Olives, His vesture already stained from the conquests coming from Bozrah. He will utterly eradicate His enemies in the valley of Jehoshaphat, fulfilling Joel 3:

> "Proclaim ye this among the Gentiles; Prepare war, wake up the mighty men, let all the men of war draw near; let them come up: Beat your plowshares into swords and your pruninghooks into spears: let the weak say, I am strong. Assemble yourselves, and come, all ye heathen, and gather yourselves together round about: thither cause thy mighty ones to come down, O LORD. Let the heathen be wakened, and come up to the valley of Jehoshaphat: for there will I sit to judge all the heathen round about. Put ye in the sickle, for the harvest is ripe: come, get you down; for the press is full, the fats overflow; for their wickedness is great." – Joel 3:9–13

God invites all of His enemies to the final confrontation. He tells them to "cause thy mighty ones to come down"—the "mighty ones" being the *gibborim* (גִּבּוֹר in Hebrew; a reference for Nephilim, angels, and fighters with supernatural prowess). They are all to come to the valley of Jehoshaphat where Jesus is using His "sickle and winepress" to complete the day of vengeance. The allusions to Jesus in Revelation 14 are stunning; this is the fulfillment of the final battle. Continuing in Joel

> "Multitudes, multitudes in the valley of decision: for the day of the LORD is near in the valley of decision. The sun and the moon shall be darkened, and the stars shall withdraw their shining. The LORD

> also shall roar out of Zion, and utter his voice from Jerusalem; and the heavens and the earth shall shake: but the LORD will be the hope of his people, and the strength of the children of Israel. So shall ye know that I am the LORD your God dwelling in Zion, my holy mountain: then shall Jerusalem be holy, and there shall no strangers pass through her any more." – Joel 3:14–17

The Messiah will return to Jerusalem as conquering king, slaughtering His enemies with overwhelming force. This is the war the prophet Zechariah predicted when he wrote: "Then shall the LORD go forth, and fight against those nations, as when he fought in the day of battle" (Zechariah 14:3). The "day of battle" is also a reference to the defeat of Pharaoh at the Exodus:

> "'*As when fought in day of battle*' – as when Jehovah fought for Israel the Egyptians at the Red Sea (Exodus 14:14; 15:3). As He then made a way through the divided sea, so will He now divide in two 'the Mount of Olives.' The object of the cleaving of the mount in two by a fissure or valley (a prolongation of the valley of Jehoshaphat, extending from Jerusalem on the west towards Jordan, eastward) is to open a way of escape to the besieged (Joel 3:12, 14). Half the divided mount is thereby forced northward; half southward; the valley running between." – *A Commentary, Critical and Explanatory, on the Old and New Testaments, Volume 1*, Robert Jamieson, Andrew Robert Fausset, David Brown, 1871, p. 734

GREAT EARTHQUAKE SIGNALS REMANT TO FLEE

The Mount of Olives bursting in two will be accompanied by an earthquake:

> "And ye shall flee to the valley of the mountains; for the valley of

> the mountains shall reach unto Azal: yea, ye shall flee, like as ye fled from before the earthquake in the days of Uzziah king of Judah: and the LORD my God shall come, and all the saints with thee." – Zechariah 14:5

Jesus' arrival in Jerusalem will trigger an earthquake reminiscent of an earlier quake that took place during the reign of King Uzziah. Although Uzziah did many honorable and faithful acts for God, he also committed a grave sin when he went into the Temple to offer incense to God. This was something only a Levite priest was permitted to do:

> "But when he was strong, his heart was lifted up to his destruction: for he transgressed against the LORD his God, and went into the temple of the LORD to burn incense upon the altar of incense. And Azariah the priest went in after him, and with him fourscore priests of the LORD, that were valiant men: And they withstood Uzziah the king, and said unto him, It appertaineth not unto thee, Uzziah, to burn incense unto the LORD, but to the priests the sons of Aaron, that are consecrated to burn incense: go out of the sanctuary; for thou hast trespassed; neither shall it be for thine honour from the LORD God. Then Uzziah was wroth, and had a censer in his hand to burn incense: and while he was wroth with the priests, the leprosy even rose up in his forehead before the priests in the house of the LORD, from beside the incense altar." – 2 Chronicles 26:16–19

Josephus, the first-century Jewish historian, provided more details on this punishment from the Lord. In addition to Uzziah being struck with leprosy, Jerusalem experienced a cataclysmic earthquake that caused a portion of the Mount of Olives to break apart:

> "Accordingly when a remarkable day was come, and a general

> festival was to be celebrated, he put on the holy garment, and went into the temple to offer incense to God upon the golden altar; which he was prohibited to do by Azariah the High Priest, who had fourscore Priests with him, and who told him, that it was not lawful for him to offer sacrifice: and that 'None besides the posterity of Aaron were permitted so to do.' And when they cried out, that he must go out of the temple, and not transgress against God, he was wroth at them, and threatened to kill them, unless they would hold their peace. In the mean time a great earthquake shook the ground, and a rent was made in the temple, and the bright rays of the sun shone through it; and fell upon the King's face; insomuch that the leprosy seized upon him immediately.
>
> And before the city, at a place called *Eroge*, half the mountain broke off from the rest on the west, and rolled itself four furlongs, and stood still at the east mountain; till the roads, as well as the King's gardens, were spoiled by the obstruction." – *Antiquities of the Jews, X, 4*, Flavius Josephus, ca. AD 93, as printed in *The Works of Flavius Josephus, with Three Dissertations and Explanatory Notes and Observations*, William Whiston, 1847, p. 200

This earthquake was so shocking and memorable that it is used to mark an epoch in the book of Amos:

> "The words of Amos, who was among the herdsmen of Tekoa, which he saw concerning Israel **in the days of Uzziah king of Judah**, and in the days of Jeroboam the son of Joash king of Israel, **two years before the earthquake**." – Amos 1:1

At the Resurrection of Jesus Christ, not only was the order of time thrown off (it was as dark as night in the middle of the day; see Matthew 27:45), but there was also an earthquake (Matthew 27:51). Psalm 18 includes a prophecy of the earthquake that will take place at His Second Coming:

> "I will call upon the LORD, who is worthy to be praised: so shall I be saved from mine enemies. The sorrows of death compassed me, and the floods of ungodly men made me afraid. The sorrows of hell compassed me about: the snares of death prevented me. In my distress I called upon the LORD, and cried unto my God: he heard my voice out of his temple, and my cry came before him, even into his ears. **Then the earth shook and trembled; the foundations also of the hills moved and were shaken**, because he was wroth. There went up a smoke out of his nostrils, and fire out of his mouth devoured: coals were kindled by it." – Psalm 18:3–8

The remnant of Judah will be surrounded by the Antichrist and the global armies of the ten kings. They will be ensnared in death as Jerusalem is conquered. When they cry out to Jesus, He will hear them and come to their rescue. His arrival will be accompanied by an earthquake. The flight of the Southern Kingdom from Jerusalem will fulfill what was foretold in Isaiah 37:

> "And the remnant that is escaped of the house of Judah shall again take root downward, and bear fruit upward: For out of Jerusalem shall go forth a remnant, and they that escape out of mount Zion: the zeal of the LORD of hosts shall do this." – Isaiah 37:31–32

The Mount of Olives that was previously fractured in a divine judgment of a sinful king will be divided once more when the True King and High Priest returns to assume His throne. The cycle of prophetic quantum repetition meets its culmination at the Mount of Olives.

MOUNT OF OLIVES: GREAT STAGE OF THE MESSIAH

Examining the significance of the Mount of Olives throughout Scripture reveals God's prophetic superposition in the plan of salvation. Consider some of the events that took place on this mountain east of Jerusalem:

- It was the place of Jesus' departure from Earth to Heaven at His First Coming:

> "When they therefore were come together, they asked of him, saying, Lord, wilt thou at this time restore again the kingdom to Israel? And he said unto them, It is not for you to know the times or the seasons, which the Father hath put in his own power. But ye shall receive power, after that the Holy Ghost is come upon you: and ye shall be witnesses unto me both in Jerusalem, and in all Judaea, and in Samaria, and unto the uttermost part of the earth. And when he had spoken these things, while they beheld, he was taken up; and a cloud received him out of their sight.
>
> And while they looked steadfastly toward heaven as he went up, behold, two men stood by them in white apparel; Which also said, Ye men of Galilee, why stand ye gazing up into heaven? **this same Jesus, which is taken up from you into heaven, shall so come in like manner as ye have seen him go into heaven. Then returned they unto Jerusalem from the mount called Olivet,** which is from Jerusalem a sabbath day's journey." – Acts 1:6–12

The disciples asked the Lord when He would return the kingdom to Israel not realizing that they were standing on the very place where it would take place: the Mount of Olives. The two angels confirmed that Jesus would return to the Holy City in the same manner He departed—

at the Mount of Olives.

- The Mount of Olives was where Jesus made His triumphal entry into Jerusalem on a donkey:

"And it came to pass, when he was come nigh to Bethpage and Bethany, **at the mount called the mount of Olives**, he sent two of his disciples, Saying, Go ye into the village over against you; in the which at your entering ye shall find a colt tied, whereon yet never man sat: loose him, and bring him hither. And if any man ask you, Why do ye loose him? thus shall ye say unto him, Because the Lord hath need of him. And they that were sent went their way, and found even as he had said unto them. And as they were loosing the colt, the owners thereof said unto them, Why loose ye the colt?

And they said, The Lord hath need of him. And they brought him to Jesus: and they cast their garments upon the colt, and they set Jesus thereon. And as he went, they spread their clothes in the way. And when he was come nigh, even now at the descent of the mount of Olives, the whole multitude of the disciples began to rejoice and praise God with a loud voice for all the mighty works that they had seen; Saying, Blessed be the King that cometh in the name of the Lord: peace in heaven, and glory in the highest. And some of the Pharisees from among the multitude said unto him, Master, rebuke thy disciples. And he answered and said unto them, I tell you that, if these should hold their peace, the stones would immediately cry out." – Luke 19:29–40

Jesus rode a donkey into Jerusalem on the first Palm Sunday to praise and adoration pouring forth from the people of Israel. They shouted, "Blessed be the King that cometh in the name of The Lord!" as He strode in triumphantly from the Mount of Olives. The Messiah told the people that He would not return a second time until they once again said, "Blessed is he who cometh in the name of The Lord," which will take place after He arrives riding a white horse, sets His feet on the Mount of Olives, and conquers the Antichrist and His armies. The prophetic similitudes through time reach their apex at this blessed mount.

- When a select group of disciples asked about the signs that would indicate the end of the world, Jesus gave His greatest prophetic sermon at the Mount of Olives:

"And as he sat upon the mount of Olives, the disciples came unto him privately, saying, Tell us, when shall these things be? and what shall be the sign of thy coming, and of the end of the world? And Jesus answered and said unto them, Take heed that no man deceive you. For many shall come in my name, saying, I am Christ; and shall deceive many." – Matthew 24:3–5

Jesus would continue to teach on many of the events of the Great Tribulation in this address, which is commonly known as the Olivet Discourse.

- The Mount of Olives also was the setting of several foreshadows of Israel's redemption. In one of the prophet Ezekiel's many direct encounters with God, the Lord prophesied the day of Israel's spiritual restoration with the one-third remnant being separated from the two-thirds who would fall for the delusion of the Antichrist:

"Thus saith the Lord GOD; I will even gather you from the people, and assemble you out of the countries where ye have been scattered, and I will give you the land of Israel. And they shall come thither, and they shall take away all the detestable things thereof and all the abominations thereof from thence.

And I will give them one heart, and I will put a new spirit within you; and I will take the stony heart out of their flesh, and will give them an heart of flesh: That they may walk in my statutes, and keep mine ordinances, and do them: and they shall be my people, and I will be their God. But as for them whose heart walketh after the heart of their detestable things and their abominations, I will recompense their way upon their own heads, saith the Lord GOD. Then did the cherubims lift up their wings, and the wheels beside them; and the glory of the God of Israel was over them above. And the glory of the LORD went up from the midst of the city, and stood upon the mountain which is on the east side of the city." – Ezekiel 11:17–23

Jesus, appearing to Ezekiel, proclaimed that a day would come when He would supernaturally redeem Israel by giving them a new heart and spirit. This, of course, is the new birth that comes through saving faith in Christ. When He finished the prophecy, the glorious presence of the Lord rode on the cherubim and stood on the "mountain on the east side of the city" - the Mount of Olives.

- One of the most famous Gospel accounts profiles the "adulterous woman." The Pharisees tried to trick Jesus into contradicting His teachings of peace, mercy, and love towards all people, as we see in the following narrative:

"Jesus went unto the mount of Olives. And early in the morning

he came again into the temple, and all the people came unto him; and he sat down, and taught them. And the scribes and Pharisees brought unto him a woman taken in adultery; and when they had set her in the midst, They say unto him, Master, this woman was taken in adultery, in the very act. Now Moses in the law commanded us, that such should be stoned: but what sayest thou? This they said, tempting him, that they might have to accuse him."
– John 8:1–6

As Jesus descended from the Mount of Olives, the Pharisees, enemies of Christ, presented the woman, who had been "caught in the very act" of adultery. Their hope, by citing the Mosaic laws on marital infidelity, was to paint Jesus into a corner by persuading Him to agree that this woman should be executed on the spot for her sin. During the end times, the Antichrist and False Prophet will deceive Israel into committing spiritual adultery via the strong delusion in order to eternally corrupt and disqualify the twelve tribes from salvation, thus "forcing" God's prophetic Word to fail.

Jesus gave a mysterious response to the Pharisees' accusation against the woman:

"But Jesus stooped down, and with his finger wrote on the ground, as though he heard them not. So when they continued asking him, he lifted up himself, and said unto them, He that is without sin among you, let him first cast a stone at her. And again he stooped down, and wrote on the ground. And they which heard it, being convicted by their own conscience, went out one by one, beginning at the eldest, even unto the last: and Jesus was left alone, and the woman standing in the midst. When Jesus had lifted up himself, and saw none but the woman, he said unto her, Woman, where are those thine accusers? hath no man condemned thee? She said, No man, Lord. **And Jesus said unto her, Neither do I condemn thee: go, and sin no more.**" – John 8:6–11

The Savior acted as though He didn't hear the treacherous words of the woman's accusers; instead, He wrote a message on the ground. Interestingly, Jesus' actions were foreshadowed by those of King David, who, when pursued by his enemies as recorded in Psalms, said: "They also that seek after my life lay snares for me: and they that seek my hurt speak mischievous things, and imagine deceits all the day long. But I, as a deaf man, heard not; and I was as a dumb man that openeth not his mouth" (Psalm 38:12–13). Now, Jesus, the Divine Son of David, was in a similar fashion ignoring the trap of His accusers.

Israel will indeed be that woman caught in adultery during the end times, and her Messiah will remove her iniquities and make her clean. Rather than destroy her, Jesus will set Israel free from the bondage of sin. The prophet Hosea was commanded by God to purchase freedom for his wife, who had abandoned him and become a harlot. Rather than punish her or leave her to die in her state of bondage, the Lord commanded Hosea to forgive her, restore his relationship with her, and love her.

The name "Hosea" (*Howshea*, or הושע in Hebrew) means "salvation"; that man of God did indeed save his wife from a life of sin and misery. "Hosea" was also the original name of Joshua, the conqueror of the Nephilim who led the Israelites into the Promised Land (before Moses renamed him; see Numbers 13:1

During the Day of the Lord, Jesus Christ, the Greater Hosea, will reclaim His beloved bride, Israel, and restore her forever. That will take place at the Mount of Olives—again, the site of so many great moments of the Messiah and the place from where He will look upon Jerusalem before He makes His Second triumphal entry. (Author's note: This is the same view from the east you will find on the cover of this book.)

TRIBE OF JUDAH FIGHTS THE ANTICHRIST AND HIS ARMIES

> "And this shall be the plague wherewith the LORD will smite all the people that have fought against Jerusalem; Their flesh shall consume away while they stand upon their feet, and their eyes shall consume away in their holes, and their tongue shall consume away in their mouth. And it shall come to pass in that day, that a great tumult from the LORD shall be among them; **and they shall lay hold every one on the hand of his neighbour**, and his hand shall rise up against the hand of his neighbour. **And Judah also shall fight at Jerusalem**; and the wealth of all the heathen round about shall be gathered together, gold, and silver, and apparel, in great abundance. And so shall be the plague of the horse, of the mule, of the camel, and of the ass, and of all the beasts that shall be in these tents, as this plague." – Zechariah 14:12–15

At His appearing, the Lord will unleash a plague that will literally melt the flesh of the enemy forces as they stand (many prophecy commentators over the years have explained this as a nuclear explosion, which it will not be, but it will have a similarly devastating effect). The following excerpt emphasizes the cataclysmic effect of Jesus' attack upon the Final Nephilim and his armies:

> "This is no cunningly devised fable. It is the word of God. The withering hand of God will be really laid on living men—men great in power and military prowess—the flower of our fleets and of our armies—men great in all that the world is seeking after. 'Come,' it

> is said to all the fowls that fly in the midst of heaven, 'come and gather yourselves together unto the supper of the great God; that ye may eat the flesh of kings, and the flesh of captains, and the flesh of mighty men, and the flesh of horses, and of them that sit on them, and the flesh of all men, both free and bond, both small and great.'
>
> Ah! how little men think, as they grasp so proudly the helm of their mighty vessel, that it is fast speeding onward to this point of overwhelming ruin! May human progress (as men now vaunt of it) be ever viewed by us in the light of these testimonies. Then they will separate us from unclean thing, and teach us to wait for God's Son from Heaven." – *The Day of the Lord—A Lecture on Zechariah XIV*, Benjamin Willis Newton, 1858, p. 21–22

This will fulfill Isaiah's prophecy that the final battle would be over in a moment:

> "Moreover the multitude of thy strangers shall be like small dust, and the multitude of the terrible ones shall be as chaff that passeth away: **yea, it shall be at an instant suddenly**. Thou shalt be visited of the LORD f hosts with thunder, and with earthquake, and great noise, with storm and tempest, and the flame of devouring fire. And the multitude of all the nations that fight against Ariel [Jerusalem], even all that fight against her and her munition, and that distress her, shall be as a dream of a night vision." – Isaiah 29:5–7

Additionally, some of Antichrist's armies *will end up fighting against each other* (Zechariah 14:13) — a similar judgment Yahweh inflicted upon Ammon, Edom, and Moab in the days of King Jehoshaphat:

> "And when they began to sing and to praise, the LORD set

> ambushments against the children of Ammon, Moab, and mount Seir, which were come against Judah; and they were smitten. For the children of Ammon and Moab stood up against the inhabitants of mount Seir, utterly to slay and destroy them: and when they had made an end of the inhabitants of Seir, **every one helped to destroy another**. And when Judah came toward the watch tower in the wilderness, they looked unto the multitude, and, behold, they were dead bodies fallen to the earth, and none escaped." – 2 Chronicles 20:22–24

Jesus' very appearance is enough to slaughter millions and disintegrate them before the eyes of their enemies. He will then inflict madness among the remaining troops, causing them to murder one another in the valley of Jehoshaphat in a repetition of the judgment that struck the enemies of the king the valley was named for. The name "Jehoshaphat" (*Yehowshaphat*, or יְהוֹשָׁפָט in Hebrew) means "Jehovah has judged." It is certainly fitting that God determined before time itself to bring the climactic end to the war against the forces of evil in this va

Once the enemy has been ravaged and scattered, the armies of Judah will join the attack to complete the defeat. This follows the same pattern of the wars for the land of Canaan in the book of Joshua, where Jesus Christ, dubbed the "Angel of the Lord" in His Old Testament appearances, directed supernatural attacks to vanquish Israel's enemies, leaving the Jewish armies to run roughshod over the often confused and decimated opposing forces.

The remnant of Judah will also gain much wealth in their victory, as they plunder gold, silver, and precious valuables from their enemies. This, too, is a cyclical rendition of the giving of gold and silver to Israel in the Exodus:

> "And the children of Israel did according to the word of Moses; and they borrowed of the Egyptians jewels of silver, and jewels of gold, and raiment: And the LORD gave the people favour in the sight of

the Egyptians, so that they lent unto them such things as they required. And they spoiled the Egyptians." – Exodus 12:35–36

CONQUEST OF ANTICHRIST FORCES SPANS 183 MILES

> "And another angel came out from the altar, which had power over fire; and cried with a loud cry to him that had the sharp sickle, saying, Thrust in thy sharp sickle, and gather the clusters of the vine of the earth; for her grapes are fully ripe. And the angel thrust in his sickle into the earth, and gathered the vine of the earth, and cast it into the great winepress of the wrath of God. And the winepress was trodden without the city, and blood came out of the winepress, even unto the horse bridles, by the space of a thousand and six hundred furlongs." – Revelation 14:18–20

The enemy forces will undoubtedly retreat when they see how quickly the Messiah and Conquering King vanquishes the Final Nephilim. Jesus and His army of holy angels and saints will pursue Satan's servants back to the valley of Megiddo, completing the shedding of blood for 1,600 furlongs. The imagery in the vision from Revelation 14 is Jesus "treading the winepress," which is symbolic of the final judgment on Earth at the Great Battle:

> "Let the heathen be wakened, and come up to the valley of Jehoshaphat: for there will I sit to judge all the heathen round about. **Put ye in the sickle, for the harvest is ripe: come, get you down; for the press is full**, the fats overflow; for their wickedness is great." – Joel 3:12–13
>
> "**I have trodden the winepress alone**; and of the people there was

> none with me: for I will tread them in mine anger, and trample them in my fury; and their blood shall be sprinkled upon my garments, and I will stain all my raiment. For the day of vengeance is in mine heart, and the year of my redeemed is come." – Isaiah 63:3–4

Jesus Christ, the Conquering King, will exact vengeance for all the evil and wickedness the world has committed for millennia. It must never be forgotten that God has set a limit on sin for all people. Once that limit has been reached from an unrepentant, God hating, Satan-worshiping populace, the consequences will be dire. There will be much blood shed at Christ's revealing because humanity has shed so much blood.

Let this serve as a sobering reminder of our need for repentance and forgiveness. No born-again Christian is forgiven because he or she "deserves it" or has somehow "earned" salvation. It was Jesus' shed blood that allowed for an atonement—a payment of the debt we owe a just and Holy God for taking away our sins. Absent the free forgiveness based on Jesus' sacrifice on the cross, all people would ever really "deserve" would be judgment from the Lord.

The distance of 1,600 furlongs has been a mysterious number in Scripture. Theologians and scholars who have converted the distance to miles often say it's equal to two hundred miles. However, in first-century Judea, which was under the rule of the Roman Empire, a "Roman mile" (five thousand feet) was shorter than the English statute mile (5,280) commonly used today.

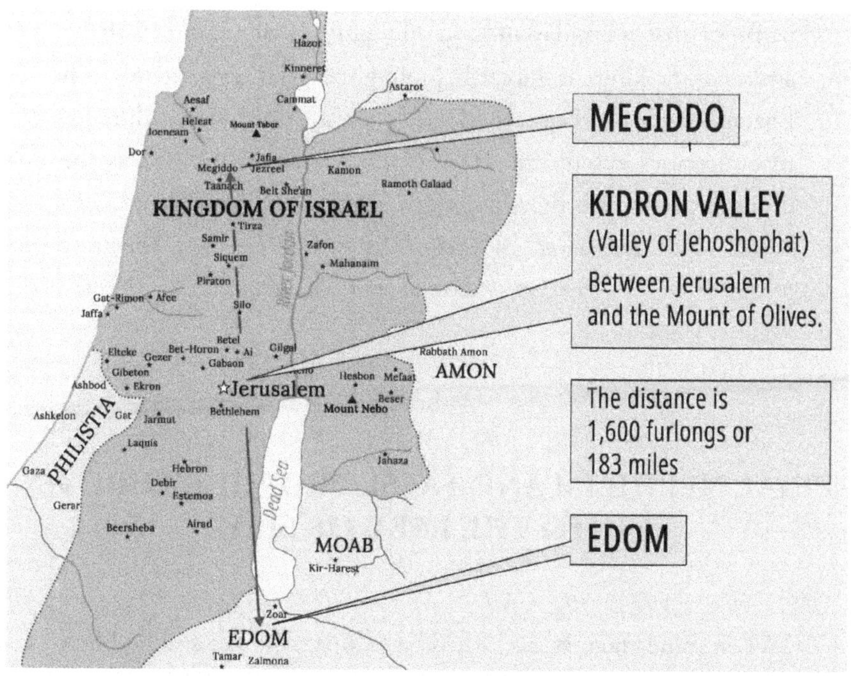

Thus, two hundred Roman miles equal approximately 183 statute miles, which is the distance from Edom to Megiddo (as seen in the map above). We read confirmation of the difference in measurements in the following:

> "'Distance of a thousand and six hundred furlongs'—200 Roman miles or about 183 English [miles]." – *The Revelation of St. John the Divine, with Notes and Introduction*, Reverend William Henry Simcox, 1902, p. 90

This is the approximate distance from Bozrah in Edom, where Jesus will retrieve the ten Northern tribes of Israel, to Jerusalem (where Christ gathers the Southern Kingdom), ending at Megiddo, where the Antichrist armies will initially gather for battle. An early-twentieth-century commentary unravels this mysterious number from Revelation 14 with the same conclusion:

> "The probabilities are that all these localities are included in 'the

battle of that great day of God Almighty;' that the hosts of the armies of the kings of the earth, joining the Beast, will extend from Bozrah, on the southeast, to Megiddo, on the northwest, a distance that measures exactly the 1600 *stadia* named in the text as the distance over which the blood flows from the wine press of God's wrath." – *His Apocalypse, Wherein Is Set Forth a Detailed Panorama of the Prophetic Wonders of Daniel and Revelation*, John Quincy Adams, 1924, p. 288

FINAL NEPHILIM AND FALSE PROPHET THROWN INTO THE LAKE OF FIRE

"When mine enemies are turned back, they shall fall and perish at thy presence." – Psalm 9:3

"And I saw the beast, and the kings of the earth, and their armies, gathered together to make war against him that sat on the horse, and against his army. And the beast was taken, and with him the false prophet that wrought miracles before him, with which he deceived them that had received the mark of the beast, and them that worshipped his image. These both were cast alive into a lake of fire burning with brimstone." – Revelation 19:19–20

For all of his blasphemies, satanic superpower, and military genius, the Antichrist poses no threat to the Lord Jesus Christ whatsoever. Just as David dispatched the God-defying Goliath with one stone, so too will Jesus instantly vanquish the Antichrist and the False Prophet with His mere presence—His divine voice and light destroying the False Messiah for good. The prophecies of the Antichrist's defeat will be fulfilled:

> "The LORD of hosts hath sworn, saying, Surely as I have thought, so shall it come to pass; and as I have purposed, so shall it stand: **That I will break the Assyrian in my land, and upon my mountains tread him under foot**: then shall his yoke depart from off them, and his burden depart from off their shoulders. **This is the purpose that is purposed upon the whole earth**: and this is the hand that is stretched out upon all the nations." – Isaiah 14:24–26

When Jesus stands upon the Mount of Olives, He will destroy the Antichrist, who will fall beneath His feet in the valley of Jehoshaphat. At the utterance of Jesus' words, the Final Nephilim will be captured:

> "And the LORD shall cause his glorious voice to be heard, and shall shew the lighting down of his arm, with the indignation of his anger, and with the flame of a devouring fire, with scattering, and tempest, and hailstones. For through the voice of the LORD shall the Assyrian be beaten down, which smote with a rod." – Isaiah 30:30–31

A third-century work attributed to Hippolytus describes the swift fashion of the conquest of the Beast:

> "But these days shall run their course rapidly; and the kingdom of the deceiver and Antichrist shall be speedily removed. And then, in fine, in the glance of an eye shall the fashion of this world pass away, and the power of men shall be brought to naught and all these visible things shall be destroyed." – "Appendix to Part II of the Works of Hippolytus," as printed in *Ante-Nicene Christian Library: Irenaeus, v.2, Hippolytus, v.2, Fragments of the Third Century,*

Translated by Reverend Alexander Roberts, 1869, p. 121

The prophet Daniel also foretold of the unique punishment reserved for the Antichrist:

> "I beheld till the thrones were cast down, and the Ancient of days did sit, whose garment was white as snow, and the hair of his head like the pure wool: his throne was like the fiery flame, and his wheels as burning fire. A fiery stream issued and came forth from before him: thousand thousands ministered unto him, and ten thousand times ten thousand stood before him: the judgment was set, and the books were opened. I beheld then because of the voice of the great words which the horn spake: **I beheld even till the beast was slain, and his body destroyed, and given to the burning flame**. As concerning the rest of the beasts, they had their dominion taken away: yet their lives were prolonged for a season and time." – Daniel 7:9–12

The Antichrist's judgment will be announced in heavenly places. Like Nebuchadnezzar, whose transformation to a human-animal hybrid was decreed by the Watchers (Daniel 4:17), the Final Nephilim's sentencing in the Lake of Fire already will have been pronounced. As punishment, he and the False Prophet will be hurled into the Lake of Fire alive—the first of this type of judgment seen in Scripture. The Lake of Fire is a unique realm of punishment, where even Hell and death will be cast into at the end of the Millennial Reign of Christ (Revelation 20:14). The warning of Isaiah 30 will be fulfilled:

> "For Tophet is ordained of old; yea, **for the king it is prepared**; he hath made it deep and large: the pile thereof is fire and much wood; the breath of the LORD, like a stream of brimstone, doth kindle it."

– Isaiah 30:33

In ancient Israel, Tophet was a large fire pit used for human sacrifice by the Nephilim-led Canaanite nations. It was located in the valley of Hinnom, to the south to Jerusalem, bordering the heart of the valley of Jehoshaphat. This was the stronghold of the Rephaim giants before Joshua led Israel into the Promised Land. And it was a location of a great deal of spiritual wickedness by Israelite kings.

But the "Tophet" in the spiritual realm is the Lake of Fire, and it is prepared and awaiting the Final Nephilim and his False Prophet. In Greek-speaking, first-century Judea, Jesus called it *ge enna* or "Gehenna," and He made it clear that it was a spiritual-realm prison:

> "Be not afraid of **them that kill the body**, and after that have no more that they can do. But I will forewarn you whom ye shall fear: Fear him, which after he hath killed hath power to cast into hell [*ge enna*]; yea, I say unto you, Fear him." – Luke 12:4-5

The same valley where the Nephilim once strode in pride thinking they had foiled the plans of God will be the exact location where the Final Nephilim will meet his doom.

SATAN LOCKED IN THE ABYSS

> "And I saw an angel come down from heaven, having the key of the bottomless pit and a great chain in his hand. And he laid hold on the dragon, that old serpent, which is the Devil, and Satan, and bound him a thousand years, And cast him into the bottomless pit, and shut him up, and set a seal upon him, that he should deceive the nations no more, till the thousand years should be fulfilled: and

> after that he must be loosed a little season." – Revelation 20:1–3

We read in the book of Revelation one final confirmation that Satan will indeed father the Antichrist. Unlike the Beast and False Prophet who are cast into the Lake of Fire at Armageddon, the Devil will be imprisoned in the bottomless pit—the same judgment handed out to the apostate angels of Genesis 6 for their fornication with the daughters of men. Note that the angel who jails the Devil also has a chain to bind him with, just as the rebel sons of God were locked in "chains of darkness" (Jude 1:7).

This will mark the end of the reign of the Antichrist. That he is a supernatural being is further confirmed when we see that at the end of a thousand years, after Satan's final revolt, the Devil will also be thrown into the Lake of Fire, where the Antichrist will still be burning *alive*:

> "And the devil that deceived them was cast into the lake of fire and brimstone, **where the beast and the false prophet are**, and shall be tormented day and night for ever and ever." – Revelation 20:10

Both the Antichrist and the False Prophet will still be alive a thousand years later, when Satan will finally be punished for good. There, they will suffer their judicial punishment for thousands of years of war, crimes, and devastation against God's kingdom and humanity. And like that, the satanic trinity will be destroyed and removed from the world forever. Not much of the biblical narrative is spent dwelling on their fate. They have never been major opposition to Jesus Christ. They are merely the final stumbling blocks to Israel's fulfillment of Scripture and the completion of the prophetic Word of God.

CHAPTER 13

THE END IS THE BEGINNING

> "And he that sat upon the throne said, Behold, I make all things new. And he said unto me, Write: for these words are true and faithful. And he said unto me, It is done. I am Alpha and Omega, the beginning and the end. I will give unto him that is athirst of the fountain of the water of life freely." – Revelation 21:5–6

With Satan imprisoned and the Final Nephilim destroyed, the world will then be reset to how it was in the beginning. The Lord Jesus Christ will restore the ravaged Earth into the state it was during the days of Noah. It won't be the perfected state that was Eden before Adam and Eve sinned, but it will be very close. This thousand-year reign of Jesus—commonly known as the Millennium—will feature distinct characteristics that set it apart from the world of today.

THE MILLENNIUM: MESSIANIC REIGN ISRAEL EXPECTED AT CHRIST'S FIRST COMING

Now redeemed believers in Messiah, Israel will find their King ruling with a theocratic government from the throne of David in Jerusalem. This is prophesied in Isaiah 11:

> "And there shall come forth a rod out of the stem of Jesse, and a

> Branch shall grow out of his roots: And the spirit of the LORD shall rest upon him, the spirit of wisdom and understanding, the spirit of counsel and might, the spirit of knowledge and of the fear of the LORD; And shall make him of quick understanding in the fear of the LORD: and he shall not judge after the sight of his eyes, neither reprove after the hearing of his ears: But with righteousness shall he judge the poor, and reprove with equity for the meek of the earth: and he shall smite the earth: with the rod of his mouth, and with the breath of his lips shall he slay the wicked. And righteousness shall be the girdle of his loins, and faithfulness the girdle of his reins." – Isaiah 11:1–5

NATIONS LEFT AFTER THE GREAT BATTLE WORSHIP JESUS IN JERUSALEM ANNUALLY

> "And it shall come to pass, that every one that is left of all the nations which came against Jerusalem shall even go up from year to year to worship the King, the LORD of hosts, and to keep the feast of tabernacles. And it shall be, that whoso will not come up of all the families of the earth unto Jerusalem to worship the King, the LORD of hosts, even upon them shall be no rain. And if the family of Egypt go not up, and come not, that have no rain; there shall be the plague, wherewith the LORD will smite the heathen that come not up to keep the feast of tabernacles. This shall be the punishment of Egypt, and the punishment of all nations that come not up to keep the feast of tabernacles." – Zechariah 14:16–19

The remaining nations, still inhabited by mortal human beings who survived the Great Battle, will be required to come to Jerusalem annually to celebrate the Feast of Tabernacles. This feast was specifically a joyous celebration

(Deuteronomy 16:14), because it was a reminder of the journey in the wilderness that led to the true home in the Promised Land. At long last, the entire world will seek to trust, believe, and follow their King, *Yeshua Ha Meshiach*. The prophet Zechariah emphasized this glorious future reality:

> "Thus saith the LORD of hosts; It shall yet come to pass, that there shall come people, and the inhabitants of many cities: And the inhabitants of one city shall go to another, saying, Let us go speedily to pray before the LORD, and to seek the LORD of hosts: I will go also. Yea, many people and strong nations shall come to seek the LORD of hosts in Jerusalem, and to pray before the LORD. Thus saith the LORD of hosts; In those days it shall come to pass, that ten men shall take hold out of all languages of the nations, **even shall take hold of the skirt of him that is a Jew, saying, We will go with you: for we have heard that God is with you**." – Zechariah 8:20–23

Israel will fulfill its original charge from God: to be a light to the world leading people to the Savior. The Jewish people will be virtual celebrities in the Millennium, as Gentiles will know that "God is with them." In fact, at the judgment following the Great Battle, Jesus will evaluate the nations who are allowed to enter the Millennium based on their treatment of Israel:

> "**When the Son of man shall come in his glory, and all the holy angels with him, then shall he sit upon the throne of his glory**: And before him shall be gathered all nations: and he shall separate them one from another, as a shepherd divideth his sheep from the goats: And he shall set the sheep on his right hand, but the goats on the left. Then shall the King say unto them on his right hand, Come, ye blessed of my Father, inherit the kingdom prepared for you from the foundation of the world: For I was an hungred, and ye gave me meat: I was thirsty, and ye gave me drink: I was a

> stranger, and ye took me in:
>
> Naked, and ye clothed me: I was sick, and ye visited me: I was in prison, and ye came unto me. Then shall the righteous answer him, saying, Lord, when saw we thee an hungred, and fed thee? or thirsty, and gave thee drink? When saw we thee a stranger, and took thee in? or naked, and clothed thee? Or when saw we thee sick, or in prison, and came unto thee? And the King shall answer and say unto them, **Verily I say unto you, Inasmuch as ye have done it unto one of the least of these my brethren**, ye have done it unto me. Then shall he say also unto them on the left hand, Depart from me, ye cursed, into everlasting fire, prepared for the devil and his angels." – Matthew 25:31-41

Those who do not go to celebrate the Feast of Tabernacles in Jerusalem will see rain withheld from their lands. This underscores that there will be a need for water and irrigation as in ancient times.

In one of her exhaustive studies of Bible prophecy, Christian researcher Helen Maclachlan noted the following regarding worship in the Millennium:

> "Here we have confirmed a most important truth, which may be learnt from many other parts of Scripture, a truth very much at variance with present (so-called) orthodox theology—namely, that every individual or every nation 'that is left of *all the nations*' which shall take part in the anti-Christian attack against Jerusalem shall afterwards year by year come up to worship Jehovah, the King of the Jews, in true Jewish fashion, as his people did of old when they came to keep the Passover and the Feast of Tabernacles.
>
> The Jews often assert they have a mission to convert all Gentiles to the worship of their God; and here we see they are right, for when these nations or individuals mingle as acceptable worshippers with

> the Jews at the Feast of Tabernacles in the Temple at Jerusalem, which is to be 'the house of prayer for all nations' (Matt. Xxi.13), then shall the prophecy of Isaiah be fulfilled." – *Notes on the Prophecies of Zechariah*, Helen Maclachlan, 1880, p. 85, italics in original

The Northern and Southern Kingdoms will finally be reunited:

> "And I will make them one nation in the land upon the mountains of Israel; and one king shall be king to them all: and they shall be no more two nations, neither shall they be divided into two kingdoms any more at all. Neither shall they defile themselves any more with their idols, nor with their detestable things, nor with any of their transgressions: but I will save them out of all their dwelling places, wherein they have sinned, and will cleanse them: so shall they be my people, and I will be their God.
>
> And David my servant shall be king over them; and they all shall have one shepherd: they shall also walk in my judgments, and observe my statutes, and do them. And they shall dwell in the land that I have given unto Jacob my servant, wherein your fathers have dwelt; and they shall dwell therein, even they, and their children, and their children's children for ever: and my servant David shall be their prince for ever. Moreover I will make a covenant of peace with them; it shall be an everlasting covenant with them: and I will place them, and multiply them, and will set my sanctuary in the midst of them for evermore. My tabernacle also shall be with them: yea, I will be their God, and they shall be my people." – Ezekiel 37:22–27

THE SECOND RAINBOW – GOD'S RECONCILIATION OF ISRAEL IS PERMANENT

In the book of Isaiah, a passage confirms that the reunion of the twelve tribes with their Messiah will be everlasting—they will never be forsaken again. The prophet emphasized this by referring back to the days of Noah:

> "For thy Maker is thine husband; the LORD of hosts is his name; and thy Redeemer the Holy One of Israel; The God of the whole earth shall he be called. For the LORD hath called thee as a woman forsaken and grieved in spirit, and a wife of youth, when thou wast refused, saith thy God. For a small moment have I forsaken thee; but with great mercies will I gather thee. In a little wrath I hid my face from thee for a moment; but with everlasting kindness will I have mercy on thee, saith the LORD thy Redeemer. **For this is as the waters of Noah unto me**: for as I have sworn that the waters of Noah should no more go over the earth; so have I sworn that I would not be wroth with thee, nor rebuke thee." – Isaiah 54:5–9

When Yahweh turns His face back to Israel, it will be a ripple through time to the rainbow after the Flood: a promise that the blessings of Israel are permanent. They will never be rebuked or experience God's wrath again.

MILLENNIAL TEMPLE: CENTER OF GLOBAL WORSHIP

Ezekiel chapters 40–48 provide one of the most amazing, detailed prophecies in all of Scripture. It lays out the topography, design, and worship to take place at the Holy Temple during the Millennial Reign of Christ. This is clearly a Temple that has never been constructed before, as its size is approximately one square mile (the Temple area measures "500 reeds" on all four sides. A reed is approximately ten feet; see Ezekiel 42:15–20). The actual "Holy Land"—the area encompassing and surrounding the Temple—measures twenty-five thousand reeds by ten thousand reeds, or fifty by thirty miles (Ezekiel 45:1).

Jerusalem will be at higher elevation than its surrounding area in the regenerated earth, providing a clear location for all the world travelers in making their annual trip to the Holy City to worship the Lord Jesus Christ:

> "All the land shall be turned as a plain from Geba to Rimmon south of Jerusalem: **and it shall be lifted up, and inhabited in her place**, from Benjamin's gate unto the place of the first gate, unto the corner gate, and from the tower of Hananeel unto the king's winepresses." – Zechariah 14:10

Most importantly, God Himself will literally dwell in the Temple during the Millennium. Jesus Christ, sitting upon the throne of David, will once again be present on earth, receiving the worship of humanity as He did during His First Incarnation and during the days of Adam and Eve when they spoke with God directly and Cain and Abel offered sacrifices to God in person. Ezekiel 43 offers a description:

> "And the glory of the LORD came into the house by the way of the gate whose prospect is toward the east. So the spirit took me up, and brought me into the inner court; and, behold, the glory of the LORD filled the house. And I heard him speaking unto me out of the house; and the man stood by me. And he said unto me, **Son of man, the place of my throne, and the place of the soles of my feet, where I will dwell in the midst of the children of Israel for ever**, and my holy name, shall the house of Israel no more defile, neither they, nor their kings, by their whoredom, nor by the carcases of their kings in their high places." – Ezekiel 43:4–7

REDEEMED ISRAEL AND THE CHURCH WILL RULE AND REIGN WITH JESUS CHRIST

> **"And hath made us kings and priests** unto God and his Father; to him be glory and dominion for ever and ever. Amen." – Revelation 1:6
>
> "And I saw thrones, and they sat upon them, and judgment was given unto them: and I saw the souls of them that were beheaded for the witness of Jesus, and for the word of God, and which had not worshipped the beast, neither his image, neither had received his mark upon their foreheads, or in their hands; and they lived and reigned with Christ a thousand years." – Revelation 20:4

All the believers who endure to the end, the saints of the Church, the believing remnant of Israel, and all of the martyrs of the Day of the Lord who will have died at the hands of the Final Nephilim will be in glorified, immortal bodies, ruling with Christ. This is the time when the mortal humans living on Earth and the sinful angels will be judged. All believers won't just inherit eternal life from Jesus Christ, but they'll also share in ruling and reigning over the Earth during the Millennium.

TOPOGRAPHY AND NATURE OF EARTH WILL REVERT TO EARLY-GENESIS STATE

In Jeremiah chapter 4, we read that the prophet received a staggering vision of the world after the pouring of the seventh vial, when God's supernatural wrath culminates with the devastating earthquake that will rock every mountain and island and destroy cities all over the globe. The destruction will be of an unprecedented scale:

> "Set up the standard toward Zion: retire, stay not: for I will bring evil from the north, and a great destruction. The lion is come up from his thicket, **and the destroyer of the Gentiles is on his way**; he is gone forth from his place to make thy land desolate; and thy cities shall be laid waste, without an inhabitant....
>
> I beheld the earth, and, lo, **it was without form, and void**; and the heavens, and they had no light. I beheld the mountains, and, lo, they trembled, and all the hills moved lightly. I beheld, and, lo, there was no man, and all the birds of the heavens were fled. I beheld, and, lo, the fruitful place was a wilderness, and all the cities thereof were broken down at the presence of the LORD, and by his fierce anger. For thus hath the LORD said, The whole land shall be desolate; yet will I not make a full end. For this shall the earth mourn, and the heavens above be black; because I have spoken it, I have purposed it, and will not repent, neither will I turn back from it." – Jeremiah 4:6–7; 23–28

The above passage sets the context in the Day of the Lord by referencing Antichrist ("the Destroyer"). The destruction of the Great Tribulation renders the earth without form and void" (*tohu va bohu* in Hebrew)—the same condition used to describe the Earth at the start of the Creation week in Genesis 1:2:

> "**And the earth was without form, and void** (*tohu va bohu*); and darkness was upon the face of the deep. And the Spirit of God moved upon the face of the waters."

The Earth was in chaos before God let His divine light shine, as recorded in Genesis chapter 1. And, as we've seen throughout this study, the prophecy ripples through time as, once again, after the seventh vial completes God's destructive judgment, laying to waste every city and shifting each mountain and island in tectonic catastrophe, the Earth will again be formless and void. It is then that Jesus Christ, the Coming King, will return and repair the Earth for His Kingdom. Isaiah 51 is one of many passages that confirms this supernatural renovation:

> "For the LORD shall comfort Zion: **he will comfort all her waste places; and he will make her wilderness like Eden, and her desert like the garden of the LORD**; joy and gladness shall be found therein, thanksgiving, and the voice of melody. Hearken unto me, my people; and give ear unto me, O my nation: for a law shall proceed from me, and I will make my judgment to rest for a light of the people. My righteousness is near; my salvation is gone forth, and mine arms shall judge the people; the isles shall wait upon me, and on mine arm shall they trust." – Isaiah 51:3–5

Israel will experience a return from its arid climate and harsh sand to lush, fertile environs akin to those of Eden. Additionally, all the world will enjoy the abundance of crops and life just as in the beginning. *Numerous passages* attest to this; here is just a small sample:

> "Let the people praise thee, O God; let all the people praise thee. O let the nations be glad and sing for joy: for thou shalt judge the people righteously, and govern the nations upon earth. Selah. Let the people praise thee, O God; let all the people praise thee. Then shall the earth yield her increase; and God, even our own God, shall bless us." – Psalm 67:3–6
>
> "Then shall he give the rain of thy seed, that thou shalt sow the ground withal; and bread of the increase of the earth, and it shall be fat and plenteous: in that day shall thy cattle feed in large pastures. The oxen likewise and the young asses that ear the ground shall eat clean provender, which hath been winnowed with the

> shovel and with the fan." – Isaiah 30:23–24

> "So shall ye know that I am the LORD your God dwelling in Zion, my holy mountain: then shall Jerusalem be holy, and there shall no strangers pass through her any more. And it shall come to pass in that day, that the mountains shall drop down new wine, and the hills shall flow with milk, and all the rivers of Judah shall flow with waters, and a fountain shall come forth out of the house of the LORD, and shall water the valley of Shittim." – Joel 3:17–18

Recall that, during the sentencing of Adam, Eve, and Satan, the Lord told the first man that the ground would be cursed, making it a struggle for him to work the plow and obtain food for crops. Life would become a hardship as the luxurious fruitfulness of God's Garden would no longer be available: "Thorns also and thistles shall it bring forth to thee" (Genesis 3:18). During the Millennial Reign of Christ, the curse on the land will be reversed:

> "Instead of the thorn shall come up the fir tree, and instead of the brier shall come up the myrtle tree: and it shall be to the LORD for a name, for an everlasting sign that shall not be cut off." – Isaiah 55:13

The "brier" is another name for "thistles":

> "Thistles and thorns are very abundant in Palestine, and occasion the husbandman much trouble and annoyance, often attaining such a prodigious size and growing so luxuriantly they must be burned off before the plow can operate. They were a symbol of desolation (Prov. 24:31).... There are no less than twenty two words in the original languages of the Bible variously translated 'thorn,' 'thistle,' 'brier,' etc., and signifying thorny and prickly plants." – *The System Bible Study or the Busy People's Bible*, The

System Bible Company, 1922, p. 317

Also note that the myrtle tree that will replace the thistles will be a special token of a covenant between humanity and God. Like the rainbow in the sky in the days of Noah that signified God's promise to never flood the Earth again, so will God give this tree as another symbol of His pledge to never curse the ground again. The Earth will be abundant with food and fruit for the entire population throughout Millennium.

The Lord Jesus Christ prophesied of this restructuring of the earth's topography and the transformation of barren, destroyed lands into lush, Eden-like paradise. He referred to it in the Gospels as "the regeneration":

> "Then [Jesus] answered Peter and said unto him, Behold, we have forsaken all, and followed thee; what shall we have therefore? And Jesus said unto them, Verily I say unto you, That ye which have followed me, **in the regeneration when the Son of man shall sit in the throne of his glory**, ye also shall sit upon twelve thrones, judging the twelve tribes of Israel." – Matthew 19:27–28

With this renewed Edenic earth, the atmosphere in the Millennium will also return to the condition it was in during the days of Noah. This will lead to extended life spans for humans who live and are born during that future time:

> "There shall be no more thence an infant of days, nor an old man that hath not filled his days: for the child shall die an hundred years old; but the sinner being an hundred years old shall be accursed." – Isaiah 65:20

Prior to the Flood judgment, Old Testament patriarchs lived to be between seven hundred and nine hundred years old. They also had children at much later ages (for example, Seth, the son of Adam and Eve, had his first son, Enos, when he was 105. Enos had Cainan an at age ninety. Cainan lived for seventy years before he had Mahaleel; see Genesis 5:7–14).

In *Judgment of the Nephilim*, I noted that, prior to the Flood, it never rained. God provided water for vegetation and plant life through a mist that sprang from geysers in the ground. This could have allowed for a hyperbaric, oxygen-rich atmosphere that facilitated prolonged life spans. Christian geologist and researcher Gaines Johnson, author of *Genesis & Geology*, said:

> "Could it be that the reason men lived longer in pre-flood days was because the Earth's atmospheric pressure was considerably higher back then and that man was originally made to thrive in a higher-pressure, higher oxygen concentrated atmospheric environment?
>
> In Hyperbaric therapy, a person is placed in a pressurized chamber and the air pressure is increased 1 to 2 times that of normal sea level atmospheric pressure (14.7 psi). Under the increased air pressure more oxygen gets into the bloodstream. This process seems to accelerate healing of wounds, promotes tissue repair, and even favorably affects metabolic rates and the performance of the hormonal systems. In fact, in researching the subject, there appears to be a wide range of medical benefits from living in a pressurized environment. It almost seems to be something that should be natural. So why isn't the world like that today if such conditions are so naturally beneficial? Perhaps before the flood, it was the natural order of things." – *More on the Windows of Heaven and Noah's Flood*, Gaines Johnson, https://www.kjvbible.org/windows_of_heaven.html

During the Millennium, with the regenerated Earth in its Edenic state, life spans will again be extended. According to Isaiah 65, someone who dies at the age of one hundred will still be considered a child, as he or she would have been during the days of Noah.

ANIMALS NO LONGER FEAR HUMANITY; NO MORE PREDATORS

One of the most well-known characteristics of the Millennium is that animals will no longer fear or attack humans. We read this prophecy in Isaiah:

> "The wolf also shall dwell with the lamb, and the leopard shall lie down with the kid; and the calf and the young lion and the fatling together; and a little child shall lead them. And the cow and the bear shall feed; their young ones shall lie down together: and the lion shall eat straw like the ox. And the sucking child shall play on the hole of the asp, and the weaned child shall put his hand on the cockatrice' den. They shall not hurt nor destroy in all my holy mountain: for the earth shall be full of the knowledge of the LORD, as the waters cover the sea." – Isaiah 11:6–9

In other words, during the Millennium, lions, tigers, and bears will be as docile as bunny rabbits. Toddlers can lie down near snakes. The harmony with animals once experienced by Adam when he was given the task of naming all of them will be restored. Recall that, like Adam, Noah was also able to have a special relationship with animals as they boarded the ark in pairs and sevens under direction from God. Noah didn't have to go out and capture the animals; they obediently came to him, as they did to Adam in the Garden.

With Jesus ruling in righteousness, this same type of covenant of peace will be established between man and animal:

> "And in that day will I make a covenant for them with the beasts of

> the field and with the fowls of heaven, and with the creeping things of the ground: and I will break the bow and the sword and the battle out of the earth, and will make them to lie down safely. And I will betroth thee unto me for ever; yea, I will betroth thee unto me in righteousness, and in judgment, and in lovingkindness, and in mercies." – Hosea 2:18–19

This is the world the awaits humanity! All those who believe in God will be resurrected to life eternal. Like Adam, who was formed from dust, every believer through history will be reformed – resurrected into a new, immortal body:

> "**And many of them that sleep in the dust of the earth** shall awake, some to everlasting life, and some to shame and everlasting contempt. And they that be wise shall shine as the brightness of the firmament; and they that turn many to righteousness as the stars for ever and ever." – Daniel 12:2-3

Christ's Kingdom will arrive, and the Earth will return to its former glory. The knowledge of and faith in God will fill the earth. The plan of redemption for all who believe will see its full fruition as God is victorious.

SATAN WILL BE DEALT HIS FINAL PUNISHMENT

> "And when the thousand years are expired, Satan shall be loosed out of his prison, And shall go out to deceive the nations which are in the four quarters of the earth, Gog, and Magog, to gather them together to battle: the number of whom is as the sand of the sea. And they went up on the breadth of the earth, and compassed the camp of the saints about, and the beloved city: and fire came down

> from God out of heaven, and devoured them. And the devil that deceived them was cast into the lake of fire and brimstone, where the beast and the false prophet are, and shall be tormented day and night for ever and ever." – Revelation 20:7–10

Released from his imprisonment in the Abyss, the Devil will set out to once again recruit the unbelieving masses in the Millennial Kingdom to rebel against God and wage war to overtake the Most High. After one thousand years without satanic influence, the mortals living in this time will barely remember the days when Satan had roamed the Earth "like a lion seeking whom he may devour" (1 Peter 5:8). Thus, it should not be a surprise to see how successful the Adversary will be in instigating rebellion against Jesus Christ one final time. The passage above states that Satan will amass an army so large that its members will be as numerous as the "sand of the sea."

Once again, this army of Satan will surround Jerusalem, seeking to destroy God's Holy City. But it will be vanquished by fire from Heaven in God's final supernatural act of judgment upon the unbelieving world.

A 19th century commentary explains how vulnerable humanity is when the last rebels join the Devil for the final judgment:

> "This extensive revolt appears clearly to intimate the necessity of a final probation, so as to separate the servants of God who remain *unalterable in their fidelity* from those *who cannot withstand temptation.* It is true, as we have proved in preceding pages, that the Millennial dispensation will have been one of undiminished blessedness; and it may appear wonderful that so large a portion of the world should be led to rebel at the instant temptations of Satan. But we know not the length of time which this may occupy.
>
> However, it fully proves, that without a Millennial dispensation, man could never have attained such universal perfection as will be

> necessary to complete the number of the human race *destined for eternal glory* in the heaven of heavens. What an awful proof of his frailty and instability, even subsequent to the Millennial period! At length the god of this world is disenchained, and once more permitted to exercise his malignant powers." – *Dissertations on Unaccomplished Prophecy*, William Snell Chauncy, 1838, p. 360

At this point, Satan at long last will meet his final destination: the Lake of Fire:

> "And the devil that deceived them was cast into the lake of fire and brimstone, where the beast and the false prophet are, and shall be tormented day and night for ever and ever." – Revelation 20:10.

Note that the Antichrist and the False Prophet will still be alive after a thousand years, suffering all that time in the excruciating torment of the flames of the lake. And the Devil will join them, ending any mention of their presence for eternity.

DEATH, HELL, AND ALL UNBELIEVERS CAST INTO LAKE OF FIRE, ENDING SIN FOREVER

> "And I saw the dead, small and great, stand before God; and the books were opened: and another book was opened, which is the book of life: and the dead were judged out of those things which were written in the books, according to their works. And the sea gave up the dead which were in it; and death and hell delivered up the dead which were in them: and they were judged every man according to their works. And death and hell were cast into the lake of fire. This is the second death. And whosoever was not found

written in the book of life was cast into the lake of fire." – Revelation 20:12–15

This describes the end of evil in the universe. All the unbelievers who rejected God throughout human history will be cast into the Lake of Fire. Death and even Hell itself (the prison no longer necessary) will be hurled into the fiery lake as well. All of the souls of the Nephilim will suffer the torment of eternal fire.

SCROLL OF TIME COMPLETE WITH CREATION OF A NEW HEAVEN AND EARTH

"In the beginning God created the heaven and the earth." – Genesis 1:1

"And I saw a new heaven and a new earth: for the first heaven and the first earth were passed away; and there was no more sea." – Revelation 21:1

"Remember the former things of old: for I am God, and there is none else; I am God, and there is none like me, Declaring the end from the beginning, and from ancient times the things that are not yet done, saying, My counsel shall stand, and I will do all my pleasure." – Isaiah 46:9–10

The culmination of God's plan of salvation will be the creation of the new Heaven and Earth, bringing everything back to the condition it was in during the time described in Genesis 1:1. Thus, the end is the beginning. Man and God will once again be in complete harmony in a universe free from sin and death. All creatures will have "the divine nature"—immortal and "in Christ," who will imbue His very Spirit into all creation. This is likely when every believer will receive their new names promised by Jesus Christ:

> "To him that overcometh will I give to eat of the hidden manna, and will give him a white stone, and in the stone a new name written, which no man knoweth saving he that receiveth it." – Revelation 2:17

When Adam was created, his first task was to name all of the creatures in the Garden. Jesus Christ, the Last Adam, will also name His children and fellow heirs in the eternal kingdom.

The end of evil will allow the true Jerusalem to descend from Heaven, unifying Heaven and Earth:

> "And I John saw the holy city, new Jerusalem, coming down from God out of heaven, prepared as a bride adorned for her husband. And I heard a great voice out of heaven saying, Behold, the tabernacle of God is with men, and he will dwell with them, and they shall be his people, and God himself shall be with them, and be their God. And God shall wipe away all tears from their eyes; and there shall be no more death, neither sorrow, nor crying, neither shall there be any more pain: for the former things are passed away. And he that sat upon the throne said, Behold, I make all things new. And he said unto me, Write: for these words are true and faithful. And he said unto me, It is done. **I am Alpha and Omega, the beginning and the end**. I will give unto him that is athirst of the fountain of the water of life freely." – Revelation 21:2–6

The dimensions of the eternal New Jerusalem will be massive. The following passage in Revelation states that it will be in the shape of a cube measuring fifteen hundred miles in length on each side:

> "And he that talked with me had a golden reed to measure the city, and the gates thereof, and the wall thereof. And the city lieth foursquare, and the length is as large as the breadth: and he measured the city with the reed, twelve thousand furlongs. The length and the breadth and the height of it are equal. And he measured the wall thereof, an hundred and forty and four cubits, according to the measure of a man, that is, of the angel." – Revelation 21:15

Note that the wall measures 144 cubits, "according to the measure of a man, that is, of the angel," affirming that humans and angels will share similar immortal, celestial bodies in eternity (thus there is no difference in their measurements and arithmetic). All those who will have trusted God will be one in Christ—free of sin, death, evil, and sadness forever. Mankind will be unified with Jesus in body and spirit. The Tree of Life will even return:

> "In the midst of the street of it, and on either side of the river, was there the tree of life, which bare twelve manner of fruits, and yielded her fruit every month: and the leaves of the tree were for the healing of the nations. And there shall be no more curse: but the throne of God and of the Lamb shall be in it; and his servants shall serve him: And they shall see his face; and his name shall be in their foreheads. And there shall be no night there; and they need no candle, neither light of the sun; for the Lord God giveth them light: and they shall reign for ever and ever." – Revelation 22:2–5

Just as the Lord started the Creation week by proclaiming, "Let there be light," so again, in the end, the divine photons of His Light will inaugurate the New Heaven and Earth. In the eternal kingdom, humanity and the righteous angels will all be one in Jesus Christ, bearing the very Name of God on their foreheads—the true Mark of life and righteousness. All in New

Jerusalem will be able to stand before the revealed Jesus Christ in His glory, as they will be "one" with Him. Jesus revealed this final step of redemption in the conclusion of a beautiful prayer found in John 17:

> "Neither pray I for these alone, but for them also which shall believe on me through their word; That they all may be one; as thou, Father, art in me, and I in thee, **that they also may be one in us**: that the world may believe that thou hast sent me. **And the glory which thou gavest me I have given them; that they may be one, even as we are one: I in them, and thou in me, that they may be made perfect in one**; and that the world may know that thou hast sent me, and hast loved them, as thou hast loved me." – John 17:20–23

This is the Omega point: humanity fully reconciled and in harmonious quantum entanglement with God the Creator. The Life of Christ, and His Light, in all believers and thus joined to Him. Hence Scripture calls all believers "the body of Christ"—literally with God and a part of God at the same time, completing the scroll of time:

> "In the beginning was the Word, and the Word was with God, and the Word was God. The same was in the beginning with God." – John 1:1–2

All believers will be in the Word (who is Christ), with God and one with God in eternity. This is not a case of Christians "exalting themselves"—it is a recognition of the transcendent magnitude of what Jesus Christ has done for all who believe in His Name. Thus, the end is the beginning and the beginning is the end. God's plan will be complete.

A FINAL MESSAGE AS THE DAY APPROACHES

> "For our light affliction, which is but for a moment, worketh for us a far more exceeding and eternal weight of glory; While we look not at the things which are seen, but at the things which are not seen: for the things which are seen are temporal; but the things which are not seen are eternal." – 2 Corinthians 4:17-18

Thank you for taking the time to read through this study. If you're not a believer in the Lord Jesus Christ or if you're unsure of where you stand with God, it is my sincere hope and prayer that you'll take the words of this book to heart and realize what an amazing message the Bible truly is. The Word of God is supernatural and divinely inspired. It is filled with many mysteries and prophecies, but most importantly, it is filled with the plan of God's salvation. It's the story of God's love for all of humanity and the absolutely amazing plan He wove through time to redeem all who desire His mercy. Don't waste time! As we know from this study, we have no control over the sequence of events laid out for our future, and we don't know which day will be our last. Acknowledge your sin before God, trust in the atoning sacrifice of Jesus Christ on the cross, and receive the free forgiveness that God lowered Himself and suffered for so that you can be with Him eternally.

If you are a born-again Christian, my prayer is that you rejoice in knowing what love our God has for us and in anticipating the amazing future that He has prepared for all of the saints. It's also my hope that studying the end times will give you a sense of urgency in the need to share the Gospel and be a true light to the world.

The Apostle Peter wrote: "Seeing then that all these things shall be dissolved, what manner of persons ought ye to be in all holy conversation and godliness.... Ye therefore, beloved, **seeing ye know these things before**, beware lest ye also, being led away with the error of the wicked, fall from your own steadfastness" (2 Peter 3:11, 17). Knowing that this world isn't going to last forever, let's not cling to it or to any worldly treasure. Let us all as believers remain steadfast, living for God, showing love to the world, and pointing the lost to Christ, knowing our Lord is preparing His return.

Finally, I know that at some point in the future, someone may be reading this book while the events described are actually taking place. You may be living through the events and circumstances that are detailed in this study. Let this serve as a witness to trust in God's Word. The things your eyes have seen and will see are only things those in society during the time this book is being written can imagine in large-budget, Hollywood films. But God tells us to walk by faith, not by sight. Don't be deceived by the Devil, his angels, or his seed. Know that Jesus Christ is returning to reclaim His Kingdom and rescue all those who believe. You may feel like there is no other option, but there is: Have faith. If you have seen the Lord correctly prophesy the events taking place around you, then believe in His victory, in His salvation, and in the Kingdom that He is preparing for His beloved saints.

May God bless you abundantly. I pray we will all see each other soon.

> "He which testifieth these things saith, Surely I come quickly. Amen. Even so, come, Lord Jesus. The grace of our Lord Jesus Christ be with you all. Amen." – Revelation 22:20–21